GW00503562

The
Pleasures of
Bibliophily

The Pleasures of Bibliophily

Fifty Years of
The Book Collector

AN ANTHOLOGY

THE BRITISH LIBRARY
AND
OAK KNOLL PRESS

© 2003 The contributors

First published 2003 by
The British Library
96 Euston Road
St Pancras
London NW1 2DB

Published in North and South America by
Oak Knoll Press
310 Delaware Street
New Castle
DE 19720

Cataloguing-in-Publication Data
A CIP record is available from The British Library
and The Library of Congress

ISBN 0–7123–4779–8 (BL)
ISBN 1–58456–097–5 (Oak Knoll)

Designed by Bob Elliott
Typeset by Hope Services (Abingdon) Ltd.
Printed in Great Britain by
St Edmundsbury Press, Bury St Edmunds

CONTENTS

❧❧

CONTENTS

FOREWORD

THE BOOK COLLECTOR owes rather a lot to James Bond. The publication in 1953 of *Casino Royale*, the first appearance of Ian Fleming's protagonist, has rather overshadowed the inauguration of THE BOOK COLLECTOR in the previous year. Yet from the first issue Fleming appeared as a member of the Editorial Board. And it was indeed Fleming who provided the crucial impetus towards the creation of the new journal. In the early 1950s he worked for the newspaper magnate Lord Kemsley and his responsibilities included a directorship of the Queen Anne Press, a Kemsley enterprise specializing in the publication of small, pretty books ('any discarded material by certain esteemed authors that could be rescued from their waste paper baskets,' as Percy Muir once put it). It was under these auspices that THE BOOK COLLECTOR began publication. By 1955, Fleming owned the press, having bought it from Kemsley for £50. He remained a member of the Editorial Board until his death in 1964 and was its majority shareholder. The role of Bond in modern bibliophily ought to be properly acknowledged.

In terms of bibliographical expertise Fleming was the junior partner. But he knew where to turn for help. In the first issue of THE BOOK COLLECTOR in Spring 1952 (Price 2s 6d,), his name is joined on the masthead with those of Percy Muir and John Hayward. Muir (1894–1979), bibliographer and bookseller, had known Fleming since the early 1930s and had been responsible for creating his remarkable collection of scientific books. John Hayward (1905–1965) was Fleming's neighbour; he lived below him at 19 Cheyne Walk in a flat he shared for a number of years with T. S. Eliot. (Eliot was himself an early contributor to THE BOOK COLLECTOR.)

For the first several years there were attempts to recruit an editor. Philip Gaskell was appointed in 1952 but was soon lured back to academic life; in 1955 he was succeeded by Christopher Dobson (later Librarian of the House of Lords), who also did not stay for long. But the main editorial burden of the journal clearly fell on Muir and Hayward, particularly the latter, even after the Editorial Board was strengthened in 1955 by the addition of John Carter (1905–1974), the eminent bibliographer and bookseller, a figure of international reputation throughout the world of books. By 1960 Hayward was Editorial Director, a role he held until his death in September 1965. He contributed relatively little to the journal in terms of articles, notes and reviews, but the informed and, at times, acerbic tone of the Commentaries, which he largely wrote, did more than anything else to establish the journal's authority, its claim to a bibliographical knowingness that was not afraid to be indiscreet or gossipy, to be on intimate terms with the world it was talking about.

Hayward was a cripple, confined to a wheelchair since the 1930s by a degenerative muscular disease that was to kill him. But he had become and was to remain an established presence in the London literary scene as editor, reviewer and anthologist, advisor and consultant. From his window overlooking the Thames he kept an alert watch on all aspects of the bibliographical world through the network of distinguished scholars and eminent friends who made regular pilgrimages to his Chelsea flat. It was to this network that THE BOOK COLLECTOR largely owed it distinctive tone of insider knowledge, its allusive grasp of the major book collecting players, both buyers and sellers and its willingness to ventilate gossip and scandal. Nicolas Barker summed it all up after Hayward's death:

Who but John would have developed the hot line to Leningrad through John Simmons – almost the only bibliographic link across the Iron Curtain? Where else would you find Nancy Cunard on the Hours Press and the true facts about the Wälsungenblut affair? To whom but John would anyone go who had something new to say about books, libraries or collecting.

The publication of THE BOOK COLLECTOR grew out of the collapse of *Book Handbook*, which characterized itself as 'an illustrated quarterly for discriminating book-lovers', of which nine parts were published between 1947 and 1952 by the Dropmore Press. The press, and hence the journal, failed in 1952, and the early issues of THE BOOK COLLECTOR are described as 'incorporating *Book Handbook*'. The relationship between the two journals did not extend beyond subject matter. From its beginnings THE BOOK COLLECTOR established itself by its ability to combine enthusiasm with a variety of approaches to bibliophily. As *An Announcement*, in the first number, put it:

Our aim will continue to be the provision of bibliographical information and entertainment, but we also intend to increase the scope and usefulness of the contents.

Regular features were created at once that have continued to the present: English (and later Foreign) Bookbindings, Bibliographical Notes & Queries, Book Reviews, as well as series that have similarly endured: Portrait of a Bibliophile, Unfamiliar Libraries, Contemporary Collectors, Uncollected Authors. And above all there had been from the outset a roll-call of distinguished contributors. The first issue established Muir, Howard Nixon and Julian Brown as regulars; contributors in the first year included Carter, Hayward, A. N. L. Munby, Michael Sadleir, W. A. Jackson, Anthony Hobson, Philip Gaskell and Sydney Cockerell. It was the capacity to draw widely on the services of those who could write best about all aspects of book collecting that quickly made the journal a familiar and authoritative part of the bibliographical landscape.

Fleming's death in 1964 created a crisis for the journal. There were protracted problems in sorting out his estate He had planned to leave THE BOOK COLLECTOR to Hayward but his sudden death left the intention unfulfilled. John Hayward's death in the following year left the journal without both its main editorial and financial pillars. In these circumstances, the surviving members of the Editorial Board, Muir and Carter, looked to a younger generation. Nicolas Barker had told the story of his recruitment as Hayward's successor, by the gang of three or four (they included Muir, Carter and Munby), after Hayward's memorial service in October 1965. He was then 32, with a full-time job, a young family and a large and growing number of commitments that were to be stretched to accommodate figures as diverse as Stanley Morison and T. J. Wise. But he was to prove an inspired choice. It is not easy to think of a comparable record of sustained commitment (Fredson Bowers's editorship of *Studies in Bibliography* comes to mind, but that was an annual, and one produced with institutional support): four issues punctually appearing each year, spread over five decades, nearly a hundred and fifty volumes, almost all with a major leader from his pen, many with reviews by him, all with significant chunks of News and Comment in his hand. It is an editorial marathon that has been run with characteristic flair.

Nicolas Barker himself has chronicled elsewhere in this volume the further crises that swiftly ensued. The death of James Shand, THE BOOK COLLECTOR's publisher, in 1966, was followed by the revelation of much financial disorder. The 1970s saw the untimely deaths of several of THE BOOK COLLECTOR's greatest early supporters—John Carter, Percy Muir, A. N. L. Munby and Graham Pollard—and changes of publisher, first from the Shenval Press to the Scolar Press and then to Smith Settle. But these and other crises have been weathered, and for 37 years THE BOOK COLLECTOR has been synonymous with Nicolas Barker and its continued survival is essentially his achievement.

But it has done much more than simply survive. It has consistently positioned itself as the leading journal for those with any interest in bibliophily in its widest sense. It is this breadth of interest that this anthology seeks to reflect. In its regular series as indeed in its special articles it has shown a breadth and quality of interest that this anthology aims to emphasise. THE BOOK COLLECTOR has, crucially, continued to be able to attract the best, to draw on a stable of writers who have been able consistently to present bibliophily as a subject both worthy of serious scholarly study and about which it is possible to write in ways that are accessible and interesting.

The *Announcement* in the first issue of THE BOOK COLLECTOR promised entertainment. It is a promise that it has consistently sought to fulfil. It has always been able to draw on a reservoir of talent that conveyed that seriousness in a way that was unclogged by bibliographical or academic jargon, that treated its readers as equals and sought to share a mutual pleasure in an absorbing topic. The articles for this anniversary volume have been chosen to indicate the range of topics that can be subsumed under the subject of book collecting, and to give some sense of the quality of lively scholarship that distinguished contributors to the journal have shown over the past fifty years. Inevitably, far too much has had to be omitted. But my colleagues on the Editorial Board of THE BOOK COLLECTOR (I am particularly grateful to Alan Bell), have helped me to ensure that the present collection is at least representative. It is our joint hope that it will give pleasure to all who enjoy bibliophily in any of its multifarious forms.

A. S. G. EDWARDS

N. J. BARKER

The Book Collector
Thoughts on Scoring a Century

I N the summer of 1965, Macmillan's the publishers, where I had just gone to work, moved from their old premises in St Martin's Street to Little Essex Street. I had been very busy, too busy for a holiday, too busy even (to my lasting regret) to go to the funeral of my old friend Cosmo Gordon, whose bibliography of Lucretius had occupied many happy hours of joint labour. In the middle of September a brief respite came and we decided to take a week off in Cambridge. We were about to depart when the telephone rang. It was John Hayward. My heart sank because his calls were never short, and as the muscular dystrophy that disabled his body (but never his mind) afflicted his mouth, it was not easy to hear what he was saying. The question turned on a review to appear in the next number of THE BOOK COLLECTOR, not by me but by someone else; without the text and with John half inaudible, I could not make out what the problem was. 'John', I said, 'it'll be easier if I can see it; we don't have to leave this minute – I'll come at once.' I put the telephone down, and a quarter of an hour later I was in the familiar, stuffy, book-lined room overlooking Cheyne Walk and the river.

I cannot remember now what difficulty John had found. It was easy to resolve with a simple direction to the printer (the Shenval Press readers were used to John, his elegant hand as well as his exigent standard of accuracy). All seemed well, and I made ready to depart. 'And you will see it's all right, won't you,' said John. 'Of course I will,' I replied, 'but you'll be here and I'll be in Cambridge – you'll be able to see to it yourself.' 'Yes, but I want to be sure that *you* will see to it too – all of it.' I was puzzled by his insistence, but gave him the assurance he wanted, said good-bye and left. That night he died.

A month later, as I sat at the back of St Luke's, Chelsea, at John's memorial service, among all his literary and bibliophilic friends, I still had no premonition of what was to follow. It was a cold grey day outside, and three or four men (I recall Percy Muir, John Carter and Tim Munby), their hands in raincoat pockets and – in John Carter's case – hat pulled down over eyes, cornered me against the north aisle. I was, they said, I had to be, the next editor of THE BOOK COLLECTOR. I protested my incapacity: I didn't have a tithe of John's bibliographic, let alone editorial skill, still less his wide circle of acquaintance; besides, editing THE BOOK COLLECTOR had been a full-time job for John and I had one already. The gang of three or four were reassuring. All I had to do was edit: others would help with the writing of editorial matter, rounding up articles and reviews; James Shand (I think his was the fourth raincoat and second hat), publisher as well as printer, would look after all the business side. All right, I said, I would see the next number through the press: that much, I realized, I had unsuspectingly promised. As to the future beyond that, it must wait.

It was John Carter who shouldered the burden of making that last number of 1965 a worthy memorial to John Hayward. He wrote to all the contributors: not one, I recall, refused – John's masterful command reached beyond the grave. It was the largest ever number, and it exists in two states: one with the correct reading in Dadie Rylands's quotation from Webster, 'As the tan'd galley-slave is with his Oare', and the other, earlier, reading 'tam'd galley-slave', of which I possess what I hope is the only surviving copy; the cancel was a last tribute to John's rigorously enforced standard of scholarly accuracy.

The future, it turned out, was full of problems. John had some years earlier passed the hat round some of THE BOOK COLLECTOR's wealthier subscribers and amassed a small fund to act as an insurance against any future crisis. Another prescient intent had been Ian Fleming's; as the main shareholder, he had planned to make over the journal to John, thus formally acknowledging, as Percy Muir put it, 'what it had long been in fact, the exclusive product of John's fertile brain'. But the intent had never been fulfilled: Fleming had died the year before John, and the Inland Revenue was still wrestling with his estate, lately swollen by the enormous success of the Bond books. I had to go and see Ann Fleming, whose wit and beauty and kindness I shall not forget. She was only too anxious that Ian's plan should go through, and was willing to give us THE BOOK COLLECTOR; but this could not be achieved until it had been valued as part of Fleming's estate and duty paid. The duty on Fleming's estate was 98%, and so John's crisis fund virtually disappeared. It seemed doubtful whether THE BOOK COLLECTOR could survive.

But before all this had been worked out, I had, in effect, yielded to the pressure not only of the first gang of friends and supporters, but of others, including the fifteen who had written tributes for that final Hayward number. Catherine Porteous, who had done secretarial work for John, and with whom I sorted out the papers and books (only partly provided for in John's will), was encouraging. Walter Oakeshott, then as always a generous friend and supporter, produced a new idea for a series, 'Collector's Piece', and the first article, on Sir Walter Raleigh's copy of Petrus d'Alliaco *Imago mundi* 1483. Stanley Morison, for whom I was also working in what passed for my spare time, gave his blessing with a remark I have never forgotten: 'You will get a lot of books to review; spend all the time and space you can spare on saying what is good about the good books; few books are so bad that neglect is not the best way of seeing them off'.

So, almost before I knew what had happened, the Spring number of 1966 came out. All THE BOOK COLLECTOR's old friends, John Simmons, Howard Nixon, Julian Brown, came across; James Walsh described the library of Bill Jackson (another recent and unexpected loss to bibliography), William B. Todd, Bent Juel-Jensen, Harry Carter, and others who came to be friends, too, provided articles and reviews. With the second number of 1966, an editorial board was formally constituted, consisting of John Carter, Percy Muir, myself as editor and James Shand as publisher. Tim Munby and Simon Nowell-Smith, both early contributors, were active in reserve. With the first number of 1967, THE BOOK COLLECTOR even achieved a little notoriety: moved by the plight of the libraries of Florence, devastated by the flood of 4 November 1966, we devoted the whole of the next issue to it, with an appeal for funds that not only produced a decent sum for conservation but also alerted the national press to the continuing need. In a modest way, THE BOOK COLLECTOR can claim to have initiated the *nouvelle vague* of book conservation that stems from the disaster.

Before the year was out, however, another and more domestic disaster struck. That November James Shand died, depriving THE BOOK COLLECTOR of a loyal friend and supporter from the outset. He saw to it that its elegant typography and immaculate presswork were maintained, like everything that came from the Shenval Press at Hertford. But he had done more: he kept the subscription records, took the money that came in from subscribers and advertisers, paid the Press, and presented the accounts to the auditors. His death came after quite a long period of ill health, concealed from us and even from himself. All the records, we now found, were in confusion: subscriptions were unpaid, copies sent to subscribers long deceased, cash figures uncertain in the last degree. Inevitably, I was drawn into the task of sorting out the confusion, and from merely editing became involved in the 'business side' that I had hoped to be spared. It was to be almost a decade before some sort of security (at least the security of knowing where you are) began to emerge.

But help of a different sort was already at hand. When, in 1966, it seemed certain that THE BOOK COLLECTOR was not to die with John, it became clear that I should need editorial help. John Carter heard that Joan Stevenson was free, following the sad and unnecessary demise of *Argosy*. We met for lunch in a rather dingy pub near the back gate of the Temple, and I realized at once that Joan had more to give than editorial experience: the loyalty once bestowed on *Argosy* would, I could see, be transferred to THE BOOK COLLECTOR. I am, in general, a poor prophet, but I got it right this time. Joan became the devoted friend and helper of all who wrote for THE BOOK COLLECTOR, not least the editor. She gave it the loyalty I had anticipated, and far more time than I had dared to hope, for over fifteen years. She took over the indexing from the admirable and long-serving Mrs E. M. Hatt of Faber's; she prepared typescripts (and in the editor's case manuscripts) with impeccable care and a curious but effective mixture of red typewriter, green ink and sticky labels. She earned the respect of the contributors and of the Shenval readers, and ruled the progress of the press with an iron hand. She became and remains to this day, a most valued friend.

We only differed, I recall, on two matters. I at first suggested that she might write a paragraph or two for 'News and Comment', but she was firm that writing lay outside her definition of her editorial role. The other matter was the definite article: I was apt to call our journal 'The Book Collector'; to Joan it was always 'Book Collector', minus the 'The', which, following, I think, her admired uncle Wickham Steed, she reserved for 'The Times' alone. Where we would have been without Joan, I cannot imagine. First at Macmillan's and then at the Oxford University Press, my daily life was full of other tasks; working with Stanley Morison ended with his death in October 1967, but then followed more work, finishing his great last book, *Politics and Script*, and writing his biography. His literary executors, Brooke Crutchley and Arthur Crook, were a great help: Brooke invited me to write a book on Morison and Robert Bridges in his handsome Christmas Series, and Arthur gave me books to review for the *TLS*.

But the increased scope of the editor's life, with bizarre interludes like the Prokosch affair; the valiant attempts of Vallance Lodge the auditors to straighten out the balance sheet; all that Joan Stevenson did to make THE BOOK COLLECTOR as accurate and as well printed as it was when John Hayward and James Shand minded it; all this could not avert the bleak sense of cumulative loss in the middle of the decade. First Tim Munby, followed only three months later by John Carter, then Graham Pollard and, in 1979, Percy Muir, the last of the founders. While they were alive, there was always someone to whom I could turn for advice and help. How much they gave, only they and I know, but our annotated bound set of THE BOOK COLLECTOR, with the authors of the anonymous pieces written in, is a partial record. More came by way of letters (John Carter, in particular, was a punctual correspondent), telephone calls, and, often enough, meetings – my last meeting with Graham a memorable and, as it proved, influential occasion.

But it was Tim Munby's legacy that proved the most important through his friendship with John Commander, then responsible for the Scolar Press which was engaged in producing and publishing books of bibliophilic interest, and for Mansell, publishers of the pre-1956 NUC and, under Tim's editorship, the series of 'Sales Catalogues of Eminent Persons'. It was John Commander who came to the rescue when the Shenval Press decided to give up hot-metal composition and printing and arranged for the journal to be printed at the Scolar Press's plant at Ilkley. Scolar's successors, Smith Settle, remain our printers and maintain a valued continuum which has now seen us through some fifty-six issues. The typesetting, still 'Monotype', was done first by Ronset in Lancashire and now by Gloucester Typesetting Services. John refreshed the typography and created the new style of covers, making use of title-page borders and other designs from famous books of the past (it was time for a change, for the old design had been plagiarized too often). Finally, and most valuable, he offered us space in the Scolar Press office, first at 3 Bloomsbury Place and then at 90 Great Russell Street. He became our publisher and a member of the editorial board. It has been a happy association, strengthened by the possession of a room of our own, and it has lasted through all the moves that have now brought us to our present premises in Covent Garden. Whether, in the face of horrifying rent increases and the imposition of the 'business rate', we shall be able to stay there depends largely on the continued support and loyalty of subscribers and advertisers.

The other sad vacancies on the editorial board were filled by Theodore Hofmann, David McKitterick and Stephen Weissman, who were later to be joined by Alan Bell and, most recently, James Fergusson.

All this time, indeed for all but thirty years now, I have been fortunate enough to have the help of Mrs Patricia Cooper. She first came to work with me as secretary when we shared a room on the *piano nobile* of 36 Soho Square, an old publishing house, first occupied by John Russell Smith, later by the Oxford University Press and then by Rupert Hart-Davis. The 'University of Soho Square' was already a home for bibliophily – it was as a member of the board of the Soho Bibliographies that I had first met John Hayward. Then and later, with only a short gap or two, Pat and I worked together, until my summons to the British Library came in 1976. At this point, wisely, Pat decided to give up full-time work, and I, even more wisely, took a deep breath and asked her if she would work three days a week for THE BOOK COLLECTOR. In a trice, it seemed, although Pat says it took longer than I think, the last muddles and confusions about subscribers, advertising and accounts disappeared. If the editorial is not quite what it was twenty-five years ago, the business side has never been in better shape.

So here we are, a hundred issues later, alive and not much changed in a world that has changed in many ways but not in one: there is still only one periodical that caters for the needs of book-collectors, booksellers and librarians. The roles of all three have changed, but not the need for a common ground where all three meet on equal terms. While that exists, THE BOOK COLLECTOR will continue. But what a change has taken place! Twenty-five years ago our world was a small one: it was a club of people to whom the individual book was something more than article of trade, a possession, or a catalogue entry. It has grown enormously since, and it is worth reflecting on the nature of that growth and the change it has brought.

Twenty-five years ago, both booksellers and book-collectors were, in their own view, each a dying breed. There were only about fifty 'serious' old booksellers, and they were, like their stock, old. Their sons wanted to go into something more technological or a merchant bank, and there was no point in stopping them because there were no old books left. There were still fewer collectors and they were old too: collecting was becoming impossible, because there were no books to collect, except at prohibitive prices; the only moderately cheerful members of the club were the librarians. Life was not what it had been, of course, and the prices were ridiculous, but one way or another they could still find books to buy. This was particularly true in America, where a great deal of inventive thought, from the Texas Sweep to the Houghton Pick, went into what was now called 'acquisition' ('collection development' was still, mercifully, uncoined). Great collections were built in this way: the one that Larry Powell and Bob Vosper built at U.C.L.A., Gordon Ray's creation at Urbana. Nor was it just straight academic libraries: the Wing Collection at the Newberry Library, the J.C.B. at Brown, had a virtual monopoly of 'the book arts' and Americana. European libraries were apt to be jealous, but even on this side of the Atlantic war-time austerity had become a thing of the past.

It was, however, pretty generally felt that this could not last. Soon the institutional libraries would tuck the last private collector under their arm, buy the last book from the last bookseller, and we would all retreat to some bibliophilic nirvana. But it has all worked out very differently. Now there are hundreds of new booksellers, hundreds of new collectors, and if the librarian can occasionally squeeze between them to pick up a book, that happens very infrequently because the acquisition budget has been cut for the tenth successive year.

What has brought this about? A number of factors come to mind. In 1965 the auction houses – Hodgson's as well as Sotheby's and Christie's (Bonham's and Phillips did not then have book sales) – were all partnerships, and the almost simultaneous decision of the big two to go public a year or two later was at once a response to the market and a major cause of its change. The 'flight from money', whether into Krugerrands or old things of all sorts, was the cause of this event, which gave the houses much greater elasticity; at the same time, they had to grow, return a larger profit each year, to satisfy their investors. This may or may not be a good thing, but it has happened. At a later date, I recall talking to Mr Taubman, not long after he had 'rescued' Sotheby's, about this. Art, he said, was not like root beer; you made root beer, you marketed it, and if you marketed right, you sold more, so you made more. Art was different, because there were only limited supplies of it; the answer to this dilemma was to persuade people to turn it over oftener: why, he said, people hold on to art for as long as thirty years – we've got to get that down to ten, or better still *three* years.

Well, no doubt people do buy and sell more than they used to, even books, though profit-taking still seems to be rarer in the book world than, say, in that of impressionist paintings. But this factor has certainly helped the book trade through what could have been a difficult stretch, when the rise in rents was making the old-fashioned shop harder and harder to maintain. Business by catalogue, stock held at home and viewable by appointment, above all book fairs, have all been fuelled by a faster turnover of stock, largely made possible by sales within the trade. It looks like the Indian rope trick or, perhaps, more like three antique dealers on a desert island – each has made a profit by the time they are rescued, but it works. Perhaps the success of book fairs has been the most startling element. In 1965, there was only the book fair at the National Book League, an agreeable but somewhat amateurish event which nevertheless was the precursor of the ABA fairs of later years. The growth of provincial book fairs, as well as the annual multiplex jamboree in London, if it provides opportunities for booksellers to meet booksellers, also gives the collector a chance to meet more booksellers in a day than in a fortnight of hard travelling.

Book fairs, then, are popular with the new collectors, and who are they? They are the product of the paperback revolution. Paperback publishing was in full swing in 1965, but some time was to pass before most new books would appear in that form. With it has come a new appreciation of old-fashioned cloth-bound hard-cover books of all sorts. Books that would once have been found on 3d. and 6d. barriers crept up to £1 and were still underpriced compared with new books. King Penguins and the 'Britain in Pictures' series began to have an antiquarian appeal. The ephemerality of new books, their short life expectancy, both as material objects and as items in the publisher's stock list, has given a new value to older and more durable books; it has also provided a welcome fillip to the booksellers who have regularly specialized in remainders as well as antiquarian books.

This may be welcome, but there is also a more sombre side to all this new growth. We live in an age of hype. The technique of promotion is inflationary: everything must be bigger, better, rarer, above all more expensive, than what went before. This is not merely due to the Press Officer and PR people employed by the auction houses and the 'arts' journalists who are their natural prey, though both have a lot to do with it. Booksellers and collectors alike, from the respectable West End houses to the shopless *marchand amateur* who 'collects' money rather than books, are galvanized by a new sense of excitement, not altogether healthy: it was just such excitement that fuelled the Kern sale in 1929 – read John Carter's *Taste and Technique in Book-Collecting* for some wise words on that and its aftermath.

Perhaps the most novel of all the new features of the trade is the 'leisure' factor. If people have less time to browse in bookshops, they have more money to spend on subjects that interest them, whether books on their trade or profession, on the area where they live, on armchair travel, or the book beautiful, something to be admired aesthetically. It is significant that places like York that have (for good or ill) devoted themselves to tourism and the encouragement of leisure have sprouted bookshops. There is no sign of any waning in this enthusiasm, nor of book fairs or any of the other new phenomena that have given such a lift to the book trade. There is even hope that modern book production is emerging from the slough of the last two decades. More books are sewn instead of perfect bound, and the quality of paper is improving, if slowly.

So, as we enter the last decade of the century, it is hard to take a gloomy view of the book trade and book-collecting. Libraries may still have some way to go before they too benefit from these optimistic tendencies, but the growth of 'Friends' groups, a greater sense of community with other parts of the book world, is something to set against the general shortage of funds.

These words were partly written in Germany, where the old book trade is as prosperous as in this country and the U.S.A. We were part of an admirable tour arranged by the Association Internationale de Bibliophilie (another body that has grown and flourished over the last twenty-five years). We had visited a number of the public and private libraries of Franconia, culminating in a visit to the library of Dr Otto Schäfer, one of the great collectors of this or any other time. From the sublime to the ridiculous: returning via Frankfurt airport, we found the bookstall there advertised itself as 'Moderne Antiquariat'. If old books, at least *in posse* (none were actually visible), can be found there, the future of the old book trade can hardly be in doubt.

But we end, as we began, with a death. Ted Dring of Quaritch's has died, and with him has gone one of the longest links with the past, for he and his father between them spanned 113 years at the great firm.

Between them they saw it in its prime, through decline in the middle of the century to reach, now, a new pre-eminence in an increasingly international world. John Hayward and Ted Dring were, in their very different ways, remarkable men, influential beyond the course of their daily lives. If we, looking forward to a next century, in some hope that THE BOOK COLLECTOR too will find new prospects and new ways of engaging the interest of its readers, it is with the reassurance that men like these have thought it worth while to devote their lives to our world.

JOHN HAYWARD

The Location of Copies of the First Editions of Giordano Bruno

SCEPTICISM is an essential part of a bibliographer's equipment. Confronted with a statement like: 'The only surviving copy'; or 'The only complete set in existence'; or 'NOT IN WING', he must at least question its validity even if he is not in a position to disprove it. The purpose of the following notes on the location of copies of the first editions of treatises by Giordano Bruno published during his lifetime (*c.* 1548–1600) is to justify the doubt raised by just such an asseveration.

According to N. Cherkashina,[1] 'there is no other collection of Bruno first editions as complete as the one in the Lenin State Public Library in Moscow. It contains 20 of the 26 Bruno first editions in existence and several of them are unique.' Although none of these claims can in fact be sustained, the collection is nevertheless a very important one, and is, with the British Museum holding, second only to those in the Bibliothèque Nationale and the Bodleian. Formed in the early years of the last century by the Russian statesman and bibliophile, A. S. Norov, and kept by him in the polished black chest in which it is still preserved, it passed at his death to the Rumyantsev Museum in Moscow and thence to the Lenin Library. It was known to Bruno's studious bibliographer, Salvestrini,[2] who records all but one of Norov's copies among those others he had located in European libraries.

First editions of Bruno's works have commonly been accounted rare and the circumstances of his life and of their publication were certainly calculated to make them so. Norov's experience as a collector in the European market led him to record in his copy of *De Monade, Numero et Figura*, that 'Giordano Bruno's first editions are more rarely found than a white crow', and from Salvestrini's census it would appear that of the commonest of them not more than a dozen copies have survived and of many of them fewer than half as many. For all his conscientiousness Salvestrini surprisingly failed, with one or two exceptions, to record the Bruno holdings of the Bibliothèque Nationale and the British Museum and overlooked completely the University and College Libraries of Oxford and Cambridge. These omissions are all the more surprising in view of the fact that Bruno spent two years in England (lecturing at Oxford during his visit) and that his

[1] In a short article, submitted to THE BOOK COLLECTOR by the Press Service of the Soviet Embassy in London, on the Bruno Collection in Moscow. Although the article was unfortunately unsuitable for publication, it subsequently led to our obtaining, through the good offices of Professor P. Bogachev, Director of the Lenin State Public Library, the photograph of the Collection, reproduced here, and a careful check-list of its contents.

[2] Virgilio Salvestrini. *Bibliografia delle opere di Giordano Bruno e degli saitti ad esso attinenti*. Pisa. 1926.

most important works were written and printed there.[3] When the copies in France and England, which Salvestrini overlooked, and those which have since been acquired by American libraries are added to his census, it will be found that some of Bruno's treatises are relatively uncommon and that only two are at present known by a single copy. It will also be seen that the Norov Collection is not the most complete and that none of its copies is unique, though this distinction may perhaps be accorded to its copy of *Oratio valedictoria*, 1588, the only known copy of any of Bruno's works with a presentation inscription.

The following short-title list and tables, while they cannot pretend to be definitive, incorporate some additional facts and figures relating to the present rarity, distribution and location of copies of the 26 first editions[4] of Bruno's writings published before his death at the stake in Rome on 17 February 1600.

SYMBOLS

STC symbols have been used for British and American libraries. Libraries of Italian and German Universities are indicated thus: Padua U, Göttingen U. Entry numbers in Salvestrini's bibliography are given after the titles *viz.* (*S.*17).

EUROPE

Paris: Bib. Nationale
Moscow: Lenin State Pub. Lib.
Florence[1]: Bib. Nazionale
Florence[2]: Bib. Magliabechiana
Florence[3]: Bib. Marucelliana
Naples: Bib. Nazionale
Rome[1]: Bib. Naz. Vittorio
   Emanuele
Rome[2]: Bib. Casanatense
Rome[3]: Bib. Alessandrina
Rome[4]: Bib. Vaticana
Venice: Bib. Naz. S. Marco
Lucca: Bib. Governativa
Milan: Bib. Naz. Braidense
Turin: Bib. Nazionale
Berlin/Marburg: The holdings
   of the former Preussische
   Staatsbib. Berlin are at
   present split between

the Westdeutsche Bib. at
Marburg and the Deutsche
Staatsbib. in Berlin
Munich: Bayerische Staatsbib.
Gotha: Ducal Library
Zurich: Zentralbib.

GREAT BRITAIN

L: London, British Museum
O: Oxford, Bodleian Lib.
O[5]:   „   Corpus Christi
O[8]:   „   St John's
O[9]:   „   All Souls
O[12]:   „   Magdalen
O[17]:   „   Balliol
O[18]:   „   Hertford
C: Cambridge University Lib.
C[2]:   „   Trinity
C[4]:   „   King's

C[6]: Cambridge St John's
C[16]:   „   Queens'
M: Manchester, Rylands Lib.
MU: „   University Lib.
   (R. C. Christie Coll.)
P: Peterborough Cathedral Lib.
E: Edinburgh, National Lib. of
   Scotland
RWD: Rothschild Coll.
   Waddesdon

USA

HD: Harvard (Houghton Lib.)
Y: Yale University Lib.
FOLGER: Folger University Lib.
HUNT: Huntington Lib.
CLSU: University of S.
   California Lib.

---

[3] See H. Sellers: 'Italian Books printed in England before 1640' in *The Library* Fourth Series, Vol. V No. 2. Sept. 1924. pp. 105–28. Bruno's printer is shown to have been John Charlewood (not Thomas Vautrollier as formerly supposed) who used Venetian or Parisian imprints to increase the sale of his books (*STC* 3932–40). John Wolfe did the same for Machiavelli. Bruno admitted to the Venetian inquisitor that 'all those books of mine which say in their imprint that they were printed in Venice, were

printed in England, and it was the printer who would put on them that they were printed in Venice to sell them more easily'.

[4] To Salvestrini's list of 25 must be added the only recorded copy of *Phitotei Iordani Bruni Nolani Dialogi Idiota Triumphans*. 8°. Paris. 1586 (Bibliothèque Nationale, R54535). The Moscow holding of '20 of the 26 Bruno first editions' includes two posthumous works.

SHORT-TITLE LIST OF FIRST EDITIONS AND LOCATIONS

1. DE UMBRIS IDEARUM. *Parisiis, Apud Ægidium Gorbinum.* 1582 (*S.*17) Paris (4 cops.), Moscow (2 cops.), Florence[1], Naples, Rome[1,2,3], Venice, Padua U, Pisa U, Marburg, Munich U; L (2 cops.), O, O[8], O[9], O[17], C[2], C[4], M, MU (2 cops.); HD, Y (3 cops.), FOLGER

2. CANTUS CIRCÆUS. *Parisiis, Apud Ægidium Gillium.* 1582 (*S.*22) Paris, Moscow, Florence[1], Naples, Rome[1,3], Venice, Marburg; L (2 cops) O, O[8], C[2], C[5], MU; HD.

3. DE COMPENDIOSA ARCHITECTURA & COMPLEMENTO ARTIS LULLII. *Parisiis, Apud Ægidium Gorbinum.* 1582 (*S.*25) Paris, Moscow, Florence[1], Naples, Marburg; L (2 cops.), O, C[2], MU; HD, Y.

4. CANDELAIO. COMEDIA. *In Pariggi, Appresso Guglelmo Giuliano.* 1582 (*S.*28) Paris, Moscow, Florence, Naples, Naples Bib. Lucc., Rome[4], Lucca, Dresden, Göttingen U, Heidelberg U, Vienna; L (2 cops.), O, O[9], O[17], C[2], C[5], MU (imp.); HD, Y.

5. RECENS ET COMPLETA ARS REMINISCENDI. [*London ?* 1583] (*S.*44. *STC* 3939) Paris (2 cops.), Moscow, Florence[1], Milan, Marburg (Part 2 only); L (imp.), O, C, C[2], E, M, MU; HUNT.

6. LA CENA DELE CENERI. [*London, J. Charlewood*] 1584. (*S.*47. *STC* 3935) Paris, Moscow, Naples (variant); L, O, O[5], O[9], C[2] (3 cops.), C[5], M, RWd (2 cops.); HD, CLSU.

7. DE LA CAUSA PRINCIPIO, ET UNO. *Venetia* [*London, J. Charlewood*]. 1584. (*S.*53. *STC* 3936) Moscow, Florence[1], Marburg, Göttingen U; L, O, O[5], O[9], C[5]; HD, Y.

8. DE L'INFINITO UNIVERSO ET MONDI. *Venetia* [*London, J. Charlewood*]. 1584 (*S.*69. *STC* 3938) Moscow, Florence[1], Naples, Marburg, Göttingen U, Zurich; L, O, O[5], O[8], O[9], C[2], C[5], MU, P; HD, Y.

9. SPACCIO DE LA BESTIA TRIONFANTE. *Parigi* [*London, J. Charlewood*]. 1584. (*S.*79. *STC* 3940) Paris, Moscow, Naples, Naples U; L, O, O[9], C[2] (2 cops.), RWd (2 cops.); HD, Y.

10. CABALA DEL CAVALLO PEGASEO. *Parigi Appresso Antonio Baio* [*London, J. Charlewood*]. 1585 (*S.*99. *STC* 3934) Heidelberg U, Zurich; L, O.

11. DE GL'HEROICI FURORI. *Parigi, Appresso Antonio Baio* [*London, J. Charlewood*]. 1585 (*S.*107. *STC* 3937) Paris, Paris Bib. Mazarin (2 cops.), Moscow, Naples, Marburg, Heidelberg U; L, O, O[12], C[2], M, MU, RWd; HD, Y, FOLGER, CLSU.

12. FIGURATIO ARISTOTELICI PHYSICI AUDITUS: *Parisiis, Ex Typographia Petri Cheuillot.* [1586] (*S.*118) Paris, Turin; O.

13. DIALOGI DUO DE FABRICII MORDENTIS SALERNITANI PROPE DIVINA ADINVENTIONE AD PERFECTAM COSMIMETRIÆ PRAXIM. *Parisiis, Ex. Typographio Petri Cheuillot.* 1586. (*S.*120) Paris, Turin.

14. CENTUM ET VIGINTI ARTICULI DE NATURA ET MUNDO ADVERSUS PERIPATETICOS. *Impressum Parisiis, ad Authoris instant.* 1586 (*S.*122)
L.

15. DIALOGI IDIOTA TRIUMPHANS. *Imprimé à Paris pour l'auteur.* 1586 (Not in *S.*)
Paris.

16. DE LAMPADE COMBINATORIA LULLIANA. *Witebergae,* [? Z. *Crato*]. 1587 (*S.*124)
Paris, Florence[1], Berlin, Gotha; c[2]; Y.

17. DE PROGRESSU ET LAMPADE VENATORIA LOGICORUM. [*Wittenberg,* ? Z. *Crato*]. 1587. (*S.*128)
Moscow, Florence[1], Naples, Romel, Venice, Berlin; L, O, O[9], C[2], M, MU; HD, Y.

18. ORATIO VALEDICTORIA. *Typis Zachariae Cratonis* [*Wittenberg*]. 1588 (*S.*132)
Paris, Moscow, Rome[1].

19. CAMŒRACENSIS ACROTISMUS. *Vitebergae, Apud Zachariam Cratonem.* 1588. (*S.*137, a much enlarged edition of No. 14, *S.*122)
Paris, Moscow, Florence[1], Naples, Rome[3], Venice, Berlin; L, O, O[9], C, C[2], M, MU; HD.

20. DE SPECIERUM SCRUTINO ET LAMPADE COMBINATORIA RAYMUNDI LULLII. *Prague, Excudebat Georgius Nigrinus.* 1588. (*S.*141. *De Lampade* is a re-issue of No. 16, *S.*124, with a new title and Dedication).
Paris, Moscow (2 cops.), Florence[1,2], Naples, Venice; L, O, O[9], C, MU; HD.

21. ARTICULI CENTUM ET SEXAGINTA ADVERSUS HUJUS TEMPESTATIS MATHEMATICOS ATQUE PHILOSOPHOS. *Prague, Ex typographia Georgii Dacziceni.* 1588. (*S.*145).
Paris, Moscow (lacks principal diagrams), Munich.

22. ORATIO CONSOLATORIA [for the Duke of Brunswick] *Helmstadii, Excusa per Iacobum Lucium.* 1589. (*S.*147).
Paris, Rome[1]; O; HD.

23. DE TRIPLICI MINIMO ET MENSURA . . . ARTIUM PRINCIPIA, LIBRI V. *Francofurti, Apud Ioannem Wechelum & Petrum Fischerum consortes.* 1591. (*S.*150).
Paris (2 cops.), Moscow (2 cops.), Florence[1,3], Naples (2 cops.), Venice, Bologna U, Pisa U, Berlin, Marburg; L (2 cops.), O, O[5], O[9], O[17], C, C[2], MU; HD, Y (2 cops.).

24. DE MONADE NUMERO ET FIGURA LIBER CONSEQUENS QUINQUE DE MINIMO & MENSURA. *Francofurti, Apud Ioan. Wechelum & Petrum Fischerum consortes.* 1591 (*S.*154)
Paris (3 cops.), Moscow, Florence[1], Naples, Venice, Bologna U, Berlin (2 cops.), Marburg, Munich; L, O, O[5], O[18], C, C[2], C[16], MU; HD, Y (2 cops.).

25. DE IMAGINUM, SIGNORUM & IDEARUM COMPOSITIONE. *Francofurti. Apud Ioan. Wechelum & Petrum Fischerum consortes.* 1591 (*S.*159).
Paris (2 cops.), Moscow (2 cops.), Florence[1], Rome[1], Bologna U, Pisa U, Marburg (2 cops.), Munich; L. (2 cops.), O, O[5], O[17], C[2], M, MU (2 cops.); HD.

26. SUMMA TERMINORUM METAPHYSICORUM. [Edited by Raphael Elgin.] *Tiguri, Apud Ioannem Wolphium, typis Frosch.* 1595 (*S.*161).
Zurich; O.

RELATIVE RARITY

2 treatises known only by a single copy.

2	„	„	„	„	2 copies.
3	„	„	„	„	3 copies.
2	„	„	„	„	5 or fewer copies.
3	„	„	„	„	12 or fewer copies.
6	„	„	„	„	15 or fewer copies.
8	„	„	by 16 or more copies.

DISTRIBUTION

[One copy only of each of the 26 treatises is included in the following holdings.]

Paris, Bibliothèque Nationale:	20
Oxford, Bodleian Library:	20
London, British Museum:	18
Moscow, Lenin State Public Library:	18
Harvard, Houghton Library:	16
Cambridge, Trinity College:	15
Florence, Biblioteca Nazionale:	14
Manchester University, Christie Collection:	13
Berlin/Marburg (*v.* note under SYMBOLS)	13

NOTE: There are also copies of 1 and 25 in a private collection in London.

JOHN HAYWARD

First Editions of Giordano Bruno
Location of Additional Copies

THE publication in the Summer Number of THE BOOK COLLECTOR of a tentative census of extant copies of the first editions of Giordano Bruno's treatises has led to 114 additional copies being reported. The fact that 80 of them are copies of treatises of which 16 or more copies had already been located tends to confirm the statistics of 'relative rarity', i.e. copies of the rare works are very rare, those of the common ones fairly numerous. Additional copies of only 4 of the rarest works have been located – three of *Cabala del Cavallo Pegaseo*, two of *Oratio Consolatoria*, and one each of *Figuratio Aristotelici Physici Auditus* and *Summa Terminorum*.

I am grateful to those librarians and others who have supplied me with additional information, and, in particular to Dr J. H. L. Pafford, Goldsmiths' Librarian in the University of London, for redeeming my regrettable failure to locate the 16 copies of various treatises in the Durning-Lawrence Collection, by virtue of which London University's holding ties with Harvard's as the sixth largest; and to Dr G. Aquilecchia for the location of more than 30 copies.

ADDITIONAL LOCATIONS

Paris[2]: Bib. Mazarin. Paris[3]: Bib. Arsenal. Toulouse: Bib. Municipale. Hague[1]: Royal Lib. Hague[2]: Masonic Lodge. Stockholm: Royal Lib. Bodmer: Bib. Bodmeriana. TCD: Trinity Coll. Dublin. UCL: Univ. Coll. London. Chatsworth: Duke of devonshire. Burndy Lib. Norwalk, Conn. USA. U=University Library.

1. DE UMBRIS IDEARUM. 1582. Paris[2] (also 2 cops. Part II), Hague[1], Stockholm, Uppsala U; E, London U, UCL (2 cops.), Liverpool U; Cornell U, Burndy (2 cops.).

2. CANTUS CIRCÆUS. 1582. Paris[2,3], Hague[1]; E, London U, UCL; Burndy.

3. DE COMPENDIOSA ARCHITECHTURA etc. 1582. E, London U.

4. CANDELAIO. 1582. Paris[2], Hague[1], Leiden U; E, London U, Chatsworth.

5. ARS REMINISCENDI. [1582]. London U, Peterborough Cathedral.

6. LA CENA DELE CENERI. 1584. Paris[2,3], Bodmer; London U, Chatsworth, TCD.

7. DE LA CAUSA PRINCIPIO, ET UNO. 1584. Paris[2], Hague[1], Leiden U, E; London U, Chatsworth.

8. DE L'INFINITO UNIVERSO ET MONDI. 1584. Paris[2], Hague[1], London U.

9. SPACCIO DE LA BESTIA TRIONFANTE. 1584. Paris[2]; Chatsworth, TCD; Burndy.

10. CABALA DEL CAVALLO PEGASEO. 1585. London U, UCL, Chatsworth.

11. DE GL'HEROICI FURORI. 1585. Paris[3], Leiden U, TOCKHOLM, ODMER; E; London U, Chatsworth.

12. FIGURATIO ARISTOTELICI PHYSICI AUDITUS. [1586.] Burndy.

16. DE LAMPADE COMBINATORIA LULLIANA. 1587. Hague[1,2].

17. DE PROGRESSU ET LAMPADE VENATORIA LOGICORUM. 1587. Hague[1,2]; London U.

19. CAMŒRACENSIS ACROTISMUS. 1588. Hague[1], Uppsala U, Lund U; London U, UCL.

20. DE SPECIERUM SCRUTINO etc. 1588. Toulouse, Toulouse U, Hague[1], Uppsala U; London U, Chatsworth.

22. ORATIO CONSOLATORIA. 1589. Leiden U, Uppsala U.

23. DE TRIPLICI MINIMO ET MENSURA etc. 1591. Paris[3], Hague[1], Groningen U, Stockholm, Uppsala U, Lund U; E, London U, UCL, London Library.

24. DE MONADE NUMERO ET FIGURA etc. 1591. Paris[2,3], Hague[1,2], Leiden U, Utrecht U, Stockholm, Uppsala U, Bodmer; E, Edinburgh U, London U (2 cops.).

25. DE IMAGINUM, SIGNORUM ET IDEARUM COMPOSITIONE. 1591. Paris[2,3], Hague[1], Amsterdam U, Uppsala U, E, London U TCD; (Copy in Cat. 45 (1956) L'Art Ancien, Zurich.)

26. SUMMA TERMINORUM METAPHYSICORUM. 1595. Paris[2].

CORRECTIONS

In the original list of locations Peterborough Cathedral Library should have been credited with a copy of No. 5 and not with a copy of No. 8. The copy of No. 8 at c[2] is missing. O[9] has a second copy of Nos. 17 and 19; F[1] has a second copy of No. 19.

JAMES M. OSBORN

Reflections on Narcissus Luttrell (1657–1732)

ALTHOUGH generations of literary historians have been familiar with the name and even with the handwriting of Narcissus Luttrell, he has remained a shadowy figure. Except for some acid remarks by the Oxonian connoisseur of sour grapes, Thomas Hearne, references to Luttrell by his contemporaries are almost non-existent. That the Oxford antiquary had ever seen Luttrell's library in London is doubtful. In July 1729, Hearne commented in his diary on the 'great and amazing collections' of 'English History and Antiquities' gathered by the 'wonderfully industrious' Luttrell and his son, 'tho' both these Gentlemen . . . are so very curious and knowing, yet I do not find that either of them hath published any thing, notwithstanding both of them are every way qualifyed to do great matters'.

But three years later, prompted by the obituary notice of Luttrell's death, Hearne wrote: 'The forsaid M^r. Luttrell was well known for his curious Library, especially for the number and scarcity, of English History and Antiquities, which he collected in a lucky Hour, at very reasonable rates, books of that nature tho' they have always bore good prices, being much cheaper than they have been of late years. But tho' he was so curious & diligent in collecting and amassing together, yet he affected to live so privately as hardly to be known in person.' Next, the reason for the sour grapes appears: Hearne had tried to borrow from Luttrell a transcript of Leland's *Itinerary*, but his application proved unsuccessful.[1]

Who, then, was Luttrell, what was he, that we commemorate him? The time for commemoration was never more appropriate, for the tercentenary of Luttrell's birth is now upon us. Moreover, just one hundred years ago public interest in Luttrell's manuscript diary, prompted by Macaulay's frequent quotation from it in his *History of England*, led to rivalry between the Camden Society and the Clarendon Press as to who would publish it. The Clarendon Press won, thanks largely to ownership of the manuscript by All Souls College, and in 1857 they published six fat volumes, containing over a million and a quarter words and carrying a title that is a masterpiece of understatement, *A Brief Relation of State Affairs*. With all its drawbacks, the *Brief Relation* remains after a hundred years one of the most valuable tool books for students of life and literature in later Stuart England.

Recently, a hundred years after the *Brief Relation*, a second publication has appeared under Luttrell's name. Entitled *Narcissus Luttrell's Popish Plot Catalogues*, and carrying

---

[1] Hearne mistakenly thought Luttrell owned 'a transcript of a considerable age' of Leland's *Itinerary*. Actually, it was a copy made in 1693 from the Harley MS; it is now at All Souls. For Luttrell's letter to Harley arranging to have the transcript made, see *Notes & Queries*, 20 July 1861, p. 44.

an introduction by F. C. Francis of the British Museum, this slim volume is the fifteenth publication of the Luttrell Society which, in turn, is now celebrating its tenth anniversary of successful existence.

I

Of the 'great matters' for which posterity honours Luttrell, foremost is our debt to him as a collector, the preserver of literature that might otherwise have perished. Luttrell began to buy books in 1675 when he was still a student at Gray's Inn. Two years later the death of his father brought him an estate that the *London Evening Post* (6–8 July 1732) described as 'a plentiful fortune'. Actually, as a group of his own manuscript records (now in my collection) shows, Luttrell's annual income was just over £300 rising to about £475, beginning in his twenty-seventh year. Even allowing for the high value of the pound in Restoration England, these documents show Luttrell's financial status has been frequently exaggerated. But the manuscripts also reveal that Luttrell was financially punctilious; he carefully followed the 'Advise to My Sonn' written out by his father, especially the injunctions, 'Live beneath your estate, not above it', and, 'Runn not into debt upon any pretence whatsoever . . . though a great bargaine bee offerd you'. Not all great book collectors have been able to follow such advice.

By 1679, Luttrell began to buy books actively and soon became an avid collector, as the *Popish Plot Catalogues* illustrate admirably. Early in 1680, an unidentified publisher issued *A Compleat Catalogue of All the Stitch'd Books and Single Sheets Printed since the First Discovery of the Popish Plot*, (*September 1678*). This was followed by a *Continuation* and *Second Continuation*, the publisher promising a new number each term, though no later issues are known. Luttrell's copies of the *Continuation* and *Second Continuation* are preserved in the British Museum, carrying abundant notations in Luttrell's clear handwriting. Of the 617 items listed, Luttrell obtained copies of all but one (T. James's rival edition of the *City Mercury*) and even added six items missed by the compiler of the catalogues.

The Luttrell Society has placed us greatly in its debt by making these two catalogues available, with a graceful and learned introduction by Mr Francis. To the information he has given, a few other points about the catalogues may be added and a few questions raised. For example, it is odd that Luttrell did not jot the date and price on the catalogues themselves, as he customarily did with other books. Also, did Luttrell have a copy of the first catalogue, and if so, is it extant? None of the five copies known to *Wing* (C5630) has any evidence connecting it with Luttrell. In passing it is worth noting that Luttrell's copy of the *Second Continuation* (*Wing* S2269) appears to be unique.

Indeed, the very fact that these catalogues were compiled and published is of considerable interest in the history of British book collecting. The publisher's purpose was stated when the three lists were re-issued later in 1680 as *A General Catalogue* (*Wing* G496), where we read on the title-page, 'Very useful for Gent. that make Collections'. This statement implies that even when the Popish Plot was at its height, enough book collectors were actively accumulating ephemeral publications to encourage the compilation and printing of these catalogues.

The extent of Luttrell's collections on this subject is revealed by his annotated copies of these two catalogues. But other evidence, unmentioned by Mr Francis, occurs in the sale catalogue of the library of James Bindley (Part IV, sold 2–8 August 1820) who had acquired many of the choicest portions of Luttrell's books in 1786. Among the folio items, lot 1130 is described as follows:

A Collection of Tracts relative to the Popish Plot, made by N. Luttrell. In the volume is a very scarce plate, representing the Solemn Mock Procession of the Pope, Cardinals, &c. through London in Dec. 1679, and other plates relating the Popish Plot.

Because this volume sold for £43 1s 0d, it must have contained an extensive group of highly desirable pieces. Probably the contents have now been scattered, but the whole volume may yet be discovered unrecognized on some library shelf.

Luttrell's annotations in the two *Popish Plot Catalogues* contain much detailed information of potential usefulness to historians and bibliographers. The most important fact revealed by overall perusal of the volumes is that the unknown compiler deliberately attempted to list the items in chronological order within each class. This is shown by the dates written in by Luttrell, for they are in chronological series within each class.[2] Judging from the two annotated catalogues, it seems likely that the compiler followed the same practice in the first catalogue, though we lack Luttrell's copy to confirm this inference.

To return to Luttrell's book buying activities, we should remember that these *Popish Plot* tracts were just one division of his collecting interests. Luttrell's collections of poetry were thus described by Edmond Malone, who in his *Life of Dryden* (1800, p. 156) was the first scholar to celebrate Luttrell's literary accumulations. After discussing *Absalom and Achitophel* and *The Medal* Malone wrote: 'Both these poems accordingly were opposed by numerous Answers, of many of which even the titles would have been lost to posterity but for the care and attention of a gentleman of that time, Mr. Narcissus Luttrell, who, having formed a very curious collection of Ancient English Poetry in twenty-four quarto volumes, distinguished by letters of the alphabet, continued his Collection by purchasing the principal poetical productions that appeared in his own time, particularly those of a political kind, which he bound up in folio and quarto volumes, according to their respective sizes. He did not neglect even the single half-sheets at that period almost daily issued from the press, but preserved them with the rest.'

Malone was in a position to know, for he himself had attended the sale in March 1786, when it took twelve days to auction off the library of Edward Wynne, grandson of Luttrell's sister, who had inherited the Luttrell holdings. As the catalogue stated, the 'Great Part of it was formed by an Eminent and Curious Collector of the last century', and the auctioneer singled out for special mention 'a very curious Collection of old English Romances, and old Poetry; with a great Number of scarce Pamphlets during the Great Rebellion and the Protectorate'. The pages of the sale catalogue show that the auctioneers took little effort to sort or describe the masses of books, pamphlets, sermons,

---

[2] Only two exceptions occur: once when Luttrell wrote 'June' where 'May' is required, and the other where the compiler apparently places an item in the wrong position. (*Continuation*, p. 16, item 12; *Second Continuation*, p. 13, item 22.)

tracts, broadsides, proclamations and news-sheets that they sold, almost by the cubic foot. Malone bought several lots, including No. 376, a 'Collection of old Plays, Gascoigne, White, Windet,[3] Decker, etc., etc., 21 vols. – 1594, etc.', for which he paid nearly forty pounds. These twenty-one composite volumes of Elizabethan quartos became the foundation of the Malone collection, one of the most superb assemblages of Elizabethan literature ever brought together by one man.

Another Elizabethan scholar, Joseph Haslewood (1769–1833), though too young to attend the Wynne Sale, later became familiar with segments of the Luttrell collections as they came under the hammer when the libraries of Dr Richard Farmer, George Steevens, Isaac Reed, James Bindley and other buyers of 1786 were dispersed in turn. Haslewood wrote the following observations in his copy of Jacob's *Historical Account of the Lives and Writings of our most considerable English Poets*, now in the British Museum: '[Luttrell] founded and in part formed one of the most extraordinary and valuable collections of fugitive poetical tracts in folio and quarto, and also broadsides and slips, relative to his own times, that are anywhere known. They exceed in interest, if not in value, the king's collection of pamphlets in the British Museum [the Thomason Tracts] and it is a matter of regret that the whole of the Luttrell collections were not, unviolated, placed in that truly national repository.'

Actually, Luttrell did give thought to the desirability of keeping his remarkable library together. Among the Luttrell manuscripts in my collection is his will, signed and witnessed 22 December 1705, wherein, among the legacies to his son Francis, he provided, 'Also I give unto my said Son all my Books, except such English ones as his mother shal think fitt to take'. But there is also another manuscript dated 1705 and headed 'Directions Left in charge to my Wife, wch I desire her to observe [after my death]'. In this document Luttrell advised his spouse, 'And for my books, wch you will also have if Frank dies intestate, you may give them to such of my Relations as will be sure to keep them & make use of them, or to some public Library, as that at Grayes Inn'. This was written, of course, nearly fifty years before the British Museum came into existence.

Still another document, dated 1706, headed 'An Account of My Estate' records that 'since my Father's death I have laid out . . . above 1,500 £ in books all wch I have by me'. This sum is the total spent in Luttrell's first thirty years of collecting, and so indicates that he put out about a £1 per week for books, a sum that seems modest considering the results achieved, though it probably brought several hundred tracts, poems and pamphlets into Luttrell's house every month. For example, the 617 items in the *Popish Plot Catalogues* cost Luttrell £9 7s 3¼d, or an average of less than twopence each. At this rate, Luttrell could have added 4,000 items a year and still have had a third of his outlay to spend for more expensive books, of which he had a fine collection in Latin and Greek, as well as standard English texts. Since his son Francis became an equally avid collector there can be little doubt that after 1705 at least another fifteen hundred pounds worth of printed matter was added to the Luttrell library.

The pages of the 1786 sale catalogue abound with tantalizing evidence of the wide

---

[3] The name Windet is undoubtedly a misprint.

range of Luttrell's collecting activities. Many of the single lots were actually extensive collections, as has been noted in Malone's purchase of quarto plays. The following examples are typical:

Lot 13   [A parcel] consisting of Petitions, Remonstrances, Declarations and other Political Matters, from 1638 to 1660, during the great Rebellion, and the whole of the Protectorate, *a very large Parcel, many of them with cuts.*

Lot 375   Collection of Sermons, from 1678 to 1688 . . . 20 vol. 4to.

Lot 377   Collection of Bills of Mortality, from 1680 to 1704, 2 vol. 4to.

Lot 397   Various scarce and uncommon Tracts on the Plague and other Physical Subjects, from the Year 1572 to the Year 1640, 12 vol. 4to.

Thus it seems clear that the *Popish Plot Catalogues* were one of the formative influences in Luttrell's life. They provided him with a pattern in collecting that he followed in one area after another.

II

Besides the great collections Luttrell gathered and preserved, we are indebted to him for a second 'great matter', his habit of recording the price and date on publications fresh from the press. Here again Edmond Malone in his *Life of Dryden* (p. 156) was first to interpret the situation: '. . . [Mr Luttrell] marked on every poem, and half-sheet, the price it cost, and the day on which he made the purchase; which he appears generally to have made immediately after its publication.' Sir Walter Scott, Haslewood, Thorn Drury, Macdonald and other scholars have taken the same reasonable attitude. But evidence to question this accepted interpretation is provided by another one of Luttrell's manuscripts in my collection.

    This volume is a thick octavo labelled on the spine 'Travel Manuscript'. On the three hundred neatly written pages Luttrell carefully describes his observations on the towns and shires of England, made on fourteen 'Travels', as he calls them, during his early manhood. The first 'Travel' in 1677, from 17 July to 27 September, took him to Cornwall and the west country where family lands were located. During the three following years Luttrell visited most of southern England and East Anglia. It is his fourteenth and last 'Travel' in 1680 that provides the crucial evidence. Luttrell's introductory note reads as follows: 'My fourteenth travell was to Lawrence Waltham to my Cosin Mr Wightwicks in the County of Berks; I began it ye 18th of August. 1680; & continued there till ye 23^d following, when he & I took out journey into ye Counties of Oxon, Glocester, Hereford, Salop, Stafford &c. & I returned again to London ye 25th of September following; in wch time I made my remarks at these places as follow.'

    During the forty-one days while Luttrell was plodding over the roads of these western shires, we should expect a gap in his purchases, if his title-page dates are indeed those of purchase. But the *Popish Plot Catalogues* now available in facsimile show no such gap. On the contrary, Luttrell has written down dates in it for more than forty items published within this span. Similar evidence occurs in the case of several earlier 'Travels', though the number of instances is smaller.

19

Fortunately, we need not rely entirely on the data jotted in the *Catalogues*, since many of the actual printed items are extant in the British Museum, at Harvard and in the collection of Colonel Wilkinson. These printed pieces carry the same dates in Luttrell's hand that he entered in the *Catalogues*, thus confirming the evidence listed there. The conclusion is inescapable that Luttrell's specific dates were not intended to record the dates of purchase as such. Indeed, the abundant evidence argues that Luttrell was noting the day of publication, which, of course, was often the day of purchase. Furthermore, corroboration for this conclusion is found on many of the tracts themselves, where Luttrell inserted the word 'Printed' before the day, month and year.

> Who at this Inſtant lyes deſparately Wounded at his
> Lodgings, near *Temple - Bar, London.*
> Printed. 17. Aprill. 1680.

Luttrell's title-page dates are therefore even more significant than has hitherto been supposed. Taking Dryden as an example, we should now consider, until disproved by other evidence, that *Absalom and Achitophel* was published on 17 November 1681; that the *Medal* first appeared on 16 March 1681/2; that *MacFlecknoe*, though written several years earlier first reached publication on 4 October 1682; and that *Religio Laici* followed on 28 November. So, too, with Dryden's other poems, plays and prologues, not to mention the many printed squibs and rejoinders that Whig party writers aimed at the Laureate's head.

Similarly in the case of other poems and pamphlets, Luttrell dates can now be used to pinpoint the actual day of publication. In order to make this information available, I have been collecting records of Luttrell dates and title-page annotations, with a view to eventual publication in chronological order. The file now numbers well over 2,300 items, gathered with the help of many scholars, librarians, and learned booksellers such as Dudley Massey and the late Percy J. Dobell. The list as it now stands has helped to solve various puzzles, but when published it may perhaps raise as many problems as it settles. Already it has yielded over fifty items 'not in *Wing*', and the possibility of many more.

In addition to details of date and price, Luttrell often wrote comments and criticisms on title-pages. Perhaps the most famous is his jotting on *The Medal of John Bayes*, 'By Thomas Shadwell. Ag^t Mr Dryden. very severe 15 May'. Luttrell's statement is the prime evidence for Shadwell's authorship of this important item of Drydeniana. When *MacFlecknoe* finally appeared in print five months later, Luttrell wrote on the title-page '2^d Ag^t Mr Thomas Shadwell A good poem Mr John Dryden 4 Octob'. Most of Luttrell's title-page comments are brief, and often are stock remarks such as, 'Against ye Whigs', 'A silly poem', or 'A scandalous thing'. In other cases he is more specific, as in the case of a satire entitled *The last sayings of a mouse lately starved in a Cupboard* (9 March 1680/1) where Luttrell's note explains, 'A jeer at Slingsby Bethel, Esq., Sherif of London'. Another beast allegory in 1727, now preserved at Harvard, carried the triple title, *Laugh and be Fat, or a Merry Tale of My grandmother's Cat, or the Drury Lane Cats in an Uproar*; this, Luttrell tells us, is 'upon ye Dutchess of Kendell', a fat cat if George I ever kept one. Sometimes Luttrell inserted annotations in the margins of the text, or filled out names left blank by the printer But the tone is usually of a man talking to himself, as on the title-page of *An Address to the Honorable City of London . . . Concerning their Choice of a New Parliament* (5 Feb. 1680/1), where Luttrell jotted, 'Good wholesome advice and touches a little to home'.

III

Besides these 'great matters' for which posterity is indebted to Luttrell there is yet a third activity in which he has not yet had his due, namely, his labours as a compiler. Luttrell's *Brief Relation of State Affairs* is deservedly the best known of these works from his ever busy pen. Examination of the manuscript shows that it has been printed faithfully according to nineteenth-century standards, with few changes except normalization. But the text lacks annotation entirely, and the index is scarcely adequate. A new, carefully annotated edition of the *Brief Relation* is badly needed.

One of the subjects that cries out for study is Luttrell's sources of information for the *Brief Relation*. The *London Gazette* and other printed newspapers were used, of course, but a comparison of his text with manuscript newsletters still awaits doing. In particular, study should be made of the collection of manuscript and printed sheets catalogued as All Souls No. CLXXI which Luttrell titled as 'State Affairs from Jan. 1678/9 unto Feb. 1681/0 being a Collection of News Letters many of wch contain diverse false stories, & scandalls, wch were then goeing in those times'. These newsletters contain many topics not in the *Brief Relation*; indeed, the lack of coherent correspondence between them and the *Brief Relation* indicates that Luttrell used other sources as well.

Significantly, some of the newsletters that apparently were sources of the *Brief Relation* are in the hand of Jacob Tonson, then a young bookseller recently set up in his own shop. Indeed, the whole relationship between Tonson and Luttrell deserves investigation. The nature of their intimacy in early manhood is revealed by a letter in my collection, dated 3 June 1680, when Luttrell was absent on his tenth 'Travel' to Epsom and other towns in Surrey. Tonson writes Luttrell as follows:

S^r

I sent to yo^{ur} mothers & they sent me word they had nothing to send to you; Mr Damosene was with me, & I hope to bring you some new Tune to morrow; there is litle news Stirring but what is in the Gazet – Nell Guyns Youngest Sonn is newly dead & all the Kings Sonns are to goe into Mourning – & ye Dutchess of Portsmouth has given Mr Duke 7 Guynys To put himself into mourning.

The marquess of Worcester is to bee Duke of Beaufort.

I cald at Mr Starkys and there is nothing of business to send to him.

S^r Yo^{ur} obleidgd Servt
Ja Tonson

June 3^d. 80
The Ld Rochester lyes a dying.[4]

[4] Alexander Damascene (d. 1719), alto singer and song writer, had settled in England in 1679; in 1695 he succeeded Purcell in the Chapel Royal.

Nell Gwyn's nine-year-old son James died in France. Rochester lingered on until 26 July.

Charles, son of Charles II and the Duchess of Portsmouth (born in 1672), had been created Duke of Lennox in 1675. Henry Somerset, the Bezaliel of Dryden's *Absalom and Achitophel*, was not created Duke of Beaufort until 2 Dec. 1682; the title was partly to reward his opposition in 1679–80 to the Exclusion Bill.

John Starkey, the bookseller in Fleet Street, may also have been one of Luttrell's agents at this time. But Luttrell's connection with Tonson, amply supported by extant letters, is reinforced by Luttrell's note on the title-page of his copy of *Absalom and Achitophel*, now in the Huntington Library, 'Ex dono Amici Jacobi Tonson. An Excellent poem ag^t ye Duke of Monmouth, Earl of Shaftsbury & that party, & in vindicaon of the King & his freinds'.

To return to Luttrell's other manuscript compilations, a number of useful volumes repose in the Library at All Souls College, Oxford. They came there in 1786, by gift from Luttrell Wynne, Fellow of the College and heir to the Luttrell Collections, most of which were sold during March of that year as part of his brother Edward's estate, in the sale mentioned earlier. Among the Luttrell manuscript compilations at All Souls the following may be cited:

Abstracts of Proceedings in the House of Commons, 1691–3 (CLVIII).
[Similar abstracts for 1698–1] (CLIX);
Abstracts of the Journals of the House of Commons (CLXXVI);
Remarkable Speeches, Letters and Verses (CLV);
Notes on Legal Cases 1660 [to *c.* 1700] (CXLV);
Calendar of papers in the Tower of London made by Luttrell in 1703/4. (CXII).

One hundred and fifty years later still other compilations were scattered among buyers when on 4 May 1936 another portion of Luttrell Wynne's inheritance was consigned by his heirs.[5] This event, known to collectors as the Pendarves Sale, included various manuscript compilations. Several are now in my collection, including an 'Account of the Parliament Rolls' from the reign of Edward II to that of Richard II (Pendarves #139) and 'A Treatise Wherein are Discussed several heads or points of Divinity' (Pendarves #135), compiled in three notebooks between 1695 and 1704. This 'Treatise' serves as a useful index to contemporary attitudes on dozens of religious subjects. Once again it shows how Luttrell made use of his book collections to condense various opinions under topic headings into a compendium for ready reference.

Another volume from the 1936 sale has recently come to rest in the Folger Shakespeare Library, a quarto manuscript labelled 'Popish and Protestant Controversies' (Pendarves #138). In parallel columns the arguments of each side are contrasted on various topics, such as 'Ceremonies', 'Dispensations' and 'Idolatry'. This manuscript provides yet another example of the impact on Luttrell of the eruption that shook England in his twenty-first year' namely the *Popish Plot*. Indeed, the Popish Plot also dominates the early pages of the *Brief Relation* in which the first sentence reads: '1678. *September*. – About the latter end of this month was a hellish conspiracy . . . discovered by one Titus Oates unto sir Edmondbury Godfrey, justice of peace, who took his examination on oath'.

---

[5] A further portion (68 lots) was sold at Sotheby's 19 Feb. 1957.

IV

A final citation of manuscript evidence is in order before we conclude these tercentenary observances. It is a letter in my collection from the eccentric bookseller John Dunton, which provides an eloquent demonstration of the reputation that Luttrell's collections held among professional bookmen. Dated 30 December 1707, it is addressed:

To M^r. Luttrell a Member of Parliament, liueing ouer against the Three Cupps In Holborn

   S^r.

I had not presumed to haue troubled you with this Letter but that I am under a Necessity of entreating your Generous assistance towards compleating a work now going to ye Press Viz. I haue all the Volumes of ye Athenian Mercuries saue the 18th and 19th volum, and The History of ye Athenian Society, and haue searcht in near an Hundred likely Places for them & can't yet find y^m. but was yesterday inform'd by Mr Goodwin Bookseller in Fleetstreet that 'tis very Probable that you haue them (as you haue bin a Good Benefactor to the Booksellers in buying most New Peices) this comes therefore humblely to Entreat, you'd lend to Mr Bell the Bookseller in Cornhill, these 3 Peices before mention'd being all 3 wanted to compleat a Supplement to *ye 3 Volumes* of ye Athenian Oracle lately Publish'd – S^r. your Generosity in this Matter will be a Reall Peice of seruice to ye Publick as I know not where to procure them ('tho ye Athenian Mercury was my own Project) and I hope that scarcity will in some measure excuse this Great Presumption. S^r. M^r. Bell ye undertaker shall when ye Supplement is Printed Present you with a Compleat Set of the Athenian Oracle for your Generosity in lending this 18th. and 19th. Volum and History of ye Athenian Society & those 3 you lend shall (when Printed) be returnd as safe as Gold and 'tho there Ualue was but 6^s all 3 when first Publish'd if you desire it y^e. Bearer hereof shall leaue a Pledge 'till they are return'd – S^r. I haue only to ask your Pardon for this Presumption, and leaue to subscribe My selfe –

your Very Humble Seruant
John-Dunton.

From ye Sword in Black Fryars
   Dec: 30th: 1707.

That the transaction was consummated is attested by the following memorandum written in Luttrell's hand, but signed by Dunton, a week after his first application:

6. Januar. 170 ⅞.

Received & borrowed then of Mr Luttrell one book in folio, intitled The Athenian Gazett or Casuistical Mercury beginning 11. July. 1693. Volumn. 11th. & ending.[ ].14.June.1697. in vol. 20th. bound in Cambridge Sort of binding; wch I hereby faithfully promise to return Safe & undammaged upon demand; & have for the Security thereof deposited in ye said Mr Luttrell's hands two guineas. & I [being] intending to make use thereof in ye publicaon of y^e [History of] Supplement to ye Athenian Oracle &c. I hereby promise to p^resent ye same Athenian Oracle Compleat to Mr Luttrell gratis, Witnesse my hand

To ye Sword in Black Fryars   John - Dunton

Thus even midway in his collecting career Luttrell's accumulations began to serve the literary public. Luttrell's books and annotations have proven increasingly useful as literary scholars have mapped out the detailed history of Augustan England. Our chief regret is that the great library was so widely dispersed. Yet today we acknowledge an obligation to Narcissus Luttrell that has increased over the centuries. We can say of this modest, curious and wonderfully industrious man, 'every way qualifyed to do great matters', what can be said about relatively few of his contemporaries – that three hundred years after his birth we stand more in his debt than has any generation before our time.

Cipher stamped in many of Luttrell's books from about 1692 onwards

Philip Hofer

PHILIP HOFER was born with a highly developed collecting instinct and it has continued to increase as through the years he has given it considerable exercise. Today if he should find himself in some part of the world where there were no books, manuscripts, or drawings available he would probably begin collecting portable objects of another type, but always ones which would appeal to a discerning taste. And when he returned to a place where the objects of his particular passion were obtainable he would immediately begin a systematic and indefatigable tour of all the book and art shops of that region.

He began book collecting before he entered Harvard in 1917 and still has the first book he remembers having bought as a 'fine' book, a copy of *Baron Munchausen*, illustrated by William Strang and purchased from N. J. Bartlett of Cornhill, Boston. In recent years he has added to it the original drawings. In college he collected in many fields including Press Books and first editions of English literature. Later when these books no longer interested him, or he had finer copies, they were dispersed at auction in 1933. Among the books then sold were fine copies of first editions of Blackstone, Boswell, Fielding, Gibbon, Gray, Pepys, Smollett and Gilbert White, all in the proper condition, although perhaps the most unusual was Richard Bull's copy of Chesterfield's *Letters*, 1774, in contemporary red morocco. That he should have then sold the Chew-Williams presentation copy of Edward Benlowes's *Theophila*, 1652, may seem odd in view of his later interest in English 17th-century book-illustration, until one realizes that he already had the much finer Bindley copy of that book, the type copy against which, since Lowndes's description of it, all other copies have been measured.

By 1927, when he had proved his ability as a businessman, and returned to Harvard to study the history of art in all its forms and thenceforth to devote himself to study, collecting, and teaching in those fields which most interested him, he already had determined that he would build a comprehensive collection which would illustrate the arts of the book, from the earliest times to the present. He has, of course, not limited his collecting to printed books and manuscripts, for his collections of master drawings and prints, unconnected with books, and his activities as trustee or adviser to numerous art museums, are another story which we must not touch at this time. For several years he was in charge of the Spencer Collection of the New York Public Library, an experience which he now regards as of great educational value but which at the time was occasionally frustrating, for some of his finest purchases, all of which were of course offered to the trustees, were quite properly pre-empted by them. Then, after a term as assistant to

Miss Greene of the Morgan Library, he came to Harvard in 1938 to establish in the Harvard Library a Department of Printing and Graphic Arts.

This Department, the first of its kind, at least in the generous dimensions with which Mr Hofer has envisaged it, for it is built around his own collection of well over ten thousand books and manuscripts, is designed to make possible the study of the history of the development of the arts of the book, from classical times to the present day, both manuscript and printed, and in all countries both Western and Oriental where those arts have flourished. Since it is located in a library which contains nearly seven million volumes, it is supplemented by countless examples which might, in many cases, have otherwise been chosen for the collection and which, in any case, are available for study and comparison.

This circumstance is of great relevance, for throughout his collecting career Mr Hofer has been far more interested in quality than quantity, in choice copies of the unusual rather than the rare but well known, in the finest of its kind rather than a complete series. His practice in regard to Press Books may illustrate this, for believing that most presses tend to a certain sameness he has chosen from the output of those he regards as important only a few examples of their best and most typical, generally copies on vellum, with drawings and proofs, and in special bindings. But in the case of contemporary presses, in the integrity of which Mr Hofer believes, he is apt to have a complete series with even, perhaps, some pieces which he has commissioned himself. Of the Ashendene Press books he has a superb selection, many on vellum and in appropriate bindings, but of most other presses while he may have proofs, drawings and other ephemera, he is likely to have only a few representative books, whereas the Harvard Library frequently possesses complete runs of ordinary copies.

All collectors are apt to spend more time bemoaning lost opportunities rather than gloating over their triumphs, and Mr Hofer has often said that he wishes he had acquired more illuminated manuscripts when they were available, at least when they could be acquired for less than the cost of a mansion. However, there has been no time during his four decades of collecting when he had a blind eye for manuscripts, though in the 1930s most of the manuscripts he acquired were calligraphic rather than illuminated. Now he must have some five hundred or more European manuscripts, not counting over a hundred single leaves, nearly half of which are classed by him as calligraphic – the borderline is often difficult to establish – and they range from the 8th to the 20th century. One hundred and forty of them were exhibited at Harvard in 1955 and the catalogue which was then published gives a better idea of their quality, variety and interest than anything that might be said in the space here available. However, it is perhaps appropriate to remark that the proportion of liturgical manuscripts is less than is usually found in such collections and that if the quality is very high Mr Hofer has on occasion acquired a fragment if he could not have a complete manuscript. He has likewise gone into fields not often trod by manuscript collectors, such as Polish and Portuguese, and has frequently acquired finely illuminated manuscripts of much later date than the range usually sought by collectors.

In recent years he has collected Ethiopian, Arabic, Persian, Turkish, Indian, Nepalese, Siamese, and Chinese manuscripts and has well over a hundred codices and forty scrolls as well as many fragments of great beauty and importance. A few years ago he began collecting Japanese manuscripts, as he has recounted in this journal (Winter, 1958) and now has over one hundred and fifty, a third dating from the 8th to the 16th century, and the rest of the 17th and 18th centuries, of considerable iconographic interest and charm.

Incunabula have interested Mr Hofer only spasmodically – the most important pieces, from an artistic standpoint, are so well known and have been so often studied that, compared to the vast prices they fetch when they are available, they provide less satisfaction than those less known. This, together with the fact that copies are available at Harvard, may explain why on various occasions Mr Hofer has parted with his copy of the first Latin edition of Breydenbach, or the first Aldine *Poliphilus*, even though he was the first to notice and publish the variations to be found in copies of the latter. (At the same time he avidly collected all the later editions of the *Poliphilus* and now has them complete, including the English 1592 edition.) The hundred and twenty incunabula which he has kept, however, are a distinguished lot and include a relatively large number of unique copies. They begin with the fine Holford copy of the block-book *Apocalypsis S. Joannis*, and among fifteen illustrated Florentine books may be mentioned the unique *Epistole et Euangeli*, c. 1500; the Tuppo *Aesop*, Naples, 1485; the *Compania del Rosario* [1485]; the Pinelli–Crofts–Crevenna–Heathcote–Heber copy of *Uberto e Philomena*, c. 1495, of which only one other is known (Plate I); Lorenzo de' Medici, *Canzone per andare in Maschera*, c. 1495; and the Cessolis, *Libro di Giuoco di Scacchi*, 1493. Among the German books are the immaculate Maihingen copy of the Ulm *Ptolemy*, 1482, the Passau *Missale*, Augsburg, 1494, with the crucifixion cut printed in four colours, and the Ingold, *Das Goldene Spiel*, Augsburg, 1472, probably the first illustrated sporting book. Two editions of the Malermi Bible, Venice, 1490 and 1494; the *Psaltir a Posledovaniem*, Cetinje, 1495, a Montenegran incunable of which only one other copy is known; a noble copy, in very fine original state, of the Sarum *Missal* printed at Rouen, 1497, likewise one of two known; and the Lyell copy of the first Spanish illustrated book, Enriquez Villenas, *Los Trabajos de Hercules*, Zamora, 1483, also deserve recording. But one could go on indefinitely for each one of his books of this period has been chosen with care either for the illustration or for its fine contemporary illumination or binding.

In the 1920s when many collectors were still concerned with collecting incunabula by presses, Mr Hofer was eagerly collecting in the 16th century, mainly for the illustrations, and with a catholicity of subject and a breadth of coverage which is truly astonishing, and, of course, today impossible to duplicate. A catalogue of the French books of this period is now in preparation for publication and perhaps it is less important to give very much detail regarding them. The Geoffroy Torys are not complete but include among more than a dozen volumes of his finest productions several extraordinary ones, such as a copy of the *Heures*, 1525, illuminated and bound by the binder of Cardinal de Granvelle, either for the Cardinal or for presentation to Charles V, and the magnificently preserved dedication copy of the 1527 *Heures*, bound in full calf, gilt, 'aux armes', for Francis I, as well as one of the very few vellum copies of the 1535 *Diodorus Siculus*. One could go on for pages recording the remarkable books from the presses of Denis Janot, Jean de Tournes, Estienne, Vascosan, and the others, but perhaps a comparison with the C. Fairfax Murray collection of French 16th-century books may be more illuminating.

PLATE I. *Uberto & Philomena Tracta damore*
[Florence, *c.* 1495.] 208 × 138 mm.
(Hofer Collection, Cambridge, Mass.)

That collection contained a few more than five hundred 16th-century books, while the Hofer Collection contains some six hundred, of which at least eighty are the same books, often the same copy. While a good many of the Murray books are more remarkable for their literary importance (those, for example, by Bruno, Montaigne, and Rabelais) or for their bindings than for their illustration or printing, there are fewer of this type in the

Hofer Collection and when they occur they were chosen because they are well printed or illustrated, such as the first edition of the *Marguerites de la Marguerite*, Lyons, 1547; the lovely little first edition of Maurice Scève's *Saulsaye*, Lyons, J. de Tournes, 1547; the unique Ronsard, *Les Figures et Pourtraicts des Sept Aages de l'Homme*, 1579–80; the fine Blanchemain copy of the first collected quarto edition of Ronsard, *Les Oeuvres*, Paris, 1567; or *Les Dix Premiers Livres de l'Iliade*, Paris, 1545, one of the handsomest of French books, in a fine large copy bound in vellum gilt, extra, for Nicholas de Herberay, which later belonged to J. A. de Thou, Montgermont, and Rahir.

If one compares the two collections in general, the Murray Collection contained a larger proportion of early romances and translations in gothic letter, frequently with 15th-century cuts, whereas the Hofer Collection has a much larger number of illustrated or finely printed books, many in roman or italic, printed in Paris and Lyons in the middle of the 16th century, the greatest period of French typography and the one which has had the most influence on later periods. Although both collections have copies of Jean Pelerin dit Viator, *De Artificiali P[er]spectiva*, Toul, 1505, and the Tory edited edition of Leon Battista Alberti's *Libri de re aedificatoria*, Paris, 1512, the Hofer copy of the first being the Dietrichstein copy and of the second a fine copy in a John Reynes binding, architecture evidently was not a subject of much interest to Fairfax Murray. It is, however, one which has interested Mr Hofer, and he has acquired fine copies of all the important French architectural books of this period, as for example, first editions of Sebastiano Serlio's *Il primo [quinto] libro d'Architettura*, Paris, 1545–47; the first complete French edition, with illustrations by Jean Goujon, of Vitruvius, Paris, 1547; the first French Alberti, Paris, 1553; one of the handsomest books of the time, the first edition of Jean Cousin, *Livre de perspective*, Paris, 1560; a complete run of the works of Philibert de l'Orme, 1561–76, and magnificent copies of the works of Jacques Androuet du Cerceau, one being the de Thou copy, as well as a fine vellum manuscript of du Cerceau. None of the books just listed was in the Murray Collection.

Among the more remarkable of the French books of this period there is room only to mention the de Seillière-Hoe copy of Robert Gobin, *Les Loups Ravissans*, Paris, Verard, c. 1503, one of the most powerful and rarest of early French illustrated books; the Gaston III Phébus, *Les Deduiz de la Chasse*, Paris, Verard, c. 1507; the apparently unique Rahir copy of the first Denis Janot Aesop, *Les Fables*, Paris, 1542, as well as the equally important Jean de Tournes, 1547 edition; five works of Gilles Corrozet, none of which, by the way, was in the Murray Collection, including the Guyot de Villeneuve–Montgermont–Rahir copy of the very rare *Les blasons domestiques*, 1539; and the first edition of Claude Paradin, *Devises Heroïques*, Lyons, J. de Tournes, 1551.

The German books of the 16th century in the Hofer Collection are nearly twice as numerous as in the Murray Collection, but many of the more important ones, from the standpoint of illustration, are in both collections. It might, however, be of interest to compare them in relation to the work of one or two artists. Of Hans Weiditz, the Hofer Collection has some eighty books with one or more cuts, just about double the number in the Murray Collection, including the Maihingen copy of the very rare Plautus, *Zwo Comedien*, Augsburg, 1518, which contains some of his earliest work, as well as the almost equally rare *Das Buechlin ... der Gilgengart*, Augsburg, 1520, the Prince d'Essling copy. Of Albrecht Dürer, the two collections are more nearly equal in number, both having nearly all the important books, but the Hofer Collection has both the Latin and the German 1498 editions of the *Apocalypsis*, the only such pair in America, as well as the 1511 edition which was the only one in the Murray Collection, and while both collections have the *Befestigung der Stett*, Nuremberg, 1527, the Hofer copy is one of two known (the other being now in Australia) with the folding cut of the siege. Hans Baldung Grien is represented by thirteen books, which include most of the important ones with his illustrations, such as Ulrich Pinder's *Der beschlossene Garten des Rosenkranzes*, Nuremberg, 1505, in a fine monastic binding from S. Erentrude's at Nuremberg; his *Speculum Passionis*, Nuremberg, 1507, with the arms of Nuremberg on the binding; and the Marcus von Lindau, *Die sehn Gebote in diesem Buch*, Strassburg, 1516. Among over twenty books with cuts by Lucas Cranach there should be mentioned an early Luther Bible, Wittenberg, 1523–4, and the *Missale Pragensis*, Leipzig, M. Lotter, 1522, which is likewise noteworthy for the full-page frontispiece of three saints now attributed to Grunewald, and (if the attribution is correct) the only woodcut by this most remarkable of German artists (Plate II). Among a number of volumes with cuts by Hans Schäuffelein, perhaps the rarest is a copy in original binding with the super-libris of the nunnery of Nonnberg, Salzburg, of Hans Leonrodt's *Hymelwag*, Augsburg, 1517. Of the seven or eight books with cuts by Hans Burgkmaier the Hofer copy of the Melchior Pfintzing, *Theuerdank*, Nuremberg, 1517, is a very fresh and clean one on vellum, bound for the Emperor Charles VI in an 18th-century imitation, a most unusual specimen, of a 16th-century-blind-stamped binding.

One can only suggest the variety and importance of this section by remarking that it ranges from the Strassburg *Ptolemy* of 1513, with the Lorraine map printed in three colours, to a volume containing five embroidery pattern books, Frankfurt, 1564–75, mostly unrecorded, bound for Princess Anna of Saxony in the style of Jacob Krause. Many of the books in this period, however, illustrate the German taste of that time by being hand-coloured, often heightened with gold, and in the fine plaque or enamel bindings of the period. Among examples of this type there may be mentioned the Petrus Apianus, *Astronomicum Caesarum*, Ingoldstadt, 1540; a 'Royal' copy of the great two-volume Wittenberg Bible, 1551, 1550; the Strassburg *Josephus* of 1578, and the rare privately published two volumes on surveying by Paul Pfinzing von Henfenfeld, *Methodus Geometrica* and *Soli Deo Gloria*, Nuremberg, 1598–9, the Lichtenstein copies. Along with these last Mr Hofer has a fine manuscript by Pfinzing on perspective, and his copy of Cyprian Leowitz's *Eclipsium* Omnium, 1554, is accompanied by the original manuscript with miniatures in gold and colours from which it was derived.

The Italian 16th-century books in the Hofer Collection number almost five hundred and are a very distinguished lot, for they include most of the well-known illustrated books as well as many unique or very rare ones which are less well known. All, or very nearly all, of the books which have cuts after Titian are represented here, including the rare chiaroscuro cut in Pietro Aretino's *Stanze in Lodi di Angela Sirena*, Venice, 1537. The *Epistole: & euagelii volgari hystoriade*, Venice, 1512, the Huth-Dyson Perrins copy, contains the only known woodcut after Marc Antonio Raimondi and the *Oscuri Passi del l'Opera Ionica di Vitruvio*, Mantua, 1558, contains a brilliant and almost unknown

S.Adalbertus. S.Sigiſmūd⁹. S.Uitus. S.wenceſla⁹.

PLATE II. *Missale Szm Ritū Setē Ecclesie Pragensis in Bohemia*
Leipzig, 1522. 308 × 210 mm.
(Hofer Collection, Cambridge, Mass.)

engraved frontispiece featuring Hercules, signed by Giorgio Ghisi after a design by G. B. Bertano, the author of the book (Plate IV).

The apparently unique copy of G. P. Ferraro's *Opera nuova historiata di Christo*, Milan, 1563, contains a series of impressions of the famous 15th-century 'Specchio di Anima' Lombard cuts. The real first edition (dated 1 March 1508) of the *Libellus de Natura Animalium*, printed at Mondovi, is an important bestiary and a rare one formerly supposed to be unique. Among a fine selection of Francesco Marcolino imprints there may be mentioned the Didot copy, on vellum, of his *Officium Beate Marie Virginis*, Venice, 1545; and copies of the first and second editions of his *Le Sorti*, 1540 and 1550, with the woodcut title signed Joseph Porta apparently based on Raphael's 'School of Athens' fresco or a study for it. (Three manuscripts of this text, Italian, French and German, evidently prepared for later editions of it, are also in the Collection.) A similar work, Sigismondo Fanti's *Triompha di Fortuna*, is here in both the first, 1526, and second, 1527, editions. Among several editions of Domenico Fontana's *Della Trasportatione dell'Obelisco Vaticano* are two variant copies of the first edition, Rome, 1590, one of which is in a fine contemporary silver and gold binding.

Among some thirty-five Florentine woodcut books of this century are several which are unique and a number which are very important, including eighteen 'Rappresentazioni'. Miss Anna Hoyt, who is making a study of the Florentine woodcut books, has stated that the Hofer Collection supplemented by those in the Harvard Library and the Boston Museum of Fine Arts furnishes a greater concentration of both quality and quantity than is to be found elsewhere in America. As examples only, there may be cited the Frezzi *Quadriregio*, 1508, the *Fior di Virtu hystoriati*, 1511, Petrarch's *Triomphi*, 1518, *Le Dodici Fatiche di Hercole*, 1550 (from Fairfax Murray) and 1568 (from Huth), Boccaccio's *Ninfale Fiesolano*, 1568, and the *Contrasti Viva e Morto*, 1572.

Among a number of books of which the literary interest is as great as the artistic there may be mentioned the Beckford–Montgermont copy of the Valgrisi 1562 edition of *Orlando Furioso*, in red morocco with the arms of Anibal, Count Altemps; the first Girolamo Porro edition of the same book, Venice, 1584, the Didot copy bound for Méry del Vic; the Ashburnham–Hoe copy of Pietro Bembo's *Lettere*, Rome, 1548, the only known copy on vellum, in a fine contemporary gilt binding; a thick paper copy of Ludovico Dolce's *Le Trasformationi*, Venice, 1553, bound possibly for Cardinal Granvelle, as well as a blue paper copy of the same book, and two coloured copies heightened with gold of the Tasso, *La Gierusalemme Liberata*, Genoa, 1590, which was probably the inspiration of the coloured copies of the London 1591 Harington *Ariosto*, the Lady Arabella Stewart copy of which on large paper is also in the Collection.

The bindings in this section are particularly fine, for besides a good many of the typical Aldine style there are unusual bindings such as one for Pier Luigi Farnese, with his upright device, the Britwell–Wilmerding copy of Giovanni Villani, *Croniche*, Venice, 1537, which is remarkable also for having a woodcut putto after Titian; and the dedication copy bound for the Emperor Rudolph II of Bernardo Parthenius, *De Poetica Imitationi*, Venice, 1577, formerly in the Wilmerding collection, in a painted vellum binding of great charm, the equal of, though quite different from, the best in the Pilloni library.

The Spanish and Portuguese 16th-century books number one hundred and seventy. They include the collection, fifty-seven volumes, of J. P. R. Lyell, the only ready-made collection which Mr Hofer has ever acquired. To that collection he has added many books of very great distinction as, for example, a vellum copy of Ludolphus de Saxonia, *Aqui acaba el vita Xpi*, Alcala de Henares, 1502, which, while only part four of the *Vita Christi*, is a very handsome volume; a copy of an otherwise unknown edition of Andreas de Li, *Repertorio de los Tiempos*, Valencia, 1501; the Herédia copy, printed on vellum, of Jacobo Marquelles, *Commentaria*, Barcelona, 1505; and an apparently unique *Passionarium Oxonense*, Burgo de Gama, 1562, with the title printed in four colours. An extraordinary pair are the Fernandez de la Gama, *Copilacio delos establecimientos dela orden dela caualleria de satiāgo del espada*, Seville, 1503, and the Portuguese *Regra: statutos: & diffincoes: da ordem de Sanctiagno*, Sebutal, 1509. Among other notable Portuguese books there may be cited the Huth–Brooke–Harmsworth copy of the first edition of *Marco paulo*, Lisbon, 1502; a very fine copy in the original vellum envelope-binding of a beautifully illustrated *O compromisso da confraria da misericordia*, Lisbon, 1516, printed in red and black (Plate III); and a fine copy in the original Portuguese dark green morocco, gilt, of the *Coronica do Condeestabre dom Muno Alurez Pereyra*, Lisbon, 1554, attributed to Fernao Lopez. It was from the full page woodcut in this book that a recent Portuguese postage-stamp was taken.

The Dutch and Flemish books of this period number well over a hundred volumes and are representative of all the major artists who were employed in the Netherlands. A number of the cuts of that most famous of Dutch woodcut books, the *Chevalier Délibéré* of 1485, are found in the William Morris copy of the *Vitaspatrum*, Leyden, 1511. Lucas van Leyden cuts appear in the Utrecht *Missale*, Leyden, 1514, and in the *Cronycke van Hollandt*, Leyden, 1517, which also has *Chevalier Délibéré* cuts. The Huth copy, one of five known, nearly all the others imperfect, of the Alardus Amstelredamus, *Passio domini nostri Jesu Christi*, Amsterdam, 1523, contains a large number of cuts by Jacob Corneliss (van Oostzanen). Among other illustrated books of particular interest may be mentioned the Willems copy of the Columna, *Historie van de Destruction van Troyen*, Antwerp, c. 1501, and what appears to be the only known copy of Cornelius van Hoorn, *Epitome*, Utrecht, 1537. The Antwerp 1503 and 1536 editions of Ludolphus of Saxonia repeat many cuts from the 15th-century editions; and the Hofer Collection contains fine runs of the usual illustrated books, such as those of Goltzius, and the liturgical, botanical, entrée and emblem books printed by Plantin. Of less obvious relevance but present in distinguished copies are the Dutch, Latin and French editions of Abraham Ortelius's atlases of 1572, 1595, and 1598; a fine set of first editions of Jan van der Noot; and a magnificent copy, with the cuts heightened with gold, of Hieronymus Natalis, *Adnotationes et Meditationes*. Antwerp, 1595, bound in elaborately tooled red morocco for Colbert, with the arms of Count Hoym let in, and later in the La Vallière and Beckford collections.

The Swiss 16th-century books again number well over a hundred and include a very remarkable representation of the book illustration and decoration of Hans Holbein, including all or nearly all his title-borders and sets of initials, all but one of the original editions of the 'Dance of Death' (the exception being the 1542 Latin edition). He also

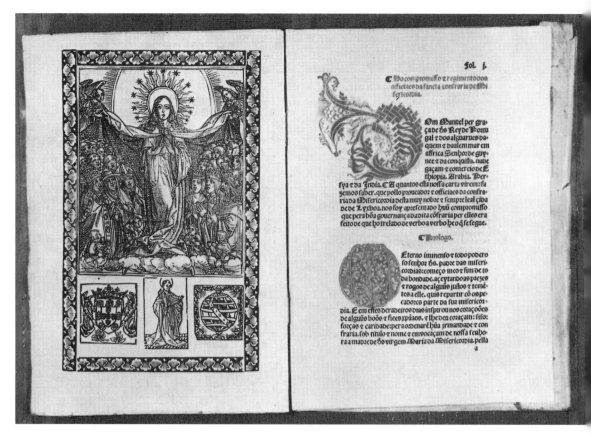

PLATE III. *O compromisso da confraria da misericordia*
Lisbon, 1516. 300 × 219 mm.
(Hofer Collection, Cambridge, Mass.)

has thirty-nine out of forty of the 'Dance of Death' proofs (Von Lanna's first and pre-ferred group of thirty-six among them). The Old Testament cuts are there in the Latin editions of 1538, 1539, 1544, 1547 (two variant copies), as well as the Spanish 1543 (two variant copies) and the English 1549. The English Holbeins are also well represented and, among many others which might be mentioned such as the *Grynaeus* there is a fine impression of the first state of the 'term' portrait of Erasmus. Among the earlier works of importance is the second edition of La Tour-Landry's *Der Ritter vom turn*, Basle, 1513, which repeats the Dürer woodcuts of the 1493 edition; the two first issued of Wimpheling's *De fide concubinarum in sacerdotes*, Basle, *c.* 1501 and *c.* 1503, with wood-cuts by the Master D. S. who also illustrated the fine *Missale Saltzburgensis*, Basle, 1510; and two copies, one coloured and the other uncoloured, of the *Von der Zurstörung der Bapstums*, Basle, *c.* 1550. Along with several handsome Gesners, Erasmuses, Fuchses, and Bibles there should be mentioned a magnificent series of Vesalius, including both the Latin and German first editions of the *Epitome*, Basle, 1546, as well as the first and sec-ond *Fabrica*, Basle, 1543 and 1555, all in original pigskin.

34

PLATE IV. G. B. Bertano, *Gli Oscuri . . . Passi del l'Opera Ionica di Vitruvio*
Mantua, 1558. 380 × 215 mm.
(Hofer Collection, Cambridge, Mass.)

The English books of this period include most of the more important ones such as Cunningham's *Cosmographicall Glasse*, 1559; Recorde's *The Castle of Knowledge*, 1556; a first *Geminus* in original vellum; a superb Saxton's Atlas, from the Hoe sale, coloured and heightened with gold, and a fine original London binding; and the Britwell copy of Tottell's *Boccaccio*, 1554, with the two magnificent 'Dance of Death' cuts. A vellum copy of the second 'Morton' Missal, Pynson, 1520, and two copies, one on thick-paper quarto, the other on large-paper folio, the latter noted above, with contemporary colouring, of Harington's *Ariosto*, 1591, are all that can be recorded by name. It is a small but select group of about forty items. Of Scandinavian books there is room only to mention the first Swedish bible ('Gustavus Vasa's') Uppsala, 1541 (1540), and the first Danish Bible ('Christian III's') Copenhagen, 1550. Seven or eight illustrated books printed in Cracow include Matthias de Miechow's *Chronica Polonorum*, 1521, *Crescentius* in Polish [1549], and the *Herbarium Polonicum*, 1568. Among a similar number of Czech books there are Wenceslaus Hajek, *Kronyka Czeska*, Prague, 1541, and the *Machsor Rosch Haschanah*, Prague, 1533, complete. Another unusual volume is the *Mishneh Torah* printed in Constantinople in 1509, with a fine title-border first used in Ixar in Spain in 1487.

Mr Hofer very early realized that the 17th century was a neglected area that, so far as book-illustration was concerned, had never been widely explored by collectors. As many of the finest of Baroque books are very large, it still remains a field that few private collectors dare enter. A measure of his success and the variety and quality of these books may be seen in his own *Baroque Book Illustration* (Harvard University Press, 1951), which has reproductions from some one hundred and fifty books then in his collection. Mr Hofer's 17th-century books now total some thirteen or fourteen hundred volumes, for since his survey was published he has acquired many books that might have been included in it had they been on his shelves when it was prepared. His territorial coverage in this century, ranging from Japan to Peru, makes a proper survey impossible. However, it may be said that he has all the illustrations by Rembrandt, and practically all, if not all, the books with illustrations engraved after designs by Rubens, Poussin, and the other major 17th-century artists who designed illustrations for books, including many rare Callots.

What Mr Hofer's pioneer treatise does not reveal is the special quality of many of the volumes in this part of his collection, their binding, provenance, and often the freshness of their condition. One of his two copies of the Duke of Newcastle's *Methode*, Antwerp, 1658, for example, is a presentation copy in fine contemporary morocco from the Beckford and Rosebery collections; one of three variant copies of Antoine de Pluvinel, *Maneige Royal*, Paris, 1623, has the arms of Louis XIII and was later in the Rochefoucauld and Earl Grey collections. The *Philostrate* of 1614 is in full red morocco with the arms of Guillaume du Vair while the 1629 edition is likewise in red morocco with the chiffres of Peiresc, du Vair's great friend; and the *Ovid* of 1619 is Gaston d'Orléans', in full morocco. Hieronymo Tetios, *Aedes Barbarinæ*, Rome, 1642, is in contemporary green morocco with black inlay having the arms of Elizabeth, the Winter Queen, and was later in the Colbert collection. The *Breviarium Romanum*, Antwerp, 1614, with ten full-page engravings after Rubens, is in red morocco with the arms of Cardinal Scipione Borghese. *Le Pastissier Français*, Amsterdam, 1655, is in a mosaic binding by Thibaron, and belonged to Elizabeth, Duchess of Manchester; and so it goes with volume after volume. *Les Tapisseries du Roy*, 1670, part of the *Cabinet du Roy*, *is* accompanied by twenty-four exquisite gouaches with gold emblems on vellum by Jacques Bailly which evidently were the source of many of the designs in that book. Indeed, among Mr Hofer's 17th-century books there are numerous royal copies and as many books bound in contemporary morocco 'aux armes' as in calf.

When one thinks of illustrated 18th-century books one inevitably envisages French illustrated books of the 'Fermiers Generaux' type in original citron morocco, *à l'oiseau, aux armes, avant lettres, et avec les dessins originaux*, of a fairly restricted type. Mr Hofer's 18th-century books, which number nearly three thousand, have relatively few of this kind beyond the great monuments – his 'du Régent', *Longus*, 1719, the first typical French 18th-century 'illustrated book', is in a Derome binding with ticket, and his *Monument de Costume*, 1789, the Edward Arnold copy in a Chambolle-Duru binding, is a much better than average copy of this last of the 'de luxe' books. He has chosen rather to collect only the best of the fête books, generally in presentation bindings, many 'Voyages pittoresques', the great illustrated books of palaces and churches, and especially the books of architecture and ornament of which he has a number of very fine copies. More particularly he has chosen to collect the little known but frequently remarkable books of science printed in France during this century when even pictures of clocks, monkeys, or shells were made with taste and verve. There are many drawings and a half dozen manuscripts to support them.

This does not mean that a French collector would not find examples of great interest and importance of the type of illustrated book which he would expect in such a collection, for Mr Hofer has, to name only a few, thirty pencil and two large wash drawings (for Ariosto) by Fragonard, two wash drawings and one red, black and white crayon by J. M. Moreau le Jeune, over ninety pen and wash drawings by Gravelot, six drawings by Chodowiecki, all done for books, copies of which are in his collection.

The English works of this period are of course not as numerous as the French but include a considerable number of fine Bewick drawings, proofs and original woodblocks, a number of Blakes including *America* and the *Vision of the Daughters of Albion*, as well as drawings and proofs, a splendid series of the works of Thomas Martyn in presentation copies or on vellum, and many unusual architectural books often in bindings of great merit. As an example of the unusual item may be cited Thomas Pennant's own copy of his *Arctic Zoology*, 1784, with many fine drawings in the margin by Moses Griffith; and a red chalk drawing by Alexander Pope, with directions to the engraver, for the frontispiece to the 1745 edition of his *Essay on Man*.

The very strong section of German books includes, to list only a very few, not only Giuseppe Galli Bibiena's *Architetture e Prospettive*, Augsburg, 1740, but also an unpublished volume containing hundreds of pen and wash drawings by him; the Bridgewater set of coloured proofs on vellum of J. C. Brand's *Cris de Vienna*, *c.* 1775; the Sebright copy in contemporary morocco of the six volume Marc Eliéser Bloch, *Ichtyologie*, Berlin, 1785, with fine hand-coloured plates; the Langton–Sykes–Thorold copy of Frederick, Lord Baltimore's *Gaudia Poetica*, Augsburg, 1770; the Paul Hirsch copy from Schloss Arklitten of Goethe's *Das Romische Carneval*, Weimar, 1789, on large paper, hand-coloured, apparently the only one known; G. Lambranzi's *Theatralische Tantz-Schul*, Nuremberg, 1716; and a fine copy in contemporary binding of that most magnificent collection of coloured views of Vienna by Karl Schutz and Johann Ziegler, Vienna, 1794–6.

For many years Mr Hofer has been interested in Italian 18th-century illustrated books and has built up his Piranesi collection with drawings, early impressions and variant states, and has obtained nearly all the sets of prints and books illustrated by Canaletto, Piazetta, Tiepolo and the Bibienas, and very special copies of books printed by Bodoni. Only recently, however, has he collected the more obscure and little-known artists and engravers. Now with a collection approaching some five hundred 18th-century pieces one can see that they really possess a charm and interest that hitherto has been little appreciated. They are nearly all on fine Italian paper, are often uncut, with generally an elaborate engraved title or frontispiece and often if no other illustration, vignettes and cul-de-lampes which fit the typography, and if not in morocco or inlaid bindings generally in the striking block-printed wrappers peculiar to Italian books of this period.

There is not space enough to describe the Dutch, Spanish, Scandinavian, Slavic, Turkish and other illustrated books of this century except to say that they contain many of great interest such as the earliest Dutch experiments in colour-printing, and a number of the noblest volumes of Spanish typography, these last nearly all in fine Spanish bindings.

For the 19th century, from the mass of finely printed or illustrated books which exist, Mr Hofer has chosen with great discrimination several thousand – I confess not to have counted them – of which the bulk are French or English. To them he has in a great many instances added original drawings for the illustrations, as for example four of the famous Delacroix wash drawings for the *Faust*, Paris, 1828, of which Goethe wrote so enthusiastically; the Prudhon drawing for the frontispiece accompanies the Longus, *Daphnis et Chloe*, Paris, 1803; and three large chalk and wash drawings by Doré for Énault's *Londres*, 1876, accompany an India paper copy of it. Besides more than a dozen other Dorés there is one of the original woodblocks of his *Rabelais*; while among more than a dozen books illustrated by Toulouse-Lautrec, including the rare *Yvette Guilbert*, as well as a nearly complete set of proofs of the *c.* 1894 edition, there are two variant copies of Jules Renard's *Histoires naturelles*, 1899, with four pencil drawings, large and small, for it. Several of the books printed by Didot are unique, printed on vellum or otherwise distinguished. The Levaillants are large-paper, the Redoutés have accompanying drawings, as does *Le Bon Genre*. The famous *Chants et Chansons de la France*, 1843, is accompanied by a large group of the original drawings, and *Paul et Virginie*, 1838, is present in every possible state accompanied by proofs and woodblocks. Daumier has long been a favourite of Mr Hofer's and I have counted at least thirty-five titles including most if not all the periodicals to which he contributed – the Fabre, *Nemesis Medicale*, 1840, is there in wrappers, boards, and contemporary morocco – but I do not know how many proofs and other odd pieces there may be though I do know there are at least a half dozen woodblocks and one great lithographic stone. Likewise the Gavarnis, Grandvilles, and Johannots are well represented. There are all the books illustrated by Manet; the André Gide, *Le Voyage d'Urien*, 1893, with plates by Maurice Denis, is a presentation copy to

Oscar Wilde; and among other notable volumes of the new art may be mentioned
Bonnard's *Parallèlement*, 1900, and Vuillard's *Paysages et Interieurs*, 1899.

The English books are equally distinguished with many special copies, frequently on
vellum, printed by Bulmer and Pickering; and there are rows of the great colour-plate
books of Ackerman, Alken, Daniel, Girtin and Nash. The *National Fields Sports* is
accompanied by two Alken drawings. Frederick Nash's *Paris and its Environs*, 1820, is
accompanied by sixty-eight drawings. Malton's *Oxford* in original parts is accompanied
by drawings, while to the complete array of the books of Thomas Shotter Boys are
added some three hundred drawings of all sizes and kinds. The John H. Clark, *On
Landscape Painting*, 1827, has all the original drawings – but the list must stop. A strong
collection of the books of the 1860s has added letters of the brothers Dalziel and drawings of A. B. Houghton and Sir J. E. Millais. There are about one hundred and fifty drawings by Hugh Thompson and others for Macmillan's 'Cranford' series.

There are several sets of drawings by Rowlandson for *Dr Syntax*, *The Dance of
Death*, *The Dance of Life*, *The English Spy*, and *The Microcosm of London*. Among some
fifty Lear drawings and manuscripts are ones for his *Nonsense Books*, *Alphabets*, *Corsica*,
Greece, and so on, together with a strong collection of presentation copies of his books.
Westall is represented by his watercolours for Crabbe's *Poems*, and H. K. Brown by the
original drawings for Lever's *Our Mess* and *The Daltons*. But there is not room to catalogue them all, for there are few books that one might expect to find in such a collection
which are not there, as well as an unusual array, including drawings, relating to the Great
Exhibition of 1851, the beginnings of photography, and many other subjects such as
botany, ornithology, the industrial revolution, paper making, and the reproductive
printing processes.

The German 19th-century books include representative collections of Senefelder,
Wilhelm Busch, including the first *Max und Moritz*, Adolf Menzel, Heinrich Hoffman,
including the rare first *Struwelpeter*, 1845, and many others. Typical of the unusual book
in this collection is a beautiful copy of Goethe's *Hermann und Dorothea*, Braunschweig,
1822, with illustrations partly printed in colour. The collection of Russian illustrated
books which consists of about one hundred titles, as well as drawings and manuscripts,
is remarkable for condition, for most of these copies came from the Imperial libraries.
Among many which deserve mention is a set of A. Agin's lithographic illustrations for
Gogol's *Mertvyia Dushi*, 1846, in the original eighteen parts with wrappers.

From the smaller national collections of this period there may be noted Andrasy's *Les
Chasses et le Sport en Hongrie*, Pest, 1857; *The Corsair of Lord Byron*, Milan, 1826, printed
on vellum and exquisitely illuminated by G. B. Gigola, one of three copies so treated; a
royal copy of *Colección de las Vistas de los Sitios Reales Litografiadas*, Madrid, 1827–32;
F. Waldstein and P. Kitaibel, *Descriptiones et Icones Plantarum Rariorum Hungariae*,
Vienna, 1802–12; the De Jonghe copy of G. L. Lahde, *Das tagliche Leben in Kopenhagen*,
Copenhagen, *c.* 1807; the original drawings for C. G. Svedman's 'Costumes of Sweden',
c. 1820; and a really superb copy of Fielding Lucas, Jr's *Progressive Drawing Book*,
Baltimore [1828].

From the 20th century Mr Hofer has gathered almost as widely as from earlier periods
and his holdings include not only most of the great classics of modern book illustration

but also many ephemera which only a trained eye would see were worthy of preservation. Early in 1961 there will be held at the Boston Museum of Fine Arts an exhibition of 'The Artist as Illustrator: 1860–1960' largely based on Mr Hofer's collection. The catalogue will show how very strong the collection now is. In surveying it for this article I could not find lacking any of the books of the masters of modern book illustration of which I had any knowledge, including Rouault, Matisse, Picasso, Braque, Dufy, Derain, etc., and their greatest works are almost always present in their finest form, as for example Picasso's *Buffon* which is one of five printed on Japan 'super nacré', with a suite on 'Chine' and the rejected plate, in a fine inlaid binding by Creuzewalt and supplemented by the *Eaux Fortes;* Rouault's *Réincarnation du Père Ubu*, 1932, one of thirty; Dufy's *Bestiare* (by Apollinaire), the artist's own copy, with original drawings and manuscript material; or Kredel's *Das Blumenbuch*, 1930, in every form, including one of two copies with quotations from the Bible inserted on every page in Rudolph Koch's calligraphic hand.

Some idea of the variety and extent of the books of the present century may be obtained by listing a few of the artists whose drawings are to be found – the books for which they were made and many others like them are all in the collection: Artzybasheff, Beerbohm, Boutet de Monville, Calder, Demuth, Disney, Dulac, Gill, Gooden, Kent, Legrand, Müller, Newell, Rackham, and many others. The shelves devoted to the Americans, W. A. Dwiggins, Bruce Rogers, and Rudolph Ruzicka, all contain many drawings, proofs, and mock-ups which are outstanding.

Besides these general collections which have been so cursorily described Mr Hofer has a number of subject collections only a few of which can be noted. His calligraphic collections contain both manuscript and printed works. A selection of his manuscripts which range from the anonymous 'Modus Scribendi', Melk, *c.* 1440, to the 20th century was shown at the Grolier Club in 1958 and those who saw that exhibition could judge of his success in gathering outstanding examples of all periods. One feature of this section which should be mentioned is the more than fifty modern manuscripts by the best of 20th-century calligraphers, which Mr Hofer has commissioned, a practice which if more frequently observed might keep this great art flourishing. His printed writing-books number more than three hundred and while this is not a great quantity they are remarkable in many instances for the condition of the copies – his *Pacioli*, 1509, is in a fine contemporary blind stamped binding (the copy chosen for the Grolier Club publication), as are his *Neudorffer*, 1538, and his *Wys*, 1549. His *Van de Velde*, 1605, is in a fine cut-vellum binding and his *Rossi*, 1598, the dedication copy, is in a silver binding, having the author's portrait repoussé. He has the *Fanti*, 1514, in original vellum, six 16th-century editions of Arrighi, and three of Tagliente. His *Juan de Ycars* include the first of 1548, and those of 1550, 1553 and 1566. To do justice to this collection would take a full chapter.

Likewise to describe in a paragraph Mr Hofer's type-specimens is hardly possible. They include the first Fell specimen of 1693 and other Oxford specimens of 1629, 1685 and 1768. Caslon and his successors are represented by specimens of 1740, 1764, 1785, 1789, 1796 and 1805, while Baskerville is there in the 1757 broadside, and Wilson and Fry are well covered. The Fournier *Manuel*, 1769, is present in the original wrappers decorated with type-ornament, and there are fine copies of his oblong *Modèles*, 1742, *Caractères*, 1764, and *Traité historique*, 1765; while the Gillé specimens of 1773, 1778 and 1815 are present in original boards, and that of 1808 is the Eugène de Beauharnais copy which has many pages on variant coloured papers, in a superb straight-grained morocco binding 'aux armes'. A dozen Bodoni specimens are there in original royal morocco, and there is one of two complete sets of all Papillon's type ornaments and vignettes. But if one listed all of Mr Hofer's type-specimens that would have meaning to anyone but a specialist one would not have done justice to them for frequently it is the odd little book, of which one has never heard and for which one would search a long time without finding another copy, that makes this, like so many other parts of this collection, so delightful to browse in.

Though they are not shelved together nor anywhere listed as a group there are many subjects which have particularly interested Mr Hofer and which perhaps would have been as good a means of surveying this vast accumulation as the chronological conspectus here used. For example, he has collected bestiaries, and particularly *Aesops* of all periods, and an account of them, beginning with his 13th-century English Hugo de Folieto, 'De Bestiis', and including his unique vellum copy of the Verona 1479 *Aesop*, variant and very fine Barlows, with a drawing, and ending with the Leonard Baskin, *Horned Beetles*, Northampton, 1958, one of thirty copies, would give a reasonably good idea of the scope of the whole collection. An even better conspectus would be obtained if one merely told of the books in this collection which have remarkably fine bindings. Mr Hofer has often said that he does not collect bindings as such and this is true in the sense that he is not interested in a fine binding on a dull edition of the *Sainte Semaine*, but in the Baltimore Exhibition of 1957–8 there were forty-one exhibits under his name, besides a few among Harvard's entries which had been given by him. This was far more than any other American collector except, of course, those of Mr Raphael Esmerian. Among the bindings in Mr Hofer's collection belonging to classes not before mentioned are two Romanesque bindings of the 12th and 13th centuries, two very early European gold tooled bindings a Ferrarese printed binding of the 15th century, and the famous Gruel triple dos-à-dos.

To collect in such a wide field a very considerable bibliographical reference collection is a necessity and Mr Hofer has accumulated several thousand of such tools. Like nearly all the great collectors, however, he has not regarded these books from a purely utilitarian standpoint – his Bayle's *Dictionarie* was Mme de Pompadour's, his *Brunet is* on thick paper, his copies of the Fairfax Murray *Catalogues* are Davies's own annotated ones, and so on. In writing this necessarily superficial account of Mr Hofer's collection I have often been reminded of the joy with which he has greeted a new acquisition, particularly one of a, to him, new kind of book, how quickly he has mastered the literature about it, if there was any, and how quickly he turned with equal pleasure to a still newer volume. May this joy continue to be his for many years to come.

John Meade Falkner, 1858–1932

THERE are four biographical memoirs of John Meade Falkner: *The Times*, 25 July 1932; *The Dictionary of National Biography, 1931–40*, by Alfred Cochrane; and the memoirs by G. M. Young and Sir Edmund Craster prefixed to the World's Classics edition of *The Nebuly Coat* in 1954. Of these *The Times* obituary is the most informative, and Sir Edmund Craster's the most sympathetic. John Meade Falkner was born on 8 May 1858 at Manningford Bruce in Wiltshire, the son of a country clergyman. He went to Marlborough and Hertford College, Oxford, where he took an undistinguished history degree in 1882. After leaving Oxford he went to Newcastle upon Tyne as private tutor to the sons of Sir Andrew Noble. When they had grown up, Falkner stayed on first as private secretary to Sir Andrew Noble, and from before 1896[1] as secretary to the firm of Sir W. G. Armstrong, Whitworth, & Co Ltd.

Sir William Armstrong, later Lord Armstrong (1810–1900) invented the application of hydraulic pressure (and of pneumatic pressure as well) to the operation of cranes and other industrial machinery; and to manufacture the apparatus he founded the Elswick Hydraulic Engineering Works in 1847. During the Crimean War he turned his attention to the manufacture of breech-loading, rifled ordnance, and for this purpose formed the Ordnance Company of Elswick in 1858. Two years later he took into partnership Andrew Noble, a captain in the Royal Artillery, who had been secretary to a committee investigating breech-loading guns. In 1863 when the British Army reverted to muzzle loading guns for another twenty years, the Ordnance Company was amalgamated with the Hydraulic Engineering Works. Sir Andrew Noble created the science of ballistics and became, like Lord Armstrong, a fellow of the Royal Society. In 1882 the firm absorbed Mitchell and Swan, shipbuilders, and became a public company under the style of Sir W. G. Armstrong & Co., with Sir Andrew Noble as vice-chairman. In 1896 they absorbed Sir Joseph Whitworth's works for making guns at Openshaw, and the style of the firm was changed to Sir W. G. Armstrong, Whitworth, & Co Ltd. Lord Armstrong died in 1900, and Sir Andrew Noble became chairman.

In 1889 Lord Armstrong's great-nephew and heir, later Lord Armstrong of Bamburgh, married the eldest daughter of General Sir John Adye (Director of Artillery and Stores, 1870–75; Surveyor General of the Ordnance, 1880–82; Governor of Gibraltar, 1882–86). Ten years later Sir John Adye's youngest daughter married John Meade Falkner. In 1901 Falkner was made a director of the Company, and on the death of Sir Andrew Noble in 1915, he was elected chairman. He resigned the chairmanship in

[1] The printed authorities all say 1897; but the new company's application for incorporation is dated 1 February 1896, and signed by Meade Falkner as Secretary.

1921, but remained a director until 1926, when the Company was amalgamated with Vickers. He died at his house in Palace Green, Durham, on 22 July 1932.

A large part of the firm's business consisted in the manufacture and export of warships and armaments, and Meade Falkner became the firm's chief diplomatic representative. The technique of salesmanship is revealed in the report of a law case[2] in which one R. L. Thompson sued the Company for salary and commission on sales in South America (Chile and Argentina) and the Far East (China, Siam, and Japan). The case was settled out of court after the first day's hearing. It was the practice of the firm to explain to each of these small countries the armament programme of their neighbours and the type and scale of armament which would be an effective deterrent. Meade Falkner was constantly abroad on these missions, particularly in the Balkans; and received many decorations from appreciative foreign governments.

Meade Falkner was a great collector of liturgical books; and his library was sold at Sotheby's 12–14 December 1932. He owned the Bangor Missal which used to be thought the sole evidence of a special Bangor rite (lot 296, £160, now in the National Library of Wales), and the 14th-century Closworth Missal, unique in having a recognizable view of the Dorset downs to the Channel as a background to the miniature of the Crucifixion (lot 295, £230, bought from Leighton for £150 (*Catalogue of MSS.* [1912] no. 217 with a reproduction of the miniature), given to the Bodleian Library in 1934 by Sir John Noble and other friends of Meade Falkner). He also possessed a long series of early printed primers and of the 17th-century manuals for Catholic priests on the English mission.

But Falkner was not merely a collector of liturgical books, he was also an expert palaeographer. He visited Oxford for three days every year, staying at the Randolph (not the Mitre). Each of those three evenings he invited to dinner one of the assistants in Bodley in strict order of seniority. He was a regular visitor at the Vatican Library: the Pope gave him a medal for palaeography; and he left £500 in his will for the use of the Vatican Library. He was honorary librarian of Durham Cathedral before 1925; honorary Reader in Palaeography in the University of Durham; and honorary fellow of Hertford College (1927). The small Cotswold town of Burford, with its wide High Street of stone houses stretching up the hill, owes its present state of preservation to the generosity of Meade Falkner; and he lies buried in its churchyard.

What manner of man he was, I cannot tell you. I never met him myself; and conversation with those who knew him has revealed nothing of the springs of action which carried him from a country vicarage to the top of one of the largest engineering firms in the world. His tastes are more apparent. He fitted happily into the domestic circle of Sir Andrew Noble. He enjoyed exploring the Cotswolds by bicycle with the younger members of the family. He relished the services of the Church of England; and he was fascinated by the past history of the things and places which he loved. He must have been an accomplished armament salesman, but he was not an industrial leader of the calibre of his predecessors, Lord Armstrong and Sir Andrew Noble. He became chairman of the Company in 1915 when they were making munitions for the 1914–18 war, and he resigned that position when the north-east coast was facing extensive and prolonged

---

[2] *The Times*, 16 Dec. 1904, p. 3.

unemployment. Apart from one or two almost conventional references to 'the dark flood threatening to overwhelm us' in *Bath* and in one of the poems, his writings never hint at any consciousness of his personal part in the Great War and the Great Depression. But this is not so out of character as it seems, because Meade Falkner wrote little after 1903; and what he did write (*Charalampia* (No. 7), *Bath* (No. 8), *Some Later Durham Bibliophiles* (No. 9) and some of the poems) is slight both in form and substance. The Meade Falkner whose literary work is listed below was an earlier and younger character, a man apart from Meade Falkner the industrial magnate.

Altogether he published two guide books (Nos. 1 and 5), three historical essays (Nos. 4, 8, and 9), three novels, and a slim volume of verse. The guide books are more than adequate, suffused with the enthusiasm of exploring the lanes of Oxfordshire and Berkshire in the company of his pupils from the North. The historical essays are very readable, though they show no original research or profundity of insight. Some of his verses have been compared to those of Mr John Betjeman (*The Times Literary Supplement*, 12, 19 December 1958, 2 January 1959); and others recall the poems of Sir Henry Newbolt, but with less vigour and more flavour. The three novels – Meade Falkner wrote a fourth novel and left it in a train – are his best work. *Moonfleet* is a first class adventure story: *The Nebuly Coat*, though not less exciting, is a richer and deeper book.

The bibliography of Meade Falkner is, with the exception of the *Poems* (Nos. 10A and 10B), straightforward enough. I know of no binding variants. A fairly large edition must have been printed of *The Lost Stradivarius*; but it always occurs in the same binding. Comparatively few copies were printed of *Moonfleet* and *The Nebuly Coat*, but the binding of the second edition in each case is an exact replica of the first. There may be later bindings of the two Murray guide books (Nos. 1 and 5), but if so, I have not come across them. Most of Meade Falkner's books are not difficult to find; but *Moonfleet* in mint condition and the *Poems* in brown wrappers are rare. The books have been described (except for No. 10A of which I know only my own copy) from the copies in the British Museum and the Bodleian Library. I have not attempted to trace separate periodical publications of the poems though some were first printed in *The Spectator*, and some were reprinted in *The Mint*. Nor have I included the annual reports of Sir W. G. Armstrong, Whitworth, & Co Ltd, parts of which were probably written by Falkner for some years before he became chairman. I have likewise excluded *The Statutes of Durham Cathedral* (Surtees Society, vol. CXLIII) 1929 because, though printed from a transcript by Meade Falkner, he had no other part in its publication.

The *Poems* in brown wrappers and the *Poems* in green wrappers present a problem. They are quite distinct editions, differently set up by different printers in different text types; but sufficiently alike for the format of one to have been copied from the other. There is no mystery about the green wrapper edition (No. 10B), of which 500 copies were printed for Mrs Meade Falkner in July 1933. When giving up her London house about 1934, Mrs Meade Falkner sold the copies which had not been distributed to her husband's friends, along with the other books in the house to Bernard Quaritch Ltd, who still have some copies in stock. The brown wrapper edition (No. 10A) looks like a piece of provincial printing and contains several obvious misprints. There has never been any popular, or even collectors', demand for these poems; and it seems inconceivable that the brown wrapper edition should be a piracy or a copy of the edition in green. The presumption, therefore, is that the green wrapper edition is the second edition set up from the one in brown wrappers. On 16 July 1933 Mrs Meade Falkner wrote from 23 Ovington Square, SW3 to Falconer Madan at the Bodleian Library:[3] '... I need not say how much I appreciate and value all you write regarding my Husband's Verses. They would never have *arrived* at being printed but for your son's [Mr Geoffrey Madan] kind help. May I now say what a real pleasure it was to us both to see him at Durham – and now he is so good in coming to see me here.' This could be interpreted to mean that Mr Geoffrey Madan supervised the printing of the green wrapper edition at London in 1933. But the more obvious and literal interpretation is that it was at Durham during Meade Falkner's lifetime that Mr Geoffrey Madan helped the *Poems* to arrive at being printed; and that the edition then produced was the one in brown wrappers.

BIBLIOGRAPHY OF MEADE FALKNER

1. HANDBOOK FOR TRAVELLERS | IN | OXFORDSHIRE | WITH MAPS AND PLANS. | LONDON: | JOHN MURRAY, ALBEMARLE STREET. | 1894.

   12°. Pp. x–(14)–242; 2 folding maps of Oxford facing p. 11; map of Oxfordshire in a pocket in the lower cover. Red cloth, lettered in gold on spine and upper cover, corners rounded, edges cut and sprinkled red, printed blue endpapers, Murray's Handbook Advertiser (64 pp.) at end.

   Imprint on the verso of the title: Horace Hart, Printer to the University. Bodleian copy received on 19 March 1894.

   Issued anonymously, but the authorship is acknowledged on the title-page of No. 4 below.

2. THE | LOST STRADIVARIUS | BY | J. MEADE FALKNER | WILLIAM BLACK-WOOD AND SONS | MDCCCXCV | *All Rights reserved*.

   8°. Pp. [viii, including one blank leaf before the half-title]–296. Blue cloth, lettered in gilt on spine; decoration in blind on upper cover; end papers with a design of white oak leaves on a brown ground, edges trimmed.

   Imprint on p. 296: Printed by William Blackwood and Sons. Bodleian copy received on 14 March 1896.

   Reprinted with *The Nebuly Coat* (No. 6):
   Penguin Books No. 487, Harmondsworth (1946).
   World's Classics No. 545, Oxford University Press (1954).

3. MOONFLEET | BY J. MEADE FALKNER | AUTHOR OF 'THE LOST STRADI-VARIUS' | [3-*line motto*] | LONDON | EDWARD ARNOLD | 1898 | *All rights reserved*.

   8°. Pp. [viii]–305. Red cloth, lettered in gilt on spine, on upper cover: MOONFLEET in gold above the arms of Mohune in silver and black, beneath the motto 'Moniet Mohune' in silver on a scroll; edges uncut.

   Imprint on p. [306]: Printed by T. and A. Constable, Printers to Her Majesty at the Edinburgh University Press. Advertisement of *The Lost Stradivarius*, pp. [307–08]. British Museum copy received on 1 December 1898.

   Reprinted:
   Second Edition, Edward Arnold, 1899.
   Nelson's Sevenpenny Library [1909].
   Arnold's Illustrated English Literature Series 'for use as a Reading-book at home and in school', four plates by Holloway. [1924.]
   New Illustrated Edition, plates by Geoffrey Fletcher, Edward Arnold, 1955.

   ---

   [3] The original letter is bound up with the Bodleian copy of the green wrapper edition.

4. POPULAR COUNTY HISTORIES. | – | A | HISTORY OF OXFORDSHIRE. | BY | J. MEADE FALKNER, | Editor of 'Murray's Handbook of Oxfordshire.' | LONDON: | ELLIOT STOCK, 62, PATERNOSTER ROW, E.C. | 1899.

8°. Pp. [viii]–327. According to the Prospectus, loosely inserted in the Bodleian copy, this was issued in three forms:

I. The ordinary edition in cloth at 7s 6d. Issued to subscribers at 6s per volume.

II. An Edition of 250 copies only, price 10s 6d nett, is printed for subscribers, on HANDMADE PAPER, and bound in Roxburgh.

III. Fifty Large Paper copies on handmade paper and bound in Roxburgh, 21s to subscribers, £1 11s 6d if unsubscribed.

The ordinary issue (No. I in the Prospectus) is in half blue cloth, claret coloured sides, spine lettered in gilt, edges uncut, and measures 231 × 144 mm. The next issue (No. II in the Prospectus) is in half black roan, dark green cloth sides, top edges gilt, other edges uncut, and measures 229 × 144 mm. The Large Paper issue (No. III in the Prospectus) is similarly bound, but measures 249 × 198 mm. Bodleian copy received on 19 August 1899.

There was a remainder issue with a new title leaf in 1906.

5. HANDBOOK | FOR | BERKSHIRE, | including Windsor, Reading, Maidenhead, Bray, | Newbury, Aldworth, The Downs, The Ridgeway, | Abingdon, Faringdon, Buckland, Cumnor, etc. | WITH 3 MAPS and 2 PLANS | LONDON: EDWARD STANFORD, | 12, 13, & 14, Long Acre, W.C. | 1902.

12°. Pp. [viii]–[xiv]–143. Red cloth, lettered in gilt on spine and upper cover, pockets for maps in both covers, corners rounded, edges cut and sprinkled red; printed dark green endpapers, Murray's Handbook Advertiser (48 pp., dated May 1902) at end.

Imprint on the verso of the title: Printed by Hazell, Watson and Viney, Ld. [sic] London and Aylesbury. The preface is signed in full, and dated June 1902. Bodleian copy received on 7 August 1902.

6. THE NEBULY COAT | BY | JOHN MEADE FALKNER | AUTHOR OF | 'THE LOST STRADIVARIUS,' 'MOONFLEET,' ETC., ETC. | LONDON | EDWARD ARNOLD | 1903 | [All rights reserved.]

8°. Pp. [iv]–372 Buff cloth, lettered on spine and upper cover in fancy letters of dark green, beneath the title on the upper cover is the Nebuly Coat in its heraldic tinctures of green and silver; top and fore-edges trimmed, bottom edges uncut.

Imprint at the foot of p. 372: Billing and Sons, Ltd. Printers, Guildford. Bodleian copy received on 9 November 1903.

Reprinted: 'Fifth Impression' 1904; and together with The Lost Stradivarius as noted under No. 2 above.

7. CHARALAMPIA (From the Greek of Trachylides, written not earlier than 1438.) in THE CORNHILL MAGAZINE, December 1916, pp. 659–679.

Signed on p. 679 'John Meade Falkner'. This is not a translation, but a cautionary tale about a Byzantine princess. It has not been reprinted.

8. BATH | IN HISTORY AND SOCIAL | TRADITION | LONDON | JOHN MUR-RAY, ALBEMARLE STREET | 1918. [The first line and the last line but one are printed in red.]

Small 8°. Pp. x–86. Stiff brown paper boards, edges trimmed; label on spine printed in red ('BATH' above an ornament); label on upper cover also in red within a single rule: 'BATH | [ornament] | BY AN | APPRECIATIVE VISITOR.'

Imprint on p. 86: Billing & Sons, Ltd. printers, Guildford, England. British Museum copy received on 28 March 1918.

9. A HISTORY OF | DURHAM CATHEDRAL | LIBRARY | BY | H. D. HUGHES, | M.A. | WITH AN | INTRODUCTION AND ADDITIONAL CHAPTER | ON |

'SOME LATER DURHAM BIBLIOPHILES' | BY | J. MEADE FALKNER, | M.A., | HON. LIBRARIAN. | *With Twenty-four Collotype Plates.* | – | DURHAM: | DURHAM COUNTY ADVERTISER, LTD. | 1925.

Small 8°. Pp. xlii–134, 24 plates and a folding plan at the end. Red cloth, lettered in black on spine and upper cover; edges uncut. Meade Falkner's contributions are: Introduction, pp. ix–xlii, and Chapter XIV, pp. 111–126. Bodleian copy received on 19 April 1926.

10A. POEMS | J. MEADE FALKNER [*probably Durham, about 1930.*]

8°. Title as above, 1 leaf; Contents pp. i–ii, 1 leaf; Text pp. 1–60; 32 leaves. No signatures. Brown paper wrappers, trimmed flush with the leaves; on front wrapper a white label printed in black within a double rectangle 'POEMS | J. MEADE FALKNER'. Set in 10-point Monotype Garamond, a design first cut in 1924. In the Contents and the Text the title of the first poem is misprinted 'DIE ASSUMPTIONS'. The chain lines in the laid paper are vertical.

10B. POEMS | J. M. FALKNER [London, July 1933.]

8°. A–E⁸ [F]². Pp. 84. Pages 5–6 and 80–83 are blank. Green overlapping wrappers, edges trimmed. On the front wrapper a white label printed in black within a double rectangle 'POEMS | J. M. FALKNER.' Set in 11-point Caslon. In the Contents and the text the title of the first poem is correctly printed 'DIE ASSUMPTIONIS'. The chain lines in the laid paper are horizontal.

Imprint on p. [84] beneath a trademark: 'The Westminster Press | 411A Harrow Road | London, W.9'. Five hundred copies were printed and paid for by Mrs Meade Falkner in July 1933.

John Roland Abbey

MAJOR J. R. ABBEY's library is well known to many bibliophiles and scholars who have been hospitably received at Storrington, under the Sussex Downs, or more recently at its present home, Redlynch House, near Salisbury. Like many other collectors, he graduated to older books through the modern private press. His first purchase, in about 1929, was of the Nonesuch Press limited edition of Donne, edited by John Hayward. Other Nonesuch, Ashendene, Doves, Gregynog, and Kelmscott Press books followed, culminating in a copy of the Kelmscott *Chaucer*, bound by the Doves Bindery, bought in 1934. In the meantime he had become interested in bindings and in 1931 commissioned examples from Sybil Pye and Roger de Coverley, some of the latter after the collector's own designs. This was followed by the purchase of a number of armorial bindings from the Rosebery sale of June 1933, and in 1935 by Grolier's copy of Origen, *De recta in Deum fide dialogus*, Paris 1556 (*Shipman.* no. 355). The Mensing, Moss, Aldenham, and Schiff sales provided exceptional opportunities for the collector of bindings. At the first of these he acquired the book which in spite of all later accessions remains his favourite binding, the Beckford–Rahir copy of Buchanan's *Psalmorum Davidis paraphrasis poetica*, Paris, 1554, bound for de Thou in olive morocco tooled in a particularly satisfying fanfare design (Mensing sale, lot 482). By 1938 there were enough English bindings for Major Abbey's friend and valued adviser, the late G. D. Hobson, to be invited to write a book on them. His *English Bindings in the Library of J. R. Abbey*, dedicated to 'Our friends and allies, the people of France', appeared, by an unhappy irony, in June 1940, at the time of Petain's armistice. Some of the continental bindings have similarly been described by G. D. Hobson's son in Major Abbey's Roxburghe Club book, on a subject suggested by Sir Sydney Cockerell, *French and Italian Collectors and their Bindings*, 1953, which studies the relationship of collectors' taste with binding design.

Parallel with the collection of bindings another interest was being developed. In 1935 Major Abbey acquired his first colour-plate book, Pyne's *Microcosm of Arts, Agriculture and Manufacture*, 1808, and with the guidance of the late George Stephenson of Messrs. Rimell he set out to form a collection of books illustrated with lithographs and aquatints which became the most distinguished of its kind in England. After Stephenson's death a Hove bookseller, George Bates, took an active part in seeking out additions to this section of the library, which ultimately numbered nearly three thousand volumes. The path to the formation of such a collection was largely uncharted, a factor which rendered the more laudable Major Abbey's decision to produce a full-dress bibliographical catalogue, (*Scenery of Great Britain and Ireland*, 1952; *Life in England*, 1953; and *Travel*, 2 vol.

1956–7). His attention to original condition, his successful search for part-issues in printed wrappers of many colour-plate books, his resolve to acquire hundreds of obscure rarities as well as the major books in the field have made the four large quarto volumes of his catalogue an indispensable work of reference, and the enthusiasm of its designer, the late Oliver Simon of the Curwen Press, ensured its typographical distinction. If Major Abbey had collected nothing else his fame as a bibliophile would be secure on the basis of the library of colour-plate books alone. As a collection, however, it had one considerable drawback, its formidable bulk, for many of the books were folios. It soon overflowed the library at Storrington and finally evicted the family from the dining-room. The pressure was only relieved by the sale of the collection to Mr Paul Mellon, through whose generosity it is destined for an American institutional library.

A by-product of the collector's intense interest in colour-plate books was the commissioning of two modern panoramas to illustrate the Silver Jubilee of George V and the Coronation of George VI. The panoramas of the 19th century had always attracted Major Abbey and he therefore had the happy idea of commemorating in this genre two of the State Occasions of the 1930s. The artist was Miss Mary McNiele and her medium a stencil, which was coloured by hand, no light task in a production of which the length was one hundred and twenty-seven feet. The result, manufactured by the Curwen Press, was most attractive: and Queen Mary, who was the recipient of copies, signified her interest and approval.

Major Abbey's collections of bindings and colour-plate books are already widely known from his published catalogues. His illuminated manuscripts are quite as remarkable, but have not been described in detail. The first, a humanistic *Cicero* written in 1476 by the scribe signing himself IO.NY. was acquired in 1934. In the 1930s Major Abbey received advice and encouragement from C. H. St John Hornby, the founder of the Ashendene Press, and after his death in 1946 Sir Sydney Cockerell, acting for his heirs, gave Major Abbey the first refusal of buying *en bloc* Hornby's substantial collection of mediaeval manuscripts. Sir Sydney asked for an answer to this proposal within twelve hours, and Major Abbey recalls the qualms with which he decided to make this major incursion into what was then, to him, an unfamiliar branch of bibliophily. He has had, however, no reason to regret the bargain, and to the Hornby manuscripts he has added a number of individual purchases as well as small groups of fine quality from the collections of the late Dudley Colman and Sir Sydney Cockerell.

Five manuscripts are earlier than the 12th century. Four of these come from the Hornby collection: a 9th-century *Evangelia*, probably from the Abbey of Poursais in the diocese of Toul; a Flemish *Evangelia* of the 9th–10th century, from the Sneyd and Michael Tomkinson collections; an Italian 11th-century *Evangelistarium;* and a glossed *Song of Solomon*, 11th century, from St Augustine's, Canterbury. The fifth, a French 9th-century St Augustine, *Retractiones*, was acquired from Sir Sydney Cockerell. Two finely illuminated volumes date from the 12th century: a Flemish glossed *Minor Prophets*, with twelve initials in coloured outline of monsters and human figures, probably from the Benedictine monastery at Anchin, near Douai, and afterwards in the Phillipps (MS 21948) and Chester Beatty collections *(Millar*, vol. I, no. 24); and a large folio *New Testament*, with an illuminated initial to each book, evidently a volume from one of the monumental Bibles produced in Northern France at this period, from the William Morris and Lawrence W. Hodson collections. Of four early Greek manuscripts, three come from the Peckover collection; two are *Evangelistaria*, one being in an early Greek stamped binding of red goatskin; the other texts are St John Chrysostom's *Sermons* and the *Catechesis* of St Theodore of Studion. The well-known *Psalter* from the Cockerell collection, with initials by various artists including William de Brailes (Plate I), and the *Missal* of the Austin Canons of St Stephen's, Dijon, with two full-page and several smaller miniatures, from the Ashhurnham and Yates Thompson collections (*Illustrations of 100 MSS*, vol. VII, pls. 8 and 9) are splendid examples of 13th-century illumination, and one of the rare mediaeval MSS of a classical text is Parisian work of the same period – Ovid's *Metamorphoses*, with other works, from the Phillipps and Hely-Hutchinson collections.

The beautifully illuminated manuscript known as 'The Ruskin Hours', Northern French work of the early 14th century, from the Ruskin, Cockerell, Chester Beatty and Colman collections, fully described by Dr E. G. Millar in his catalogue of the Chester Beatty Library (vol. II, no. 64), is probably the finest work of mediaeval miniature-painting in the library. Justinian's *Institutiones*, the first volume only (the second is in the Musée de Cluny, Paris) written in Bologna, has a series of miniatures of excellent quality executed in Paris in the latter half of the same century in the style which Henri Martin attributed to the 'Maître aux Boquetaux' – a name which covers several different ateliers; this comes from the White Knights, Henry Drury, and Hornby collections. English 14th-century art is represented by the *Belknap Hours*, perhaps executed for Sir Robert Belknap, Chief Justice of the Common Pleas, who died about 1400. This has much illumination of good quality, and although the binding is not of interest, the edges retain their original decoration. Later work includes two Utrecht Books of Hours of the first quarter of the 15th century which are among the finest Dutch work of this period (A. W. Byvanck, *La Miniature dans les Pays-Bas Septentrionaux*, pls. XXXII and XXXIII); the Hours of Jeanne Cauchon, a Rheims manuscript of about 1460 with much lively decoration, from the van Zuylen collection; *Libri Salomonis et Epistole*, a Flemish manuscript of about 1500 with miniatures, beautifully written and in brilliant condition, from the Huth collection; and the very richly decorated *Monypenny Breviary* (Plate IV), executed at Bourges in the early 16th century, perhaps by Jean de Montluçon, for Alexander Monypenny, a Scottish official at the court of Louis XII. The last (which is in an inlaid Parisian mid-16th-century binding, probably by Claude de Picques) was studied by A. van de Put in *Proceedings of the Society of Antiquaries of Scotland*, Vol. 56, 1922. A recent acquisition (from the Lucien Graux sale in 1957) is the Sainte Chapelle Hours, France, *c.* 1500, a fine manuscript on vellum with fourteen large and thirty-two small miniatures, including two by a Neapolitan artist and another depicting the relics in the Sainte Chapelle.

St John Hornby, as a printer, was naturally interested in the roman and italic hands of the 15th century and the library is particularly strong in humanistic manuscripts. Most of the great scribes are represented, and several minor ones: Pierantonio Salando, of Reggio; Sigismondo de Sigismondis, of Carpi; Johannes Marcus Cynicus, of Parma; Joacchinus de Gigantibus; Raphaello de Berti, of Pistoia; Nicolaus Antonii de Riciis,

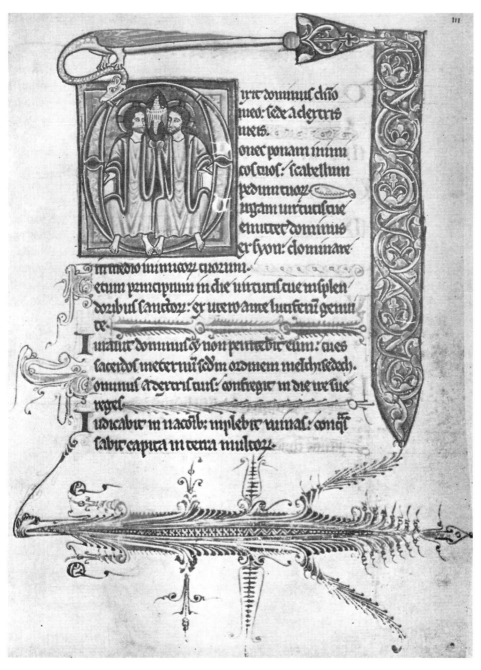

PLATE I. Illuminated by William de Brailes and other artists
Psalter. England, 1250. 178 × 130 mm. Bound by Katherine Adams
(Abbey Collection)

Damianus de Oliva, and Johannes Petrus de Spoleto. Among the famous Renaissance patrons whose arms occur in manuscripts in the library, are Pope Sixtus IV, Matthias Corvinus (a *Martial*, not recorded by Hevesy, perhaps *Fraknoi*, Appendix E, no. 80), Cardinal Bessarion, Pope Leo X, the Aragonese Kings of Naples (*Ausonius:* De Marinis, *La Biblioteca Napoletana dei Re d'Aragona*, II, p. 22; and Petrarch, *Sonetti e Canzoni*, not recorded by de Marinis) and Francesco Maria I, Duke of Urbino. A few other Renaissance manuscripts must be mentioned for the fine quality of their illumination: a Florentine St Jerome, *Epistolae*, with distinguished 'white vine-leaf' initials; a Florentine *Lucretius*, decorated by Attavante for a member of the Pazzi family; a Tuscan *Propertius* written in an italic hand with the arms of Agostini della Seta, of Pisa, from the George Dunn and C. S. Ascherson collections; and a beautiful small Florentine *Virgil* (Plate III), from the Vernon collection.

Books printed on vellum are a natural complement to illuminated manuscripts. In this category must be mentioned Francesco Filelfo, *Orationes et Opuscula*, Milan, Pachel and Schinzenzeler, 1483, with an illuminated border on the first page containing the arms of Ludovico il Moro as Duke of Bari; and *Recueil de peintures antiques*, by P. S. Bartoli and the Abbé Rive, 3 vol. Paris 1783–7, splendidly coloured and bound in blue morocco by Derome le Jeune. The last belonged to Sir Thomas Phillipps and perhaps before him to Paris d'Illens who is said to have paid Derome 450 livres for the binding.

Some of the continental bindings which fell outside the scope of Major Abbey's Roxburghe Club book may be briefly mentioned. A Parisian Romanesque binding of the 12th or early 13th century comes from the monastery of Admont in Styria (no. XLVI in G. D. Hobson's list, *English Binding before 1500*, Appendix B), and a Limoges enamel binding (Plate II) was acquired at the Aldenham sale in 1938. One of the rare gilt bindings by the *atelier de Louis XII* covers a copy of Jean de Pins' lives of St Catherine of Siena and Filippo Beroaldo (Bologna, 1505); apart from a few isolated examples of earlier dates, this workshop was the first in France to produce gilt bindings. A copy of the first edition of the *Hypnerotomachia Poliphili* (Aldus, 1499) is bound in Parisian early 16th-century gilt calf, and the first edition of Aristotle (5 vol. in 6, Aldus, 1495–8) is in a series of magnificent morocco bindings of about 1560 by a craftsman who worked also for Grolier. Three 'sunk-panel' bindings of Lyonnese type belong to the latter part of the century; the exquisite pointillé ornament of the 17th century can be seen on a superb inlaid example, with painted edges, covering a devotional book *(Exercice Spirituel*, Paris 1654); and the 18th century is splendidly represented by a total of eighteen inlaid bindings, including the one by Derome with a painting of the Annunciation signed *Dulin pinxit*, from the Schiff collection (Michon, no. 334); an almost complete set of P.-P. Dubuisson's plaques, and some exceptional copies of the famous illustrated books: the Lamoignon copy of the 1734 *Molière* in blue morocco; the Oudry *La Fontaine*, 1755–9, in contemporary morocco with dentelle borders and the arms of the duc de la Vrillière; the Fermiers Généraux *La Fontaine*, 1762, in an olive morocco binding 'de présent' after a design by Gravelot; and the *Monument du Costume*, first edition (1784, etc.) in contemporary French calf, from the Russian Imperial Library.

The German series starts with a splendid example of *cuir ciselé* work, from the Kyriss collection, and continues with many incunabula in blind-stamped bindings, including

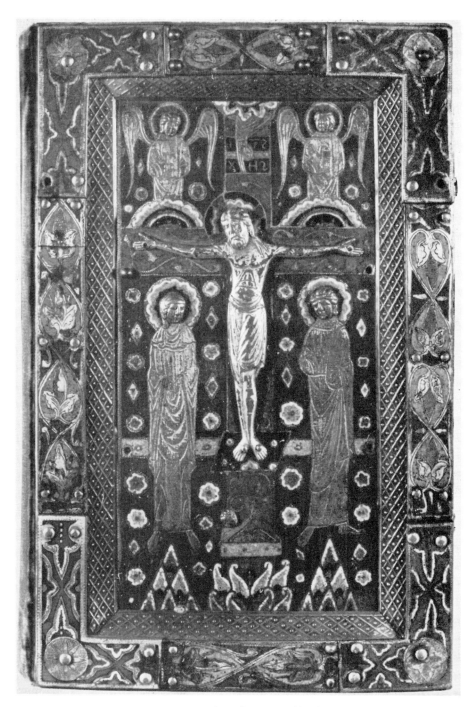

PLATE 11. A Limoges champlevé enamel binding, *c.* 1250
Psalter. France, on vellum, 13th century. 273 × 178 mm.
(Abbey Collection)

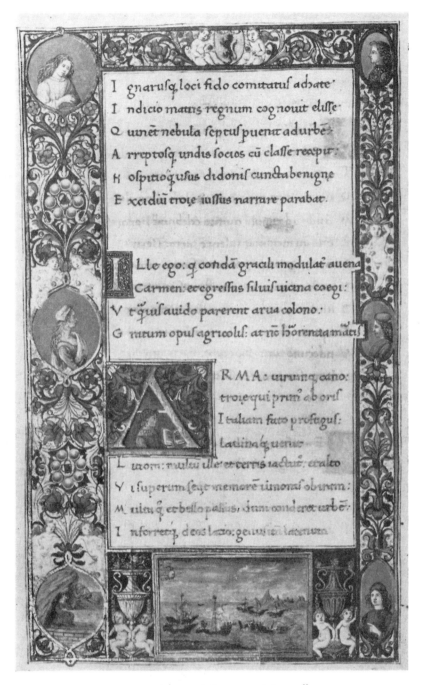

I gnarusq; loci fido comitatus adhate·
I ndicio matris regnum cognouit eluffe·
Q umet nebula septus puenit adurbê·
A rreptosq; undis socios cū classe recepit·
H ospitioq; usus didonis cuncta benigne
E xcidiū troie iuffus narrare parabat·

Lle ego: q; condā gracili modulat’ auena
Carmen: et egreffus siluis uicina coegi:
V t q̃uis auido parerent arua colono·
G ratum opus agricolis: at nc̄ hōrentia mārtis

R M A: uirumq; cano:
troie qui prim’ ab oris
I taliam fato profugus:
latiiaq; uenit
L itoru: multu ille et terris iactat’: et alto
V i superum seuit memore iunonis obiram:
M ulta q; et bello paffus: dum conderet urbē·
I nferretq; deos latio: genusui[...] latinum

PLATE III. A humanistic manuscript on vellum
Virgil, *Opera*. Italy, Florence *c.* 1470. 178 × 114 mm.
From Yates Thompson, Lord Vernon, St John Hornby (Abbey Collection)

PLATE IV. The Monypenny Breviary
Manuscript. France, Bourges, early 16th century. 241 × 140 mm.
With 50 full-page miniatures attributed to Jean Jacquelin de Montluçon (Abbey Collection)

one from the library of the Nuremberg humanist, Hieronymus Münzer, Hartmann Schedel's friend. These are followed by the gilt and painted work of the Renaissance: the extraordinary round binding whose edges bear the painted arms of Julius Echter von Mespelbrünn, Prince Bishop of Würzburg (illustrated in *Buch und Bucheinband* [*Loubier Festschrift*], 1923); Fraulein Dorothea zu Sachsen's arms are similarly painted on the edges of a binding by Caspar Meuser; bindings with portrait-panels of Luther and Melancthon, painted, by Matthias Gartner, of Augsburg or Munich, and gilt, by Thomas Krüger of Wittenberg – the latter containing inserted drawings of the two reformers attributed to Hans Cranach the Younger; a remarkable specimen by a Munich binder – now identified as Leonhard Ostertag – who worked also for Philip Eduard Fugger and used large historiated ornaments in gilt; and the dedication copy to the Archduke Ferdinand of Tyrol of Gerard de Roo's *Annales rerum ab Austriacis Habspurgicae Gentis Principibus gestarum*, 1592, with the Archduke's elaborate coat-of-arms, perhaps by Georg Barreutter (the two last from the Oberndorff collection).

Some outstanding bindings come from other countries. One of the very rare mediae-val embroidered bindings formerly in the Cockerell collection and illustrated in colour by G. D. Hobson, (*Bindings in Cambridge Libraries*, pl. III), and a Ferrarese woodcut wrapper of St George, the Dyson Perrins copy, are Italian. From Spain there are several *mudéjar* bindings, one of which is gilt (*Horae* of Dominican Use, perhaps written at Cordoba: Henry Thomas, *Early Spanish Bookbindings*, pl. 88) and an 18th-century inlaid binding by Antonio Sancha. From Holland come three lavish products of the Magnus family, one, in green morocco, covering, curiously enough, an English Prayer Book and Bible, 1679–83. The famous Buda workshop is represented by an example with the arms of Ladislas Jagellon, who continued to patronize it after Matthias Corvinus's death, and from the other side of the Atlantic comes an early 19th-century Mexican binding by Francisco Acurdo: nor must we forget to record the representative series of silver bind-ings which was described by Mr J. F. Hayward in *The Connoisseur*, October 1952.

Major Abbey's interest in bindings has continued to be the reverse of wholly anti-quarian. Throughout his collecting career he has consistently extended his patronage to living binders, both in this country and in France. He was certainly one of the first col-lectors outside France to commission a binding from the greatest French master, M. Paul Bonet, with whom he has had friendly transactions from 1937 onwards. During the dark days of the Occupation M. Bonet bound a book for Major Abbey which had been left with him before the war and more recently has executed a binding for him decorated in a design based on the owner's arms, the first heraldic binding which he has undertaken. A number of modern French bindings, including several by Rose Adler, were bought in Paris in 1949 when Major Abbey was preparing the exhibition which was sponsored by the Arts Council of Great Britain in that year.[1] The English series in the same exhibition illustrated, with ninety specimens, the work of every major figure in the craft since Cobden-Sanderson. The collection contains splendid examples of the work of Sybil Pye, Katharine Adams, Douglas Cockerell, and Mr Roger Powell as well as of a number

---

[1] *cf.* the annotated catalogue, *Modern English & French Bindings from the Collection of J. R. Abbey*, with an Introduction by Philip James and sixteen plates.

of young British binders, some of whom have been encouraged by receiving from Major Abbey their first commissions: and the work of talented amateurs is also represented, notably Lady Hester Bourne, who has contributed two exquisite modern needlework bindings.

Several other groups of books in the library are worthy of mention. There are, for example, between eighty and ninety *incunabula* in contemporary bindings. The reference library, which fills a separate room, is particularly noteworthy. Rich, as one would expect, in the standard works on manuscripts and bindings, it also embodies two special collections to which Major Abbey has paid particular attention. He has assembled a set of the publications of the Roxburghe Club, which is now nearing completion and includes a considerable number printed on vellum; and, as befits a collector who has himself produced a noble series of catalogues, he has been energetic in the acquisition of library catalogues, especially those which have been privately-printed in small numbers. This impressive series of the records of past bibliophily is by no means the least interesting feature of Major Abbey's library, which must in its entirety rank as one of the most remarkable in private hands today.

J. C. T. OATES

An Old Boot at Cambridge

THEY say that the author of a certain learned work, having seen the *nomarchs* of his typescript safely through galley and page, was not a little put out when they all emerged on publication as *monarchs*: and it is, of course, primarily in the hope of causing some similar confusion in the pages of THE BOOK COLLECTOR, and only secondarily for the benefit of boot-lovers at large, that I draw attention to an old boot in the University Library at Cambridge.

That an old library should contain an old boot need occasion no surprise. Libraries, both private and institutional, were long regarded as proper repositories for coins, medals, fossils, mathematical and scientific instruments, and curiosities of all kinds. Most college libraries had, in a cupboard, a more than metaphorical skeleton, and when Zacharias Conrad von Uffenbach visited Cambridge in 1710 he was shown (in the words of J. E. B. Mayor's translation of the *Merkwürdige Reisen*) 'a *cranium petrefactum*, or rather an *incrustatum*', brought from Crete in 1627, at Sidney Sussex; 'a tolerable magnet, and in a bag some lenses for *tubis astronomicis*', at Emmanuel; and at St John's a box containing 'all kinds of florentine marble, a fine fossil *fungus marinus*, and an english cheese petrified'. The University Library possesses an écorché figure in boxwood and a model skeleton in ivory presented by John Banister in 1591; among the contents of the cabinet given by George Lewis, Archdeacon of Meath, in 1726, was 'the Figure of a Chinese Idol in Alabaster in a sedent posture . . . placed as in a chariot whereby it can be drawn out of the Cabinet for the better seeing' (Samuel Dale's Diary, ULC MS Add. 3466); and in 1743 the Hon. George Townshend gave an Egyptian mummy. Other donations of this kind are recorded: on 24 June 1771 'A Bow & Arrows brought from one of the late Discoverᵈ Islands in the south seas by Commodore Byron', the gift of Richard Farmer; on 1 July 1803 'the famous Statue of the Goddess Ceres . . . Also the column placed on the Tomb of Euclid', the gift of Edward Daniel Clarke and John Marten Cripps; and in February 1815 (also Clarke's gift) 'Dresses &c. of the Esquimaux Indians in Hudson's Bay; brought by his Majesty's Ship Rosamond in 1814', including 'Seal Skin Boots of the Men, Waterproof' and 'Boots of the Women'. And so I come – I will not say *at last* – to footwear.

I was led to the book which led me to the boot by an entry in the University's Audit Book for 1706–07: 'Given by Vote to a Protestant Lithuanian Ministers Widow who presented yᵉ University wᵗʰ yᵉ New Testament translat. into yᵗ language by her husband & others 05.07.6.' The book was easily found and identified by an inscription on its fly-leaf: 'Presented to the University Library this new Testament translated into the Lithuanian language by Mʳ Ramsey & others, whose widow Mʳˢ Ramsey made a present hereof

58

together with a Lithuanian Boot & Shoe. 1707.' (Plate I) An enquiry in the Library's Anderson Room, which is reserved for the study of rare printed books and manuscripts (and where else could a man reasonably enquire for an old boot?), was at first received less seriously than it deserved, but on my persistence an old boot was soon discovered in a cupboard together with, *inter alia*, the doeskin satchel in which Henry Fylongley, sheriff of Warwickshire and Leicestershire kept his *computus* roll for 1458 and a copy of *Granta* for November 1951, as originally issued in a half-pint beer-bottle, mint and unopened.

In bibliographical terms (and here McKerrow and Bowers were unhelpful) the boot, being tall (13 ins.), narrow (3¼ins.), and a small fitting (8½ins. from toes to heel), might be called an agenda duodecimo. I took it to Mr Harthan, who looks after old books at the Victoria and Albert Museum, and he called in Mr King, who looks after its textiles and old boots. They reported as follows:

The workmanship appears to be of late 17th–18th century date, and the boot is of the type known as 'Polish'. There was a considerable vogue for 'Polish' costume in western Europe during the second half of the 17th century, as an informal dress for adults and even more for children . . . Rembrandt's 'Polish Rider' (*c.* 1655) wears boots of this kind. A rather similar pair, also with iron heels, now in the Livruskammaren of the Nordiska Museet, Stockholm, is said to have been worn by Charles XI of Sweden (1660–97) when a boy. These boots are illustrated in E. Jäfverts book *Skomod och skotillverkning från medeltiden till våra dagar*, Stockholm, 1938, pl. 25 (b). The general view . . . is that the Cambridge boot is a child's 'Polish' boot, probably late 17th century, and quite possibly (in view of the tradition) Lithuanian in origin.

Of the widow's Lithuanian shoe there is no trace; but one wonders how many pieces of footwear she distributed among the curious before retiring, bootless yet not without profit, to the obscurity whence she came.

Her remaining gift, *Nanjas Testamentas wiesƶpaties musu Jeƶaus Kristaus*, Karalaućiuj [i.e. Königsberg], 1701, a quarto of 244 leaves, is a book of some rarity, at least in this country, there being no copy in the British Museum, the Bodleian Library, or the library of the British and Foreign Bible Society (see Darlow and Moule, *Historical Catalogue*, &c., No. 6368). It has a dedication in Latin to Frederick I of Prussia from the *Ecclesiarum Evangelicarum Litvanie hinc inde dispersarum Ministri & Seniores*, and contains a cursory account, also in Latin, by Bernhard von Sanden, Professor of Theology at Königsberg, of the first vernacular translations of the Bible, of the origins of the Lithuanian language, and of the first books printed in it. The text has alternative words put in brackets where the dialect of the Prussian Lithuanians differs from that of the Russian. The translation is mainly the work of Samuel Bythner, one of a commission appointed by the Lithuanian Synod to undertake the translation and printing of the Lithuanian Bible after Chylinski's version had failed to gain the approval of the authorities. Its historical background has recently been explored in great detail by Stanislaw Kot in one of the introductory essays (printed in both English and Polish) in *Biblia litewska Chylińskiego*, vol. ii (Poznań, 1958), but I found no mention of the widow's husband here. Eventually I was advised to consult the same writer's 'Anglo-Polonica' (*Nauki Polskiej*, XX. 49–140), and here, in all the alluring lucidity of a language which I could not read, was a paragraph devoted to Tomasz Ramsaeus with references to surviving letters and other writings by

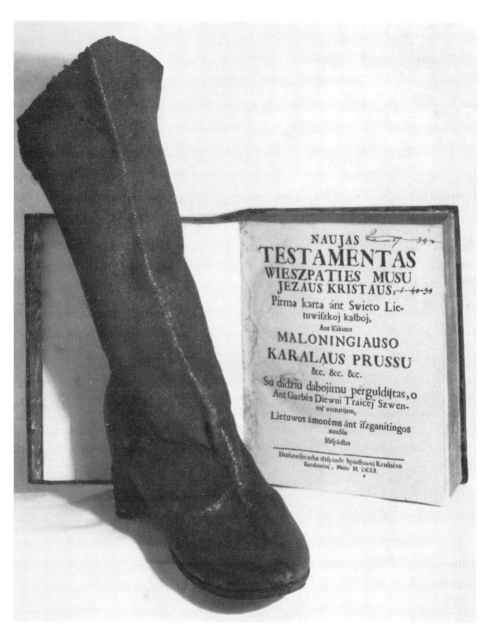

NAUJAS
TESTAMENTAS
WIESZPATIES MUSU
JEZAUS KRISTAUS,
Pirmą kartą ánt Swieto Lie-
tuwiſzkoj kałboj,
Ant Iſſikimo
MALONINGIAUSO
KARALAUS PRUSSU
&c. &c. &c.
Su didżiu dabojimu pérguldijtas, o
Ant Garbés Diewui Traicej Szwen-
toſ wienatjam,
Lietuwos źmonéms ánt iſzganitingos
naudôs
Iſſſpáuſtas

Drukawôjo arba iſzſpiaude Spáuſtuwoj Reuſnéro
Karalauciuj, Métu M. DCCI.

PLATE I. Lithuanian Boot and New Testament
Presented by the Widow Ramsay in 1707 to the University of Cambridge
(Cambridge University Library)

him. Interpreters having been called in, I decided to examine all this material for myself and to follow the boot's trail as far as it would lead. The only reference in English to Ramsay (as he usually spells his name when writing English) which I have found is in an article by Dr Nicholas Hans in *The Slavonic and East European Review* for December 1958 entitled 'Polish Protestants and their Connections with England and Holland in the 17th and 18th Centuries'. Dr Hans here states that Ramsay studied at Edinburgh University, where a Scottish emigrant merchant had established a fund for the education of a Calvinist student from Lithuania. This may well be so, though Ramsay's name does not appear in the admittedly incomplete records of that university. On the other hand, if he was indeed a Bachelor of Divinity, as he claims in some of his letters, he cannot have received that degree from Edinburgh, where it was not instituted until the 19th century.

Ramsay published at least three works:

1. *Climax Panegyrica vitæ serenissimi ac celsissimi principis, Jacobi Eboraci & Albaniæ Ducis, &c. Fabrefacta per T. Ramsæum. Londini, Excudebat Nathaniel Thompson, Anno Domini MDCLXXXII. Wing* R213. 4°, fourteen leaves; dedication (to James, Duke of York) in verse, text in prose. The British Museum copy is inscribed 'Nobilissimo Domino E. Browne M.D. Mecenati suo. d.d. Author'. Edward Browne (1644–1708) was the eldest son of Sir Thomas Browne; he travelled extensively in Europe, 1668–73, and settled as a practitioner of medicine in London in 1675.

2. *Apostrophe ad Idaliam Matrem de Redivivo Cæsare, Serenissimo Invictissimoque Carolo II Britanniarum Monarcha, &c. Occasione Statuæ in Regio Londinatum Excambio positæ. Authore T. Ramsæo Lituano. Londini, Typis Johannis Darby, Impensis Authoris. MDCLXXXV. Not in Wing.* Copy in Bodleian Library (see below, letter no. xii). 4°, eight leaves; dedication (to the Duke of Albemarle, Chancellor of Cambridge University, and to the leading members of the University) in prose, text in verse. The occasion is described by Echard, *History of England*, iii (1718), 716: 'The King being at the Height of his Glory, most Men seem'd ready to fall down and worship him; and this Year [1684] a famous and Noble Statue was erected to his Honour, in the Middle or Centre of the Royal Exchange. It consisted of the exact Figure of his present Majesty, done in Grey Marble, erected upon a curious Pedestal of the same; and the Statue was in the Garb and Habit of a *Roman Cæsar*. The Work-man that cut it was *Mr. Grinling Gibbons* . . . This was perform'd at the Charge of the *Hamborough* Company, at five Hundred Pound Expense . . . The King was so fully pleas'd with this Performance, that he gave special Orders that no Person should so much as Copy it in any Print, without the particular Leave of the said Mr. *Grinling Gibbons*.' Ramsay's pamphlet has an engraving of the statue (Plate 2) opposite the dedication, and two other engravings of it are listed by F. O'Donoghue, *Catalogue of Engraved British Portraits in the British Museum*, i. 404–5. The statue did not survive the fire which destroyed the Royal Exchange in 1838. M. Whinney and O. Millar, *English Art, 1625–1714* (1957), pp. 246–7, have little doubt that the statue, 'though commissioned from Gibbons, was executed by Quellin'. Ramsay's dedication refers to past kindnesses received from the University.

3. *Elogium fælicis fati Britanniæ, sub auspiciis serenissimi ac potentissimi Gulielmi III. Mag. Brit. Franc. & Hyber. Regis; exerti A Supremo Gentis Senatu. Concinnatum a Thoma Ramsæo Lituano Theol. Londini, Impensis Authoris Anno MDCLXXXIX. Wing* R214, also

listing another edition (?) dated 1690 (R215). 4°, ten leaves; dedication (to Parliament), dated *Lond. ex Musæo Idibus Junii 1689*, and *Præfatio Valedictoria ad Britannos* in prose, text in verse, or at least printed as such, there being no apparent metrical scheme.

Manuscripts of two other pieces survive:

a. Elogia Ejaculatoria in praesentem statum Illustrissimi ac Celsissimi Principis Iacobi Ducis Monmouthiensis compilata per Thomam Ramsaeum Lithuanum SS. Theol: Cand. & V.D.M. Anno 16⁷⁹⁄₈₀. Bodleian Library, MS Tanner 466 (18). Six leaves, of which 5ᵛ, 6 are blank, save for the endorsement. Dedication (to William Sancroft, Archbishop of Canterbury), dated *Hackniae 16⁷⁹⁄₈₀ Jan. 23*, in prose, text in verse, of a kind (cf. No. 3 above). See below, letter No. iv.

b. De cataractis oculorum ex Quarta, Quinta, et Sexta Parte Ὀφθαλμοδουλείας Georgij Bartesij Germani Ophtalmiatri. Dissertatio Theretico-practica e Germanico in Latinum conuersa per T.R. British Museum, MS Sloane 2520. Fifty-seven leaves. Undated (but Sloane 699, a transcript in another hand, is dated 1694). On leaf 2ʳ: Pensum Nobilissimi & Experientissimi Dni Franc: Bernard M.D. Celeberrimi deductum per T. Ramsæum Lituanum. This is a translation from Georg Bartisch's Ὀφθαλμοδουλείας *Das ist, Augendienst*, of which editions were printed at Dresden (1583), Frankfurt a.M. (1584), and Sultzbach (1686). Francis Bernard (1627–98) was reputed to possess 'the largest collection of books on physic ever made in England' (*DNB*). They were sold at auction after his death; the printed sale-catalogue includes a copy of the 1583 Bartisch (*Libri medici in folio*, No. 533) and Ramsay's *Elogium fati Britanniae* (*Appendix*, Bundle 1), the latter doubtless a gift from the author.

I have been able to add one letter (No. xiv of my list) to those summarily mentioned by Dr Kot:

i. Bodleian, MS Tanner 461 (38). To William Sancroft, as Dean of St Paul's, in Latin. Undated, but from its content earlier than No. ii. Signed by Ramsay as *SS. Theol: Candidatus*. Begins with some reflections on the mutability of fortune; the writer formerly wanted for nothing but is now reduced to begging at the doors of others, his remittances from Lithuania having ceased because of the Turco-Polish war; he needs money to pay his debts and to enable him to return home; encloses testimonial letters in order to introduce himself.

ii. Bodleian, MS Tanner 40 (118). To Sancroft, as Dean, in Latin. Dated 2 Feb. 1677 (therefore N.S., since Sancroft was consecrated Archbishop of Canterbury on 27 Jan. 1677/8). Signed as No. i. Addresses Sancroft as an old benefactor; the writer has been ill for four weeks and has spent on medicines all the money he has collected, including donations from Stillingfleet and Tillotson; after much fulsome praise of Sancroft's generosity, begs his signature to the enclosed testimonials, with which he hopes to obtain further relief from the bishops now assembling in London for the meeting of Parliament.

iii. Bodleian, MS Rawlinson Letters 59 (116). To Sancroft, as Archbishop, in Latin. Undated, but soon after 27 Jan. 1677/8. Signed as Nos. i, ii. Congratulates Sancroft on his elevation, wishes him long life, &c.; contrary to expectation is still in England, the persecution of the Church in Lithuania being such that to return thither would be a foolish temptation of providence; has therefore stayed in London and with the permission of the Bishop has opened a school of grammar and rhetoric; has few pupils but many debts; asks for help.

iv. Bodleian, MS Rawlinson Letters 59 (115). To Sancroft, in English. Dated 23 Jan. 1679/80, from Hackney. Signed by Ramsay as B.D.; sent by a bearer (Mrs Ramsay?). Regrets the necessity of applying to Sancroft once more, after the year's interval which his Lordship had commanded; is very sick and has no means of maintenance, his school being dispersed because of his sickness; implores aid and promises never to be 'truble-some' again; encloses a 'small present'. Cf. manuscript *a* above, which must be the present in question.

v. Bodleian, MS Rawlinson Letters 51 (119). To Sancroft, in English. Undated, but from its contents later than No. iv. Signed 'Thomas Ramsay a Lituanian Minister'. Implores aid; encloses a certificate of his troubles and two letters written to him in French by 'Lady Holles Widow of the lately lamented Lord'; the writer's wife is bearer of this letter and will give Sancroft further details; encloses a present. Denzil Holles, 1st Earl of Clare, died on 17 Feb. 1679/80 and was survived by his third wife Esther, *née* Le Lou, of Colombiers in Normandy. She died in 1684 (*Registers of Westminster*, ed. J. L. Chester, Harleian Soc., x, p. 4), So that Ramsay's present, unless a manuscript, was most probably a copy of *Climax Panegyrica* (1682).

vi–x. See *Ecclesiae Londino-Batavae Archivum*, ed. J. H. Hessels, iii, Pt. 2, No. 4391. Two letters in English to the Elders of the Dutch Church in London and three in Latin to the Rev. Mr Opdebeek. All undated, but dated *c.* 1680 by Hessels, who reproduces one in full and gives the substance of the others. Variously signed as *M. of the Gospell; Lithuanus V.D.M.; Lith. S.Th. Cand.; Lithuanus; a Lithuanian, B.D.* These letters may cover at least two years; Mrs Ramsay was the bearer of two of them. Ramsay refers to help received from the French Church in London; he is working on two books and so needs assistance; he describes one of them as *Historia modernae conspirationis* (i.e. the Popish Plot?) and says it will be published soon; the other, of which he sends the begin-ning for perusal, is 'intended to clear the innocency of the purer party of Protestants and to shew the folly of them which calls them Schismatics and denies a true Ministry to be amongst them'. I have not identified either work, if indeed either ever saw publication. Ramsay's reception by the Dutch seems to have been tepid.

xi. Lambeth Palace Library, MS 674 (36). 'For the Rev. Dr Spencer Mr of Beñett College', in Latin. Undated, but perhaps not before 1685: John Spencer was master of Corpus Christi ('Benet') College, Cambridge, 1667–93, Signed with name only. Offers two books, one in Latin, 'which I have dedicated to you as an acknowledgment of the gratitude I owe You', the other in English, dedicated to the King; Spencer will excuse the mistakes (caused by hurry) in the former, and will see from the latter the writer's progress '*in pronunciando vestro Schibolet*'; asks for help now that he is about to return at last to his own country '*post gravissimum meum meorumque morbum, post amissa omnia*'. The Latin book may possibly be *Apostrophe ad Idaliam matrem* (1685), which, though not dedicated to Spencer himself, is dedicated to the Chancellor and Heads of his University. I have not traced to Ramsay any book in English. The words *meum meo-rumque* are the first indication that Ramsay has a family as well as a wife.

xii. Bodleian, MS Ashmole 1136 (17). To Ashmole, in English. Undated, but not before 1685. Signed with name only. Ramsay has met Ashmole but once, but ventures to approach him nonetheless; complains of debts, sicknesses, and misfortunes, which even the little book enclosed as a present has not escaped, 'for I but scarcely saved some few of them (as out of the destruction of Troy) out of the Printers house, whose forms, seats and other instruments were broke the day before I was to receive these Exemplaries, because of printing of some either prohibited or not licensed pamphlet'; is resolved to return to Lithuania, but has no resources; has a wife and child to support; will send the former for an answer.

On 1^v is a verse to Ashmole, *Nobilissimum Mecænatem*, taken from Martial (*Epigr*. iv. 14. 6, 10–11, 13–14). The pamphlet enclosed was *Apostrophe ad Idaliam Matrem* (1685) and is now Ashmole 1021 (9): it has additional manuscript material prefixed to it, as Ramsay says in his letter ('I have adjoyned to it some other trifles'), and it fits with other descriptive clues therein ('The Object is dead, but his memory lives' and 'the (though now deceased, yett then when it was written living) King'). Its printer, John Darby, was convicted in the Court of King's Bench in Feb. 1683/4 of printing *The Speech of the late Lord Russel* in the previous July (Echard, *History*, iii. 711, Plomer, *Dictionary of Printers, 1668–1725*, p. 97). I have not found that he was involved in any similar trouble late in 1684, the probable time of printing of Ramsay's pamphlet. W. H. Black, *Catalogue of the Manuscripts bequeathed by E. Ashmole*, &c. (1845), p. 972, says that this letter and the following 'seem to have been sent together': but this is impossible since Ramsay has one child in No. xii, two or more in No. xiii.

xiii. Bodleian, MS Ashmole 1136 (18). To Ashmole, in Latin. Undated, but from its content later than No. xii. Signed as *Lithuanus*. Opens with rhetorical compliments and proceeds to the usual appeal; mentions *suspirans uxor et nutu adgementes infantuli*; ends with two sets of three elegiac couplets, the former *in Chymici apud Oxonienses Phrontisterij cum Theatro Connubium*, the latter to the King of Poland.

xiv. Public Record Office, S.P.32 (Will. & Mary I), No.118. To Charles Talbot, Earl of Shrewsbury, in English. Dated 1 Aug. 1689. Signed with name only. Encloses a 'piece of ingenuity' as a present; writes confidently of his resolution to return home, 'there to serve the Protestant interest to power'; needs help, however, if he is to do so, all his property having been seized by his landlord and creditors. The 'piece of ingenuity' enclosed must have been a copy of *Elogium faelicis fati Britanniae* (1689).

xv. Bodleian, MS Ashmole 1136 (16). To Ashmole, in English. Undated, but from its content very near No. xiv. Signed with name only. Is about to repair to his own country; encloses 'the monument of a small ingenuity' in gratitude for kindnesses received; will call to say goodbye on Friday, when (as he delicately hints) he will give Ashmole an opportunity of listening to the tale of his 'toe palpable necessities'. The present enclosed was again the *Elogium* (1689), of which there is a copy, Ashmole 1021 (3).

Here the series ends, leaving two questions unanswered: Did Ramsay ever return to Lithuania? And did he help to translate the New Testament into Lithuanian, as his widow claimed? According to Dr Kot's account, work began on this translation in 1682; if Ramsay had been employed upon it during his stay in England it is inconceivable that he omitted to mention in his letters so telling a recommendation, seeing that a Lithuanian translation had been canvassed and supported, both publicly and privately, in England for some twenty-five years. He may, perhaps, have taken some part in the work after 1689, but it is impossible to believe that he made any important contribution to it. The tale of his iterated disasters has a certain Slavic charm, but his works are utterly insignificant. His prose, whether English or Latin, is intolerable, save when desperate circumstances force him (as in letters Nos. iv and v) to go straight to the point, and his verse is worse than his prose. He never got beyond the mental age of the Advanced Level, being addicted to sinfully show-off devices, such as acrostics and anagrams, and quite unable to resist quotation and allusion, both biblical and classical. The opening of letter No. xii shows him in full flight, and sinking like a plummet under the weight of what he himself liked to call a 'subitaneous ingenuity':

If tears could change their colour by any artifice; with them I might write to You; for, they, being the effects and Attendants, could also be the truest Representers, of my Grieff. Butt, since Nature admits of no Variation, in (as they call them) elementary matters, without a new Ingredient, I am forced to convey unto Your Honour my tears in an inky dress; noways doubting, but that by the most polished Telescope of Your subact judgment, You'l discern in the same draught, the different Natures of Salt and Vinegar . . .

As for this article, Ramsay would have supplied the appropriate tag without difficulty: *ne sutor ultra crepidam* – which means, roughly: bibliographers should beware of boots.[1]

---

[1] I am indebted to Dr R. Auty, of Selwyn College, and Dr L. R. Lewitter, of Christ's College, Cambridge, for indispensable help in the preparation of this article.

DAVID FOXON

John Cleland and the Publication of the
Memoirs of a Woman of Pleasure

I HAD not intended to deal with Cleland's notorious *Memoirs of a Woman of Pleasure* in my study of 'Libertine Literature in England, 1660–1745';[1] my dates were carefully chosen to exclude it. I had, however, discovered in the Public Record Office an important letter by Cleland on the subject, and just as the last part of my article was going to press a vital piece of bibliographical evidence turned up by chance after eight years' waiting. On looking at the published literature, including the new American edition,[2] it was clear that there was still a good deal of confusion that could be straightened out, and though I can give no final answer to all the problems which surround the publication of the book, at least some facts can be finally determined. I am greatly indebted to Mr John Hayward and Dr E. J. Dingwall for the use of their notes and observations.

The earliest advertisement I have found for the first volume is in the *General Advertiser* for Monday, 21 Nov. 1748:

> *This Day is Published*, (*Price* 3s.)
> MEMOIRS of a WOMAN of PLEASURE.
> Written by a PERSON of QUALITY.
> Printed for G. FENTON, in the Strand.

Subsequent advertisements drop the reference to the 'person of quality'.

The second volume is advertised in the *London Evening-Post* for 14–16 Feb. 1749:

> *This Day is publish'd, Price* 3s.
> *The Second and Last Volume of*
> MEMOIRS of a WOMAN of PLEASURE.
> Printed for G. Fenton, at No. 12, in Exeter Exchange in the Strand.

Later the imprint becomes 'Printed for G. Fenton, and sold at No. 12, in Exeter Exchange. . . . Where may be had, the first volume, price 3s.' Both volumes are advertised together at 6s in the *General Advertiser* of 27 March 1749.

After a considerable period of silence the government, apparently stirred by the bishops, went into action. On 8 November 1749 a warrant[3] was issued by Newcastle to seize the author, printer, and publisher. The result is two informative documents, the first

---

[1] *v.* THE BOOK COLLECTOR, Spring, Summer, Autumn 1963.

[2] G. P. Putnam's Sons, New York, 1963.

[3] *Copies taken from the records of the Court of King's Bench* (1763) p. 45.

being Ralph Griffiths's statement[4] taken before Lovel Stanhope, the Law Clerk in the Secretary of State's office, on 13 November:

Being shewn a Work in Two Volumes intitled "Memoirs of a Woman of Pleasure London printed for G. Fenton in the Strand 1749" & being asked whether he knows who is the Author, printer or publisher thereof, he says That some time last Winter his Brother Fenton Griffith came to him & asked his advice whether it would be safe for him to Publish the said Book, That at that Time there was only one of the said Volumes finished & the said Fenton Griffith giving the Examinant a discription of the said Volume the Examinant did advise him to publish it & the Examinant believes he did publish the same at his the said Fenton Griffiths Shop in Exeter Exchange in the Strand & supplied the Booksellers with it.

The Examinant says that his Brother told him that he had the Copy of the said Work from one J. Cleeland who the Examinant believes, from what his Brother has told him, is the Author of the said Work.

That the second Volume of the said Work was published by his said Brother about Seven Months since.

The Examinant says that his said Brother has told him that Thomas Parker of Jewin Street in Aldersgate Street printed both the first & second Volume of the said Work.

The Examinant says that he has sold about Sixty sets of the said Work now shewn to him.

This at last makes clear that the imprint 'for G. Fenton' is a simple cover for Fenton Griffiths, though one is entitled to wonder whether Ralph Griffiths was as detached an observer as he makes out. Fenton Griffiths does not seem to have been found by the authorities at the time, or by anyone since.

Cleland wrote his own statement on the same day in the form of a letter to Stanhope;[5] it is a delightful piece of special pleading in all its varieties:

Sir,

Called on to give an account of my Share in the Memoirs of a *Woman of Pleasure*; whatever may be the degree of guilt incurred by it, I shall at least deserve your favourable report by a most candid, and plenary detail of all the circumstances of it: Some indeed impertinent to a formal, judicial examination, but which may serve to abate much of the rigour urged against me.

The plan of the first Part was originally given me by a young gentleman of the greatest hopes that ever I knew, (Brother to a nobleman now Ambassadour at a Foreign Court,) above eighteen years ago, on an occasion immaterial to mention here.

This I never dreamt of preparing for the Press, till being under confinement in the Fleet, at my leisure hours, I altered, added to, transposed, and in short new-cast: when, on showing it to some whose opinion I unfortunately preferred to my own, and being made to consider it as a ressource, I published the first part. And not till near four months after the Second: which had been promised, and would most surely have never been proceeded to had I been in the least made sensible of the first having given any offence: and indeed I now wonder it could so long, escape the Vigilance of the Guardians of the Public Manners, since, nothing is truer, than that more Clergymen bought it in proportion, than any other distinction of men.

And such at least was my tenderness of adding the fault of prophaneness to that of wantonness, that in the second Volume, where the Story of the Flagellant is told, and which I fished for in actual life, I substituted a Lay-character, to that of a Divine of the Church of England, of

---

[4] PRO, SP 36/111/159. I have expanded the contractions of the original.

[5] PRO, SP 36/111/157, 158.

whom the Fact, with little variation, is sacred Truth: as may, if doubted, on a slender enquiry be traced, and verified.

In short, my offence was really of itself a very severe punishment: condemned to seek relief, not only from the meanness of writing for a bookseller, but from becoming the author of a Book I disdain to defend, and wish, from my Soul, buried and forgot.

This too would probably be the Case, if the pious indignation of my Lords the Bishops will give them leave to consider that they can take no step towards punishing the Author that will not powerfully contribute to the notoriety of the Book, and spread what they cannot wish supprest more than I do. To say nothing of its giving occasion for this very natural question: why slept this zeal so long? and waked not but till the Book had had its run, and is dying of itself, unless they choose to give it new life?

May I support these arguments by an Example chosen from a Number? It is not eight months since the Son of a *Dean* and Grandson of a *Bishop* was mad and wicked enough to Publish a Pamphlet evidently in defence of *Sodomy*, advertised in all the papers.[6] This was perhaps rather overlooked than tolerated – What was the consequence? Why, it is at this instant so thoroughly forgot that few I believe know that ever such a Pamphlet existed: Whereas, if My Lords the Bishops had been so injudicious as to stir this stench they might have indeed provoked the public indignation, but its curiosity too: and all to punish a crazy wretch, who would, I dare swear, not be unambitious of taking Vanini[7] for his Model.

Thus far, sir, in mitigation rather than defence of my fault. I submit however gladly the whole to his Grace's decision. If the innocence of my intention, the circumstances in which I committed it, and even my present low abject condition, that of a writer for Bread, all are not sufficient to give, in his Grace's Eye, a less grave and serious turn to this affair, than a prosecution in form, in complaisance to this Episcopal Representation, which is however certainly of the latest; I must of course submit to superiour power. But it will be some alleviation to the rigour of my fate, if his Grace would permit me to be the *only* victim in this affair, and I do assure you, sir, if it proves of any service to the Reformation of manners, I shall not complain of being the victim; But it is really little more than Justice to acquitt, and deliver from longer confinement those poor People now under punishment for *my* fault: as they certainly were deceived by my avoiding those rank words in the work, which are all that they Judge of obscenity by, and made them think the Line was drawn between them, and all danger of Law whatever.

I scarce think it necessary to mention here, that, From the Messenger's house,[8] in the heat of my resentment at being treated like a common malefactor, I wrote a Letter to Mr Stone,[9] and probably a very impertinent one, but I take for granted that he must be too much the gentleman to use it against me: Especially since his not vouchsafing me any answer, was, from one of his extream politeness, mortification enough to a gentleman, who measuring other hearts by his own, would pay ten times more tender respect to the natural Jealousy of the distrest, than where, there is so little, and so vulgar a merit in paying it, to Fortune, and Power.

As for you, Sir, I shall not intrench on your time with anything so vain and useless, as compliments from a Place like this, where my head is even so disordered that I can hardly write common

---

[6] There seems little doubt that the reference is to *Ancient and Modern Pederasty investigated and exemplified* which was listed among the books published in April 1749 by the *Gentleman's Magazine*. I have not traced a copy. Cleland's reference seems to have led to action: SP 44/134/9 contains a letter of 20 Jan. 1750 from Newcastle to the Attorney General sending the examinations of Thomas Cannon, the author, and John Purser, the printer, and requesting their prosecution. The further history of Cannon can be seen in a petition printed in *Notes and Queries* ser. 2, vol. 8, pp. 65–6.

[7] Lucilio Vanini, the Italian freethinker, burnt at the stake for atheism in 1619.

[8] The Messenger to the Press at this time was Samuel Grey, appointed in 1729.

[9] Andrew Stone, one of the Under-Secretaries of State.

sense, or common English. That Humanity you have showed me, is my security for your saying to yourself for me all that I ought to say, and with the more effect, in that I, from motives of diffidence, and respect, omit to say more.

> I am, Sir, with the most profound sense of your goodness,
> Your most obliged, and most

Dartmouth Street obed^t, humble Servant
Monday the 13th. Novr. 1749.   J. Cleland

On 24 November 1749, Stanhope wrote from the Secretary of State's office to John Sharpe of the Attorney-General's office[10] enclosing six recognizances in £100 taken before him for the appearance of the persons named at the Court of King's Bench on the last day of Michaelmas term. They were

John Cleland of St. James's Place . . . Esqr
Thomas Parker of Jewin Street . . . Printer & Stationer
Ralph Griffiths of St Pauls Churchyard . . . Bookseller
Bispham Dickinson of London, Bookseller
Robert Sayer of Fleet Street, London, Printseller
Matthias Darby of St. Martins in the Fields, Seal Engraver

The first three are, of course, author, printer, and publisher of the *Memoirs*. Whether the other three were involved in this or another case there is nothing to show.

It seems clear that the first three were not deeply intimidated, for in the *General Advertiser* of 8 March 1750 the following advertisement appears:

> *This Day is Publish'd,*
> *Compleat in One Pocket Volume, Price bound* 3s.
> MEMOIRS of FANNY HILL.
>
> *If I have painted Vice in its gayest Colours, if I have deck'd*
> *it with Flowers, it has been solely in order to make the worthier,*
> *the solemner Sacrifice of it to* VIRTUE.   Vide p. 273.
>
> Printed for R. Griffiths, at the Dunciad in St. Paul's Church-yard.
> *Of whom may be had, in Two Volumes, Price* 6s.
> Memoirs of the celebrated Mrs. *Lætitia Pilkington.*

The entry in the catalogue of books in the *British Magazine* for March gives more information: 'Memoirs of Fanny Hill, (being the story of a heroine of a book published sometime since, entitled, Memoirs of a woman of pleasure, 2 vol.) divested of its obscenity . . .' This is quite clearly an abridgement, but the Bishop of London, Thomas Sherlock, was not at all convinced of its virtue. He wrote to the Secretary of State:[11]

Temple 15 March 1749.

My Lord Duke
    Your Grace ordered a prosecution against the Printer and publisher of the *Memoires of a Lady of Pleasure*. The same Bookseller, one *Griffiths* (as I apprehend) has published within a few Days a Book called *Memoires of Fanny Hill*, the Lewdest thing I ever saw; It is, I am told, the same with the other, after leaving out some things, which were thought most liable to the Law and to expose

---

[10] SP 44/85/161.   [11] SP 36/112/139.

the Author and publisher to punishment – But if there is not Law enough in the Country to reach this vile Book after all the pretence to correct it, we are in a deplorable condition.

I beg of your Grace to give proper orders, to stop the progress of this vile Book, which is an open insult upon Religion and good manners, and a reproach to the Honour of the Government, and the Law of the Country.

I am My Lord
Your Grace's
most obedient & most humble servant
Tho: London.

On the same day, 15 March, a warrant was issued for the author, printer and publisher of *Fanny Hill*,[12] and on 20 March Griffiths made the following statement before Stanhope:[13]

The Examinant says that upon the Suppression of a Book Intitled the Memoirs of a Woman of Pleasure he applied to Mr. Cleeland the Author of it, & desired him to strike out the offensive parts of it & compile a Novel from it which might be inoffensive, which the said Mr Cleeland did & called it "Memoirs of Fanny Hill" which the Examinant is the proprietor & publisher of.

The Examinant says his motive for asking that Favour of Mr. Cleeland was that Mr. Cleeland owed him a Sum of money & as Cleeland was going abroad he thought it was the only Method to get his Debt paid.

Says he does not think there is any harm in the said Book & that had the King's Messengers given him Notice that the said Book gave offence, he would have Cancelled the whole Edition.

At the same time a bookseller called William Owen made a statement that he had bought two copies from Jacob Robinson of Ludgate Street and 'lent one of them to an officer to read for sixpence'.[14]

Still Griffiths seems to have been unconcerned, for in his periodical *The Monthly Review* for March 1750 (published early in April) he reviewed *Fanny Hill* in the following terms:[15]

Though this book is said to be taken from a very loose work, printed about two years ago, in two volumes, and on that account a strong prejudice has arisen against it, yet it does not appear to us that this performance, whatever the two volumes might be, (for we have not seen them) has any thing in it more offensive to decency, or delicacy of sentiment and expression, than our novels and books of entertainment in general have: For, in truth, they are most of them (especially our comedies, and not a few of our tragedies) but too faulty in this respect. . . .

As to the step lately taken to suppress this book, we really are at a loss to account for it; yet, perhaps, all wonder on this head will cease, when we consider how liable great men are to be misinformed, how frequently obliged to see with other men's eyes, and hear with other people's ears.

⁎ The news-papers inform us, that the celebrated history of *Tom Jones* has been suppressed in *France*, as an immoral work.

On 12 April 1750, Newcastle, the Secretary of State, wrote to the Attorney-General a letter[16] reciting that Ralph Griffiths has been apprehended for printing and publishing

---

[12] *Copies taken from the records of . . . King's Bench*, p. 46.

[13] SP 36/112/145.

[14] SP 36/112/147.

[15] Vol. II, p. 431. Griffiths's authorship of the review is known from his file copy of the magazine in the Bodleian.

[16] Sp 44/134/28; the copy is textually corrupt.

' "Memoirs of Fanny Hill", being an extract of a book entitled "Memoirs of a Woman of Pleasure", the author printer and publishers of which you have already had directions to prosecute'. He requested that Griffiths and Owen should be prosecuted on this new charge if there was sufficient ground. Nothing seems to have happened as a result of this request, and on 27 November 1750 Newcastle wrote again, including the names of other printers and booksellers who were probably charged with other offences:[17]

> The following persons, viz¹: Robert Sayer, John Cleland, Ralph Griffith, Thomas Parker, Charles Moseley, Henry Chappelle, Charles Corbett, William Owen, and George Bickham, being bound to appear upon their recognizances, in the Court of King's Bench, I am to signify you his majesty's pleasure, that you should prosecute them for the several crimes and offences of which they stand indicted . . .

Here, alas, the story fades into uncertainty. I have been unable to trace any action against these men up to the end of Hilary Term 1753.[18] There remains only the testimony of John Nichols, first in the *Gentleman's Magazine* (February 1789, p. 180) and then in a slightly altered form in his *Literary Anecdotes* vol. 2 (1812) p. 458n. Having told of Cleland's being reduced to the debtor's prison, he goes on:

> . . . In this situation, one of those booksellers who disgrace the profession, offered him a temporary relief for writing the work above alluded to,* which brought a stigma on his name, which time has not obliterated, and which will be consigned to his memory whilst its poisonous contents are in circulation. For this publication he was called before the Privy Council, and the circumstances of his distress being known, as well as his being a man of some parts, John Earl Granville, the then president, nobly rescued him from the like temptation by getting him a pension of 100l. a year, which he enjoyed to his death.
> * The sum given for the copy of this work was twenty guineas. The sum received for the sale could not be less than 10,000l.

The suggestion that Griffiths made £10,000 out of the *Memoirs* seems rather the fantasy of a jealous rival than a reasonable estimate; one wishes one could be sure of Nichols's other statements. Granville became Lord President of the Council on 17 June 1751, but there is no trace in the registers of the Privy Council up to the end of 1753 that Cleland ever appeared before them; indeed, it was not the sort of business they dealt with. It remains possible that Granville arranged a pension for Cleland – probably, no doubt, in the hope that he would lend his pen to the service of the government. One wonders whether Griffiths escaped legal action under a similar agreement – though the *Monthly Review* gained a good reputation for dispassionate criticism.

There remain the bibliographical problems. For a change, a number of copies of different editions survive or are reliably reported, and the problem is to determine which is the first edition. (It is always possible that the first edition has been lost; but since it enjoyed such a long period of immunity from legal action, it should be the most likely to survive.) We may, I think, safely discard the undated editions *Memoirs of* ********** **

---

[17] SP 44/134/32.
[18] At this point there is over a year's gap in the 'Great

Dogget Books'. A search of the Controlment Rolls and of the indictments has also been without result.

************, which Guillaume Apollinaire put first in his bibliography.[19] Since the first edition was advertised and referred to in the documents by its full name, the coyness of this title must be later – typographically it looks later as well.

This leaves us with four editions in which the title-page reads, with minor variations: MEMOIRS OF A WOMAN OF PLEASURE. VOL. I. [II.] *LONDON:* Printed for G. FENTON in the *Strand*, MDCCXLIX. G. Fenton, of course, is that shadowy character Fenton Griffiths; and the date 1749 in both volumes is natural enough even though the first was published in November 1748. The variations in the editions may be listed thus:

A. Oval woodcut ornament on title-page. Date as 'M.DCC.XLIX.' 12°: A–I¹², K⁶; A–K¹², L⁶, M². Pp. [1–3] 4–227 [228 blank]; [1–3] 4–255 [256 blank]. 25 lines of type per page except vol. I, pp. 194–227 which are set unleaded, giving 29 lines. Headlines: *Memoirs of a | Woman of Pleasure*. With a sodomitical description in vol. II, pp. 177–9. BM, Yale, Bay. Staatsbibliothek Munich, Bibliothèque Nationale. (Plate I*a*.)

B. A similar oval woodcut ornament on title. Date as 'MDCCXLIX.' 12°: A–I¹², K⁶; A–K¹², L⁶ (L6 not seen, presumably blank). Pp. [1–3] 4–228; [1–3] 4–250 [?251–2 blank]. 28 lines of type throughout. No headlines. Without the sodomitical passage. Mr Graham Greene. (Plate I*b*.)

C. Ornamental group of type-flowers on title. Date as 'MDCCXLIX.' 12°: A–I¹², K⁶; A–K¹², L⁶ as B, with which it corresponds page for page. No headlines. Without the sodomitical passage. BM, *Rothschild Catalogue* I, no. 643. (Plate II*a*.)

D. No ornament on title. Date as 'M,DCC,XLIX.' Not seen; pagination reported by Apollinaire as 172; 187. Bay. Staatsbibliothek Munich (vol. I only).

Since it forms an important part of the argument, here is the description of the abridged version. No copy has been located, but there is a description and some photographs in a collection of notes put together by Michael Sadleir and now in the possession of Dr E. J. Dingwall.

MEMOIRS OF *FANNY HILL*. *If I have painted* Vice *in its gayest Colours, if I have deck'd it with Flowers, it has been solely in order to make the worthier, the solemner Sacrifice of it to* Virtue. *LONDON:* Printed for R. GRIFFITHS, in St. *Paul's Church-Yard*. [No date, but 1750.] 12°. A[3ll.] B–M¹², N[5ll.]; pp. [i–vi] [1] 2–273 [274 blank]. (Plate II*b*.)

The work has been recast in the form of 11 letters (the last misnumbered 'xv'); it contains all the incidents of the original but the overall length has been reduced to something over half. Since the photographs include only the first and last pages of text, it is not possible to determine how much obscenity has been removed. No doubt copies are so rare because it was suppressed within a week of publication.

It is convenient to remove D from the list of four candidates for the first edition of the *Woman of Pleasure*; further argument will, I hope, confirm this step. The use of commas in the date 'M,DCC,XLIX' suggests a foreign origin, as does the fact that it is known by Apollinaire's description and a copy in Munich. The pagination is the same as a dated edition of 1781 described by Ashbee.

If we apply the same sort of general principles to A, B, and C, we can say that the

[19] In *L'Œuvre de John Cleland* (Paris, 1910), p. 133, dating it 1747 or 1748. There are apparently two editions, one in the collection of Mr C. R. Dawes, pp. 232; 252 (A–I¹², K⁶, L²; A–K¹², L⁶) and two copies of the other in the Bibliothèque Nationale, pp. 228; 252. The untidy collation of Mr Dawes's copy suggests that it is the earlier; it has an MS inscription dated 1759.

MEMOIRS

OF A

WOMAN

OF

PLEASURE.

VOL. I.

LONDON:
Printed for G. Fenton in the *Strand,*
M.DCC.XLIX.

PLATE 1*b*. A later imitation. 158 × 97 mm.
(Mr Graham Greene)

MEMOIRS

OF A

WOMAN

OF

PLEASURE.

VOL. I.

LONDON:
Printed for G. Fenton in the *Strand*
M.DCC.XLIX.

PLATE 1*a*. The first edition. 156 × 95 mm.
(British Library)

MEMOIRS

OF

FANNY HILL.

*If I have painted Vice in its gayest Co-
lours, if I have deck'd it with Flowers,
it has been solely in order to make the
worthier, the solemner Sacrifice of it to
Virtue.*

LONDON:

Printed for R. GRIFFITHS, in St. *Paul's
Church-Yard.*

PLATE 11*b*. The lost first edition of *Fanny Hill* [1750]. 164 × 94 mm. (From a photograph in the possession of Dr E. J. Dingwall)

MEMOIRS

OF A

WOMAN

OF

PLEASURE.

VOL. I.

LONDON:

Printed for G. FENTON in the *Strand.*
MDCCXLIX.

PLATE 11*a*. Another early edition. 170 × 105 mm. (British Library)

a. *Memoirs of a Woman of Pleasure*, 1749. (British Library)

b. *Memoirs of a Woman of Pleasure*, '1749'. (Mr Graham Greene)

c. *Memoirs of a Woman of Pleasure*, 1749. (British Library)

d. *Memoirs of a Woman of Pleasure*, '1749'. (Mr Graham Greene)

PLATE III. Ornaments of Thomas Parker and their imitations referred to in the text: reproduced actual size.

e. Memoirs of a Woman of Pleasure, 1749. (British Library)

f. Travels . . . of William Bingfield, 1753. (British Library)

g. The Frisky Muse, 1749. (British Library)

PLATE IV. More ornaments of Thomas Parker. Ornaments *f* and *g* are found in the photographs of the lost *Memoirs of Fanny Hill* [1750].

changeover from woodcut headpieces and ornaments to the use of combinations of printers' flowers took place about 1750; some printers were quicker to take up the fashion than others. In general, though, the woodcut is typical of the first half of the century, and therefore A & B are likely to precede C. Similarly an irregular collation is more typical of a first edition than a regular one, since it is more difficult to estimate precisely the length of manuscript than of printed copy. On these grounds A would precede B & C: note not only the additional signature M^2 in vol. II but also the closer setting of type in sig. I of vol. I; these abnormalities are ironed out in the other editions.[20]

There is next the question of the sodomitical passage in vol. II. All editions record how Fanny's chariot had a breakdown on the way to Hampton-court, and how while waiting in an inn she observed a homosexual encounter in the next room. Only edition A includes two paragraphs which give the physical details in Cleland's usual periphrastic style. It has been widely accepted that these two paragraphs are a later addition, and they have been related to a note added by Bohn to his edition of Lowndes's *Bibliographer's Manual* (1864):

... after this had appeared the language was considerably altered for the worse by Drybutter, the bookseller, who was punished for it by being put in the pillory in 1757.

All attempts to find evidence to elucidate this statement have failed, but the suggestion that Drybutter added these two paragraphs scarcely fits the charge of altering the *language* for the worse. It seems to me highly improbable that Cleland, having deliberately led up to this scene, would not make the most of it as he did everywhere else. Moreover the references to sodomy in Cleland's letter trying to exculpate himself suggest that this point was being pressed against the book. If an indictment is ever discovered I would not be at all surprised to find this passage quoted in the charge. Subsequent publishers might then have a possible plea of innocence by claiming they had omitted the passage objected to. All this suggests to my mind that edition A which contains this passage is in fact the first edition.

The clinching evidence is that of the woodcut ornaments. Edition A uses three; the distinctive oval on the title-page (Plate III*a*); a rectangular cut of a common style with Cupid playing a lute (Plate III*c*) on the first page of text; and a double cornucopia of fruit and flowers (Plate IV*e*) at the end of vol. II. Of these, *a* is found on p. 48 and *e* on p. 26 of *The Frisky Muse . . . By Rigdum Funnidos* (London: printed for and sold by the author, 1749: BM); *c* appears on p. 1 of vol. 2 of *The Travels* and *Adventures of William Bingfield* (London: printed for E. Withers . . . and R. Baldwin . . . 1753: BM). These two books have other cuts in common to confirm that they came from the same printing shop.[21] Unfortunately there are no decisive breaks or signs of wear in the cuts which would establish the sequence in which these books were printed; but at least we have a rather naughty book of verse printed in 1749 by the same man who produced edition A.

---

[20] In the *Memoirs of* ********** ** *************mentioned above it is interesting that one edition has an extra L^2 in the first volume; this suggests that A was used as copy and the compression of the text in I^{12} was not noticed when the copy was cast off. This would therefore be the earlier of these two editions.

[21] The stock of ornaments is a mixed one, and looks as though it was acquired second-hand. There are certainly three cuts and probably more which belonged to Henry Woodfall in the 1730s; Woodfall senior died about 1747.

Fortunately the photographs which are all that we have of the *Memoirs of Fanny Hill* show three ornaments. The one on the title-page (Plate IV*g*) appears on p. 42 of *The Frisky Muse*, and the one which heads the text (Plate IV*f*) is found in the same position in vol. I of *The Travels*. This too was therefore produced by the same printer. We know that the abridged *Memoirs of Fanny Hill* were printed for Griffiths in 1750; and when we find that the same printer was responsible for an edition of the *Memoirs of a Woman of Pleasure*, it is hard to escape the conclusion that this edition was the original one printed for Griffiths. In that case the printer was Thomas Parker, and like Griffiths and Cleland he was not deterred from making money out of *Fanny Hill* by the threat of court proceedings against the *Memoirs of a Woman of Pleasure*.

From this accumulation of evidence it seems clear that A is the first edition.[22] Edition B, which resembles it so closely, poses a problem. The key may be that it contains a frontispiece and eight hand-coloured mezzotints in each volume[23] which on expert evidence cannot be earlier than 1760. Most of them have volume and page references which fit edition B (and would approximately fit A and C as well). This suggests that we have a publisher planning an illustrated edition in the 1760s. The plates could be produced quite discreetly as required, but stock of a two-volume novel is not easy to conceal. It seems possible that the production of a reprint which could be explained away as a 'remainder' of the first edition might have its attractions – superficial attractions, no doubt, rather than any real preservative value against determined investigation; but this sort of publishing with its false dates and imprints is often satisfied with such rough cover. The woodcut ornaments on the titles and at the head of the text (Plate III, *b* and *d*) are very similar to those in edition A, but they were probably already in existence and borrowed for this book: I have not traced their ownership.

Editions C and D, like the undated *Memoirs of ********** ** ************, cannot at present be dated at all precisely; probably they never will be. Since it is in the highest degree improbable that Cleland ever revised the text, this is not of importance for textual study; if, as I hope I have shown, A is the first edition, we have the nearest we can get to Cleland's text, and it is not corrupt. But it would be nice to trace a copy of the abridged *Memoirs of Fanny Hill*.

---

[22] It would not be surprising if there had been more than one edition printed for Griffiths in 1749, but all four known copies are certainly from the same setting of type in those pages of which I have had photostats.

[23] The frontispiece to vol. I is probably a late insertion or replacement. The overall design of the plates is the same as some of the engravings attributed to Gravelot in an edition dated 1766 recently acquired by the BM: cf. *Cohen-de Ricci*, col. 243.

ARTHUR RAU

Henry George Quin, 1760–1805

ALTHOUGH he rates encomiastic mention by Dibdin, it may be doubted if many readers of this article will have heard of Henry George Quin unless they happen to have seen his collection 'in situ' or the few volumes from it included in the exhibition of Treasures of Trinity College, Dublin at Burlington House in 1961 and briefly described on pp. 18 and 19 of the Catalogue.[1] His name did not occur in an article on the exhibition by R. L. S. Bruce-Mitford in the *Museums Journal*.[2]

Henry George Quin was born in 1760 at Dublin as the third son of Dr Henry Quin (1717 or 1718–91) and his wife Anne, *née* Monck. Henry Quin had been admitted MB, Dublin in 1743 and MD there in 1749 (in the interval he had become a Doctor of Medicine of Padua). An eminent and very prosperous medical practitioner, he was known in his later years as a liberal patron of the arts; he befriended and patronized James Tassie, the maker of glass gems, and William Mossop, Ireland's most famous medallist.[3] Henry George followed his two elder brothers to Harrow and in extant letters written home he makes precocious and sophisticated comments on friends and relatives who entertained him in London on his way to and from school. From Harrow he went in 1776 to Trinity College, Dublin, graduating BA there in 1781, after which date he seems never to have done a stroke of real work, his nearest approach thereto having been to land the comfortable sinecures of 2nd Chamberlain of the Exchequer on 6 September 1788 and of Clerk of the Quit Rents on 16 December 1794.[4] On 23 September of that year he had made his will, bequeathing the Bibliotheca Quiniana to the Provost and Fellows of Trinity College. Of his life thereafter we know practically nothing until his death by his own hand in Dublin on 16 February 1805; the jury duly recorded a verdict of suicide, advancing no reasons for his action, and more than a century and a half later they can only be surmised. A miniature portrait of Henry George Quin is in the possession of his collateral descendant, Mr Cormac Quin, by whose courtesy it is reproduced here (Plate I).

Quin may be assumed to have begun collecting in 1784, the year in which he bought, almost certainly from Payne, the first four or five of the 127 titles (14 were later extruded and three not found after his death) in his Catalogue, more or less chronologically arranged by order of acquisitions. Bound in red morocco and written in his own hand, with notes and prices paid, it has been preserved with the books, which now comprise 110

[1] By F. J. E. Hurst, deputy Librarian, to whom, as to the Librarian, Dr H. W. Parke, and to Mr W. O'Sullivan, Keeper of Manuscripts, I am grateful for assistance.

[2] Vol. 61, No. 1, 1961.

[3] For further information about Henry Quin see

T. Percy C. Kirkpatrick, *Henry Quin, M.D. . . .* , Dublin, 1919.

[4] *Liber Munerum Publicorum Hiberniae*, III, 119 and 124.

PLATE I. Henry George Quin
From the miniature in the possession of his collateral descendant,
Mr Cormac Quin. 73 × 57 mm.

titles in 156 volumes. To the same year can be assigned his purchase of a copy, bearing his signature and that date on the title-page, of Edward Harwood, *A View of the Various Editions of the Greek and Roman Classics*, London, 1775, which does not form part of the Bibliotheca Quiniana and was presented to the Library in October 1894 by the Rev. T. W. Carson, Vice-Provost; also absent from Quin's Catalogue are five volumes of the Latin Classics, Dublin, 1745–47, in local bindings, acquired by him in 1788–90, which entered the Library on 28 March 1843. The *Harwood* is important because it contains, in Quin's hand, auction records of editions which he bought and it shows his early interest in the ancient classical authors who form one of the two main sections of his library; the other is Italian literature, this section being crowned by his fine copy of the Foligno *Dante*, 1472 (Plate II). For the origin of this interest we also have evidence, albeit more inferential, for it may be assumed from what is known of Dr Henry Quin that talk in his house[5] ran not infrequently on his student years in Padua and on Italian art.

In 1785–6 Quin went on the Grand Tour and we know all about the latter part of it from the second and third volumes of his MS 'Travelling Diary'. The first has unfortunately disappeared but, by jobbing backwards from the extant volumes, we can reasonably infer that he started off in the summer of 1785 in the company of his friend Truell

[5] It still stands, at 101 St Stephen's Green, and is now St Patrick's Nurses' Home (see tile illustration in T. Percy C. Kirkpatrick, op. cit.).

(probably Robert Truell, BA, Dublin, 1777 and DD, 1796) and that they spent some time in Paris, where Quin bought books from de Bure and left some to be bound by Derome (presumably Nicolas-Denis Derome, le Jeune, who, according to Thoinan,[6] 'mourut vers 1788'). The second volume was presented in 1946 to Trinity College Library, through its Friends,[7] by Dr T. Percy C. Kirkpatrick who had acquired it from the family of J. R. Garstin; a note by the latter in the volume states that it had been given to him in 1890 by 'Richard Quin, J.P. Monasterboice, being the foreign Note Book of his ancestor – grandfather? – presenter of the Bibliotheca Quiniana to Trinity College, Dublin', but this is not quite accurate, for Henry George Quin, a bachelor, had no descendants and Richard Quin was the grandson of his older brother, Thomas (J.) Quin. The third volume has remained in the family and now belongs to Mr Cormac Quin who has allowed quotations to be made from it in this article. In the absence of the first volume it is perhaps hazardous to generalize too freely from the 'Travelling Diary', but it is clear from what we have that Quin's aesthetic judgement matured very fast on the Tour and we have a very vivid picture of him not only as a book collector but also as 'un homme moyen sensuel' (perhaps, indeed, not so 'moyen').

The first entry in volume 2 is dated 2 October 1785 'in the Valley of Chamouni, Savoy', and, after visiting Geneva and other Swiss towns, Quin arrived on the 20th in Turin where he does not seem to have gone to any bookshop or library, but saw a great deal of one Signora Gastildi, 'a person who was considered the prettiest woman in this town which abounds with that commodity'; she had 'the most roguish eyes that ever leered' and squeezed his hands 'most agreeably', his last entry before he left the town being: 'N.B. The sensations of these last evenings have appeared to me like a dream.' In Milan too he remarks on 'women much prettier than in England' and is shocked at the high price of lodgings; he refers in passing to 30,000 volumes stacked in the Brera and belonging to Count Firmian of which the sale was 'to take place next year'. On 6 November he was at Verona where he visited a bull-fight, 'disappointing'; some of the women spectators were in men's clothing, which gave them 'a most disgusting, forbidding appearance; there were two very pretty ones standing near me this evening, yet I do really think I could not have been persuaded to kiss them.' In Padua he remarks on the scarlet cloaks, no doubt remembering his father's graduation there some 40 years earlier. From 10 to 15 November he was in Venice where he visited the library of San Marco and was disappointed in the printed books but impressed by the manuscripts; the local oysters too were disappointing, lacking 'the fine flavour of the Carlingford'. From Venice he went back to Padua and then to Ferrara along roads so bad that they called forth the comment: 'I wish to God there was a hot poker thrust into the fundament of the Doge.' After a short visit to Bologna he arrived on 29 November at Florence, where he had an encounter with 'an Englishman who I could almost swear is a young Painter for he is one of the greatest coxcombs I ever saw'. Of the Laurentian library he writes: 'It consists entirely of manuscripts, about 6000 arranged in a very curious manner. The Room is just like Lady Arabella's Asylum with pews and the Books are chained down on sloping desks … The Librarian was very civil to us, among other manuscripts he showed Virgil of the

[6] *Les Relieurs français*, 1893, p. 255.   [7] See their *Annual Bulletin*, 1946, pp.6 and 7.

COMINCIA LA COMEDIA DI
dante alleghieri di fiorenze nella q̄le tracta
delle pene et punitioni de uitii et demeriti
et premii delle uirtu: Capitolo primo della
p̄ma parte de questo libro loquale sechiama
inferno : nel quale lautore fa prohemio ad
tucto eltractato del libro:·

N EL mezo delcamin dinr̄a uita
mi trouai p̄una selua oscura
che la diricta uia era smarrita
Et quanto adir q̄ler̄a cosa dura
esta selua seluagiā aspra eforte
che nel pensier r̄enoua la paura
Tantè amara che pocho piu morte
ma pertractar del ben chio uitrouai
diro dellatre cose chi uo scorte
I non so ben ridir come uentrai
tantèra pien disonno insuquèl punto
che la uerace uia abandonai·
Ma poi che fui appie dum colle giūnto
ladoue terminaua quella ualle
che mauea dipaura el cor compuncto
Guardai inalto et uidde le suoe spalle
uestite gia deraggi del pianeta
che mena dricto altrui perogni calle
Allor fu la paura un pocho cheta
che nellaco del cor mera durata
la nocte chio passi contanta pieta

PLATE II. The Foligno *Dante*, 1472
Editio Princeps of *La Commedia*. a2 recto. 282 × 200 mm.
(Bibliotheca Quiniana, Trinity College, Dublin)

4th [afterwards altered to '5th'] century and Ptolemy's Geographie . . . By the Librarian's desire we entered our names in a Book kept for the purpose. . . '. He sounds even more impressed by the Grand Duke's collection of cameos and intaglios in an oval room where he spent an hour – 'my father would have staid twenty at least'. But the chief object of interest to Quin in Florence was the Medici Venus which, or rather whom, he visited every day. Of his first visit he says: 'On my entrance into the celebrated room I had very singular sensations; Truell thought me mad, for the first thing I did was to make a most idolatrous bow to the Venus.' On another occasion: 'I stole into the Tribune when no one was there and fervently kissed several parts of her divine body.' On 1 December: 'I placed a chair by the pedestal, and mounting on it, I applied my lips to different parts of the statue. At first I kissed it as one would any piece of marble, but upon my conscience, at last I began to conceive it was real flesh and blood, and my favours increasing in proportion, I don't know what I should have done had not my sensual Reverie been interrupted by an ill-looking fellow who came into the room and jawed me terribly [there surely speaks the Harrow schoolboy] for dusting the chair-covers.' On 7 December before leaving Florence he went to the gallery 'and took leave of my Darling'.

After spending a whole day at Siena 'en route' Quin arrived on 11 December in Rome to remain there, with trips to the environs, until towards the end of February 1786. As volume two of the 'Travelling Diary' ends with Quin setting out on 31 January for Tivoli, Kirkpatrick[8] wrongly inferred that he proceeded thence directly to Naples; the third volume, however, whose existence was unknown to Kirkpatrick, starts on 1 February at Tivoli and then records Quin's return to Rome for about three weeks. A week after his arrival there he had gone to the Sistine Chapel where he saw the Pope: 'he put me in mind somewhat of Alderman Warren'; later he complains of the Pope's 'squeamishness in signing death warrants (which is very inconvenient in this rascally country').￼ On 2 January he went to the Vatican Library where he saw some of the more celebrated manuscripts but could not examine any printed books as the presses were locked. He had to pay the 'under Librarian, who is an Abbé, four pauls for showing me the Library. This shameful system of venality has gained such ground here that I do verily believe that if you were to intrigue with the Princess Borghese herself she would expect the *mancia*; this is the word in Italy for tipping.' But, as in Florence, he was more excited by cameos and intaglios than by books. On 29 December a 'virtu merchant, Signor Milondo' had brought him some cameos and mosaic snuff-boxes and later the same day he went to see Pichlar from whom he ordered a cameo, subsequently delivered; on 16 January he went to see a collection of antique cameos and intaglios of which he bought a number, perhaps as presents for his father, and on the 26th he 'accidentally stumbled into a vertu shop where I expect I shall spend a good many sequins' and did. His occasional visits to book shops and inspection of book-stands produced 'nothing worth the carriage'.

Quin's social programme in Rome was very full and he was taken up soon after his arrival by Cardinal Bernis, 'an unaffected old man, frequently troubled with the gout', and no wonder, for 'he is almost the only person who gives dinners in Rome . . . the wines

---

[8] Op. cit., p. 53.

various and excellent.' At one of these parties, on 20 January, Quin sat by the Pretender, 'the bottle has been the sum of his table for many years and the consequence is that his legs swelled to a great size'; his daughter, whom Quin calls 'Miss Pretender', was thought to be in Lesbian relationship with one Countess O'Donnel, a Frenchwoman. On 27 January Quin was again at the Cardinal's: 'Princess Ruspoli the prettiest woman there. The English as usual together in a clump. Every one of the Italian ladies had their Cicisbeos dangling after them, I wish to God Princess Ruspoli would take me into her keeping. She is a handsome likeness of the John Beresford family. One of the old Trouts was an Irishwoman, Princess Giustiniani; her name was Mahony.' Quin claims that the French were very unpopular with the Italians and implies that Countess O'Donnel's affair was only one of many scandalous tales about them, men and women. On 14 February he records, first, that he steals the fig-leaf of the Apollo Belvedere (whom he had already compared unfavourably with his beloved Medici Venus) and, second, that he visits the library of the Palazzo Corsini, with its valuable old editions of the classics and Italian authors 'from the year 1470'; he finds the illustrated Aretino, from which he copies some sonnets, less obscene than he had expected, and compares the Giunta *Boccaccio* with his own, to the advantage of the latter (this is No. 14 in the Catalogue where Quin notes that he paid de Bure 432 livres for it – presumably on his visit to Paris in the previous summer – and Derome 15 livres for the binding).

On 24 February, after passing through Velletri and Fondi, he arrived in Naples whose King he described as 'the best billiard player [Quin had played a lot of billiards in Rome], the best shot, the keenest sportsman and the greatest blackguard of any crowned head in Europe'. Quin paid the usual homage to the obscene artefacts at Pompeii and had the usual trouble with a pimp; he found very few fine-looking women in Naples and was delighted to be back, on 23 March, in Rome with his 'Roman flame, the daughter of the Venetian Ambassador . . . she is but 17 and a most magnificent piece', quite different, he implies, from the 'ugly bitches in Naples'. On 6 April he records a meeting with 'Shard and Chappelow, both of whom had made great purchases of prints and books'; it is to be assumed that their taste was less eclectic than Quin's. There followed the Holy Week ceremonies about which he expresses himself in terms redolent of Protestant prejudice; his worldly self admired the way in which 'the Duchesses of Albany and Cumberland managed matters very well so as not to meet'. One of his last visits in Rome was to Piranesi and on 22 April he left the city, 'with regret', for Perugia, Cortone, Arezzo, and Florence, arriving back there on the 27th. The next day he records: 'At Rome I had determined that the Backside of the Borghese Hermaphrodite was the most perfect one in the world but on paying a visit today to that in the Gallery I am almost tempted to change my Opinion. It is really most difficult to determine which of the two is the most beautiful.' On the 28th he 'spent the whole of the morning in the Gallery. Have found out a happy *Succedaneum* for Cantharides. Put a smooth doe-skin glove on your hand, get up on a chair by the Venus de Medici and shutting your eyes pass your hand gently over all the parts of its body, this operation being repeated two or three times the nervous system will be thrown into an agreeable and innoxious state of Pride.' On 1 May he is back again: 'gazed for about an hour at the Venus. Gross mortals think her breasts and Bum are not large enough but they should recollect that the Statue is meant to represent a Girl about

15 or 16 and therefore these parts should not be exuberant.' He tries a silk stocking on the statue, 'to measure the length of leg . . . I shall preserve the stocking as a sacred relic and treasure it up in the same place with the tin figleaf which I stole from the Nudities of the Apollo of Belvedere' . . . The same day he left Florence – not an hour too soon, surely.

Between 2 May and 7 June he was, nowhere very long, in Pistoia, Lucca (he admired the women's 'bums'), Leghorn, where he read Thomson's *Seasons* on the ramparts and negotiated in vain through the bookseller Masi for a copy of the Letters of Lucrezia Gonzaga belonging to one of the latter's customers; Lerici, Genoa (he was tempted by a Landino *Dante*), Ventimiglia (the girls 'very pretty; to be the paragon of perfection a Girl should have a Lucchese bum and Vintimiglian Bubbies'), Nice, Antibes, Porquerolles, Toulon, where he enjoyed French cooking after being so long in Italy, Marseilles, Aix-en-Provence, Avignon ('finest strawberries'), Nismes, Montpellier, Pezenas, Beziers, Perpignan, and Figueras. On 10 June he arrived in Barcelona and stayed there for ten days; he spent a lot of time in the bookshops but found everything very dear and the booksellers unwilling to reduce the prices of the few books that interested him. (Of one dealer, in the Plaza del Angel, he wrote: 'perhaps it is an Instance of his honesty that he would not abate any prices', but he managed to buy two or three from another, in the Calle Grande). One day the frigate *Phaeton* arrived 'with Lord & Miss Keppel & Lord Pembroke' which event, for some reason, provoked the following entry: 'The only thing to be said in favour of the Inquisition was that this frightful Engine of Church Tyranny has been of some service in checking a Vice that has taken too deep a root in other Countries of Europe. By the way one word as to this filthy Crime. We in England brand the Italians with the name: yet it is certain that in Italy it is known by the Name of *Peccata Inglese*. The number of these unfortunate Animals that have been banished from England and obliged to take refuge in Italy has given rise to this odious synonima [*sic*].' Quin's own sex-life, such as it was, in Barcelona did not depart from the usual; one day he stood on his inn-balcony and ogled a pretty girl in the opposite house, on another he commented: 'women's bums are not only broad but project most exceedingly.' As it was too hot to go further into Spain, he returned to France, arriving back at Perpignan on the 23rd when he confided to his Diary: 'literally and truly taking them in the Lump the Women of France are *less handsome* than in any other country I have yet seen – in this I include Ireland, England, Scotland, Switzerland, Italy & Spain'. By way of Narbonne, where he 'bowed . . . most profoundly' to the tomb of one of his 'Royal Ancestors, Philip the Hardy, King of France', he arrived at Castelnaudary where he met 'a charming widow of about 32, a very agreeable kind of Piece', who asked him whether he had been poxed in the course of his travels and warned her young son of this danger. From 28 June to 2 July Quin was in Toulouse, where he was struck by the tales, which he was to hear elsewhere too, of Queen Marie Antoinette's 'extravagance & Bitchery'. At a bookseller's an elderly gentleman introduced himself as 'Mr Hackman who had travelled all over Europe on foot'. Truell, who had fallen ill in Rome, had meanwhile gone home, and Quin's travelling companion at this time was one St George on whose good looks Hackman 'seemed to dwell too narrowly . . . therefore we thought it prudent to take our leave of him as soon as convenient.' But the highlight of Quin's stay in Toulouse was of course a visit to the McCarthy Library, 'the choicest rarest and most splendid Private Collection I ever saw ... Psalter of 1457, Bible of 1460, illuminated manuscripts, first editions of the Classics, the veritable Giunta Boccaccio (agreeing with de Bure's description), Spaccio dela bestia trionfante, Bandello ... among other books, no Spanish Romances or the Teseide of Boccaccio, almost all in morocco, very few in russia, perhaps the odour offends him. Count McCarthy had for two and a half years with him an English bookbinder whom he had brought over with him from London.[9] ... Where he was able to pick up these books God knows. ... from Askew, Préfond, La Vallière, Mead, Crofts, &c. ...' Unfortunately Count McCarthy was out of town but the Abbé of the same name, whom Quin at first took to be the owner's brother, showed him the Library.

From Toulouse Quin went via Agen to Bordeaux where he stayed from 5 to 13 July, visiting the theatre, some booksellers (with no success), and a dealer who tried to sell him some antiques so obviously false that 'tomorrow I intend to produce a pack of cards & tell him that Hannibal played with them at Capua'. St George returned to Ireland by sea from Bordeaux and Quin sent some of his things along with him; he would have liked to send his father some truffles but the season was not right. On 18 July, after passing quickly through Angoulême, Poitiers, Tours, and Orléans, Quin was back in Paris (where he found 'three long comfortable pleasant letters' from his mother) and remained for nearly a month.

Now we see Quin entirely wrapped up in his books. On the 20th within a couple of days of his arrival he calls on de Bure in the morning for his box of books and in the evening goes to Derome for his Elzeviers and other books being bound but found him not at home. Meanwhile he had attended, in the afternoon, the first session of a book sale at the Hôtel Bullion[10] and comments on the fact that 'at French sales 4 persons should be thought required to do what one does in England or Ireland' (a state of affairs which still holds). On the 21st after another vain attempt to find Derome, he goes shopping: 'I am all on a sudden growing a great Buck.' Then he opens his box of books and finds that 'comparing the dimensions of my Giunta Boccaccio with those of Prince Corsini's I find that the margin is very little greater than mine. That is some comfort.' Then he bought a *Boiardo* (No. 18 in the Catalogue) and a *Giolitti Amadigi* (this he must have eliminated later) from Molini, after hunting for them all over Italy: 'After all Paris is the place to get scarce books in any language.' On the 22nd he goes to Bailly's where he sees more books which tempt him: *Bandello*, Clarke's *Caesar*, large-paper Baskerville *Ariosto* and, on returning to his lodgings, finds that Derome has delivered the Elzevier *Ciceros* and other books he had bound while Quin was away. On the 24th he returns to the Hotel Bullion and bids for the *Marguerite de la Marguerite* (lot 388) as far as 30 livres at which figure he lost it. On the 25th, before dealing with his books he comments: 'Here the execution and breach of the law follow very closely – it was but the day before yesterday that a young man was murdered in a bawdy house in the rue Valois & tomorrow the girl who cut his throat & the two men who assisted her are to be hanged at the Place de Gesvres. That is

---

[9] See the article by Charles Ramsden: 'Richard Wier and Count MacCarthy Reagh' in THE BOOK COLLECTOR, Autumn 1953, pp. 247–57.

[10] I have been able to identify this sale of which I have the catalogue; it was of the library of 'M. ***' and was held at the Hôtel Bullion from 20 to 29 July (excluding Sunday, 23) by Leclerc & Dupuis.

all right.' (Unlike the Pope.) In the afternoon he went back to the Hôtel Bullion where he met 'Edwards of Pall Mall the bookseller brother to the Bookbinder of Halifax; he tells me my Ariosto [probably No. 1 of the Catalogue] is not yet finished; bid for the Giunta Boiardo by Berni [lot 432; No. 20 of the Catalogue where it is glossed 'de chez Bullion'] & got it for a Louis. This very edition sold at Croft's for 4 guineas.' On the 27th he goes to Derome and pays him for the Elzevier Ciceros and 'gave him my Boiardo & my Giunta Boccaccio to bind . . . God send the leaves may not be *rognés*'. On the 28th he goes to Belin for books, 'to Didot's to look at the famous edition of Tasso . . . on excellent paper & incomparably good type with cuts in the bad French taste . . . & not worth the price demanded for it'. On the 28th he moves to the Palais Royal for which he had been yearning for days; on 1 August he calls on Edwards, takes a quick look at St Sulpice, visits booksellers on the quai des Augustins and gets 'priced catalogues of Randon de Boisset & Limar sold by de Bure in March, several books sold ridiculously high'; on the 2nd he visits picture galleries, crosses the Seine by ferry, and goes to Laurent, bookseller in the rue de Tournon, Edwards's friend who is to send the latter's books to London. On the 4th, at the Bibliothèque du Roi he meets his 'old Harrow fag, Lord Elgin, a very good kind of fellow' and together they go to the Manuscript room, consisting of 60,000 volumes, and on the 7th he sends his own box of books to Laurent to be sent to England with Edwards's. On the 8th the pipe of the 'commodité' at his hotel bursts and he is obliged to keep at a distance all day because of the intolerable stench, but he improves the shining hour by following 'Colombe and her sister Adeline round the Palais Royal gardens. Colombe is one of the most magnificent voluptuous looking Pieces in Paris'. On the 11th he 'went to the Bibliothèque and turned over the *Voyage Pittoresque de Naples* [presumably Saint-Non's work, 1781–6] . . . met an English collector a Mr Pretville, rather pretentious and his niece too', on the 12th he calls on Derome, who promises the rest of his books for the morning; on the 14th he has to go back and scold him for having lettered some books wrong and on the 15th, when the Diary ends, he mingled with the holiday crowds in the Champs Elysées.

Back in Dublin he devoted himself to his library, buying from Robson, Edwards and, mainly, from Payne who acted for him at the Soubise, Pinelli, and other sales; he sent books to be bound by Edwards of Halifax, Roger Payne, and Kalthoeber (No. 86 of the Catalogue, a *Longus* of 1786, acquired, it would appear, in 1789, being glossed 'bound and ornamented according to my directions by Kalthoeber'). In 1790 he went abroad for the second and last time, to attend the Crevenna sale in Amsterdam whence he brought back some of his greatest treasures and also the auctioneer's hammer which came to Trinity College with the books; it is inscribed as follows:

Malleum huncce
Bibliothecae Crevennae sub hasta Amstelodam posita
ipsi viro clarissimo
Honoris causa acceptam retuli;
Utpote qui ad hastam illam ab Hibernia accedens
Permultos magni pretii Libros
et inter alios
Virgilii Spirensis exemplar

Membranis vetustissimis et auro contra aestimandum
Pecunia redemeran meique juris feceram
Henricus Georgius Quin
Eblanensis

III. ID. JUN. MDCCXC.

(This Vendelin of Speyer *Virgil*, 1470, one of 14 incunabula and one of 17 books printed on vellum in the Collection, is recorded in the Catalogue as costing £200, of which, it would seem, £7 10s was the cost of re-binding by Roger Payne.)

Quin's copy of the Crevenna sale-catalogue did not come to Trinity College with the books, but was presented in March 1891 by Devonshire John Rowan; with it came Quin's *Gouttard*, 1780, *La Vallière* 1783, *Crofts*, the same year, *Mead*, 1785 (bound with some other catalogues) and *Bibliotheca Parisiana*, 1791 sale-catalogues, and a copy of Lair, *Index*, 2 volumes, of the same year, acquired by him in 1792. In the Crevenna catalogue (vol. I, p. lxxxiii) there is the following note in Quin's hand: 'I went to Amsterdam on purpose to attend this sale and indeed my acquisitions amply repaid my journey. They were the most unsophisticated books I ever saw.' In this day and age it is interesting to reflect on this early use of the word 'unsophisticated' to describe an ancient book and to realize that when Quin wrote 'repaid' he was not thinking of a future profit on resale or of an eventual fiscal advantage. Not that his mind was unattuned to finance, for the note quoted above goes on to explain in detail how each under-the-hammer price in florins was converted, after addition of the Amsterdam sales-tax and export duty, into a final cost in Irish currency, to be entered in the Catalogue. Thus the only manuscript now in the collection (another was a *Petrarch*, one of the three mislaid books), Boccaccio, *Il Philostrato*, was figured at £5 13s 9d and among other purchases at the sale were, for the same price, the Aldine *Scriptores de re rustica*, 1514, on blue paper, in a binding of no value, and, for £2 5s 6d, another Aldine, the *Quintus Smyrnaeus* of c. 1504, in a typical humped-spine 'Greek' binding made for Henri II and Diane de Poitiers (Plate III); the prices paid for these two books compared with their value today give cause for thought both absolutely and relatively. Other books from Crevenna were: three splendid 18th-century French morocco bindings with coloured onlays all unrecorded by Michon[11] (one of them, on Morlini, *Novellae*, 1520, is cited by Brunet;[12] the others, typically, cover works by Giordano Bruno, the binding on Quin's *Spaccio de la Bestia*, 1584, being the same as on *La Cena* of the same date at Aix-en-Provence, reproduced as plate XXXIV by Michon, the editio princeps of Boccaccio, *Teseide*, Ferrara, 1475 (relatively expensive at £113 15s; was there a bid from McCarthy?[13]) *Theuerdanch*, 1517, on vellum (£56 17s 6d), Petrarch, *Trionfi*, Parma, 1473, and one of the two Mahieu bindings (*Hobson* LX) in the collection; the other, 'ex libris Charles Ford' (*Hobson* XXVII), Quin did not buy until 1800. The last entry, dated 1801, in the Catalogue is D. Heinsius, *De contemptu Mortis*, Leyden, Elzevier, 1621, glossed 'Exemplar unicum Impressum in Membranis. This is the only Elzevier on vellum that exists'; the second part of this statement, if it means that the Elzeviers printed no other book on vellum, may well be true, but the first is certainly not,

---

[11] *Les Reliures Mosaiquées du xviile siècle*, 1956.

[12] III, 1909.

[13] See p. 457 above.

PLATE III. Bound for Henri II and Diane de Poitiers
Quintus Smyrnaeus, Παρλειπόμενσ Ὁμήρου, Aldus, Venice, c. 1504. Citron morocco.
The Crevenna copy. 160 × 95 mm (the hump on the spine adds 6 mm to the height)
(Biblioteca Quiniana, Trinity College, Dublin)

as there are at least two other such copies, that presented to Rutgers, now at The Hague, and a copy sold for £38 17s (Quin's cost him £34 2s 6d) in London at the Singer sale, 1818, and subsequently in the possession of Lloyd. (Willems[14] was led astray by Van Praet,[15] usually so accurate, in identifying the Singer-Lloyd copy with Quin's, still in Dublin). Incidentally, Miss Shipman[16] too departed from her normal standard of accuracy in deriving only three of Trinity College's six Grolier bindings from Quin, whereas all but her No. 513 were his; moreover, light may be thrown on her not very consequentially described No. 423 by the fact that entry No. 112 of the Quin Catalogue, 'Gratii de Venatione . . . 1534 . . . Exemplar Grolierii' was subsequently expunged and glossed 'This book I returned to Mr Payne on account of several of the leaves being stained. Hen: Geo: Quin 1793'.

In his will made, as already noted, in 1794 Quin gave exact instructions for the preservation of his books in one bookcase and that 'the words *Bibliotheca Quiniana*, in capital letters, two inches in height, and gilt on a dark-coloured ground, be put on the top of the two central doors of the aforesaid book-case, one word on each door'.[17] Furthermore the bookcase was to be placed in 'the Manuscript Room . . . exactly in the centre of the side of the room, opposite to the door of entrance'. However, in 1802 the library of Greffier Fagel, comprising over 20,000 printed books and some manuscripts, catalogued for sale by Christie's in March of that year, was bought privately by the Erasmus Smith Board for presentation to Trinity College.[18] Its installation meant that by the time Quin died and his will had been proved, on 6 March, 1805, there was no space in the Manuscript Room for his bookcase, which some 'mauvais coucheur' attempted on that pretext to retain, with its contents, for the Treasury. Thomas Quin, Henry George's brother, writing about this on 2 July, to 'Jackie' Barrett, the librarian, foresaw grave legal difficulties, but they had been resolved by 13 September when the bookcase was released and everything handed over except the three mislaid items and a few books still with 'Payne' (either the bookseller or the binder). The last of the latter was received on 27 April 1806, since when this tiny but choice collection – a true 'cabinet de bibliophile' – preserved in its bookcase, now against a wall of the Deputy Librarian's room, has been one of the glories of Trinity College.

[14] *Les Elzevier*, 1880, p. 54.

[15] *Catalogue des livres imprimés sur Vélin . . . dans des Bibliothèques tant publiques que particulières*, 1824–8, vol. II, pp. 95–6 and vol. IV, p. 73.

[16] *Researches concerning Jean Grolier*, New York, 1907, pp. 342 and 359.

[17] See the illustration in Kirkpatrick, op. cit.

[18] See Parke, *The Library of Trinity College*, 1961, p. 10.

Imago Mundi

O NE of the attributes of a collector's piece is that it has about it more than meets the eye at first sight – that it should be, as that notable collector of pictures, Captain Spencer Churchill, said, a 'rescue'. And if it has a story of exceptional good luck in its acquisition, so much the better. This collector's piece seems to fulfil both these requirements.

Some five years ago now, a friend wrote to say that there was to be a sale in one of the large houses in her village in East Kent and that she thought some of the books might be of interest. It was a sale of miscellaneous effects: furniture, ornaments, carpets, books. It was due to take place the day before Oxford term began so that I could not hope to attend it. But one of the view days happened to be possible, if I was prepared to spend most of the day in the train, and have about three hours to look about me at the other end. I went, and on the way studied the catalogue. Its compiler was no bibliographer. But it was clear that there were unusual books; and I noticed an item singled out, with several others, for heavy type, which simply read *Imago Mundi*. Everyone has heard that Cardinal Pierre d'Ailly's *Imago Mundi* was one of the books used by Columbus; and that Columbus's own heavily annotated copy is actually known. The book, written early in the 15th century, is a cosmological treatise of outstanding significance for the geography and the astronomy of the renaissance, and it contains a discussion of the possibility of reaching Asia by the western route across the Atlantic. It was this idea which interested Columbus in the book; this idea indeed which actually sent him across the Atlantic himself, in 1492. Could this conceivably be another copy of that famous work? I had no reference books available, and no idea how many editions had appeared of the d'Ailly. But I marked it, with half a dozen others in the sale, to be examined.

The books had all been moved out of the house for the sale, into a garden hut. They were soft and clammy to handle, for there was a thick, moist fog. In spite of the fog, the house was crowded and there were numbers of people in the hut, looking at the books, also. Several evidently had an eye for the same sort of thing as I. I went through my marked items rapidly. A *Sowerby* had once been magnificent, an uncut copy. But there were some volumes missing, and it had suffered from damp. There were others of interest. But it was the *Imago Mundi* which kept my attention. With glances at my competitors in case they should see how interested I was, I went back to it again and again. It was obviously an incunable. The first leaf had been repaired by pasting another over it, but I managed to hold it to the light and read *Bibliothecae Colbertinae* below. It had a fine series of cosmological diagrams as its first gathering (Plate I is an example), including a diagrammatic map of the world (Plate II). But it also had notes in a hand with which I was

Hec figura feruit qrto capitulo: In qua circulus principalis repfentat orbê lune : infra quê funt quattuor elemêta ꝗ ónia generabilia ꝗ corruptibilia. Ignis ê calidus ꝗ ficcus immediate poft fperâ lune fituat): ibi tam pur9 ꝗ clar9 q̇ ê inuifibilis. Aer eſt calid9 ꝗ humidus in tres regiones diuif9. Quaꝝ fupma fpere ignis iungitur ꝗ vtraq̇ cû celo de oriente in occidentê mouet. Aqua ê frigida ꝗ humida q̇ inter aerem ꝗ terrã naturaliter fituatur. Sed tñ vna pars terre q̇ ê minus graui, q̇ alia fupeminet ꝗ pro magna portione difcooperit aquis vt fit habitabilis. Maxima ãt pfunditas oceani ê.riiii.miliarıũ vt quidã a marinariis inuentû eê aſſerũt. Dicêtes etiã q̇ eade̅ pfundi tas minor ê q̇ dupla ad diſtantiã centri mũdi ꝗ cêtri terre. Terra ê frigida ꝗ ficca q̇ figurã habet quaſi rotundã. Cuius circuit9 cõtinet. CCC.lx.portiones totidê gradib9 celi correfpõdentes: ꝗ cuilibet gradui correfpodent in terra feptingẽta ſtadia : quoꝝ octo valẽt miliare: ꝗ duo miliaria leucã. Vnde cõcludunt aliqui totũ circuitũ terre continere quindecim millia feptingenta ꝗ quinquaginta leucas.

Correfpoꞇe ã
gradiũ celi Nõ
ad portiones
terre

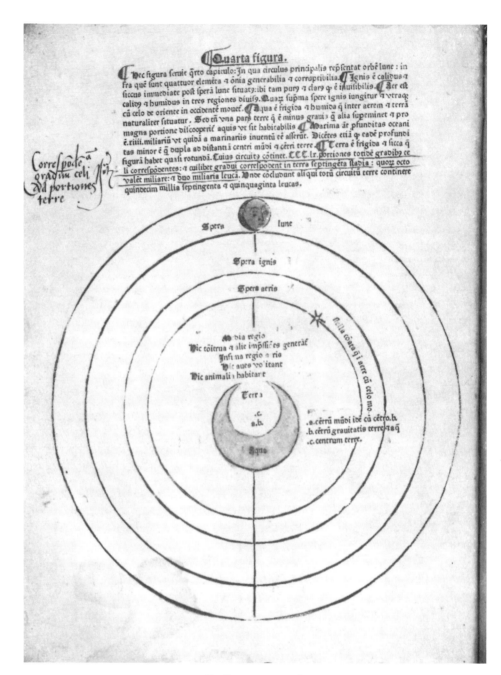

Spera lune

Spera ignis

Spera aeris

Media regio
Hic tõitrua ꝗ alie impſſiões generãt
Infima regio ꝗ ría
Hic aues vo icant
Hic animalıa habitant

Medıa cõuens qñ aer cũ celo mo.

Terra
.c.
a.b.

a.cêrũ mũdi ibe cũ cêtro.b.
.b. cêtrũ grauitatis terre qaꝗ
.c. centrum terre.

Aqua

PLATE I. Pierre d'Ailly: *Imago Mundi* (Louvain, 1483).
One of the eight cosmological diagrams; the marginal note is in the hand of
the mid-16th-century annotator.

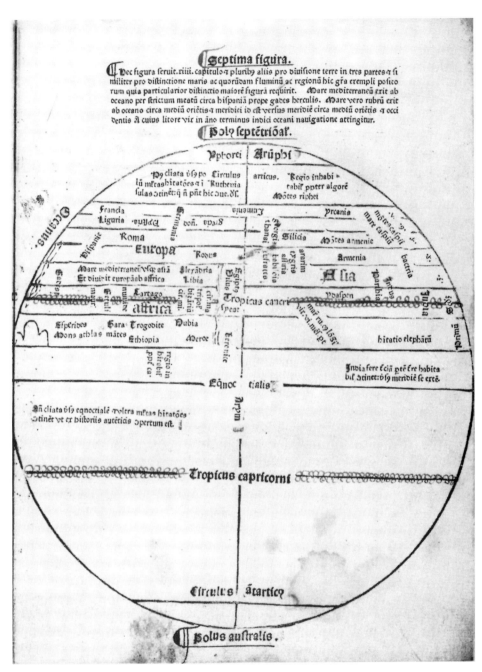

PLATE 11. The deletion of the two tropics, in one of the earliest links made in the book, is probably due to the owner's conviction that an uninhabitable torrid zone (an idea handed down from antiquity in the work of Macrobius, and known in the 15th century from the text) is out of date. This idea is vestigially preserved in this map, with the inscription (*regio inhabitabilis propter ca* [*lorem*]). The deletion is in a different ink from that used for the Raleigh annotations.

familiar. Since I worked on Phillipps MS 6339, which turned out to be a notebook prepared by Sir Walter Raleigh when he was writing the *History of the World*, I had looked at every Raleigh document and letter that I could locate. This was surely Raleigh's hand? The annotations in it were few, some 60 or 70 words all told; the book had been studied in the mid-16th century by a more copious annotator, and before him again by others who had marked passages here and there, their notes in every instance being (like the original) in Latin.

My friend, to whom I dared not voice my hopes, kindly agreed to bid for any book I wanted. How high would I go? I set a figure a good deal higher than I could reasonably afford. Then on the way home I reflected that, whatever else this was, it was an astronomical text of the 15th century, and as such would almost certainly be saleable, if the worst came to the worst. So I sent a wire from Charing Cross: 'Half as much again'.

The sale was next day. Once again there was thick fog. But (though it may have kept off some of the professionals) it did not deter at least one strong competitor. Yet the increased bid saved me. *Imago Mundi*, with its tattered mottled calf binding, was mine.

It was some time before I had a chance to do anything more than turn the leaves and examine what I thought to be the Raleigh notes. The conviction grew that the attribution was sound. Then it began to appear what a rarity the book itself anyhow was. *Book Prices Current* did not record a single copy sold during the period of its compilation; Milton Waldman in his book on *Americana* mentioned it as one of the quite unattainable pieces. The only American copy (out of three or four recorded) of which details were available lacked six leaves. I was to find (and this surely is a common experience) that it was not so rare as the reference book seemed to suggest. Polain, *Catalogue des Livres du XV siècle*, showed that this, the only 15th-century edition, was printed at Louvain in 1483. And my copy was complete save for the last blank, with all the eight full-page diagrams in the *Imago* section.

But how were we to demonstrate that the latest annotator was actually Raleigh? The book would clearly anyhow have to be rebound, and I hoped that when Roger Powell took up the pastedown sheet on the first leaf, and revealed (as I already knew he would) the mark of the *Bibliotheca Colbertina*, something else might appear. There was indeed a long inscription by one of the earlier owners, not including, unfortunately, his name – at best there is only a relic of it, as yet indecipherable. But there was no trace of Raleigh. This was not indeed surprising, for I have not yet found reason to think that he inscribed his name in any of the books which he used while he was in the Tower. The only one I know which carries it he seems to have inscribed somewhere between 1582 and 1593.

Fortunately, however, a list of those books is known. It is unpublished, though its existence has been recorded in various articles I have written about Phillipps MS 6339. So I asked the present owner if I might consult it, and sure enough among the works it contained was *Imago Mundi*. '. . . Haskelii Geographica, Pii 2 cosmographia, Antonini itinerarium, Sardus de moribus gentium, Casmanni scholae philosophicae, Imago Mundi, Petrarch de remedio fortunae, Aulus Gellius' – runs this section of that remarkable list (Plate IIIa), which is not only the bibliography for the *History of the World*, but in its entirety an extraordinary record of Raleigh's interests at the time. Even without this evidence it could readily have been shown that Raleigh used Pierre d'Ailly, for he quotes him by name: Petrus de Aliaco.

We knew, therefore, that Raleigh had had a copy of this rare book with him when he was working on the *History of the World*. Mr Neil Ker told me that to him the hand of the mid-16th-century annotator looked English. One of these earlier notes can be seen in the margin of Plate I. But we can be more positive. His notes draw attention to various statements in the text that have an English interest. In the chapter on the parallels of latitude, for example, he underlines many countries, rivers, etc., when he reads their names, but when he comes to a mention of 'Albion, id est Anglia' he adds in the margin 'nota', followed in a moment by 'Albion, Anglia' in his bold hand. Nor is this unique. In Ptolemy's list of the 'Provinces of the whole world', several are underlined, but again it is 'Anglia' which is alone singled out for marginal attention. The annotator is interested when Pierre d'Ailly mentions an English authority, and in others when he is talking about 'Britain'. The same hand is responsible for a fascinating note on a passage in which Pierre d'Ailly speaks of the extent of the inhabited world as 37 degrees 45 minutes of latitude, and explains that beyond these latitudes even Ptolemy allows considerable habitable regions; 'etiam hoc nostro aevo' says the annotator 'offensae sunt nonnullae insulae habitabiles' in the regions beyond these parallels. He was interested, like his contemporary Dr John Dee, in Calendar reform. As Dee would have done, he paid close attention to the astrological passages, those in which Pierre d'Ailly speaks of Christ fulfilling the law of the stars, or about astrology and free will. And it is in these subjects, and in the geographical notes, that his annotations go beyond simply drawing attention to the passage marked, and provide independent comment. He shared Dee's interests, and may perhaps have belonged to his circle. He may even conceivably have borrowed, or acquired, the book from Dee himself, for I have sometimes suspected that Dee himself drew and lettered an unusual manuscript diagram on the first leaf, and was responsible for some calligraphic notes on other passages also. Professor E. G. R. Taylor has examined a photograph of this diagram. She described it as 'the nautical triangle, or more generally the right-angled triangle which Ptolemy demonstrated could give mutual bearings or distances on the globe according to the data in hand'. To assert that the hand of the diagram is Dee's beyond doubt is in my view impossible with a calligraphic script of this kind. But the Roman lettering certainly shows, in the form of the letter *e* with its prolonged horizontal, one of the most marked characteristics of Dee's hand (though it is to be found in other italianate hands of the period), and we know from Dee's library list (in the Bodleian Library) that he also possessed an *Imago*. On balance, however, I doubt the Dee ownership, because this is surely the kind of book which he would have covered with his own notes, whereas those in the hand that might be Dee's are but few. The main point, however, is established beyond doubt: that our copy was in the hands of some English scholar in this mid-16th century. The earlier owner, who writes out four lines of the *Aeneid*, regretting that he is no longer young, was perhaps from his hand French. But of this I am not certain.

Many of Dee's books are known. The number in Oxford libraries alone runs into some scores. But, so far as I am aware, none of those belonging to Raleigh when he wrote out the list in Phillipps MS 6339 has yet been identified. The task of going through the

PLATE IIIa. Raleigh's reading list, showing *Imago Mundi*
(Phillipps MS. 6339)

PLATE IIIb. The hand of the second English annotator; a note of the main
geological features through which the lines of latitude pass.

later, 'Raleigh', annotation in my *Imago* was easier than I could have wished. One would have liked the notes in this hand to be more extensive, yet the results may I think be regarded as conclusive. Phillipps MS 6339 has an English note about 'Cham' the son of Noah, Plate IV, which bears a close resemblance not only in content but also in hand, to corresponding notes in the margin of the *Imago*, Plate IV*b, c*. They are here reproduced so that the reader may see the almost exact correspondence in the writing of the name 'Noe' – he will notice that the correspondences between the words as written in *a* and *c* are considerably closer than between *b* and *c*, though the two latter are both from the margin of the *Imago*, on adjacent pages, while *a* comes from the notebook – as well as the general similarities. Mr Neil Ker pointed out the distinctive character of the letters 'c' and 'h', not invariable in the case of 'c', but frequently recurrent, in Raleigh's hand.

The plates (lxxxiv, lxxv) in Greg's *English Literary Autographs* show the variety in the hands which Raleigh wrote. But there occurs in each of them from time to time this distinctive 'c', finished with a horizontal top stroke that is no part of the curve of the letter. This 'c' is a departure from the italianate style of the hand as a whole. It can be seen a number of times in Plate IV*g*, from the notebook, and twice in IV*b* and IV*e* from the *Imago*. In the characteristic 'h', the left-hand down stroke is stopped early, at the top of the line as it were, and the curve brought round from that point. Again, we can readily find a parallel in the *Imago* notes for this idiosyncrasy. 'Raleigh' had noted, too, the *Imago's* reference to Ninus, from whom Nineveh was named: 'Ninive a Nino rege nominata' being his note – slightly shaved by the 17th-century binder – and on the opposite page a similar note about Assyria. Here it is not the notebook (though its versions of the word Assiria or Assyria [Plate IV*f, g*] – it has both forms – are illustrated for comparison with the *Imago* note) but the *History* itself that provides the parallels:

It may be understood that *Assur*, the Founder was the sonne of *Shem*; and *Assur* the destroyers were the Assyrians . . . hence it came to passe, that as *Semiramis* was counted the Foundresses of the Citie which she onely finished: so also *Ninus* of *Nineve* [1634 ed. pp. 162–3].

It seems indeed to have been the occurrence of these names on opposite pages in the *Imago* that brought them together in the text of the *History*. Most of the notes are not of great interest. In two margins (fol. 40 recto and fol. 89 recto) he jots down a calculation of the number of the fixed stars. I have not yet run to earth what he had in mind when he made this calculation, though his interest in astronomy is well known. He possessed a Copernicus, and in the *History* he mentions the work of Galileo. The majority of his notes were simply names or phrases. 'Pathalis Insula', 'Pigmaei homines', 'Herculis mors', 'Augusti mors' and such like. In a passage dealing with Roman history, he calls attention to Caesar's modification of the calendar. In one which discusses the main divisions of latitude in the northern hemisphere, he copies in the margin the names of the geographical features – cities, rivers, mountains – through which the lines of latitude run (Plate III*b*). This is characteristic of an interest in geography which is one of the main features of the library list, and may be regarded as one of Raleigh's greatest contributions to the study of history; which, he insists, should be based on an understanding of geography. Opposite the famous eighth chapter – the one noted above as having inspired Columbus's voyage – he notes the mention in Esdras that six parts of the earth

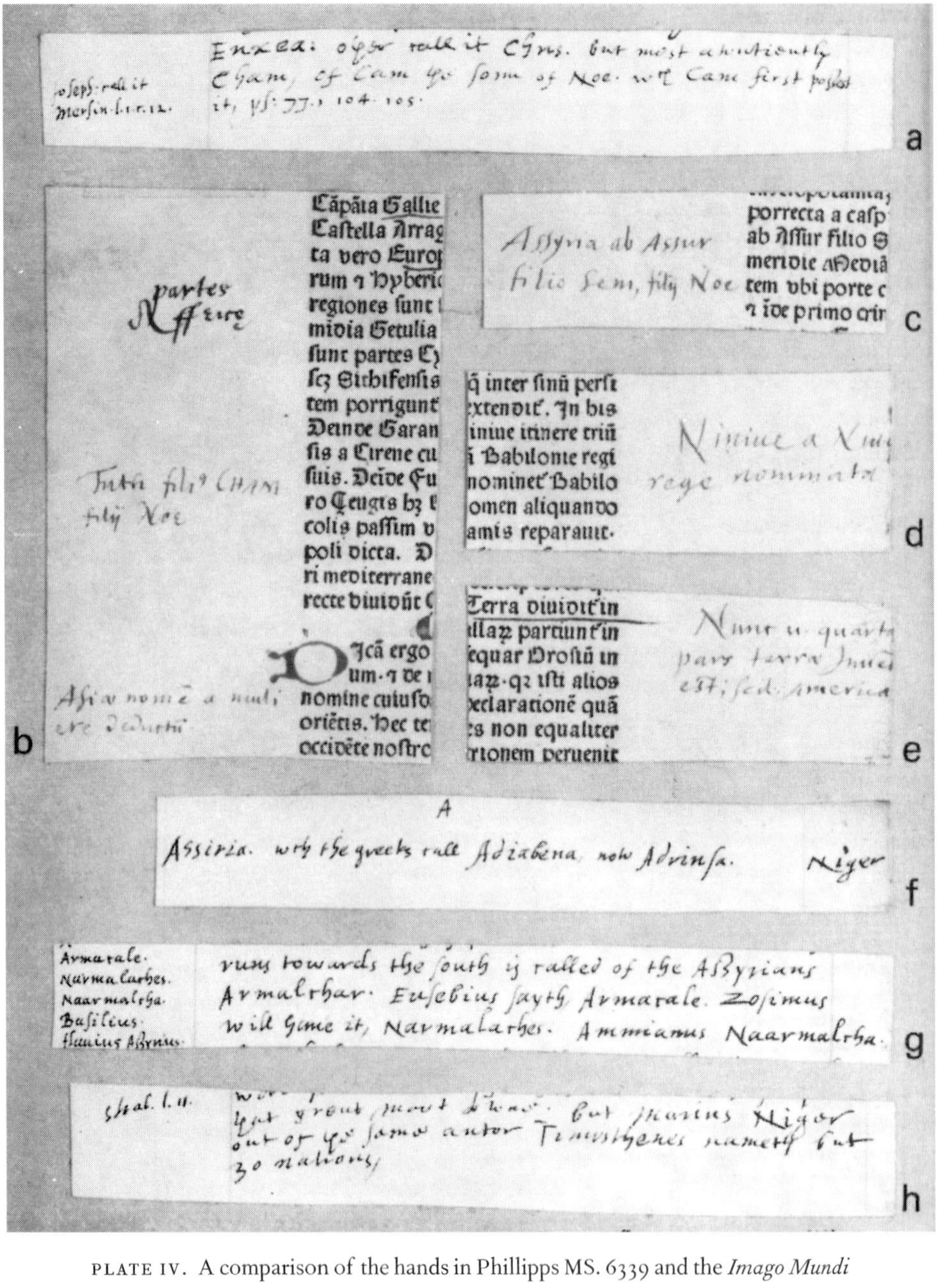

PLATE IV. A comparison of the hands in Phillipps MS. 6339 and the *Imago Mundi*

are inhabited and the seventh covered by water; and notes also the reference to the help Alexander the Great gave Aristotle in his geographical investigations, and the similar help given to Seneca by Nero. One would dearly like to know whether he was thinking of Elizabeth when his eye caught that passage. One note however is of surpassing interest, and in it we glimpse another Raleigh, not simply the author of the *History of the World*. 'Terra dividitur in tres partes', says Pierre d'Ailly, 'Scilicet Asyam, Africam, et Europam'. 'Nunc et quarta pars terrae Inventa est', notes the margin, 'scilicet America'. It is a momentary flash of Raleigh's vision of the greatness of America.

As one further proof of the amount of work done by Raleigh himself on the *History* (for which Ben Jonson, talking after dinner to Drummond of Hawthornden, indicated that he – Ben – with others had been largely responsible) this book is important, but it has a greater significance than that. For this, one of the most interesting books in the history of exploration, belonged to the man to whose inspiration and effort the first English settlements in Virginia were due. And it is a start on the task of identifying his library. What happened to Raleigh's books after his death is not known. But there is a letter from Lady Raleigh (published in Edwards, *Life and Letters of Sir W.R.*, II, pp. 413–14) which gives us a hint that they may have been immediately dispersed.

I beseech your Ladyship [Lady Carew] that you will do me the favour to entreat him [Sir Thomas Wilson] to surcease the pursuit of my husband's books or library; they being all the land or living which he left his poor child . . . Sir Thomas Wilson hath already by virtue of the King's letter fetched away all his mathematical instruments . . .

The library of his intimate friend, the 'Wizard Earl' of Northumberland (imprisoned with him in the Tower) is already being explored by Mr G. R. Batho. It is possible that between Raleigh's library and those of his two friends, Northumberland and Dee, we shall discover some overlap. For Dee was selling books to buy the necessities of life when Raleigh began to compile his library. And Northumberland was still buying books when Raleigh went to the scaffold. But there is no trace of Northumberland's hand in this *Imago*, and if a book exists, for it may do, with notes in it by those three members of the so-called School of Night, that treasure has yet to be identified. For the moment we have to be content with Raleigh's copy of the *Imago Mundi*; in itself a collector's piece.

The Iniquity of Oblivion Foil'd

I FELL in love with Sir Thomas Browne's *Hydriotaphia* (*Urne Buriall*) *and the Garden of Cyrus* at the age of 18. We were not taught 'English literature' at Eton; you were supposed to do your own reading. But there was an optional course in one's senior years called 'extra studies', conducted by the late George Lyttelton: an assistant master much relished for his lordly air and jovial bulk, his affable, worldly style, and his capacity (remarkable even in a famous cricketing family) for hitting any bowler who gave himself airs out of the ground for six, not just once, but two or three times in an over. Among much else of worth, he introduced us to Sir Thomas Browne; and I can still hear, after more than 40 years, his orotund declamation of the marvellous last chapter of *Urne Buriall*, the magical conclusion to *The Garden of Cyrus*. With his encouragement I prevailed upon my sceptical tutor to allow me, for my last Fourth of June, to choose a selection from the former for my contribution to those recitations annually delivered (in full dress and knee-breeches) by members of the Sixth Form at Eton under the misleading name of 'Speeches'.

I was already a collector of early editions of the classics. I was not, and never have been, a collector of first editions of English literature. The only exception on my shelves today (aside from the books of contemporaries bought as they came out) is one which I happened on by accident and acquired by luck. You can guess what it is (8vo, 1658, Keynes no. 93).

In 1928, a year or so after I went into the rare book business, I was invited by Desmond Flower to provide an up-to-date text for a grand edition of Browne's two precious essays then preparing for publication by Cassell's, to be illustrated by my friend Paul Nash; which, with his noble designs, printed by Oliver Simon at the Curwen Press, was in due course published in an edition of 215 copies in 1932 (an unpropitious year for 15-guinea books: but time has tripled it). In preparation for this task I equipped myself with every published edition, from the second onwards, and a copy of the Noel Douglas replica of the first, which was obviously – at the going price of £15 or £20 – out of my reach.

In 1929 I was in Percy Dobell's shop in Bruton Street, looking for some Restoration books for a customer of ours at Scribners. Sir Thomas Browne was somehow mentioned (by me, I suppose). And dear Mr Dobell, with that gentle, apologetic air which earned him Richard Jennings's nickname of 'Piteous Percy', said, from behind his immense, his pre-eminent authority in the books of the 17th century, that he had a copy of the first edition of *Urne Buriall and the Garden of* Cyrus with marginal corrections which he believed to be in the author's hand and which he ventured (ventured! to an ignorant youth) to think I might like to see. I knew, by now, of the author-corrected copies in the Osler collection at McGill and in the library of Trinity College, Cambridge, because Mr (as he then was) Geoffrey Keynes had drawn readings from them; indeed, I had examined the Trinity copy, first used by a still earlier editor, Charles Sayle. But Keynes, then as now our prime authority on Sir Thomas Browne, had doubted that the corrections in the Dobell copy were in the author's handwriting: there are plenty of copies of the book with contemporary marginal transcriptions from the errata – an example is shown in Plate IV for comparison with Browne's own script below – so that scepticism is the rule. And he had passed the same discouraging verdict on a second copy with MS corrections which Dobell, almost more apologetically, now admitted that he also had in stock.

He produced the two volumes from some recess in the back room – he didn't like, he said, to keep them in front, because, although *he* had thought the corrections were the author's, it seemed they weren't; so that he didn't quite know how to describe them, nor indeed how to price them. In the presence of so much humility from so learned a bookseller I did not consider offering any opinion. But for an aspiring editor who was also an aspirant in the rare book business, the chance was not to be missed. I asked if I might take the two copies on approval, for full study: yes, I might. Would he please put a price on them? Well, it was *very* difficult but – say £25 each, or £45 if we took them both?

I carried them off, and reported, in high excitement, to my chief (I was still very much 'on approval' at Scribners). Charles Kingsley did not pretend to know much about Sir Thomas Browne, still less about his handwriting: the less obvious 17th-century first editions were not much in Scribners' line; and £45, or even £25, was money in those days. He was sceptical (he was a Yankee from Vermont); and naturally enough, in face of the great Keynes's opinion. But he was a kindly man, and I suppose he didn't want to pour cold water on my enthusiasm. So, after some wrinkle-browed thought, he said: 'All right, you go ahead and do some work – some real work – on these two copies. In your spare time, you understand. If, when you have finished, you can convince *me* that either of them is right, we'll buy it – I agree with you that it would be a bargain at the price of the two. If both of them turn out to be right, Scribners will buy them both – and you can keep the less good copy as a bonus. Fair enough?'

I went to work. In due course I satisfied myself, by comparison with the Trinity copy, photographs of the Osler copy (sent with a friendly pat on the back by Dr W. W. Francis), the Browne manuscript material in the British Museum and elsewhere, that the corrections in both copies were the author's. I convinced Charles Kingsley. Sir Geoffrey Keynes examined the evidence I had assembled, took another and closer look, and magnanimously endorsed them. The Scribner copy, in much the finer condition of the two, though with fewer corrections (it was earlier in the private collection of Elkin Mathews, the publisher) is now, after some wandering, in the Lilly Library, Bloomington, Indiana. The other copy, which was once John Towneley's (de Ricci, p. 88) and which has since had to be rebound, became, and still is, mine.

In 1958 I was able to record (in Appendix A to the Cambridge University Press edition of the two essays) 12 author-corrected copies of the first edition, of which three were then in private hands; mine being no. 5, with 43 corrections; and no further examples have been publicly reported. No. 3 has since gone, with the library of Dr Lawrence

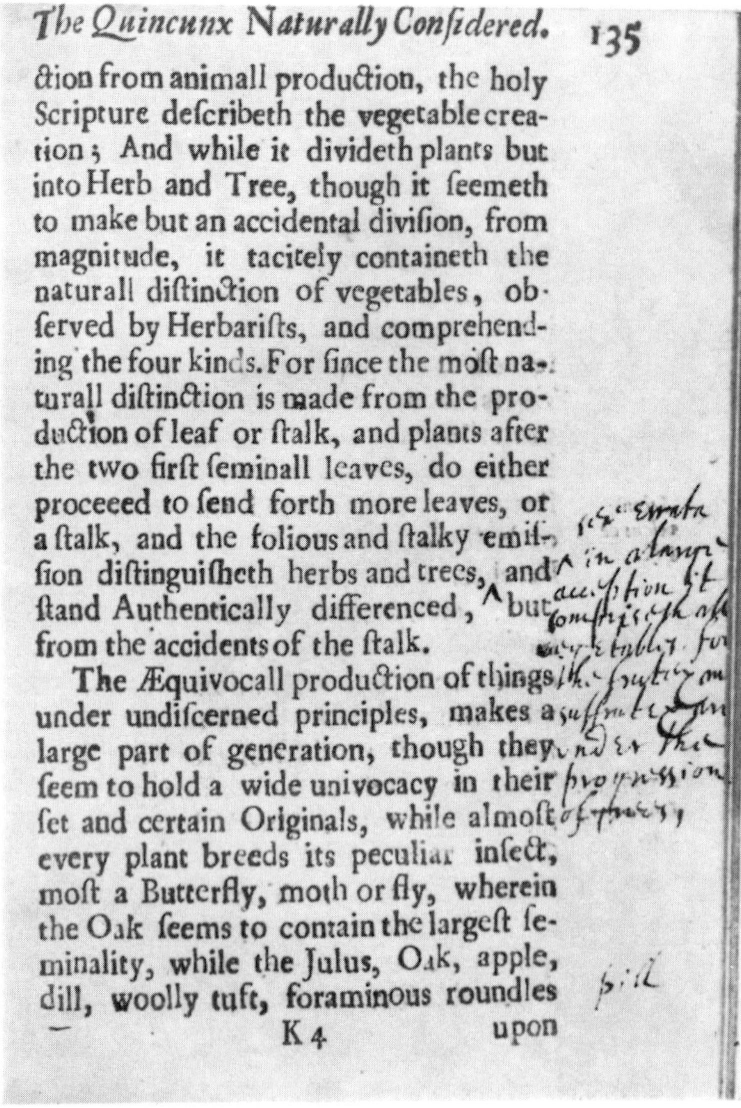

&ion from animall produ&ion, the holy
Scripture defcribeth the vegetable creation; And while it divideth plants but
into Herb and Tree, though it feemeth
to make but an accidental divifion, from
magnitude, it tacitely containeth the
naturall diftin&ion of vegetables, ob-
ferved by Herbarifts, and comprehending the four kinds. For fince the moft naturall diftin&ion is made from the pro-
du&ion of leaf or ftalk, and plants after
the two firft feminall leaves, do either
proceeed to fend forth more leaves, or
a ftalk, and the folious and ftalky emif-
fion diftinguifheth herbs and trees, and
ftand Authentically differenced, but
from the accidents of the ftalk.

The Æquivocall produ&ion of things
under undifcerned principles, makes a
large part of generation, though they
feem to hold a wide univocacy in their
fet and certain Originals, while almoft
every plant breeds its peculiar infe&,
moft a Butterfly, moth or fly, wherein
the Oak feems to contain the largeft fe-
minality, while the Julus, Oak, apple,
dill, woolly tuft, foraminous roundles

K 4   upon

PLATE I. The Osler Copy

Sir Thomas Browne's *Hydriotaphia*

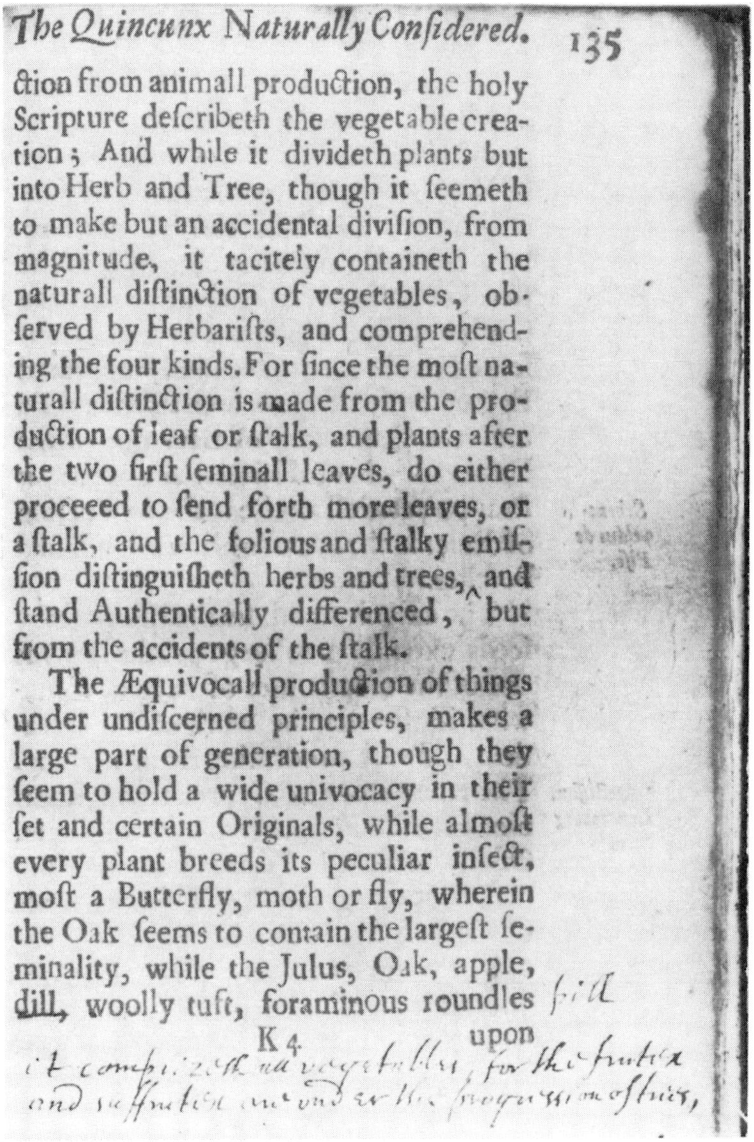
The Quincunx Naturally Conſidered. 135

ction from animall production, the holy Scripture deſcribeth the vegetable creation; And while it divideth plants but into Herb and Tree, though it ſeemeth to make but an accidental diviſion, from magnitude, it tacitely containeth the naturall diſtinction of vegetables, obſerved by Herbariſts, and comprehending the four kinds. For ſince the moſt naturall diſtinction is made from the production of leaf or ſtalk, and plants after the two firſt ſeminall leaves, do either proceeed to ſend forth more leaves, or a ſtalk, and the folious and ſtalky emiſſion diſtinguiſheth herbs and trees,^ and ſtand Authentically differenced, ^but from the accidents of the ſtalk.

The Æquivocall production of things under undiſcerned principles, makes a large part of generation, though they ſeem to hold a wide univocacy in their ſet and certain Originals, while almoſt every plant breeds its peculiar inſect, moſt a Butterfly, moth or fly, wherein the Oak ſeems to contain the largeſt ſeminality, while the Julus, Oak, apple, dill, woolly tuft, foraminous roundles fill

K 4 upon

it comprizeth all vegetables, for the frutex and suffrutex are under the progression of trees,

PLATE II. The Carter Copy

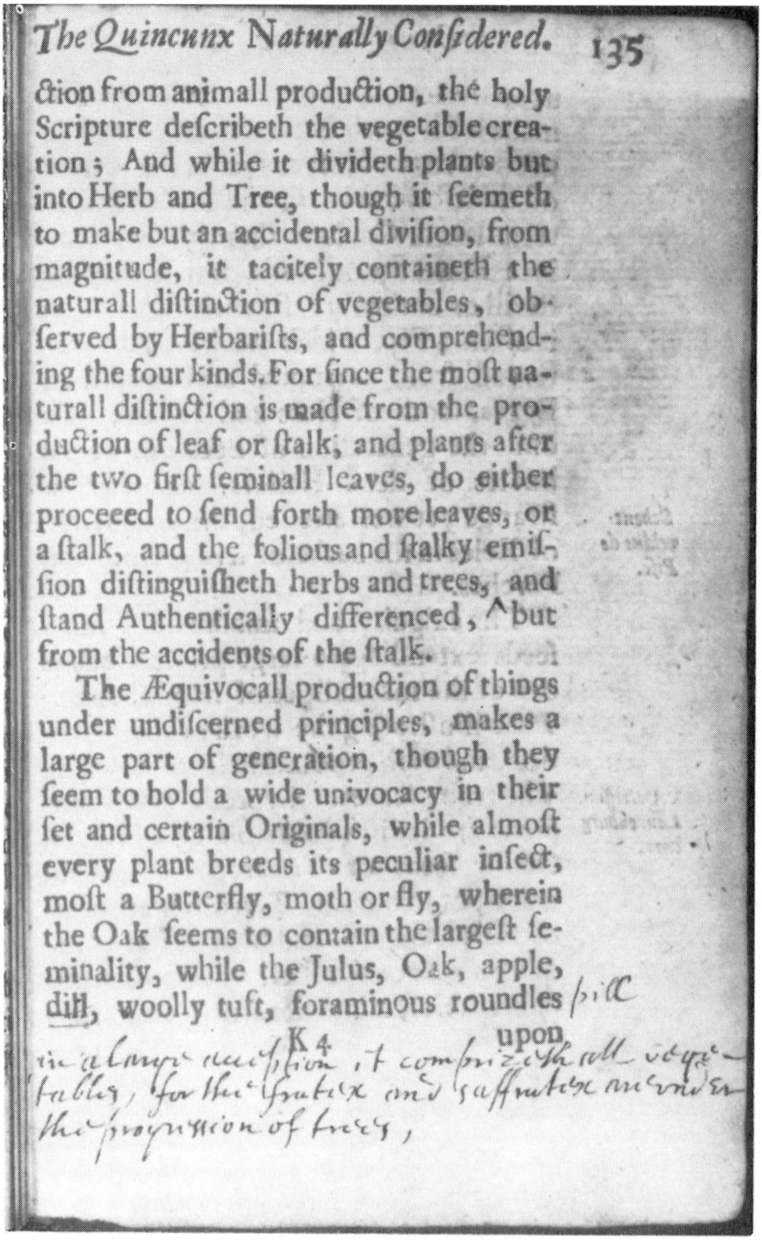

The Quincunx Naturally Considered. 135

ction from animall production, the holy Scripture describeth the vegetable creation; And while it divideth plants but into Herb and Tree, though it seemeth to make but an accidental division, from magnitude, it tacitely containeth the naturall distinction of vegetables, observed by Herbarists, and comprehending the four kinds. For since the most naturall distinction is made from the production of leaf or stalk; and plants after the two first seminall leaves, do either proceeed to send forth more leaves, or a stalk, and the folious and stalky emission distinguisheth herbs and trees, and stand Authentically differenced, ^but from the accidents of the stalk.

The Æquivocall production of things under undiscerned principles, makes a large part of generation, though they seem to hold a wide univocacy in their set and certain Originals, while almost every plant breeds its peculiar insect, most a Butterfly, moth or fly, wherein the Oak seems to contain the largest seminality, while the Julus, Oak, apple, dill, woolly tuft, foraminous roundles pill

K 4 upon

in a larger acception, it comprizeth all vegetables, for the frutex and suffrutex are under the progression of trees,

PLATE III. The Yale Copy

ction from animall production, the holy
Scripture defcribeth the vegetable creation; And while it divideth plants but
into Herb and Tree, though it feemeth
to make but an accidental divifion, from
magnitude, it tacitely containeth the
naturall diftinction of vegetables, ob-
ferved by Herbalifts, and comprehending the four kinds. For, fince the moft naturall diftinction is made from the production of leaf or ftalk, and plants after
the two firft feminall leaves, do either
proceeed to fend forth more leaves, or
a ftalk, and the folious and ftalky emul-
fion diftinguifheth herbs and trees, and
ftand Authentically differenced, but
from the accidents of the ftalk.

The Æquivocall production of things
under undifcerned principles, makes a
large part of generation, though they
feem to hold a wide univocacy in their
fet and certain Originals, while almoft
every plant breeds its peculiar infect,
moft a Butterfly, moth or fly, wherein
the Oak feems to contain the largeft fe-
minality, while the Julus, Oak, apple,
fill, woolly tuft, foraminous roundles
upon

K 4

R. Reynolds of the Ford Hospital, Detroit, to the University of Alabama. No. 9, which then belonged to Dr Eli Moschcowitz of New York, was after his death sold at Sotheby's[1] (9 November 1964, lot 84, £480) and when last heard of was still – surprisingly, of course, to me – on the shelves of Messrs Dawson of Pall Mall.

My current census, therefore, is as follows:

1. Avery Library, Columbia University, New York
2. Osler Library, McGill University, Montreal
3. Reynolds Library, University of Alabama
4. Trinity College, Cambridge
5. John Carter, London (the Towneley-Dobell copy)
6. Durham University Library
7. British Museum (the Salter copy)
8. Princeton University Library
9. The Moschcowitz copy (Messrs Dawson, London)
10. Lilly Library, Bloomington, Indiana (the Elkin Mathews–Dobell–Scribner–Beyer–Scribner copy)
11. Yale University Library (once with Tregaskis)
12. Cornell University Library.

As the cognoscenti know, Sir Thomas Browne's manuscript corrections in the copies of the first edition which he gave away or found on the tables of his friends – it was very inaccurately printed – seem to have been haphazardly made. Half a dozen of the known survivors contain between 40 and 50: the Avery copy has as many as 77; the Cornell copy has no more than three. Some corrections are found in most copies, some in a minority, a few in one copy only. The substantial addition on p. 135 is here reproduced from four of the 12 (by courtesy of McGill, Yale, and Indiana Universities).

---

[1] The executors of the Moschcowitz estate had dutifully approached both Sotheby's New York office and our then rival (now affiliate) Parke-Bernet. They told me later that an influential factor in their decision to consign the library to London had been their discovery in the Moschcowitz copy of my sheets of notes (1930 and 1956) on its corrections: a nice example of bread upon the waters.

Collecting Modern Imprints

S ome bookshop proprietors have the habit of trying to guess their customers' interests, by looking over the books the customers select, so that they can mention other related books currently in stock. Although I have encountered many such dealers, I have never yet found one who correctly guessed my reason for choosing whatever books I picked out; and when I have finally confessed the motive for my selection, some of the dealers have not been able to conceal their incredulity, occasionally tinged with ridicule. In one shop where I found a copy of Vincent Fuller's *The Long Green Gaze* 1925, the clerk assumed that I was interested in mystery stories and mentioned a particularly good one which he had just purchased as part of a private library. When I replied that I was not looking for mystery stories at the moment, he concluded that I must be a devotee of crossword puzzles, for he was acquainted enough with the Fuller book to know that in it the resolution of the plot turns on the solution of a crossword puzzle. He therefore directed me to his understandably meagre supply of used crossword puzzle books, and I was forced to reveal that I was buying the book not because it was a mystery about crossword puzzles but because it was published by B. W. Huebsch. This statement left him at a loss, since he could not immediately lay his hands on another book published by Huebsch.

I do not mean to imply that the majority of dealers have never heard of imprint-collecting, for even the most unscholarly and provincial bookshop owner would not find anything unusual in an interest in Elzeviers, or Baskervilles, or Kelmscotts, or even Stone & Kimballs. Indeed, such dealers often have a shelf reserved for private press books or 'gift editions' (invariably, in the United States, those of the Heritage Press); and they recognize that a major aspect of collecting has always been the search for books bearing the names of printers or publishers who played a significant role in the history of printing or book production. Bibliographies, like Philip Gaskell's of Baskerville and Sidney Kramer's of Stone & Kimball, have served to emphasize the importance of certain imprints and have caused dealers to be on the lookout for them; it is not uncommon, for example, to find – even in the average bookshop – the phrase 'Stone imprint' pencilled into a book as a justification for its higher price. Book-dealers, in other words, are well aware of imprint-collecting because particular imprints have been publicized by collectors and scholars.

What came as a surprise to the dealer I have mentioned is that anyone would collect the output of a modern commercial publisher – not a printer, or a designer, or a private press, but an 'ordinary' trade publisher. If many people collected such imprints, the idea would not have appeared novel to him, so his reaction is indicative less of ignorance on his part than of general indifference on the part of collectors. The interests of collectors have usually centred on particular authors or subjects; when collectors have sought books for their imprints, they have normally been concerned more with printing than with publishing, more with the work of fine (or historic) printers than with the products of important (or interesting) publishers. Although the uses of a publisher-collection are obvious, the traditions of bibliophily have not encouraged such collections, just as the emphasis on first impressions has tended, until quite recently, to turn attention away from many textually significant later impressions.

Even if the value of a publisher-collection as a research tool seems obvious, so few such collections exist – either in private hands or in institutions – that some comment on this approach to collecting is perhaps in order. For the private collector, the attractions of collecting publishers' imprints are both financial and scholarly: in this area an individual need not spend much money to bring together a collection which makes a contribution to learning. For the institutional collector, the same advantages of course still obtain, since a relatively small outlay will procure a collection which can bring increased prestige to the institution as a research centre; the difficulty, however, from the rare-book custodian's point of view, is that the process of forming this sort of collection is extremely time-consuming, since the antiquarian book trade is not organized in such a way as to make an efficient procedure of the search for books by imprint. That is to say, one cannot quickly check a dealer's catalogue (except in rare cases) to see whether any books with a given imprint are listed, since there is usually no imprint index; and one generally does not have much success in presenting a dealer with a blanket request for a particular imprint, for his stock is not arranged by imprint and he cannot keep many such requests constantly in mind. Instead, one must perform the research necessary to construct a check-list of the imprint and then request the specific titles in the usual fashion and institutional purchasers rarely have the time for this kind of research on any significant scale. Imprint-collecting is therefore a peculiarly appropriate form of collecting for the private individual: in pursuing it, he is not duplicating (or attempting to duplicate) the collections formed by institutions with considerably more money at their disposal, but he is performing a valuable service which institutions are not so well equipped to perform; indeed, one may predict that institutional libraries will look to individual collectors as the source for this kind of collection ready-formed, to complement their author collections.

Of the two basic attractions which imprint-collecting has for the individual, the monetary perhaps requires less comment than the scholarly, since it is even more self-evident. In the case of publishers' imprints, a large part of the output of any given publisher is likely to be of little intrinsic interest – and therefore at least for 19th- and 20th-century publishers, inexpensive. If one has decided to collect Mitchell Kennerley imprints, for example – because of Kennerley's distinguished typography as well as his willingness to experiment with the 'new' literature and to give a hearing to unknown writers who later became famous – one would have to purchase such works as E. Temple Thurston's *The Garden of Resurrection: Being the Love Story of an Ugly Man* 1911 and Elsa Barker's *Letters from a Living Dead Man* 1914. If one chose B. W. Huebsch – an ideal example of the one-man experimental firm which had a great impact on modern literature – one would be forced to procure Emily M. Bishop's *Daily Ways to Health* 1910. All these books are quite cheap – and rightly so – when one finds them (they are not easy to locate); but they are essential for understanding the range of interests of these two publishers and the context out of which the more important books emerged. Thus a great number of books which are cheap, regardless of their scarcity, because they are of almost no interest in themselves, take on value when they are placed in a collection of other books bearing identical imprints.

At the same time, it goes without saying that the collector of modern publishers' imprints will not find all his desiderata so inexpensive. As collectors have always recognized, when one's own interests converge with another's on a particular item, prices must inevitably rise. Since Kennerley published work by Edna St Vincent Millay, Vachel Lindsay, Van Wyck Brooks, D. H. Lawrence and Joseph Hergesheimer, and Huebsch brought out early volumes by Sherwood Anderson and James Joyce, a collector of Kennerley and Huebsch imprints finds himself in competition with many other persons for books by these authors, and he must accordingly be prepared to encounter high prices (high, that is, in comparison to those asked for the average books of these publishers). H. G. Wells's *The Door in the Wall* (Kennerley 1911) is sought by both Wells and Goudy collectors; *Philip Dru, Administrator* (Huebsch 1912) is in demand by those interested either in its anonymous author, Colonel E. M. House, or in Woodrow Wilson's administration in general. A number of books bearing any given imprint, in other words, will be comparatively expensive; but the difference between imprint and author-collecting is that, with imprints, the lesser (and often scarcer) items are not likely to be costly, whereas with authors – at least important or 'collected' authors – the scarcer (and often lesser) works are decidedly expensive. In the case of printers' imprints this difference may not always be so great, for the quality of the typography and design of books printed by the Goudys or the Grabhorns, for instance, may have attracted enough attention for their prices to be high regardless of the merit of their contents. But this observation only reinforces the basic point: collecting imprints involves picking up many books which are of little interest except for their imprints, and, since relatively few imprints (both publishers' and printers') have been of interest to collectors, it follows that such books will generally be cheap.

If it is true that a large part of the output of any publisher is insignificant, or at least dull, what is the reason, one may ask, for going to the trouble of assembling all the volumes bearing that publisher's imprint? The fact that most of them are cheap is of course not a sufficient justification, though it is related to a quite important reason: for the lack of general interest in a book (with its resulting low price) does not necessarily mean that the book is useless but may instead indicate that the uses to which it can be put have previously been overlooked (or not widely recognized). If one grants that the history of publishing and printing is a legitimate field of inquiry, then complete collections of the output of individual publishers and printers, the raw material for such study, become desirable from a scholarly point of view, and in those collections each book, however trivial, plays its role. That collections of this sort have not been frequently formed in the past is no sign that they do not have purpose or value; and, for the very reason that they have not been formed so often as other types of collection, the person who turns his

PLATE I. Stone & Kimball Ephemera
Letterhead of 1894 (215 × 139 mm); leaflet for summer 1899 (6 pp., 140 × 70 mm); order form
for David Swing's *Old Pictures of Life* 1894 (2 leaves, 173 × 110 mm)
(Tanselle Collection)

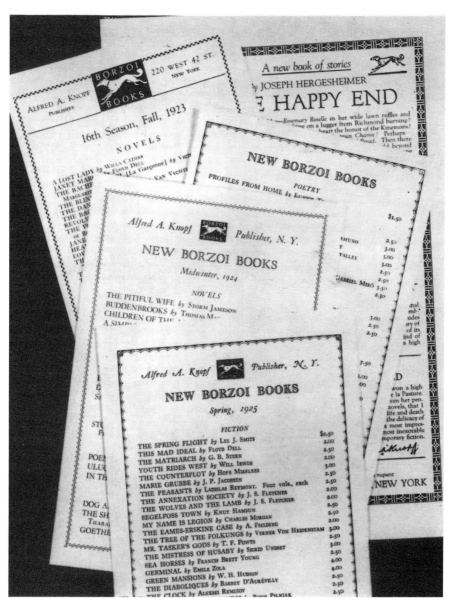

PLATE 11. Knopf Ephemera
Rectos of advertising leaves for fall 1923 and winter 1924, and recto and verso of leaf for
spring 1925 (178 × 116 mm); broadside advertising five novels, 1919 (243 × 166 mm)
(Tanselle Collection)

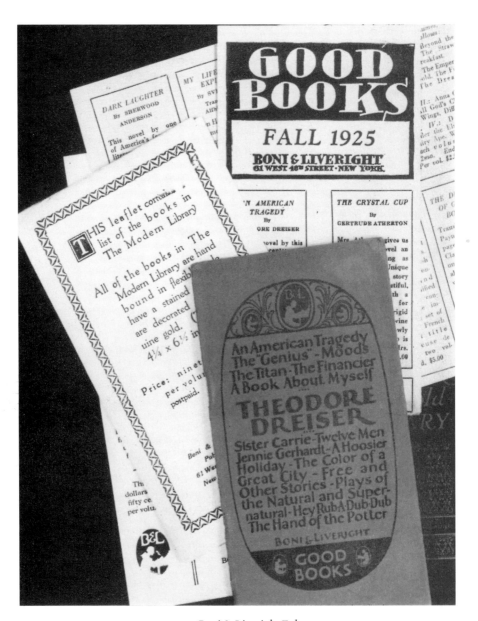

PLATE III. Boni & Liveright Ephemera
Front cover and pages 2–3 of the leaflet for fall 1925 (8 pp., 160 × 87 mm); leaflet for the
'Modern Library' (6pp., 160 × 90 mm); *A Book about Theodore Dreiser and His Work* 1925
(24 pp., 154 × 83mm); leaflet for the 'Black and Gold Library' (4 pp., 129 × 95 mm)
(Tanselle Collection)

PLATE IV. Huebsch and Kennerley Ephemera
Huebsch mailing-list form (140 × 107 mm); Kennerley shipping label (121 × 83mm);
broadside, advertising Kennerley's 'Little Omar Classics' 1907 (134 × 87 mm)
(Tanselle Collection)

attention to them and builds up an integrated one can make an especially significant contribution to knowledge.

When a number of related books are physically brought together, connections between them and generalizations about them often become apparent which would have escaped notice if the volumes were examined separately. In any case, drawing all the books issued by one publisher from an ordinary library stack requires previous knowledge of what titles to request – information which can sometimes, but not always, be extracted from the standard reference works of the book trade or from the publishers themselves. Some publishers, whose records no longer exist, were negligent in sending copies of their books to the *Publishers' Circular* or *Publishers' Weekly* offices for listing and prepared no catalogues or comprehensive advertisements. In such cases, a separate assemblage of the actual books is the only source for writing a history of the firm or for reconstructing its list; and, even when some form of external information is available, a collector constantly on the alert for a particular imprint often turns up titles (or editions) not otherwise recorded for that firm. There is no substitute, in other words, as far as the study of publishing history is concerned, for collections of books arranged by imprint and consciously formed with that purpose in mind.

Such collections also serve useful purposes in the historical, textual and bibliographical study of the authors involved. In the same way that accurate literary history demands extensive knowledge of the minor literature of a period, against which the major works can be viewed in perspective, an acquaintance with the entire output of a publisher enables the student of a particular author to see more clearly the contemporary position which that author's writings occupied. Thus John Murray's predilection for non-fiction, particularly in his 'Home and Colonial Library' helps account for the changes he requested in Melville's *Typee* 1846. Similarly, textual work on *Typee* would be facilitated by a collection of the 'Home and Colonial Library', if not indeed of all Murray's publications from the late 1840s, so that one could more reliably ascertain the degree to which a uniform house style existed and was imposed upon *Typee*. And, bibliographically, this collection would illustrate Murray's customary practices in regard to binding and the general physical appearance of his books, helpful collateral evidence for classifying various issues or states of *Typee* and perhaps for dating changes in binding designs, endpaper styles, and the like. There is no question but that modern textual and bibliographical scholarship would greatly benefit from readily accessible publisher-collections of this sort, for bibliographers are increasingly more aware of the fact that whatever book they are examining was not the only one with which its publisher (or printer) was concerned and that it must be examined in the context of the other books which he was producing at the same time.

The historical value of an imprint collection can be increased in various ways, by extending it both in breadth and in depth; and an individual who has nearly completed a collection of one publisher or a group of publishers has a number of options open to him for considerably enhancing the significance of his library. If I may turn to my own collection for a moment as an illustration, I can suggest a few of these directions. In the belief that there was a clearly defined group of American publishers, in the first three decades of this century, who were willing to take risks on new and experimental young writers and who thus bore the same relation to the large established houses as the 'little magazines' and 'little theatres' did to the popular commercial magazines and the Broadway theatre, I have been attempting to assemble the total output of these 'little publishers' as one way of illuminating the literary milieu of a major period in American literary history. My principal attention has therefore been given to five imprints – Boni & Liveright, Huebsch, Kennerley, Knopf (pre-1930) and Seltzer – but not to the exclusion of many lesser ones that served a similar function, such as Egmont Arens, N. L. Brown, Laurence Gomme, Lieber & Lewis and Frank Shay.

A list of the authors published by these firms reads like a roll-call of the leading figures in early 20th-century literature. Boni & Liveright could boast of T. S. Eliot, e. e. cummings, Theodore Dreiser, Eugene O'Neill, Conrad Aiken, Hart Crane, William Faulkner, Robinson Jeffers, Edgar Lec Masters, Waldo Frank, and H. D. Knopf in the early years published H. L. Mencken, Willa Cather, George Jean Nathan, Wallace Stevens, T. S. Eliot, Conrad Aiken, Carl Van Vechten, Adelaide Crapsey, Floyd Dell, Arthur Davison Ficke, Witter Bynner and Arthur Waley, and he was the American publisher for the Sitwells, Dorothy Richardson and Katherine Mansfield. Huebsch's list included Sherwood Anderson, Van Wyck Brooks, D. H. Lawrence and James Joyce, while Kennerley was the first publisher of Edna St Vincent Millay and Vachel Lindsay, and Seltzer brought out many of D. H. Lawrence's works (in some cases before they appeared in England) and the Scott Moncrieff translation of Proust. Although these publishers were essentially similar – in their interest not only in whatever was new in literature but also in liberal approaches to political and social issues – they nevertheless had distinctive characteristics. Kennerley and Knopf, for example, devoted considerable attention to typography and produced the most handsome volumes physically; Huebsch expressed his concern with economic and political questions by publishing the work of Thorstein Veblen and many books on India; Knopf – to an even greater extent than Seltzer and Huebsch – made European fiction known in the United States; and Boni & Liveright – even more than Seltzer and Kennerley – issued great quantities of fiction, often with sensational titles, to help offset the small sales of their poetry, drama and essays. The related smaller publishers reflected the same interests on a lesser scale: N. L. Brown and Lieber & Lewis were particularly drawn to foreign writers, while both Shay and Arens published plays performed in the little theatres of New York, and Gomme (who was associated with Kennerley in the Little Book-Shop Around the Corner) issued poetry (Joyce Kilmer, Braithwaite's annual anthologies, *Eight Harvard Poets*) and essays by John Jay Chapman.

Since all the publishers in this basic group had their headquarters in New York, one way to expand the collection in breadth was to represent other sections of the country. Accordingly, I have added to the list certain publishers of Chicago (Covici-McGee and R. F. Seymour, who, despite frequent lapses in taste, served as outlets for writers of the area, such as Harriet Monroe, A. D. Ficke, Alice Corbin, Ben Hecht and Maxwell Bodenheim), San Francisco (A. M. Robertson and Paul Elder, both interested in book design and in local writers), and Boston (John W. Luce – influential promoter of foreign literature – and Badger and Four Seas – early and illustrious examples of the 'vanity' publisher, whose lists included E. A. Robinson, William Faulkner, Conrad Aiken and

Gertrude Stein). Indeed, the geographical extension could well proceed abroad, for a characteristic of most of these publishers was their effort to promote the 'new' writers of England and Europe, as well as of the United States, copies of the overseas editions of the works they published, therefore, would form a useful adjunct to the collection, valuable both for an investigation of their relations with other publishers and for textual study.

Another principle of expansion, besides the geographical, is the chronological. In order to illustrate the American publishing scene in the years just preceding my main period of concentration, I have selected for extensive collection several of the most interesting publishers of the 1890s: Stone & Kimball and Way & Williams of Chicago, William Doxey of San Francisco, R. H. Russell of New York, and Copeland & Day and Lamson Wolffe of Boston – publishers whose names often appeared in joint imprints with such English firms as John Lane and who illustrate (in both the content and the design of their books) most aspects of the *fin de siècle*. Then, to place all these publishers of the 1890–1930 period in the context of the whole development of American publishing (and printing), I am trying to put together a selection of books which will represent every year from about 1775 to the present and every part of the country. Such a group of books, if carefully limited and controlled, can sometimes reveal basic patterns and trends more effectively than can a large library, where those patterns may be obscured by the exigencies of housing and classification. All forms of publication should ideally be included (such as the literary annuals, the cheap reprints in elaborate bindings, the paper-covered series of the 1890s, the paperbacks of the 1940s); and even the years covered by the main collections (that is, 1890–1930) are to be represented, so that there will be at hand a sampling of the output of the major established firms against which to view the work of the newer, more experimental publishers. A card catalogue of the entire collection, indexing the books not simply by author and title but by imprint, place and year as well, can be developed into a useful tool for research particularly since few library catalogues are organized in this fashion for 19th- and 20th-century books.

If techniques such as these broaden the range of an imprint collection, there are other ways of increasing its depth – particularly by giving attention to later printings, dustjackets, ephemera and manuscripts. Thus, for my main publisher-collections, I am concerned with obtaining not simply the first impression of each book but every impression. To have all the successive printings of a work together is naturally of inestimable value for textual study and descriptive bibliography; in addition, many of these publishers carefully identified and dated each impression on the verso of the title-page, and sometimes – when a publisher's records do not survive or are inaccessible – the only way to establish the printing history of a work is to examine these dates in the books themselves. In any case, one would expect a collection organized around publishers to contain material illustrating those publishers' practices in handling later printings and showing the relative popularity of their books in terms of the numbers and dates of new impressions. Because copies of later printings have not been sought after so assiduously as those of first impressions, they are generally much cheaper; but for that reason they have often been discarded and are sometimes scarcer than the firsts. This part of a publisher-collection can therefore be built up at a moderate cost and at the same time be extremely valuable for historical and bibliographical research.

The same points could be made about the other ways of strengthening a collection in depth. Like later printings, dust-jackets are frequently disregarded and difficult to locate but sometimes contain material not elsewhere available (such as the texts of comments by well-known persons) and are essential for descriptive bibliography and for understanding a publisher's style of advertising and design. Similarly, any kind of ephemera – advertising leaflets, broadsides, promotional pamphlets, catalogues, bookmarks, subscription blanks, and so on – reflect the character of the publisher, sometimes preserve information that would otherwise be lost, and often are desirable items in their own right. Among my Boni & Liveright material is a brochure issued in 1925 to promote Dreiser's books, containing essays by Sherwood Anderson, Edgar Lee Masters, and H. L. Mencken; my Kennerley collection includes one of Kennerley's blue shipping labels, which is also an example of Goudy typography. Finally, it goes without saying that any sort of manuscript material – even seemingly routine letters or inscriptions to or from a publisher – may shed light on that publisher's relations with his authors or on his general method of operation.

All this is obvious, but not many collectors over the years have formed collections of this sort. In a day when the kinds of books which have traditionally been collected are fetching extremely high prices and are rapidly disappearing into institutional collections, the private collector – or even the librarian of a young institution – may find himself turning into less familiar (and therefore, perhaps, more exciting) paths. I have described the collecting of modern publishers' imprints as one such direction – one in which an individual of limited means can have the satisfaction of manipulating a considerable quantity of books, sometimes insignificant in themselves, in such a way as to create (through imaginative selection, arrangement and cataloguing) a context that reveals their potential importance. Mitchell Kennerley in 1945, long after he had stopped his own publishing, wrote an article for the *American Mercury* (LX, 361–6) to explain the fascination of unusual imprints and the pleasure of finding them on the bargain tables of used-book stores. He was describing a casual approach to collecting, but he recognized the historical value which an imprint can lend to an otherwise dull book. And he would have agreed that, true to the highest traditions of bibliophily, much of the excitement comes from putting together and shaping an entity within which individual items take on significance, for only through this process can order and some degree of understanding be brought to the past.

Archdeacon Francis Wrangham, 1769–1842

'A STILL more formidable visitation', Sir Walter Scott wrote to his friend Morritt in 1829 when he was much pestered by visitors at Abbotsford, 'was that of Archdeacon Wrangham full fraught with prize poems, charades and Latin versions of English nonsense.' That says a good deal about the enthusiastic and infinitely engaging clergyman and bibliomaniac whose career and achievement Michael Sadleir recorded so sensitively in *Archdeacon Francis Wrangham, 1769–1842* (1937). Sadleir's essay, a Supplement to the Bibliographical Society's Transactions, was followed two years later by his paper in *The Library* drawing on an extensive series of letters from Wrangham to Sir Samuel Egerton Brydges which Sadleir had acquired from the Phillipps collection. The monograph and its supplement were reprinted (without appendices) in *Things Past* 1944, but the Wrangham-Brydges letters – although so recently known – have so far evaded my persistent enquiries. The loss is regrettable, as there was probably more to be found in the correspondence than Sadleir used in his principally bibliographical discussion. The search has been rewarding, with new friendships made and new studies undertaken in its course, and hundreds of the Archdeacon's letters to other correspondents have come to light in libraries, record offices and private collections. This new correspondence confirms Sadleir's impression of an attractive personality and an affectionate father, of a conscientious clerical dignitary with a consuming passion for rare books and eccentric bibliographical detail. I hope it will be used in due course for a short biographical work amplifying many parts of Michael Sadleir's essays. Bibliographically, too, there is still much to be said about the Archdeacon's own works: his taste for limited editions and coloured-paper copies will probably attract and confuse collectors of his works indefinitely. Some years ago Messrs B. C. Bloomfield and C. B. L. Barr discussed in THE BOOK COLLECTOR various extracts from Wrangham's *The Works of Thomas Zouch* (Sadleir 47); a whole box of assorted blue-paper offprints from this book awaits full investigation in York Minster Library. The intricacies are endless and would have delighted the Archdeacon himself, but they deter the less enthusiastic, who can take refuge in his correspondence. This article draws on some of his unpublished letters to show a little of the breadth and fervour of his interests as a collector, author and minor man of letters.

Wrangham was pictured magniloquently by Dibdin (*Reminiscences* 1836, pp. 392–5): 'The Archdeacon yet continues to woo his muse in his miscellaneous and wide-spreading library. He is yet as rapturous as ever over the charms of BIBLIOMANIA; and stretching himself at length in the Elizabethan chair, in the midst of his *Plantins* and *Elzevirs* – as he sees the last glimmer of day tipping the Cheviot-hill-tops – he exclaims with his beloved Horace,

Sit BONA LIBRORUM et provisæ frugis in annum
COPIA, ne fluitem dubiæ spe pendulus horæ.'

(The hills were Wolds and not Cheviots, but admirers of the Doctor will allow him a little latitude.) Another, less florid description is to be found in the diary of Wrangham's friend and protégé the Scarborough bookseller John Cole (1792–1848: *DNB*), whose autobiographical journal is now Add.MS 153 in York Minster Library. The Archdeacon introduced himself to Cole in a characteristic manner, writing 'I have a great many duplicates of old Books. Would you like to have them? and on what terms?' Cole went out to Hunmanby, where he urged Wrangham to print the catalogue of his library. He was accordingly lent a copy of 'that portion of his Private Catalogue then printed' and was allowed to make extracts. A year later (in October 1823) he went to press with his *A Bibliographical and Descriptive Tour from Scarborough to the Library of a Philobiblist in its Neighbourhood*:

This brought me [Cole wrote in his journal] into intimate connexion with Archdeacon Wrangham, whom I found a man of great taste, and an admirable corrector of the press; indeed, his editorial powers have long been celebrated, being possessed, from his peculiar studies, of that kind of erudite mind, so admirably adapted to the minutiæ of editorship, and grammatical nicety of expression . . . In person Archdeacon Wrangham is very tall, and slenderly formed, with a countenance, if I may so describe it, of classical elegance, very like that of the Revd Clayton Mordaunt Cracherode, M.A., as given in the *Repertorium Bibliographicum*: I mean much of that expression of countenance, not so much a likeness of features. I have heard the Archdeacon preach with much pleasure. Although not eloquent or energetic, there is a captivating sweetness of poetical intonation in his delivery, which seems to proceed from the depth of that source of feeling – the human heart. In his compositions there appears a remarkable conciseness and felicity of expression. In his rich canonicals flowing gracefully round his tall figure, on a Visitation day, the Archdeacon looks, as I have seen him, venerable.

Cole's *Tour* gives a few details of the Wrangham library drawn from the then incomplete catalogue. More importantly it shows how much the bookseller was influenced by Wrangham's taste for restricted editions and coloured tirage: Cole's own writings are protean, but only a few copies of each of his many works were printed.

John Cole's admiration of the Archdeacon's prose style is unusual. Wrangham was celebrated in his own time for a certain elevation of expression which today gives his prose writings an aura of innocuous quaintness. There was nothing bombastic about it, merely a rather self-conscious orotundity. Sydney Smith advised him 'Don't use hard words and say odd things in the pulpit . . . no man respects more your attainments and liberal sentiments than I do – but in words you have peregrinity and sesquipedality.' Wrangham's prospectus for the *General Sea-Bathing Infirmary, Scarborough* (Scarborough 1811: not in Sadleir) is an example:

The Baths will be established in the Lower Town; in order to remove unpleasing objects from the public eye, and to consult economy as well in the rent of the building, as in procuring Water from the Sea. The obtrusion, indeed, of offensive spectacles (which does not, however, appear to have proved any annoyance at Margate) will be guarded against with every possible precaution.

Sometimes his delight in words is bibliographically appropriate. In 1808 he wrote to

Leigh Hunt, on the verge of imprisonment, about *The Examiner*: '. . . I shall be obliged to you likewise for the title-page, preface, etc., as *I* shall assuredly bind you up, whatever the law may do.' A letter congratulating Whewell on becoming a Fellow of Trinity is less happy: 'Of your becoming so, even on your first sitting, there would be little question indeed: but I always rejoice wherever hope is exchanged for certainty. It is for younger bosoms to enjoy the flutter of expectation.' The Archdeacon (as 'a sort of fiddler in verbal criticism') wrote to Archibald Constable pointing out minor defects in the language of *Rob Roy*, and to Lockhart listing inconsistencies or repetitions in *Kenilworth* ('in the prodigality of genius trifles are overlooked'). Yet he urged on William Blackwood the verses of a friend, that they might have 'the advantage of being obstetricated by your skilful hand'. And to John Marshall on his retiring from Parliament in 1836: 'Amid the storms of St. Stephens, the calmest of minds may pardonably be moved from the moderation [of Temper], and passion lead up to an occasional triumph over philosophy.' As Archdeacon addressing Churchwardens, however, he was commendably direct:

Hilston Church. Your *very damp* Church requires ventilation by introducing at least a casement in the chancel window . . . The ivy at the south side must be kept thin, the pews painted, the hatchment at the north side repaired or (better) removed, the chancel which is deplorable, underdrawn;
    A new Prayer Book, folio, for the Minister, and his old one repaired for the Clerk.

Wrangham was a very active ecclesiastical administrator.

One of the most interesting correspondences to have come to light is a packet of Sydney Smith's letters to Wrangham, now in the Fondren Library of Rice University. Smith habitually destroyed all his incoming letters, so the correspondence is one-sided; but it is the largest group of letters to the Archdeacon to have survived, and shows both parties from a pleasing angle. Sydney Smith enjoyed teasing Wrangham, and the letters from Foston to Hunmanby soon develop from stilted professional formalities to a much more humourous relationship in which book collecting is a perpetual theme of mirth. Sydney's well-known advice to Mrs Wrangham was 'If there be a single room which you wish to preserve from being completely surrounded by books, let me advise you not to suffer a single shelf to be placed in it; for they will creep round you like an erisypelas till they have covered the whole'. In his letters, Sydney could wish 'Health and respect, promotion in the Church, rare books, innumerable purchases, laudatory reviews and all other good things to the Vicar of Hunmanby'; or on another collector's downfall, 'I congratulate you upon Ford's bankruptcy (no book collector has any feeling in his own line)'; and in March 1825, 'Poor Parr, Poor Elmsley, Great Grecians are quaking – take care of yourself in these easterly winds'. Much of their correspondence is concerned with clerical business, where Smith found Wrangham an inexhaustible source of intelligence – 'to apologise to you for asking for information is as it were to beg pardon of the cow for milking, or of the pump for taking water from it'. Perhaps he remembered the long list of corrections which the Archdeacon, *more suo*, had sent after Sydney Smith had written his attack on the public schools in the *Edinburgh Review* several years previously. When Lady Copley solicited the Archdeacon's vote in a Cambridge election through Sydney Smith, the intermediary did as requested ('Handsome women are not to be answered by reason'), but he reported that the Archdeacon would probably relish a line from the Attorney General himself. If not, he continued, 'then the avenues to Mr Wrangham's heart are the Granthams, the Duke of Leeds, the Archbishop of York. I have told him (Heaven forgive me) that I have repeatedly seen his Works lying on your table, with an elegant silk string in them, and highly perfumed – that the A[ttorney] G[eneral] and yourself had an insatiable anxiety respecting everything he did, and said – and that I had a sort of roving commission from you to collect his fugitive verse and prose.'

Wrangham sometimes tried to secure copies of Sydney Smith's works from the author. But in 1812 he received a reply to a request for a couple of pamphlets that 'I suspect they are long since hurried away to the confectioner – the season for hot tarts is just over, and few pamphlets have escaped'. And in 1824: 'I should with the greatest pleasure send my Sermon to Mr [Basil] Montague but I have not one single copy left, not if you were to offer me for it Wrangham's Works in 7 vols 8vo – such an exchange as has never taken place since the days of Glaucus and Diomedes. I printed only 250 copies, and the Sermon has received a value from its limited supply, which it never could have done from its merits – something of this nature has been heard of I believe at the Roxburghe Club.'

Wrangham's taste for aristocratic society and his well-known pursuit of the rare in literature made him relish to the full his early membership of the Roxburghe Club. In 1822, soon after his election to Sir Alexander Boswell's place, he wrote to Blackwood that 'Having recently been elected a member of the 31, or Roxburghe Club, I may perhaps tax your friendly nature with a request that you would endeavour to recollect a few books, the *rarest* of the rare, of which a reprint might be acceptable to my colleagues, as I shall be called upon in my turn to present to the Club something of the kind, and have not yet anything of a moderate size in my collection, except indeed Bieston's Bayte and Snare of Fortune [?1550, *STC* 3055], which would suit my purpose'. Wrangham eventually chose Henry Goldingham's *The Garden Plot, an Allegorical Poem, inscribed to Queen Elizabeth* 1825 [Barker 40 and p. 16], an elegant piece of printing, which Dibdin chastised as 'unworthy' in his *Reminiscences*. His strictures provoked a dignified reply from the Archdeacon:

In returning my most heartfelt thanks for the very kind manner in which you have characterized me in many parts of your *highly interesting* volumes, for the suggestion of literary employments so highly flattering to me, and for the friendly honesty of your censure of my poor Garden-Plot, I ought I know to attach a formal disclaimer of all fitness, &c., but it would at once be too formal and too hypocritical for the habits of our intercourse. I will therefore only *meo more* note two or three slight errata in your extracts relative to me which I hope you will soon be called to set right in a second edition.

The Archdeacon was able to hail Sir Walter Scott as a brother 'in one respect at least … in my capacity of Roxburgher'; the kinship became closer when after some anxiety he was also awarded 'the green ribband of British Literature, the Bannatyne Club'. Wrangham was elected in 1828 with Lord Spencer (a fellow-Roxburgher), to whom he wrote in 1829 suggesting his own translation of Buchanan's Epithalamium on the marriage of Mary Queen of Scots for the Club. In the event the poem was printed with a few others at Chester in 1837, a mere by-product of Wrangham's Bannatyne activities: it is dedicated to Scott's memory and to Samuel Rogers. The Archdeacon's election to the Bannatyne probably led to his visit to Scotland in 1829, when he called at Abbotsford. Scott does not appear to have been much irritated by Wrangham's 'formidable visitation', as he commended him warmly to David Laing, the Secretary of the Club: 'I have no doubt that you will contrive to be of use to him when he comes to Auld Reekie he being a worthy brother of the Bannie'. The Archdeacon, for his part, was much gratified by his reception at Abbotsford, writing to Scott at the end of the year that 'we shall ever remember, with perhaps unequalled satisfaction, the journey across the Ettrick, through the woods of Yarrow, to the Newark Tower. They were scenes before all but consecrated in my imagination, and (by an unusual result) they have been exalted in being realized.'

Scott was not his only acquaintance in Scotland. There was William Blackwood, to whose *Magazine* Wrangham contributed much verse in its early years. His letters to Blackwood give details of his publications and characteristically seek small quantities of offprints for himself. For example, he wrote to Blackwood in 1819:

If you would accept a few sonnets closely (and, I hope, not inelegantly) rendered from Petrarch for your Magazine, on condition of throwing me off a dozen copies of each sonnet as a single leaf of pink 4to paper (printed only on one side), which could be forwarded with your monthly packet to Mr Baldwin for me, and could they reach me cheaply and safely I should be glad to send them to you. I have already had 40 printed by Sir E. Brydges at the Lee Priory Press.

Similarly, when his *Pleiad* (Sadleir 46, 67) was being reprinted in Constable's Miscellany, he begged the publisher to send proofs, although the copy was very accurate ('even in the punctuation, about which I am systematically particular'), and remarked that 'Half a dozen or a dozen fine paper copies will be as many as I will trespass upon you for'. Wrangham was as careful a corrector of his own work as of others. When asking Blackwood for a proof he remarked 'I know my own scrawl too well, not to distrust the perspicacity of those who are to read it, even if you have an Argus for a Compositor, and a Lynceus for a Corrector of the Press'.

The Archdeacon's attempts to procure privately printed rarities occupy many of his letters. His relationship with Blackwood as a customer of the bookshop and a contributor to the *Magazine* led to his asking for a copy of the suppressed eight pages of the notorious 'Chaldee MS.' article, 'as needful to the integrity of my set of your Magazines, with which I am highly pleased. I ask this as a ravenous collector.' Six months later, when Blackwood had failed to reply, Wrangham reverted to the point when asking for offprints of a contribution:

If a dozen copies should be thrown off on paper, either coloured or not, as you please, of a 4to, and a dozen of an 8vo size, I fear you would think me exorbitant in my claim of retribution, particularly as I mean to add my *earnest* request for a copy of the Chaldee MS. withdrawn from a former number – as a *Collector* (not to be even shown without your permission) – and for any little trifle you may at any time print a few copies of for private distribution.

There is no evidence that Blackwood complied with this request for the suppressed 'Chaldee' pages, but he might well have been able to appease him at the time of George IV's visit to Edinburgh in 1822, when the Archdeacon asked: 'If any little rarities, or *unpublished* feuilles volantes appear on the occasion of His Majesty's visit, pray remember me: I shall not grudge the carriage of a special packet.'

In 1834 Wrangham wrote to Sir Thomas Phillipps announcing that he had just sent off his Bannatyne voting-paper signed in the baronet's favour. To this blandishment he added:

Being an assiduous, and not unsuccessful collector (though perhaps deemed an importunate beggar) of unpublished works, and knowing Sir Thos. Phillipps' press by reputation, the Archdeacon ventures to solicit a few specimens – if any such remain on hand – and will be happy to make a similar return.

Phillipps obliged, but the Archdeacon could only regret having no MSS to satisfy the other collector, offering only his *Flaminio* (Sadleir 69) instead.

Other friends were put under contribution. James Montgomery's *Whisperer* 1797 was winkled out of him in 1822. William Hone's *Every-day Book* was praised, but the Archdeacon asked suggestively 'Do you throw off any copies on larger paper, or otherwise discriminated?' Sometimes the volumes Wrangham sought had a real literary interest as well as an enticing rarity. A reading of Lockhart's *Life of Scott* in 1839 led him to remark to the author that 'I suppose it will be hopeless' to procure three of Scott's early or privately-printed works. In 1836 he had hinted to Dawson Turner that 'I fear you cannot minister to my capacity as a collector of *unpublished* productions, by procuring me a copy of young Hallam's exquisite volume – it is quite a gem, as far as I had time to examine it at his friend's Milnes Gaskell's'. A year previously, a copy of *The Close of the Eighteenth Century* had evaded the grasp even of so enterprising a connoisseur of prize poems:

Dr. Arnold presents his best compliments to Archdeacon Wrangham, and is sorry that it is not in his power to send him any copies of the Prize Poems of former years at Rugby, as he is not even in possession of any himself. But at the same time he fears that had he been able to send them, they would have disappointed Archdeacon Wrangham's expectations, as Clough's Prize Poem is more than an average specimen of their merits.

Wrangham's predominant (but never exclusive) passion made him one of the principal contributors to John Martin's *A Bibliographical Catalogue of Books Privately Printed* 1834; the Archdeacon's letters survive in an interesting volume of Martin's correspondence in the British Library (Add. MS 37965). Wrangham sent many lists of titles, all in his minute hand, and revised the text of Martin's prospectus in 1830. By January 1833 Martin was able to announce that the volume was 'at length fairly in the printer's hands', and enquired whether a copy of the earliest book he recorded, Parker's *De Antiquitate Eccl: Brit:* folio 1572, existed in York Minster Library. Wrangham replied eagerly, sending details of several more of his own private productions. He was delighted (to the extent of listing 41 errata) when *Martin's Catalogue* was finally published in 1834, and remarked of the large-paper copy he had ordered:

The delight of possessing your beautiful volumes makes me *almost* insensible of Mr Arch's bill, by which they were accompanied . . . I believe however with my family I ought not to indulge in the luxury of large paper copies, and I have hitherto restrained myself in that particular, so that the Magna Chartas which I possess have been (I think with no exceptions) presents. I must make up this prodigality by economy in some other quarter.

Cost was always a serious consideration. He could not be sure whether his nearly complete *Morte Arthur* of 1529 was unique, because (as he wrote to Lord Spencer) 'I have none of the expensive guides to Bibliography, which Mr. Dibdin has so copiously and with so much ability furnished to the *Affluent*. However blessed with *present* competency, a clerical father of six children must restrain his strong desire of possessing such enviable, and alas! by him unattainable volumes'. It was prudence rather than parsimony which led him to use Baldwin of Paternoster Row as agent for receiving parcels. The delivery of catalogues was also a source of alarm, as he reminded Mrs Priestley of St Giles, London, in 1813; her catalogue had cost him 4s 8d by the mails, but sent through Baldwin it would have cost him nothing. ('This he mentions, not only as entitling him to some deduction in the event of his giving an order out of it, but also as a suggestion with regard to the best method of transmitting the catalogue in future.')

In January 1815 he asked William Blackwood for details of some eighty items from his unpriced catalogue of 1812, '*with their lowest prices attached*, it being customary with many London booksellers considerably to lower their charges upon such as, after a certain interval from the circulation of their catalogues, still remain on hand'. A similar request in 1819 remarked that 'as my object in this sequestered corner is rather to have an extensive than an expensive library', only cheaper items were required. For his new books he relied partly on the generosity of Blackwood and others sending him 'friendly enclosures'. He told Lockhart that 'I do, with half a dozen children and the insecurity of professional income (though mine is not, all, of that description) find the purchase of *new* books rather oppressive, and I may truly add, less to my taste than the tattered and dusty old, so that I am obliged to peep at Peter's Letters, &c. in a friend's library'. He was never above giving a strong hint when a complimentary copy was possible.

In February 1816 Wrangham had asked Lord Spencer to frank his letter to 'a very enlightened and intelligent young bookseller', adding 'He has often curious books, at an early age edited a selection from Carew's poetry, indicating no small taste, and has lately published a few numbers under the title of *Bibliographical Memoranda*'. This was John Fry of Bristol (1792–1822: *DNB*) with whom the Archdeacon had been corresponding for some years. Sadleir (Supplement, pp. 429–30) refers briefly to their friendship, adding Wrangham's contributions to Fry's periodical to his bibliography. Over seventy letters from Wrangham to Fry survive in Manchester City Library to show the development of a business relationship into a literary intimacy cut short by the death of the promising antiquarian. They are spiced with the pardonable anxieties of a voracious collector of renowned persistence.

Fry shared many of the Archdeacon's interests and the letters are written to a fellow enthusiast as well as to a practising bookseller. Wrangham bought, and quite extensively, from Fry's occasional catalogues, remarking of one of them that 'I see that Fuller's Worthies stood at £2.10s. That I think I could afford, but I must forbear from the Gulls Hornbook, Cardinal Wolsey's Tracts, and the 1597 Psalms a while longer. The time will come however, I hope, when I may request you to procure for me the Bibliomania, and some of the Bibliographical Guides . . . with some of the many late reprints'. Wrangham asked Fry to be particularly watchful for first editions of Southey ('He is a very great man') – a reminder of his close association with the Lake poets in early life. But the main commercial transactions between the Archdeacon and the Bristol bookseller seem to have been in kind. 'By what line of Canal can I forward my duplicates?' Wrangham asked in 1815, '(upon you I rely implicitly for sending me other books to their value)'. The slowness of forwarding boxes by water, and Fry's failure (usually through illness) to acknowledge them promptly, were frequent annoyances.

Wrangham lent Fry his incomplete copy of Robert Southwell's *St Peter's Complainte* 1636 for use in a reprint. Fry was able to perfect it with spare pages or facsimiles, and returned it much improved in its binding. 'I scarcely recognized my old friend Southwell', Wrangham remarked, 'with his new and very splendid face. For the loan you have more than made amends by the completing of the copy. In every way I am shamefully a profiteer by your kind attentions.' A common interest in books of the period led to Wrangham's sending rather breathless lists of recent acquisitions, few of them as interesting as the *Synonima* of Johannes de Garlandia, 1518, a Wynkyn de Worde of which Fry published a description in his *Memoranda*. Wrangham took a keen interest in these notes, and in their format. Writing in 1815 about the fifth number, he remarked 'I am such a friend to method and uniformity [that] I must take the liberty of protesting against your varying the size of your meditated continuation . . . I am always rejoiced when I find an apparent 12mo, by its signatures, to be a cut down or dwarfish 8vo, if others of that same origin stand on the 8vo shelf. I suppose some expense is spared by reducing the 4to to the lower size, but that to bibliomaniacs is generally I should suspect not a primary object.'

Wrangham in return sent Fry details of his own publications, mentioning his intention to print various items on his (*i.e.* John Cole's) private press at Scarborough, using the specially-commissioned Bewick woodcut of Hunmanby church and parsonage which is characteristic of so many of his volumes. As early as 1815 he mentioned the possibility of producing a catalogue of his library: 'But that must I fear be the work of some distant year, if ever a year of *leisure* is to be mine – and much of bibliographical knowledge remains to be acquired to do some of my volumes justice.' Two years later, Wrangham was still 'dallying with a Catalogue', but only an enumeration 'to guide my intelligent bibliographical friends to some curiosities . . . Even so, the mere aggregation will be in itself a curiosity, which if confined to 50 copies – half for sale – might indemnify me from a great part of the expense. What do you think?' The *Catalogue* was not issued until 1826; few of its 70 copies were distributed.

Quite early in their correspondence the Archdeacon had admonished his young friend 'If at three or four and twenty the health begins to feel the effect of nightly lucubration, it is indeed the first of duties by consulting it to guard against the unavailing remorse of a disoccupied and exhausted old age'. But Fry's health, which often interrupted the correspondence, got worse; he died in 1822. On hearing the news, Wrangham wrote to Bristol: 'From the slight intercourse with him which it fell to my lot to be favoured with, I was greatly impressed by his intellectual powers, and anticipated from his rare union of talent and industry rich and lasting fruits.'

Wrangham himself enjoyed robust health for most of his life. In 1827 a postscript to one of his occasional letters to Wordsworth reads 'I enjoy, thank God, very good health in general. My hair to be sure is gone – but then there is always at the worst, or best, the resource of a wig. The Episcopal one, of course, is out of the question.' Though he never attained the highest ranks, he enjoyed a distinguished clerical career in the northern province, and the close friendship of his metropolitan. It was at Bishopthorpe that Dibdin saw him on his *Bibliographical and Antiquarian Tour in the Northern Counties . . .* (1838, pp. 228–9), when his visit to the Archbishop's seat 'was not a little clouded by the wan and altered appearance of my old friend, Archdeacon Wrangham. We had, however, a good gossip, as well as an animated resuscitation of former times; and if my friend's figure be now inclined at a gentle angle, and his step comparatively hesitating, there were two graceful *woodbines* twining about him, in the character of daughters, to render his appearance the more picturesque.'

Late in life, only a little while before he published *A Few Epigrams: Attempted in Latin Translation by an Old Pen nearly worn to its Stump* (Sadleir 77), Wrangham wrote to William Whewell, now Master of Trinity, offering his adopted college a thousand volumes of tracts from his collection. Characteristically, he fussed over the sending of the catalogue. 'Non sum qualis eram', he had written by an amanuensis (to whom a transcriber must record his gratitude), and it was not until shortly before his death that the College received the books. They are the largest group to have survived intact from the Wrangham collection, which under the terms of his Will was dispersed by Sotheby over twenty days in 1843. The library he assembled was his principal monument and deserves closer attention. As a minor poet in, from and between several languages he has little claim on the attention of posterity. But as a creator and collector of the rare and the curious he is full of interest to the bibliophile, and his extensive correspondence confirms it.

NOTE: I am grateful to the Rt Hon. Earl Spencer for permission to quote from Wrangham letters at Althorp, and to the authorities of the following institutions for allowing me to quote from unpublished MSS in their keeping: The Bodleian Library (letters to Dibdin and Phillipps); British Library (letters to and from Arnold, Hone, Martin and Mrs Priestley); East Riding County Record Office (re Hilston Church); Fondren Library, Rice University (to Sydney Smith); Manchester Central Library (to John Fry); National Library of Scotland (to Blackwood, Constable, Lockhart and Scott); Trinity College, Cambridge (to Marshall, Turner and Whewell); York Minster Library (diary of John Cole). To my friend Mr C. E. Wrangham, owner and improver of the Sadleir collection of Wranghamiana, I am indebted for much helpful advice over many years.

ARTHUR FREEMAN

Harry Widener's Last Books
Corrigenda to A. E. Newton

SOME episodes in the history of bibliophily have assumed for us all, through tale and re-telling, the proportions of folklore or myth. There are Blandford and Spencer pursuing the Valdarfer Boccaccio at the Roxburghe sale, David Casley at the Cottonian burning (or Erostratus at the Alexandrian), the bakings of Betsy, John Warburton's cook, Rossetti and Swinburne at the penny-stall with Omar, the butcheries of Bagford, the parsimony of John Brand, Flaubert's ultimately murderous bibliomaniac, the depredations of Count Libri, the fabrications of W. H. Ireland, Simonides, Vrain Lucas and the masterful Chalon – as well as our personal favourites among finds, failures and miraculous near-misses. Prominent among these remains, no doubt, for most biblio-fabulists, the celebrated tale of Harry Widener's last book: but one may wonder how well the memory of that youthful collector is served by a concoction of fantasy and pastiche which has passed, in its main author's own estimate, as 'in all the history of book-collecting . . . the most touching story'. Story indeed, but given Harry himself dwelling deeply, moodily, from early age upon the testate survival of his name and memory – which a great Library has now ensured – there seems no need to sanction by silence an improbably pathetic and certainly inaccurate narrative of his last acts as collector. And it is scarcely iconoclastic, or even untoward, to set right that sentimental part of A. E. Newton's 'Word in Memory', when the precocious achievement of its subject needs no bookman's bush, no terminal embroidery, nor a moral as trite as it is pointless to the sad accident he suffered.

By now generations of bibliophiles have revelled in the capricious, opinionated, error-fraught and incomprehensibly delightful books-about-books of A. Edward Newton, self-appointed publicist of the escalation, from Hoe and Huth to Kern and The Crash, of book collecting in America (as occasionally in Britain, via or by British). The American Dibdin, for expansiveness, stamina, eccentricity and infectious exuberance – not to say magisterial inanity, categorical false modesty, and wit more like the bludgeon or clenched fist than the velvet glove or Ivory Hammer he so often disparaged – Newton first broke into popular attention with *The Amenities of Book-Collecting and Kindred Affections* (Boston 1918), thirteen personable essays in memoir, nostalgia, and hobby-horse. The last of these is 'A Word in Memory', devoted to Harry Elkins Widener, born 1885 at Philadelphia, died 15 April 1912 on the *Titanic;* its conclusion may be quoted in full:

We lunched together the day before he sailed for Europe, and I happened to remark at parting, 'This time next week you will be in London, probably, lunching at the Ritz.'

'Yes,' he said, 'very likely with Quaritch.'

While in London Harry spent most of his time with that great bookseller, the second to bear the name of Quaritch, who knew all the great book-collectors the world over, and who once told me that he knew no man of his years who had the knowledge and taste of Harry Widener. 'So many of your great American collectors refer to books in terms of steel rails; with Harry it is a genuine and all-absorbing passion, and he is so entirely devoid of side and affectation.' In this he but echoed what a friend once said to me at Lynnewood Hall, where we were spending the day: 'The marvel is that Harry is so entirely unspoiled by his fortune.'

Harry was a constant attendant at the auction rooms at Sotheby's in London, at Anderson's in New York, or wherever else good books were going. He chanced to be in London when the first part of the Huth library was being disposed of, and he was anxious to get back to New York in time to attend the final Hoe sale, where he hoped to secure some books, and bring to the many friends he would find there the latest gossip of the London auction rooms.

Alas! Harry had bought his last book. It was an excessively rare copy of Bacon's 'Essaies,' the edition of 1598. Quaritch had secured it for him at the Huth sale, and as he dropped in to say good-bye and give his final instructions for the disposition of his purchases, he said: 'I think I'll take that little Bacon with me in my pocket, and if I am shipwrecked it will go with me.' And I know that it was so. In all the history of book-collecting this is the most touching story.

The death of Milton's friend, Edward King, by drowning, inspired the poet to write the immortal elegy, 'Lycidas'.

> Who would not sing for Lycidas? –
> He must not float upon his watery bier
> Unwept.

When Shelley's body was cast up by the waves on the shore near Via Reggio, he had a volume of Keats's poems in his pocket, doubled back at 'The Eve of St. Agnes'. And in poor Harry Widener's pocket there was a Bacon, and in this Bacon we might have read, 'The same man that was envied while he lived shall be loved when he is gone.'[1]

The errors in the above lines are no less remarkable than the unacknowledged reflections. Newton has in fact gotten wrong the specific Huth sale, Hoe sale, Harry's presence at the first, his commissions, and even the identity of the 'last' book; he has also appropriated, from the London journalist A. C. R. Carter, Quaritch's remarks ostensibly made to himself, as well as the allusion to Milton and the passage from Bacon – the last unfortunately a kind of howler. Let us simply begin again with the narrative as it might better be told.

The celebrated lost Bacon, *Essaies* of 1598, was lot 386 in the first Huth sale of printed books, begun 15 November 1911 at Sotheby's, and Harry Widener was not really a major competitor at that sale. Neither did he place any commission with Quaritch on the Bacon; and in fact he was back in America when it sold. He had sailed for England in July, following the gaudy first session of the Robert Hoe sale in New York (24 April–5 May 1911) at which he, like many others including Quaritch, came away largely in disap-

---

[1] A. Edward Newton, *The Amenities of Book Collecting* (Boston 1918), pp. 353–5.

pointment.[2] For at the first Hoe sessions emerged the raw power of Henry E. Huntington, bidding through George Smith, who carried away half the sale's value, including the 42-line Bible on vellum, richly illuminated ($50,000 over Harry's grandfather P. A. B. Widener), Daniel's *Delia* 1592 ($3800 over Rosenbach-for-Harry), and the Ashburnham copy of Bacon's *Essaies* 1598, at $1575. This slight duodecimo was reputed at the time to be actually scarcer than the first edition of the preceding year, which it is not, but it does render *Meditationes Sacrae* in English for the first time and is indeed rare if textually unimportant.[3]

Harry arrived in England via the *Amerika* in time only for the August lull, but he would have known what to expect, at best, from the Huth books. In February Quaritch had published and circulated a handlist of 'The Rarer and most Important Books in the Huth Library', and clients of the firm began to make known their ambitions comparatively early. Harry must have viewed the books for the first sessions while in London, but his final allocation of funds to the sale was, as he himself frankly allowed, modest. He may well have spent $25,000 with Rosenbach after the frustration of Hoe, Part One,[4] but when he returned to America his letters to Quaritch[5] speak glumly of 'bad times' and economical measures. Newton, who characterized Harry as 'a man of almost unlimited means', might have been shocked to read that he had 'managed to accumulate £500' for the first Huth sale [Harry Widener to B. A. Quaritch], and that he bid on no more than six or finally seven books. Harry's original desiderata were lots 1 (H. A., *The Scourge of Venus* 1613, £20, lost at £60), 19 (*Academy of Compliments* 1640, £20, lost to White at £26), 109 (a very rare Wynken de Worde, £40, lost to the British Museum at £128), 366 (*A Report of the Truth of the fight about the Iles of Acores . . . betwixt the Reuenge . . . and an Armada of the King of Spaine* 1591, £200, to Quaritch at £300 – but see also below), 448 (Thomas Bancroft, *Epigrammes* 1639, £40, bought at £38), and 502 (Nathaniel Baxter, *Sir Philip Sidneys Ourania* 1606, £15, bought cheaply at £9); but he expressed particular enthusiasm for the Revenge-Azores pamphlet, then not attributed, as it now is, to Sir Walter Ralegh. Adding up his commissions meticulously, Harry noted that they amounted in all to less than £500, but for the Azores pamphlet he would stretch a point: 'Use all your strength on that one book,' he urged Quaritch, although his limit was set nominally at £200.

The one addition to Harry's commissions is slightly puzzling, and almost certainly a last-minute decision. In the Quaritch commission book is entered a £600 bid for lot 292, *The Story of the moste noble and worthy Kynge Arthur* (1557), but while the extant invoice places it in normal sequence, Quaritch records put it in at the end. Quaritch bought it for Harry at £210, over another, earlier commission for Rosenbach of £200, and the possibility does remain that Bernard Alfred found the notion of outbidding one Philadelphian for another especially piquant – for it is by far Harry's largest Huth bid, and bespeaks both urgency and perhaps urging. Rosenbach and Bernard Alfred Quaritch were (by no means surprisingly) convivial friends, but friendship would not at

[2] See the account in Westley Towner, *The Elegant Auctioneers* (New York 1970), pp. 258–80; dates of Hoe sales are variously misreported, notably by De Ricci.

[3] Cf. James Spedding, ed., *The Works of Francis Bacon*, VI (1861), p. 535.

[4] Edwin Wolf II [with John Fleming], *Rosenbach* (New York 1960), p. 74.

[5] Quaritch MSS bound into the firm's record copy of Huth, Part One.

all preclude such a caprice. And it is worth recalling that Rosenbach's first encounter with Quaritch, early in 1907, ended with the latter executing a bid – for Harry's mother, and for Harry, as it happened – on the Locker-Van Antwerp First Folio, which he procured for the record sum of £3600, while the collector was in his last semester at Harvard; later there would also be the matter of a Mazarine Bible for Harry's grandfather from the second Hoe sale.

At all events Harry spent £557 plus commission at the first Huth sale, was billed on 22 November 1911, and paid in full by 13 December. Quaritch had had bigger fish to fry, meanwhile. Bidding through the firm, as if in testimony to its enormous prestige, were American collectors like Beverley Chew, Henry Wagner, W. A. White, H. C. Folger, J. P. Morgan and Widener (Huntington would follow), closer to home Dyson Perrins, St John Hornby, Fairfax Murray, Schwerdt and Osler, the Marchesa di Melzi, Edouard Rahir, and the Bibliothèque Royale de Belgique, Eton, Bodley, and the British Museum. And of course Quaritch himself was active, purchasing for stock among other lots the very 1598 Bacon and its far more costly predecessor of 1597. Almost without pausing along the way to total domination of the sale, Quaritch arranged the disposal by treaty of the entire Shakespeare section (lots 1187 to 1228, although one must note that several unlisted quartos had been ceded to the British Museum earlier) to Alexander S. Cochran of New York, who presented the splendid assembly to the newly established Elizabethan Club at Yale.

Huth Printed Books, Part One, had been Quaritch's oyster, and among his purchases for stock was the Azores pamphlet, lot 366, at £300. As Harry engaged to take this it was transferred into his 'bought' column, with the normal commission of ten per cent. More dramatic were the Bacons, *Essaies* 1597 having fetched the sensational price of £1950, or, as the newspapers delighted to describe it, over £1000 an ounce for the text. Quaritch had had commissions from two eminent American collectors, one of £700 (apparently withdrawn) and one of £30 [*sic*], but his final customer was probably Cochran once more, for the copy is now at the Elizabethan Club with the Huth Shakespeares. And the 1598 edition cost £200, although Quaritch obtained an allowance of £10 from Sotheby's 'as sigs. and catchwords on A3, 6, 7 and 10 are cut into'.[6] Virtually all newspaper accounts of the sale stressed the *1597* cost, and Quaritch was careful to emphasize his purchase of the second edition as well; so *1598* obtained its publicity. Harry Widener did not then buy it, however, and it remained in the Grafton Street stock until April 1912.

Harry's four Huth books were despatched by Quaritch in a tin-lined box via the *Carpathia* – ironically, the vessel first to reach the *Titanic*, on a subsequent crossing. Bernard Alfred's next encounter with the young collector was only three months hence, at the less spectacular second portion of the Hoe sale in New York. Here, in the absence of Huntington himself, Quaritch fared far better than he had previously, taking more than a quarter of the total sold on 8 and 15 January 1912 for $123,000. On home turf Rosenbach may have bid for Harry in the main (certainly the fine set of *The Spectator* came to the Widener Collection that way) but Quaritch did buy one book, Dekker's *Whore of Babylon* (1607), at $860 plus ten per cent, for the same client. And he visited the Wideners before returning to England.

<hr />

[6] Quaritch records, in Huth, Part One, as above.

At Philadelphia Quaritch sold Harry the drawings by Luke Fildes for Dickens's *Edwin Drood* (£300), fleshing out a collection of Dickens which was among the first enthusiasms of the collector. More important, he sold, to Peter A. B. Widener, Hoe's second (paper) copy of the 42-line Bible, which had just cost $27,500 in New York. This latter transaction may again have been one of the complex Rosenbach-inspired split commissions, if it is true, as Rosenbach's biographers assert,[7] that Quaritch turned over a quarter of the 'commission' on this sale. If so Harry knew nothing of it; he wrote to Luther Livingston on 10 March of the *Drood* sketches, tacking on (with strict injunctions that it was still secret) news of the Bible acquired from Quaritch by his grandfather. 'Is it not great?' he asked, wistfully adding, 'I wish it was for me but it is not.' The Bible today lies in a glass case in the Widener Room at Harvard alongside Harry's Van Antwerp First Folio.

If the transaction were a secret among the Wideners, it was not so with Quaritch; for, once more in London, Bernard Alfred informed his journalist friend A. C. R. Carter of its sale: 'I know that you take an interest in Mazarine Bibles. I suppose you know that the one I bought in the Huth Sale is now in Mr. J. P. Morgan's library.

'I thought perhaps you would like to hear the fate of the copy I bought in the Hoe Sale in New York last January. Just before I left America I sold it to Mr. P. A. B. Widener of Philadelphia . . . [16 March 1912].'[8] Now Quaritch was back in London, and Harry was to come: in the same letter of 10 March he had told Livingston, 'I am saving every cent I can for the next Huth sale' – apparently reappraising his failures in earlier Huth and Hoe sessions – 'where I am really hoping to get a number of books . . .'[9] In fact he lost nothing he bid on, eventually, although he did not live to know it. He was going on a brief trip to England, he explained, 'on Wednesday', via the *Mauretania*, to return on 10 April, in time for at least part of Hoe, Part Three, via the *Titanic* on its maiden crossing.

In less than a month in London Harry viewed the books of Huth, Part Two, and made some purchases from dealers' stock in the shops. Among these was, at last, the 1598 Bacon from the preceding November's sale, for which Quaritch charged him £260 – a profit of £70 – on 1 April 1912; Harry took eight other books as well, totalling £361 12s 6d, but the Bacon is marked 'delivered' in the original invoice, and the others were shipped.

However, none of these was in fact Harry's 'last book', nor even his last purchase from Quaritch. Subsequent statements from Quaritch to the Estate list '1 Gibbon's Decline & Fall of Roman Empire [and *Miscellaneous Works*],[10] 1st edition uncut, half morocco, 9 vols. 4to. 1776–1815,' as billed to Harry himself on 11 April at £12. The billing must have postdated the transaction, for the *Titanic* sailed on Wednesday 10 April, but it was certainly not part of the group charged up on 1 April, and the delay of a day or two is not unusual in Quaritch records. Nor could this be, I think, one of Mrs Widener's purchases after the disaster and before the completion of the collection as catalogued, which a subsequent July entry in the Quaritch ledgers (for re-bound George

[7] Wolf [and Fleming], p. 76.

[8] MS in my possession.

[9] MS in the Widener Collection, Harvard College Library. I must thank Miss Martha Shaw and Dr W. H. Bond for their invaluable assistance, as also Messrs E. M.

Dring and P. N. Poole-Wilson of Quaritch.

[10] Cf. *A Catalogue of the Books and Manuscripts of Harry Elkins Widener*, ed. A. S. W. Rosenbach, I (Philadelphia 1918), pp. 215–16.

Meredith first editions) no doubt was. In fact the set of Gibbon is actually the last data-ble acquisition now extant – although one other perished book may have been bought even later, and several lots obtained at auction posthumously (as the result of com-missions from Harry) may claim to be his *very* last books. But I know of no book in the present Widener Collection actually bought by Harry himself and technically owned by him later than these handsome Gibbons – curiously once more the works of a sceptical philosopher and historian.

It is hardly to be imagined, though, that Harry frequented no other shop but Quaritch's during his last weeks in London. In 1939 a London bookseller G. W. Michelmore wrote to the Librarian of Harvard offering a book for sale, with a story behind it. He recalled that 'on the morning of the day upon which the *Titanic* sailed on her first and last voyage, young Harry Widener called at Messrs. J. Pearson, 5 Pall Mall Place, and purchased a tiny duodecimo volume entitled *Hevy news* [i.e., *newes*] [*of an hor-ryble erthquake which was in the Citie of Scarbaria in this present yere of .xlii. The xiii, day of June. And also how that a Citie in Turky is sonke*] . . . I was Chief Assistant to J. Pearson & Co. at the time and interviewed Young Widener. After the purchase of the above vol-ume which he put in his pocket, Mr. Widener asked how long it would take him to get to Euston Railway Station, for his train to Liverpool to catch the boat.'[11]

The book Michelmore describes is a four-leaf black letter pamphlet of 1542 (*STC* 21808), printed by Richard Lant at London, a translation of a German account of an earthquake near Thessaloniki in Turkish Greece. It was the Inglis copy, and had been listed at £70 in a lush Pearson catalogue of *Two Hundred Extraordinarly Important Manuscripts and Autograph Letters* [*sic*] (item 82, then termed unique). Subsequently copies have surfaced in the Longleat library, in a Britwell sale (1919, bought by Quaritch for Harmsworth and now at Folger), and among Sir Thomas Phillipps's residual printed books. The last came via Messrs Robinson to the Widener Room in 1950 as the gift, appropriately, of Harry's brother George D. Widener, Jr and is one of the few serious volumes to have been formally added since the donation of the original books and dedi-cation of the Library. Another might have been the Luttrell-Birkenhead copy of Bacon's 1598 *Essaies*, presented anonymously to Harvard College (and now in the Houghton Library) in 1926.[12]

Michelmore's letter goes on to offer for sale a copy of the German original of this nar-rative, which Harvard already possessed among its extensive holdings from the collec-tion of Count Paul Riant. And so just possibly the tale told was a pitch for the offering, given especially that the train Harry boarded left at 9.30 a.m. – rather early for prelimi-nary shopping – and that its destination was Southampton, not Liverpool (and it there-fore left from Waterloo, not Euston). Nor is there a bill from Pearson for *Hevy Newes* among those invoices presently in the archives of the Collection. But indeed the Inglis copy seems itself to have vanished, and it is finally reasonable to suppose that Harry did buy the book. If so it was a grim last or near-last purchase: one may recall his intense enthusiasm for the pamphlet in the first Huth sale about the sinking of the *Revenge*, and speculate on the direction his library may have been beginning to take.

---

[11] MS in the Widener Collection.
[12] There is an excellent account of *Hevy Newes* by W. A. Jackson, *Harvard Library Bulletin*, VI (1950), pp. 248–50.

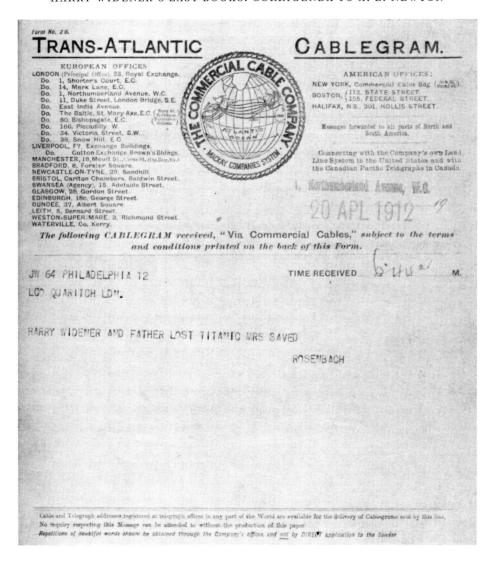

The second Huth sale began on 5 June 1912, seven weeks after the wreck of the *Titanic*, but in Harry's name and presumably upon his instructions before embarkation Quaritch bought no less than 18 lots – in fact every book bid on. Possibly the limits were raised or removed by Mrs Widener, but these were almost certainly Harry's own original commissions and choice of desiderata. Technically the last book bought was Drummond of Hawthornden's *Forth Feasting* 1617, lot 1490. Also in April 1912, at the sale of Lady Ashburton's books, Quaritch purchased to the account of Mrs Widener ten Carlyle association volumes or lots (billed and shipped with the April Huth books on 29 June), which are again most likely Harry's selections. There are however no limits whatever listed in the invoice, and the group cost a stiff £210 plus commission. The last book bought was Carlyle's annotated copy of John Sterling, *Essays and Tales* 1848, at £17 5s 0d.

Had the *Titanic* not sunk, Harry would have arrived in New York in the middle of the third, last, and perhaps the least of the Hoe sales; any commissions before his intended appearance would have been handled by Rosenbach, but we know of no purchases resulting. Wolf and Fleming describe Rosenbach's bidding directly after the disaster as 'listless', due principally to his despondence, and the Caxton *Confessio Amantis* which Harry had wanted went predictably to George D. Smith for Huntington. Later Rosenbach was to supply a major portion of the present Widener Collection to the bereaved mother, at prices which his biographers rather disingenuously excuse as a gesture to grief: 'Mrs. Widener desperately wanted to spend a lot of money for what she bought, and the more she spent the better she liked it . . . if the prices had been half what she paid, she would have been half as pleased, and would have looked elsewhere for books to buy'.[13] Some of the material then supplied might bear excusing as well, but Rosenbach maintained his advisory monopoly and was engaged to prepare a catalogue of the final books and manuscripts. Assistants may have done much of the actual composition, although Dr R. himself provided the preliminary memoir, which gives the first printed form to the 'book in the pocket' detail mentioned by Quaritch in his letter to Carter of 3 June 1912.

And in the process of restructuring a myth it is a pleasure to be able to think the last part of it most likely true, for the anecdote is indeed an attractive one. Rosenbach's 'memoir' of Harry is prefixed to the first volume of the final Widener catalogue, the Robert Louis Stevenson collection, issued in 1913, and it is very much one of Newton's unacknowledged sources. 'We come', writes Rosenbach, 'to the most touching, most pathetic, withal the most glorious incident in the romance of book-collecting . . . [Harry] had purchased from Mr. Quaritch the rare second edition of Bacon's Essays (1598), of which only a few copies are extant. He said he would take it with him, as he did not want to trust it with the other volumes that he had bought. He would keep it in the dispatch box, with which he always travelled. Just before the "Titanic" sank he said to his mother, "Mother, I have placed the volume in my pocket; little 'Bacon' goes with me!" This is surely the finest anecdote in the whole history of books.'[14]

It is difficult to imagine that Rosenbach would falsify or misrepresent a story emanating from the family he was serving with both memoir and catalogue. Either Mrs Widener endorsed that 'finest anecdote' or Rosenbach could never have printed it; indeed she was on one of the last boats lowered from the port side of the sinking vessel, where her husband George, son Harry and Philadelphia friends saw her away.[15] There is no real reason to doubt this portion of the story; one may assume that Quaritch as well heard of it directly or indirectly from the same source by 3 June.

To return to Newton, and the origin of the Widener-Bacon legend: what follows may be anticlimax, but the original myth depends upon it. A. C. R. Carter was a most competent correspondent for the *Daily Telegraph* (London) whose articles on book collecting, auctions and personalities are outstanding in a period much devoted to each. His rela-

---

[13] *Rosenbach*, p. 79.
[14] Widener *Stevenson Collection*, ed. A. S. W. Rosenbach (1913), p. 9.
[15] Cf. conflicting accounts presented by Archibald Gracie, *The Truth about the Titanic* (New York 1913), and other contemporary testimony summed up by Geoffrey Marcus, *The Maiden Voyage* (London 1959); but Gracie, p. 44 and p. 181, is probably dependable in declaring Mrs Widener's boat *not* the last cut from the port side.

tions with the firm of Quaritch, both before and after the death of Bernard Alfred in 1913, were so close as to render him almost an ally in mufti. His own accumulation of letters and clippings survives in part, and contains a great deal to do with the firm and its owners. Nonetheless he is a trustworthy witness and to him Bernard Alfred Quaritch revealed much that he might not otherwise have committed to paper. On 3 June 1912 he wrote thus to Carter:

Perhaps it might interest you to know that Harry E. Widener who was drowned on the Titanic has left his Library to Harvard College ... it includes the Van Antwerp & Locker Copy of the 1st folio. Should you care to see his Catalogue [i.e, the privately printed quarto of 1910][16] I could lend it to you ... Young Widener was only 26 [*sic*] and a very enthusiastic book-collector, with his wealth had he lived he would no doubt have gathered one of the most remarkable libraries in America. He was a most amiable young man & greatly liked by everyone who came into contact with him. Absolutely devoid of side and affectation.

He had the second edition of Bacon's Essays from the Huth Sale in his pocket when drowned ...[17]

Despite the potential fictionalizing of the last observation – which turns out to be substantially likely – Carter absorbed most of Quaritch's communication when he came to write his memorial for Harry, a day later, on the very opening of Huth, Part Two.

The *Daily Telegraph* of 5 June 1912 contains a piece headlined 'An American Lycidas', into which Carter placed both Quaritch's epitomes and some literary reflections of his own:

From Mr. Quaritch's bag in the great Huth sale, the second part of which begins today at Sotheby's, Mr. Harry Widener purchased much. For example, says Mr. Quaritch, 'he had the second edition, 1598, of "Bacon's Essaies," from the Huth sale, in his pocket when drowned.' The pathos of this is irresistible, and one cannot help thinking of the young philosopher reading that essay in which the memorable passage occurs [here Carter quotes from 'Of Death', which however was not contained in the 1598 version of *Essaies*: it appeared first in the 1612 edition, and in the form quoted only in the 1625 final version] ... 'He was absolutely devoid of side and affectation,' said Mr. Quaritch yesterday. Much has been written, and we have aided and abetted, concerning the disposition of American plutocrats to treat the prizes of literature in the terms of steel rails. Harry Widener represented in himself the renascence of the old type of bibliophile, of which even we in England are losing the pattern ... in that essay of Bacon, from which we have already quoted, is a fitting epitaph on this bright American lad: 'The same man that was envied while he lived shall be loved when he is gone.'[18]

Alas, Newton's scissors-and-paste appropriation of Carter's and others' reflections perpetuates not only the very wording, but the errors which might be pardoned in a newspaper journalist's article under a deadline. We find Milton and Lycidas in Carter, Shelley in Rosenbach's preface to the Stevenson catalogue (and the part about the page doubled back if altogether apocryphal), Carter's very own 'steel rails', the letter of Quaritch as

---

[16] Quaritch subsequently presented to Carter the copy of Widener's 1910 catalogue which came with his purchase of Sidney Colvin's library.

[17] MS in my possession; apparently this is the first known statement of the 'pocket' detail, although it must

have derived from another source.

[18] Carter's piece appeared anonymously in the *Daily Telegraph* for 5 June; there is a further word in the same newspaper on 6 June.

quoted by Carter ('side and affectation') presented as is Quaritch had 'once told me' – steel rails and all![19] Rosenbach contributes 'the most touching', 'little Bacon', and perhaps 'the whole history of books'; but it is again Carter who has lent Newton the final quotation from Bacon. And unfortunately so, for 'in this Bacon we might have read' no such words: they are not only from a much later essay, but even in the 1625 version they are expressed simply as 'Extinctus amabitur rerum'. To read Newton's or Carter's epitaph one requires James Spedding's properly bracketed paraphrase-translation, in his still standard edition of Bacon published in 1861 (VI, 380). Perhaps the sentiment is less ostentatiously pious, but one might prefer from an essay actually present in the 1598 duodecimo, 'Of Expence', to substitute the following as *sortes Virgilianae*: 'Riches are for spending, and spending for honour and good actions. Therefore extraordinarie Expence must bee limited by the worth of the ocasion; for voluntarie vndoing may bee as well for a mans countrie as for the kingdome of heauen. But ordinarie expence ought to bee limited by a mans estate, and gouerned with such regard, as it be within his compasse, and not subject to the deceite and abuse of seruants and ordered to the best shew . . .' These are good words for collectors: as a magnanimous but rational collector of books Harry Widener seemed very well to understand them, and to manage his own fortunes 'within his compasse'. And as a collector, a calling which he himself thought both primary and noble, he is best remembered today.

'Too much magnifying of man or matter doth irritate contradiction', says Bacon (1625); so the ultimate achievement and personal reputation of Harry Widener ('absolutely devoid of side & affectation') may deserve from us now something better and hence less theatrical than the ubiquitous 'last' anecdote has hitherto demanded.

---

[19] The tale of Newton's final falling-out with Bernard Quaritch Ltd is recounted by Gordon Ray, 'The World of Rare Books Re-Examined', *Yale University Library Gazette*, Vol. 49 (1974), pp. 109–10.

ALAN G. THOMAS

Solomon Pottesman

WITH the death of Solomon Pottesman, universally known as 'Potty', the world of antiquarian books has lost one of its most learned and eccentric figures. After two years at London University studying philosophy and psychology,[1] he spent a short time in his father's tailoring business, found the life uncongenial, and turned to book-selling. Entirely self-taught in bibliography, blest with an exceptionally retentive memory, he knew the dates and details of scores of thousands of books and had a deep knowledge as to why they were important. This knowledge was at the service of all. Meet him in the street and he could tell you not only the reference books you should consult, but also their shelf-numbers in the British Museum Reading Room. Though, by the time he had finished pouring out information, there was small need for any further research. Long before that book was published, he was a veritable walking *Printing and the Mind of Man*.

With these advantages he could have become one of the leading antiquarian booksellers of his generation but they were sacrificed to the grand passion of his life, the collecting of his own library. This might be described as a 'poor man's Broxbourne Library', for it was his ambition to represent, with as early a book as possible, every town in which incunabula had been printed. 'Inkies', to him. To this end he sacrificed not only all the comforts, but also all but the very minimal necessities of life, living alone in conditions of eremitical austerity. True, he had often to be content with imperfect or battered copies, but these, when he started to collect, more than forty years ago, could be picked up for unbelievably low prices.

With every moment of every day spent ferreting around among old books, Pottesman developed an uncanny power of sensing the presence of interesting printers' waste or early documents hidden under the endpapers of old bindings. Thus he recovered leaves of printing by Caxton and others which differed in setting from the published books, but his greatest prize was 'my Shakespeare discovery'. Francis Meres, writing in 1598, stated that Shakespeare had followed *Love's Labour's Lost* with another play, *Love's Labour's Won*. Scholars have searched for this ever since, but no copy has ever been seen or even recorded. In 1953 Pottesman removed from a copy of Thomas Gataker's *Certaine Sermons* 1637 some sheets from the ledger of Christopher Hunt, a bookseller working in Exeter in 1603, recording his transactions and stock. And there, among other plays by Shakespeare, adjacent to *Love's Labour's Lost*, was *Love's Labour's Won*.

The supreme example of how Pottesman stalked his prey is provided by 'My Oxford

---

[1] In 1960 he privately printed a pamphlet, *Time and the Playground Phenomenon*, and was bitterly disappointed when it passed unnoticed. At the time of his death he was engaged in another venture into psychology.

Book'. One day in the North Library of the British Museum he observed a neophite bookseller examining an early binding, his own property. 'What've you got there?' 'I think this may be an Early English binding.' In a flash Pottesman realized that this was not only an English binding, but that it covered one of the rarest of English incunabula, John Lathbury, *Liber Moralium Super Threnis Jeremiae*, printed at Oxford, by Theodoric Rood, in 1482. It was, indeed, in a contemporary, probably original, Oxford binding of blind-stamped calf over oak boards by Rood and Hunt. Keeping the information to himself, he asked if the book were for sale. No, the bookseller was preparing his first catalogue and this was to be the star piece. How to secure the book without rousing the suspicions of its owner? From then on, once a week, he called and offered modest books for sale, with always the kindly enquiry, 'How's your catalogue getting on?' At last came the day when he arrived to find them stuffing the catalogue into envelopes. 'Oh, so your catalogue's ready. Are the books for sale now? How much for the binding?' '£650.' 'Do you give 10% to the trade?' Pottesman carried off the great prize, though after long reflection he refused to accept the ten per cent. About the same time the inferior Chatsworth copy, in 18th-century calf, sold at Christie's for £9000 and, almost immediately, Pottesman turned down an offer of £15,000.

It must be admitted that all his geese did not turn into swans, and he was a bit inclined to say 'it is certain that . . .', when he should have said 'I hope . . .'. Much of his optimism was lavished upon STC and Wing books containing signatures like Cotton or Mather, which he hoped to connect with the Pilgrim Fathers.

All these books were separately wrapped in brown paper, packed into suitcases and squirrelled away in a series of bank vaults and strong rooms, never seen by anyone except their owner. During certain winters, when there was danger of the Thames overflowing its banks and flooding the underground strong rooms, Pottesman would be in an agony of apprehension. 'Why don't you move them to some high ground, like Highgate', I would suggest. But he never did. His fear of flooding extended to his flat. Fearing that the lavatory cistern might burst and flood his books, he had it disconnected, and flushed the lavatory with a bucket.

No sale of early books was complete without him. At Sotheby's he had his own chair, on the staff side of the table upon which books are laid immediately before being held up for sale. This unique point of vantage often enabled him to snatch a last minute bargain.

Completely uninterested in any book printed later than about 1700 (unless it had promoted a major scientific discovery), it was beyond his comprehension that other booksellers could value works printed in later years. So, with the best of intentions, he endeavoured to ward them off from making purchases which he regarded as ill-judged. Further, when he had secured some prize at auction, his enthusiasm overflowed, and he had to tell a colleague why some apparently insignificant book was so important.

Or, when some incunable was knocked down for several hundred pounds, Pottesman would turn to his neighbour. 'I've got a copy of that. Do you know what I gave for it? Ten pounds, at Hodgson's, and there were two other books in the lot which I sold for twenty pounds.' All this while the wretched bookseller would be trying to follow the sale and might be bidding for some later book which Pottesman regarded with contempt, the *Kelmscott Chaucer*, for example. There was no staving off the torrent of information, so that, more often than not, the *Chaucer* would be knocked down to a less encumbered buyer. Whereupon Pottesman would congratulate his neighbour. 'You had a lucky escape there, you might have been landed with it.' Should the bookseller have persisted against all odds, and secured the *Chaucer*, Pottesman would console him, doubtfully, 'Well, I suppose it will be all right, if you get rid of it *quickly*'.

Exasperation was not confined to booksellers. Sales clerks and auctioneers had to suffer his irritating habit of moving about during sales, and the appalling time it took him to write a cheque: 'I once made a mistake writing a cheque', he would say if reproached.

Pottesman never launched out as a major bookseller. Not for him the tedious side of bookselling – invoices in quintuplicate quoting order number, applications for export licences, providing photocopies, filling in customs declarations, packing and posting, submitting to the inordinate delays of some customs authorities before releasing books and the worse delays of some institutions or governments in paying for them. All this would have taken him away from the books themselves. Booksellers made better customers.

As an example of his offerings, he picked up, somewhere, for about five pounds, a fine copy of the sixth edition (unrecorded by either Sabin or Wing) of *The Bay Psalm Book* 1688. He sold it to me for a little over two hundred, and as item 100 in my catalogue 20, it was snapped up by the John Carter Brown Library.

One day in 1972 I was unpacking my Sotheby purchases when Pottesman turned up. They included a *Horae B.V.M.* printed at Rouen in 1520, which had previously passed through the same rooms in 1930. 'What've you got there?' Before I could examine the book myself it was snatched from my hands. 'Hey, this is interesting, here's a York rubric.' After this had been purchased by the Minster Library, with help from The Friends of the National Libraries, the librarian, Mr. C. B. L. Barr wrote: 'Printed liturgical books of the use of York are not much less rare than manuscript texts, and York Minster Library has been fortunate to secure this copy of the Book of Hours, printed, like several of the other editions, in France. The present copy is apparently the only known exemplar of this 1520 edition, which has not previously been recorded, e.g. by Hoskins or the S.T.C. The book was formerly (Sotheby's, 3rd March 1972, lot 8) identified from the colophon as of English i.e. the common Sarum use (*secundum morem & vsum anglicanum*), but the bookseller Mr. Alan G. Thomas perspicaciously noticed a single rubric (facing fol. i recto) . . . Inspection at York quickly confirmed that the contents are indeed of the use of York . . .' Let me openly confess that these were but borrowed plumes. The 'perspicacious bookseller' was Pottesman.

Pottesman was an unmistakable figure. Indoors or out he never removed his cloth cap. He always wore the same tieless brown shirt, under which, during bad weather, he would strap around his chest two or three copies of *The Times* as protection against the cold. He was invariably festooned with brown paper parcels. The books inside those parcels changed, but the same pieces of ever more creased brown paper and greasy string remained with him for years. It took him ten minutes to unwrap even the smallest parcel, and the same time to reassemble it. All this became more noticeable when, in recent years, security precautions had to be enforced at the British Museum and elsewhere. Queues of frustrated would-be readers waited impatiently behind him. He lived but a

PLATE 1. Solomon Pottesman 1904–78
(*photographed by Keith Fletcher*)

few hundred yards from the Museum and it might have been his private library, so regularly did he haunt it, while during the annual week's closing he was like a lost soul.

Living alone, he became almost totally eccentric, quite unaware that other people had to catch trains, keep appointments, eat regular meals or attend to their own business. The clock, such a hard taskmaster to the rest of us, hardly affected him. The only occasions when he was forced to pay attention to the time was the start of an auction sale and the evening closing of the British Museum Library. He would telephone me at about 1.30 p.m. Knowing that any conversation with him must last at least half an hour I would say:

'Potty, we are in the middle of lunch. May I ring you back?' 'Oh, really? What time is it then? I've only just got out of bed.' Johnson remarks, somewhere, that an actress is no more interested in the rest of a play from which her part has been extracted, than a shoe-maker is interested in the rest of a hide once he has cut enough to make a pair of shoes. The same simile might be applied to Pottesman and everyday life. Entirely wrapped up in his own private world, Pottesman could be a veritable Ancient Mariner. No matter how pressed for time his involuntary listener might be, he would embark at great length, perhaps for the fiftieth time, on 'my Shakespeare discovery'. Tom Thorp recalls that on days when, with only half an hour left before closing time, he still had three important letters to write, Pottesman would come into the shop and nothing on earth would put a stop to the flow of his conversation.

Potty generally came to see me about six in the evening when the bookshops and the auction rooms had shut. This timing saved our friendship. I had finished work for the day and was ready to relax. Armed with a pot of tea or a bottle of wine, I sat back to enjoy his company.

After completing the deal, there would be a flow of information on bibliography, the early scientists, classical authors and the early civilizations of the Middle East. Then comments on those he liked or disliked, heroes such as Dr Scholderer and H. W. Davies, the learned bibliographer and bookseller who had been kind and tolerant to him in his youth. Except for the very elderly or august, his phrase of acceptance was, 'He's a nice boy'. This accolade was especially applied to learned men who had treated him with courtesy. Julian Roberts, then of the British Museum, now Keeper of Printed Books at the Bodleian, was the very embodiment of 'a nice boy'. I was gratified to learn, from his family, after the funeral, that I came into this category. 'Alan's a nice boy'. They were a bit surprised that the nice boy was aged sixty-six.

Finally, after about two hours I would have to say: 'Now, Potty, you really must go, or our dinner will be burned.' He was very reluctant to go. Ahead of him stretched loneli-ness and the squalor of his flat. He smoothed out the creases in his brown paper with glacial slowness. Seeking to delay his departure he would keep saying, 'Let me see, now, what was I going to say'. These tactics continued until the front door was actually opened. Then the hypochondriac took over. 'Shut the door quickly, Alan. Our winters are killers.'

Time and again, over ten years, we invited him to stay for dinner. He might have had a meal, wine if he wanted it, warmth, comfort and welcoming friendship. But he invari-ably refused. It could hardly have been a question of 'kosher', for I have observed him eating in cafes which would have discouraged a goat. His family, to whom he was totally devoted, told me that he would not consent to join them at the dining-table. Right at the end of his life he discovered a home from home, the cafeteria in the newly rebuilt YMCA round the corner from his flat. Saddened by the thought of him sitting alone on Christmas Day (he had refused our invitation to dinner), I rang him from time to time, but received no answer. He had spent all day in the YMCA.

One of his antidotes to loneliness was film musicals from Hollywood's golden age, especially those featuring Jeanette Macdonald and Nelson Eddie. Some bibliophile hap-pened to pass a cinema showing *Blossom Time* when the audience was coming out on a

Monday evening. He was a bit surprised to observe Pottesman among them. It so happened that he passed the cinema on Saturday, and again witnessed the emergence of Pottesman. 'So you've seen the film twice', he remarked. 'No, I've been every night.' Fortunately, he was able to join the Starlight Cinema, under the arches of a railway bridge, a club entirely devoted to musicals. 'I didn't bother to see them when they first came out', he once confided to me, 'but I like them now because they take me back to a less violent age.'

His love of musicals also took him to Ken Russell's eccentric and erotic film on the life of Tchaikowsky. He thought this a bad piece of work. Was he upset, I wondered, by the homosexuality, the sexual intercourse in train corridors or similar incidents with which Russell had packed the film? No. That had all passed over his innocent head. What really riled him was the omission of his favourite symphonies.

Pottesman's interest in music was very real. He was a brilliant pianist and, as a young man, had seriously considered earning his living as a musician. But, he decided, quite rightly I am sure, that the emotional strain and the difficulties of the profession would prove too much for his nerves. Few of his bibliographical acquaintances knew of this talent. One day Jacques Vellekoop went to live in Bedford Court Mansions, where Pottesman's flat was situated. Pottesman observed Jacques's splendid concert grand, originally made for Irene Scharrer, being moved in. 'That's a nice piano you've got, Mr. Vellekoop, I'd like to have a go on that.' 'Well, come up and have a drink and try it.' Pottesman sat for ages on the piano stool. 'I'm very rusty. I haven't owned a piano for fifteen years. When we inherited auntie's furniture there wasn't room for my piano, so Mummy made me sell it.' Whatever Jacques was expecting to hear, he was amazed when Pottesman broke into a brilliant rendering of Chopin's Ballade in A Flat. Then, 'I love Mozart, too, Mr. Vellekoop.' And so on, for over an hour.

Happily, until the last eighteen months of his life, Pottesman enjoyed uninterrupted good health. This did not prevent him from being a hypochondriac, perpetually anticipating the return of minor ills which had occurred decades before, or further effects from the fall he had suffered during the blitz. During his last stay in hospital it was agony to observe him, he was so shrunken and withdrawn. He spoke in a croaking whisper that was hard to understand and, for the first time ever, with me, he was irascible. Worst of all, he seemed to have lost all desire to live. 'They can't keep me here, can they? I want to die at home, among my books.' He told me the name of the book which first recorded the disease from which he was about to die. And then, for the last time, I saw that big smile spread across his drawn face. 'I've *had* that book.'

In an attempt to renew his interest in life, after important sales I used to take the catalogues and read them to him, including prices and buyers, while he commented. Just at this time I had the good fortune to buy the Pforzheimer copy of the Fust and Schoeffer *Durandus* 1459. 'That was a good buy. Do you know what's important about that book?' I trust it will be believed that I had not paid twelve thousand pounds for a book without knowing something about it, but to encourage him I pretended not to know. 'You *ignoramus*. Nobody who is so ignorant should be allowed to own so important a book.' Then, for the last time, if only in scarcely audible whispers, I heard him launch forth into bibliographical expertise.

Shirley, my wife, had written him a cheering letter, recalling how, when the 18th-century collector, Isaac Gossett, lay stricken with illness he was miraculously restored to health by the mere sight of one volume of the Pinelli copy of the *Complutensian Polyglot* on vellum. Following this I lugged the heavy folio *Durandus* (all copies were printed on vellum) round to the Middlesex Hospital. Pottesman was too weak to handle it himself. 'Show me the illuminations', he said. I turned the pages while he distinguished the printed from the pen-drawn decoration. I lifted his fragile hand and laid it on the vellum page. But, alas, the days of bibliographical miracles, it seems, are over. That was the last time I saw him conscious.

The next evening, Saturday 1 July, I called again, but he was sleeping. The thick white hair, which he had hidden for so long under his cap, was like snow. His face was suffused with serenity. I crept away. Shortly after I left, his devoted niece, Ruth, arrived, and they had a little conversation. Next morning, about three a.m., he died in his sleep.

In the whole history of the antiquarian book trade there can have been no man who caused so much exasperation, who, time and again, drove his colleagues to the point of explosion. Yet it is surely a tribute to the warmth of his unforgettable character, to his learning, to his enthusiasm, to his almost childlike sincerity and integrity, that those who knew him best, those who suffered the more frequently, are those who miss him most and mourn him most deeply today. It is touching to observe that, during his last illness and since his death, no other bookseller, however eminent, however crowded the room, has ventured to sit in Potty's chair.

POSTSCRIPT. Since the above was written, Sotheby's have held their first sale of the Pottesman library, Incunabula and 16th-century Books, 15–16 Oct. 1979. The total realized was £195,448. (There will be further sales.) While preparing the catalogue the Hon. William Ward made a remarkable discovery. Examining the Oxford Lathbury, 1482, he noticed that vellum sewing-guards inserted in the middle of each quire consist of lateral fragments in three typesettings of John Kendale's Indulgence, licensed by Sixtus IV, to raise money for the defence of Rhodes against the Turks: one of 21 lines (only about 18 words of approximately 280 are missing) was printed by Caxton in 1480, and hitherto known only from two fragments at Trinity College, Cambridge, no. 207 in Duff's *Fifteenth-Century English Books*; a further 3½ lines (of 17) were printed at London by Lettou, 1480, also only known by a single copy BL, Duff 208. And finally, 4½ lines printed by Caxton (in type 4 as in Duff 207) *hitherto unrecorded*, probably printed not much before or after what has been called up to now his second edition of 1480. The book (purchased by Quaritch for £25,000) therefore contains material printed by the prototypographers of Westminster, London and Oxford.

It is ironic that Pottesman, the master of the hidden fragments, should have kept this book (in his private strongroom below Harrods) for nine years without being aware of this exciting aspect. Had he kept it at home, poring over it, sooner or later, he must have realized that his most treasured volume was greater than even he had hoped.

GEOFFREY KEYNES, KT.

'To the Nightingale'
Perhaps an unrecognized poem by William Blake

TO THE NIGHTINGALE

Come lovely Chantress of the lonely Bow'r
(Allured by vernal airs to chequer'd shades)
And lightly sit upon the moss grown tree,
Near where the dark stream glides, and the soft flow'r,
Rears its enamel'd head to grace the glades;
Come there and wildly pour thy mellow Minstrels'y.

And I with open ears will drink thy Song,
With cautious trembling steps advancing near,
Chiding the low hung boughs that bar my way,
Then gently stretch my weary limbs among
The Fern, and part the woodbine shoots, and peer
About to find thee perch't upon the bending spray.

O then begin thy undulating note,
Check't by faint Echos from the distant grove,
And oft recall the sweetly wandring air;
Till, bursting forth, the jolly peal shall float
upon the Breeze, and tell a tale, to move
Bald Apathy, or smooth the wrinkled brow of Care.

And may no Hind thy secret haunt disclose,
Or wanton Heifer near the thicket stray,
Rudely to break thy song, thy breast affright;
But whilst Attention hears thy gentle lay,
Soft Eve advance, clad in Her mantle gray,
And Cynthia's silvry beams illuminate the night.

THE relations of William Blake with the virtuoso, George Cumberland, have been under close scrutiny in recent times by Professor G. E. Bentley of Toronto University and myself. We both made a detailed survey of the Cumberland papers in the Manuscript Department of the British Library. Professor Bentley extracted for his volume, *Blake Records*, Oxford, 1969, all Cumberland's references to Blake in his letters. I had gathered my material for a general account of Cumberland's relations with Blake during both their lives. This was published in THE BOOK COLLECTOR, Spring 1970, and was reprinted with revisions in my *Blake Studies*, Oxford 1971. I had already pointed out in my *Bibliography of Blake*, New York, 1921, the probability that the two men had met as early as 1784 because of a reference in Blake's satire known as *An Island in the Moon*, assigned to this year. It was, indeed, most likely that they had become acquainted by attendance at the *salons* of the 'bluestocking' Mrs Mathew, wife of the Revd A. S. Mathew, frequented also by Blake's friends Flaxman and Stothard.

Blake no doubt told this circle of acquaintances about the poems he had written as a boy and it is reported that he would sometimes sing his songs to the assembled company, who were delighted, and Flaxman, with a few others, collected enough money to cover the cost of printing a small edition of a selection. The consequence was the production of *Poetical Sketches*, perhaps fifty copies being given to Blake to distribute as he wished. Between twenty and thirty copies are known at the present time to have survived, a few being found among his effects after his death in 1827. Blake rather unkindly repaid his friends by satirizing them in *An Island in the Moon*, though there is no evidence that they ever saw it. The manuscript survived and about the year 1880 came through the hands of Samuel Palmer's son, Herbert, to the Rossettis and so to Mrs Gilchrist, widow of Alexander Gilchrist, Blake's biographer. Mrs Gilchrist did not appreciate Blake's sometimes coarse sense of humour and is thought to have destroyed the two or more leaves now missing from the manuscript, which as a whole is of great interest to Blake scholars for its literary content, having early drafts of several of the *Songs of Innocence* and other fragments. It has another value in the present context in the opening sentence on the leaf following those that are missing.

This begins:

—them illuminating the Manuscript.
'Ay,' said she, 'that would be excellent'.
'Then', said he, 'I would have all the writing Engraved instead of printed, & at every other leaf a high finished print – all in three volumes folio – & sell them a hundred pounds apiece. They would print off two thousand'.[1]

In this passage Blake seems to be laughing both at himself and at foolish talk coming from George Cumberland. This concerned Cumberland's own proposal in a letter to his brother, Richard Denison Cumberland, dated 3 January 1784, and later published in Henry Maty's *New Review and Literary Curiosities and Literary Intelligence*, 1784, vol. vi, p. 318 (reprinted in the first edition of Mona Wilson's *Life of Blake*, Nonesuch Press, 1927, pp. 318–19). He had first mentioned 'multiplying copper plates' in a letter to his brother of 29 September 1783. In January 1784 he wrote again:

The occasion of my writing today is to send you the enclosed specimen of my new mode of Printing – it is the amusement of an evening and is capable of Printing 2000 if I wanted them – you see here one page which is executed as easily as writing and the cost is trifling, for your copper is worth at any rate near as much as it cost, besides you are not obliged to print any more than you want at one time, so that if the work dont take you have nothing to do but cut the copper to

---

[1] *Complete Writings*, ed. Keynes, p. 62.

pieces or clean it – but if it does you may print 4 editions, 2000 and then sell the Plate as well – all this can only be read with the help of a looking glass as the letters are reversed – I know that would be none to you or to anyone who reflects and knows that glasses are always at hand – but it will be none *to the crowd* by and by, for we may begin with printing Debates of great news and then they will condescend to the Mirror for information and so discover there is no trouble; however we have a remedy for this defect also, for in printing 20 we can have 20 more right by only taking the impression while wet, in fact this is only etching words instead of Landscapes, but nobody has yet thought of the utility of it that I know of. The expense of this page is 1/6 without reckoning time which was never yet worth much to authors and the copper is worth 1/6 again when cut up. In my next I will tell you more and make you also an engraver of this work – til then keep it to yourself. (BL, Add. MS 36494, f. 232)

With this letter Cumberland enclosed a print of an anonymous poem entitled 'To the Nightingale', either written backwards on copper as any professional engraver was able to do, and then printed so that it was reversed for ordinary reading, or made as a counter-proof from a print taken from a copper plate on which the poem had been written forwards.

In his paper in Maty's *New Review* entitled 'New Mode of Printing' Cumberland had written:

It had long been considered by the author of this paper, in the course of his practice of etching on copper, that a new mode of printing might be acquired from it by writing words instead of delineating figures on plates. As this is in the power of almost every man, it requires only to know the facility with which it may be accomplished for it to be generally practised.

The inventor in January last, wrote a poem on copper by means of this art, and impressions of it were printed by Mr. Blake, in Exchange-alley, Cornhill, which answered perfectly well, altho' it had cost very little more time than common writing. Any number of impressions, in proportion to the strength of the biting in, may be taken off.

This is followed by an account of the ordinary process of etching of which Cumberland called himself the 'inventor'. The mention of 'Mr Blake in Exchange-alley, Cornhill' as printer of the plate introduces an element of confusion. The address was that of William Staden Blake, a journeyman engraver known to have been working in Exchange-alley. But did Cumberland really mean this individual as being the printer? Perhaps he made a mistake through knowing both Blakes. His letters were sometimes very carelessly written. It was William Blake, the artist, who was more likely to be interested in Cumberland's 'invention'. Soon afterwards, in the early 1790s he was giving Cumberland much help in making the plates to illustrate his poems and for his *Thoughts on Outline* 1796, and was executing inscriptions on his etched plates, Cumberland not being able to write backwards on copper. If Cumberland had himself etched the specimen print sent to his brother, it must have been a counter-proof made on the rolling press of one or other of the two Blakes.

There is no evidence that Cumberland ever used the method he claimed to have invented for making a larger number of copies of any document.

In August of 1979 Professor Robert Essick of the University of California was working on my collection of Blake's engravings and, after looking at the print of the

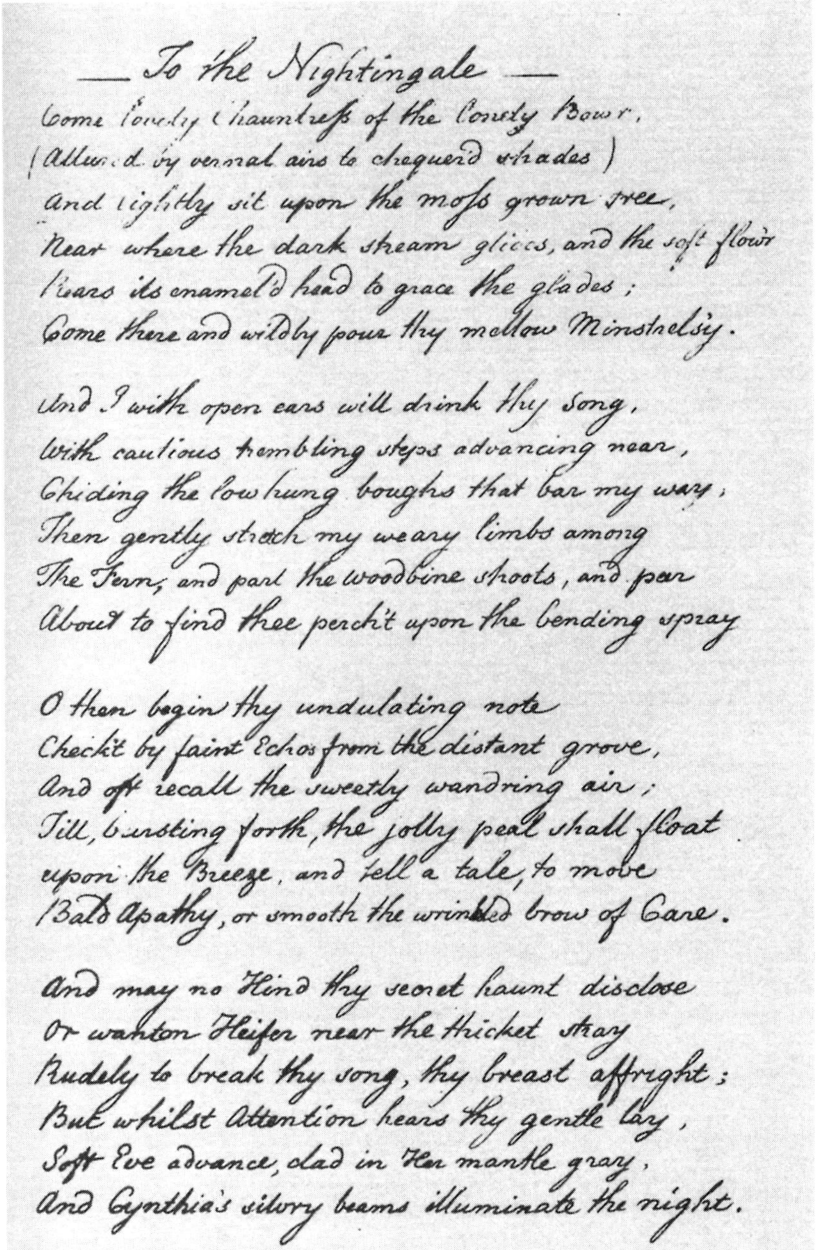

_ To the Nightingale _

Come lovely Chauntress of the lonely Bow'r,
(Allur'd by vernal airs to chequer'd shades)
And lightly sit upon the moss grown tree,
Near where the dark stream glides, and the soft flow'r
Rears its enamel'd head to grace the glades;
Come there and wildly pour thy mellow Minstrelsy.

And I with open ears will drink thy Song,
With cautious trembling steps advancing near,
Chiding the low hung boughs that bar my way;
Then gently stretch my weary limbs among
The Fern; and part the woodbine shoots, and peer
About to find thee perch't upon the bending spray

O then begin thy undulating note
Check't by faint Echos from the distant grove,
And oft recall the sweetly wandring air;
Till, bursting forth, the jolly peal shall float
upon the Breeze, and tell a tale, to move
Bald Apathy, or smooth the wrinkled brow of Care.

And may no Hind thy secret haunt disclose
Or wanton Heifer near the thicket stray
Rudely to break thy song, thy breast affright;
But whilst Attention hears thy gentle lay,
Soft Eve advance, clad in Her mantle gray,
And Cynthia's silvry beams illuminate the night.

PLATE 1. 'To the Nightingale', etched by Cumberland 1784

Nightingale poem, remarked on the close resemblance in the style of the script to Blake's hand in both manuscript and copperplate examples. When I examined the print myself, I was bound to admit that he was right. For many years I have possessed two scrap-books containing collections of prints by Cumberland, the larger one having on the fly-leaf the small bookplate engraved for him by Blake just before his death in 1827. Cumberland had evidently made this collection himself; the smaller one is signed by a member of the Cumberland family soon after the death of the elder Cumberland, and again has a print of 'To the Nightingale' pasted inside the cover.

The copper-plate hand of the later eighteenth century was conventional and it is difficult to judge with certainty the authorship of any particular example, but the resemblance of the Nightingale text to Blake's hand is very striking, especially in the writing of his prose pieces 'Woe cried the Muse' and 'Then she bore pale desire' ascribed to 1788 or earlier. This applies to both the capital letters and to the lower case letters such as d and r, both occurring in two forms. It might have been written out by William Blake in January 1784 to shew Cumberland how easy it was to do, though it did not solve his difficulty in writing on copper backwards unless the prints were counter-proofs. In the opinion of Mr Iain Bain all three prints (two in my collection, one in the British Library) are counter-proofs. All of them have deeply impressed plate-marks, but this does not exclude their being counter-proofs, which are made by placing a second sheet of paper on the wet print and passing it again through the press without removing the plate, so that the plate-mark will appear again on the second sheet.

When I began to read the poem again with proper attention to its style of composition, I suddenly became aware that it gave me a strong impression of belonging among the pages of Blake's *Poetical Sketches* 1783, although it had not found a place there. Both style and language suggested Blake's juvenilia, and though the subject was conventional in its many Miltonic echoes, the cheerful rather than melancholy tone, with its reference to 'the jolly peal', was unconventional. The verses were not to be found in any of the obvious possible sources.

The six-line stanzas of 'To the Nightingale' have a rhyme sequence of abc/abc. It can perhaps be presumed that Blake arranged the poems in *Poetical Sketches* in chronological order. The first seven have no rhymes at all, but those that follow exhibit a variety of rhyming modes, shewing that the young poet was experimenting in this and other irregular forms, even making variations in the number of lines in the stanzas of a single poem. There is none with a rhyming pattern similar to that in 'To the Nightingale'.

I confess with shame that I have possessed the prints of 'To the Nightingale' for many years without having thought about the author of the poem, but I have not concealed it, having reproduced it in my article on Cumberland in 1970. No one has until now come forward with the suggestion that it should be added to the Blake canon.

It has to be remembered that if the print were proved to be a counter-proof, then it must have been written by Cumberland himself, since he was incapable of writing backwards. As already stated, this question was settled by Mr Iain Bain, an expert in the making of copper-plate prints. By measuring my two prints he shewed that the impressions were in slightly different positions on the paper in relation to the plate-marks, proving thereby that the prints were counter-proofs and that therefore the etching had been done by Cumberland. This was confirmed by Mr Nicolas Barker, of the British Library, who made a close examination of the Cumberland manuscripts in the Library and came to the conclusion that the formal hands of Blake and Cumberland were very much alike and not easy to distinguish, but that the writing of my print was more like Cumberland's hand than Blake's. The print accompanying Cumberland's letter to his brother was exactly the same as my two and was a counter-proof.

These conclusions all agree with Cumberland's statement that he wrote the poem on copper and that one or other of the Blakes made the counter-proofs on a rolling press. If the author of the poem was William Blake, then Cumberland presumably possessed the manuscript from which he copied.

These circumstances do not give rise to any difficulties concerning the possibility of Blake's authorship. It may be supposed that the choice of poems included in *Poetical Sketches* was primarily Blake's own from among those written during his boyhood and adolescence. It is known that the printing was arranged for him by his friends, whose opinions may have been sought, and it was certainly they who gave the collection to the printer. The note printed on the first leaf apologizing for 'the irregularities and defects to be found on every page' would not have been included by Blake himself. Cumberland was very likely to have been one of the friends from meeting Blake at the house of the Revd A. S. Mathew. The manuscript of a rejected poem such as 'To the Nightingale' (perhaps regarded as too conventional a subject) could easily have remained in his possession, though afterwards lost, since it is no longer to be found among the Cumberland papers.

The circumstantial evidence concerning the origin of the poem does not offer any impossibilities in attributing the authorship to William Blake, but is it impossible to exclude Cumberland himself? He was not afraid to try his hand at writing poetry and published two poems, illustrated with a few of his own etchings, in 1793. One of these, entitled *Lewina the Maid of Snowdon*, does not offer anything comparable with the copper-plate poem now under consideration, but the other, *A Poem on the Landscapes of Great Britain*, does have a relevant passage (pp. 6–7)

> How sweet it is to mark the deep'ning shade,
> By varying forms enchantingly display'd.
> The ancient trunk, low stooping to the ground,
> By the blind ivy clasp'd in volumes round;
> The graceful bandage of the pendant vine,
> The waving cypress, and the nodding pine;
> The lime sweet-scented, or the holly bright,
> The tow'ring poplar trembling at her height;
> But most the oak's broad venerable head
> Affords my soul a pleasure mix'd with dread;
> In spring the nightingale's belov'd retreat,
> In summer pleasant, as in autumn sweet.
> Ever the refuge of the weak and fair,
> The painter's idol, and the prince's care.

There foxglove's purple spires surround each root,
There the pale eglantine projects her shoot,
Whose blushing tints with softest union meet,
In ornamental neatness simply sweet;
Above, in flaunting circles loosely born,
Th'aspiring honeysuckle crowns the thorn;
Like a gay mistress, innocently bold,
She woos his straggling limbs with wanton fold;
Whilst the dark ivy fring'd, and moss-clad vine,
Grasp the distorted trunk with snaky twine.
At our first step, the solitary jay
Shoots thro' the glades, and thrids the wiry spray;
Nor aught is heard but songs of birds around,
And silence reigns for voice of human sound;
Save when the ploughboy, with provincial squeal,
Calls the stray cattle from their sav'ry meal.

and so on – and on for many pages. I do not believe that it is possible to attribute 'To the Nightingale' to Cumberland. I can offer this opinion with confidence and with the suggestion that there may have been some influence operating in the opposite direction. Yet I do not have any great opinion of myself as literary critic, and have therefore sought the help of academic opinion in various quarters, hoping to find support for my valuation of 'To the Nightingale'.

My first appeal was to Dr Michael Phillips of Edinburgh University, himself a close student of Blake. He was greatly interested and thought I was probably right in making the attribution to Blake, who would have composed it while writing his other juvenile poems printed in *Poetical Sketches*. He began a search for the poem in other possible places, but did not find it. He examined among works by earlier poets, *Lyric Poems* by Philip Ayres, 1687, and *Miscellany Poems* by Anne Finch, Countess of Winchelsea, 1713, but was not able to suggest that these writers could have even influenced the author of 'To the Nightingale'. Dr John Beer, of Peterhouse, Cambridge, well known for his Blake scholarship, was inclined to support my attribution and drew attention to the carrying over of a phrase from one line to the next, such as *peer/about* and *float/upon* in 'To the Nightingale', and finding that Blake had used the same mode in many instances in *Poetical Sketches*. Apart from mannerisms of this kind he was much struck by comparison of the poem with Coleridge's 'The Nightingale' of 1798. Not only are there many echoes of 'To the Nightingale' in Coleridge's lines, but he also draws attention in a footnote to his having quoted Milton's description of the nightingale as:

'Most Musical, most melancholy' bird,

following with his own exclamation

A melancholy bird! Oh! idle thought!
In nature there is nothing melancholy,

following up his argument with a reference to 'the merry nightingale'. Most poets have followed Milton in regarding the song of the nightingale as 'melancholy', whereas the writer of 'To the Nightingale' has the lines:

> Till bursting forth, the jolly peal shall float
> upon the Breeze, and tell a tale to move
> Bald Apathy, or smooth the wrinkled brow of Care.

Dr Beer then wonders whether Coleridge could have seen the poem printed in some place not yet discovered. So wide a search has now been made for the source of the poem that this seems to be very unlikely indeed. On the other hand we have no knowledge of how many copies of his counter-proof print Cumberland may have circulated. It could have happened that Coleridge saw one in 1784 or later and so have adopted the same attitude.

Having quoted these lines from 'To the Nightingale' I may draw attention to what I regard as the strongest possible evidence in favour of Blake's authorship, namely the phrase 'Bald Apathy', a most unusual conjunction of words with characteristic capitalization. Blake might have had in his mind the figure of Tiriel, the old bald-pated tyrant, whose name was given to the earliest of the illustrated poems, never carried to completion. In the remainder of the line the words 'smooth the wrinkled brow of Care' are almost repeated in a phrase found in the prose piece of about the same date, 'Then she bore pale desire', where Blake wrote: 'Care sitteth in the wrinkled Brow'.[2]

In this context it should be noticed, as corroborative evidence of Blake's authorship, his use of the phrase 'jolly peal'. He repeated the epithet *jolly* three times in *Poetical Sketches*: twice in 'To Autumn' ('And tune thy jolly voice to my fresh pipe', and 'Thus sang the jolly Autumn as he sat'), and once in 'Song' ('And the jolly swain laughs his fill'). Thereafter he used the word only in association with Chaucer's 'Jolly Company' in *A Descriptive Catalogue* and elsewhere. In his poetical writings he substituted 'jocund' three times and 'merry' no less than thirty-six times.

Dr Roger Lonsdale, of Balliol College, Oxford, who has an exceptional knowledge of occasional poetry, reported that he did not recognize 'To the Nightingale'. He drew attention to Joseph Warton's poem with the same title from his *Odes on Various Subjects* 1746, of which he enclosed a copy. Its possible relation to our poem both verbally and in content justifies its being quoted here:

> O Thou, that to the moonlight vale
> Warblest oft thy plaintive tale,
> What time the village-murmurs cease,
> And the still eve is hush'd to peace,
> When now no busy sound is heard
> CONTEMPLATION's favourite bird!
>
> Chauntress of night, whose amorous song
> First heard the tufted groves among,
> Warns wanton MABBA to begin
> Her revels on the circled green,

---

[2] *Complete Writings of Blake*, ed. Keynes, Oxford, 1978, p. 42.

When'er by MEDITATION led
I nightly seek some distant mead;

A short repose of cares to find,
And sooth my love-distracted mind,
O fail not then, sweet PHILOMEL,
Thy sadly-warbled woes to tell;
In sympathetic numbers join
Thy pangs of luckless love with mine!

So may no swain's rude hand infest
Thy tender young, and rob thy nest;
Nor ruthless fowler's guileful snare
Lure thee to leave the fields of air,
No more to visit vale or shade,
Some barbarous virgin's captive made.

Blake was so well read in poetry even in his youth that he would certainly have been familiar with Warton's verses and, in his mood of making pastiches and 'imitations', with his mind wide open to Warton's influence. Dr Lonsdale feels inclined to place 'To the Nightingale' midway between Warton's and Keats's poems on the same subject.

Professor John Holloway, of Queen's College, Cambridge, author of a critical study of Blake's juvenilia,[3] agreed that 'To the Nightingale' recalled to him Blake's *Poetical Sketches*; it seemed to possess what he would call 'Blake's quality of apprehension and to be, indeed, a quite beautiful piece'.

Having received so much encouragement from these academic sources, I now wish to confront a wider field of comment with the proposition that 'To the Nightingale' is most probably a rejected poem from William Blake's repertory considered for inclusion in *Poetical Sketches* in 1783.

I should add that obvious sources of information, such as Miss Crum's 'Index of First Lines' in the Bodleian Library and Granger's *Index* have been consulted. I have searched myself through the contemporary volumes of *The Monthly Magazine, or British Register*, containing a great amount of the minor verse printed over the relevant period. A Japanese scholar, Toshihito Sato, has searched through the pages of forty other contemporary magazines, reviews and miscellanies without result. It is remarkable that the poem was not included in William Allingham's *Nightingale Valley, a Collection, including a Great Number of the Choicest Lyrics and Short Poems in the English Language* 1860. It seems unlikely that Allingham would have missed so good a poem if it had been printed in any easily accessible volume.

It seems to be unlikely that any documentary proof of Blake's authorship of the poem will ever be found. Its authenticity must rest on critical opinion.

---

[3] (Studies in English Literature) *Blake the Lyric Poetry*. Edward Arnold (1968).

'Munby Ltd'

I T is fifty years since I first met Tim Munby. I suppose that I could, if need be, fix the exact date, as it was the first day of the Michaelmas term at Cambridge in 1932. As a scholar I was given rooms in College at King's and on my staircase there were two other Freshmen, both from Clifton. I went upstairs to make their acquaintance and there I met yet another Cliftonian, whose breezy cheerfulness and erudite humour appealed to me immediately. Soon we were fast friends and Tim, who was in digs, adopted my room as his base in College – even to setting up his last there when, in a fit of economy, he decided to mend his own shoes. His hammering and singing, like one of the Seven Dwarfs, was not conducive to my studies, but luckily it was a craze that did not last long.

More importantly, he left his books in my room, including the latest treasures that he had picked up at David's and the other antiquarian bookshops of Cambridge. For he was already a keen and knowledgeable book collector and his tales of his adventures in the dark and dusty cellars of Bristol (the scene of one of the most sinister tales in his book of ghost stories *The Alabaster Hand*) fascinated me. At that time we were both reading Classics and I remember him working on an early edition of Herodian with manuscript notes in the margins that he thought might be by the great Stephanus. But his real interest was in the obscurer English poets of the 18th century and he soon infected me with his enthusiasm. At first I tried to stand out for the Classics, and a Leyden Martial of 1661 and a little Amsterdam Lucan 1712 still lurk somewhere on my shelves. But I could not long resist the lure of those quarto poetical pamphlets, so delightful to look at and handle as well as to read, with their wide margins and clear print, their sharp wit and delicious absurdity. I became, and have remained ever since, a devoted collector of English 18th-century verse.

It was typical of Tim's generous spirit that he welcomed this trespasser in his own field and our friendly rivalry only brought us closer. We made a pact that we would always go *together* to David's shop on Friday morning, when the old man unpacked the lots that he had bought at Hodgson's the day before; and the same applied to our Saturday visit to his sixpenny stall in the market. As the eager crowd hovered each Friday over the tea-chests from which David was pulling and pricing book after book, the excitement was intense. We all knew his secret code and anything that he marked from 'g/–' to 'o/l' would be snatched from his hands, as this was within our price range (1/– to 2s 6d). I remember a tug-of-war between Tim and the Public Orator, T. R. Glover, over some particularly choice item and on another occasion we went outside and tossed a coin for Gay's *Poems* 1720, quarto. (I won and still cherish this shabby volume.) Tim also introduced me to the London booksellers and we conducted many an exciting raid on McLeish's in Little Russell Street or David Low's in Cecil Court or, best of all, Frank Norman's in Whitfield Street, where we would plunge into the dusty cellar and emerge loaded with grime and quarto first editions of such luminaries as William Whitehead and Edmund Cartwright, Macnamara Morgan and 'Peter Pindar', for which he charged us an average of 1s apiece.

Tim himself told something of the story in his article in the *Times Literary Supplement* dated 11 May 1973 on 'Book Collecting in the 1930s', where he explained how his part of our joint collection came to pass into my possession. He asserts that he had to sell it to me in order to pay his college bills; my own recollection is that he had begun to collect illuminated manuscripts, a rather expensive hobby that demanded the sacrifice of his former love. He was liable to such wayward fancies, as I regarded them, and I remember being astonished, on a visit to Cambridge after the war, to find that he was – as he put it – 'moving into armour', which was cluttering up all the landings of The Knott. But nothing ever weaned him away from his devotion to the nymph Bibliography, whom he began to woo while still up at Cambridge with his article in the *Book Collector's Quarterly* no. XVI 1934 on the variants of Christopher Anstey's *Election Ball*. In his *TLS* article Tim credits me with a hand in this project, but at that time bibliography for me was a mystery of which I was hardly aware. He would sometimes quote to me Iolo Williams's *Points in Eighteenth Century Verse*; but I was content with the simpler descriptions in Dobell's great *Catalogue of XVIIIth Century Verse* 1933 with its 3216 entries, giving the number of leaves as well as the usual details of format, edition, plates, half-titles, advertisements – and, of course, prices. Dobell was our bible and I remember Tim's excitement when I came back from a visit to Winchester with an early miscellany that I had picked up for 3s at Gilbert's bookshop. He rushed to Dobell and showed me the price – nine guineas! a fortune! For it was Lintott's *Miscellaneous Poems and Translations* 1712, in which appeared the first version of Pope's *Rape of the Lock*.

Anyway, soon after we went down in June 1935, Tim offered to sell me his collection, an offer which I eagerly accepted. I could not, of course, afford to buy the whole lot at once, so for the next two years or so I had the pleasure and thrill of receiving regular lists of about a dozen books per month, spiced with tempting quotations and jaunty comments in Tim's inimitable style. Few of the lists, scribbled on the backs of old calendars and such, were dated, but I estimate that they covered a period of some twenty-four or twenty-five months between autumn 1935 and the end of 1937. Fortunately I kept them and they form not only a nostalgic record of the astonishing prices of that happy era but a very characteristic collection of 'Munbiana'.

Most of the lists are without heading or date, presumably enclosed with a letter, of which I have only one left, dated 30/10/35 from Quaritch's, where he was then working. Whether this was the first of the lists I cannot be sure, but it was certainly one of the earliest. The total bill for nine items (covering three original numbers of *The Spectator* 1712, a folio first edition of poetical *Essays* 1737 by 'Hesiod' Cooke, Thomas Warton's *Ode for Music* 1751 in quarto, three more quartos (not firsts), a couple of octavos and another folio in poorish condition (John Dennis's *Court of Death* 1695), came to 16s 9d. This was fairly typical of the early lists; it was only gradually that Tim yielded up his favourite treasures, the Popes, the Ansteys, the Bath-Eastonians. But for Christmas 1935 he produced a special 'Catalogue' with a title-page on which is pasted 'an original XVth century woodcut, cut by some Vandal from the Nuremberg Chronicle 1493'. The contents were choice and carefully angled towards my particular interests, quarto pamphlets, preferably satirical, and the works of the Wykehamists. (I was trying to make a special collection of the poets of my old school, Winchester, who included not only Collins and Young, but John Philips of *The Splendid Shilling*, Somervile of *The Chace*, William Whitehead the Poet Laureate, Joseph Warton the pre-Romantic, 'sonneteering Bowles' and many more obscure poetasters, down to William Lipscomb who won the Oxford Prize in 1772 for his poem on *The Beneficial Effects of Inoculations*.) In his Christmas list Tim found for me another Wykehamist, William Crowe, whose *Lewesdon Hill* (second edition, quarto, 1788, 1*s*) was praised by Wordsworth and Coleridge. Then there was a specimen of another favourite *genre*, the Hermit poem, in *The Anchoret*, 4to, 1776, by Nathaniel Tucker (first edition, 1*s*); some 'rousing satires' like *The Brutes of Cam* (first edition, 4to, 1776, 1*s* 6*d*) and *The Triumph of Dulness* (first, 4to, 1781, 1*s* 6*d*), which both attacked Cambridge, and other such titbits, fifteen items in all including eleven first editions for a total of £1 2*s* 6*d*!

But the real joy of this list was that it was the first in which Tim began to expand his notes with irresistible salesmanship. For example:

Ecclesiastical Gallantry: or, the Mystery Unravelled. 4to. 1778. First edition. (2/–)
A poem written round a cause célèbre of the time – a vicar visiting his whore found his curate there and in a fit of pique brought the matter before the ecclesiastical courts. The bedroom scene receives graphic treatment.
ΜΕΛΗ ΕΦΗΜΕΡΙΑ 4to. Oxford. First edition. (2/–)
The author seems to have been a several-bottle man. Many of the poems are to Bacchus:
> *Ruddy Bacchus ever sporting*
>   *Lifts on high the airy soul;*
>   *Still the God's kind influence courting,*
>   *Bumpers after bumpers roll.*
Specimens of the Poetry of Joseph Blacket, with an account of his Life . . . by Mr. Pratt. 8vo. 1809. First edition. (2/–)
Reading between the lines in the introduction one can see that our friend Sympathy Pratt, thoroughly nettled at the success scored by Capel Lofft, in his discovery and patronage of Bloomfeld, set out to introduce the works of Blacket to the world.

Not every list was thus annotated; it depended on how busy Tim was at the time and several, like the one headed '*Munby Ltd Autumn List No.* 1 (1936), are simply businesslike catalogues with no more than the prices and brief bibliographical notes. Yet these are in themselves of considerable interest, reflecting as they do the state of the antiquarian book market of those days, in which Tim was closely involved through his work at Quaritch's and later at Sotheby's. They also illustrate again and again Tim's own generosity, e.g.:

The Spectator 1711–12.
I picked up a run of the original newspaper issue in folio sheets and have been breaking it up and selling separately. The run is very roughly Nos. 248–553 with many gaps. If you would care to have a few of the numbers as specimens I will try to supply the ones you want (I rather want Sir Roger de Coverley

myself). A complete folio Spectator *is rather expensive, about £70; but I am supplying odd sheets at 9d. each.*

A volume (folio, contemporary ½ vellum and marbled boards) containing –
Tickell, T. *A Poem for . . . the Lord Privy-Seal*. Fifth edition. 1713.
Tickell, T. *An Epistle from a Lady in England . . .* Fifth, 1717.
Tickell, T. *An Ode occasioned by . . . Earl Stanhope's Voyage to France*. First edition. 1718.
Tickell, T. *To the Right Honourable the Countess of Warwick*. Manuscript of 4 pp. folio.
Young, E. *A Letter to Mr. Tickell on the Death of Addison*. Second edition. 1719.
Young, E. *On the Late Queen's Death . . .* First edition. 1714.
Eusden. *A Poem . . . on the Birth of a Prince*. First edition. 1718.
Welsted, L. *An Epistle to . . . the Duke of Chandos*. First. 1720.

I expect you remember the fantastic price which I paid for this, and while wanting to give you a bargain I feel disposed to make a bit of a profit on it. Dobell seems to list the firsts to about 30/– a time and the others at about 10/–. Would you think it exorbitant of me to ask 2/6 apiece for the firsts and 1/– for the others, i.e. 14/– for the volume – say 12/6, reduction on bulk?

Miscellaneous Poems by Several Hands, viz. Dean Swift, Mr. Parnel, Dr. Delany, . . . Mr. Concanen & others. Published by Mr. Concanen. 8vo. First edition. 1724. (5/–)
This is really quite a decent book and quite rare. We sold a copy at Q's for £3/3/–. It has a fair amount of Swift firsts in it, also a good Parnell poem . . . This is a poor copy, but even so I think it is worth 5/–.

Browne, Moses. *Piscatory Eclogues*. 8vo. First edition. 1729. (7/6)
Is this exorbitant? Cp. Dobell's price (£2/10/–) and Maggs recently catalogued it even higher.

The Loss of Liberty. A Poem. Folio, uncut. London, 1733. (3/–)
I hope this doesn't seem dear. Uncut folios are a bit expensive. D(obell) wants 12/6 for a cut one.

Harte, Walter. *Poems on Several Occasions*. 8vo. London, 1739. (4/–)
These are the sheets of the first edition of 1727, re-issued with a cancel title and the preliminaries suppressed . . . See Williams Points in C18V . . . I hope it doesn't seem a bit dear – it cost me 7/6.

Lloyd, Robert. *Poems*. 4to. 1st ed. 1762. (6/–)
I bought this I think from Gilbert of Winchester for 6/–. Is it worth this to you? I have just sold Q's copy for 21/–, though I see Dobell only asks 10/6.

(Chesterfieldiana) *The Fine Gentleman's Etiquette; or, Lord Chesterfield's Advice to his son, Versified*. By a lady. 4to. First edition. 1776. (3/6d)
I believe this is rather rare. The only copy I found as having sold at auction fetched the quite fantastic price of, I think, £5/10/– in 1927 or thereabouts.

Park, Thomas. *Sonnets & other small Poems*. 8vo. 1st ed. 1797. (3/6)
Do you know T. Park? He was a great Hampstead light and our local historian. His verses are very charming . . . You may think this a bit dear, but it cost me 6/–, I think. I bought it here (Hampstead) where he is at a premium. It is one of 200 copies.

Collins, John. *Scripscrapologia; or, Collins's Doggerel Dish of All Sorts*. Post 8vo. with portrait . . . Birmingham, 1804. (6/6d)
A lovely book – see Williams Points for a most enthusiastic write-up . . . I hope you wont think this dear – it is a really scarce book and has come into prominence since I. A. Williams has written it up – I have seen it catalogued at 30/– or so.

I am glad to say that I had the sense to pay those 'exorbitant' prices and all the treasures mentioned still rest on my shelves. But the most extraordinary bargain of all (though neither of us realized it at the time) was an item in one of the later lists with no comment whatever simply 'Pope, A. *Essay on Man*. First collected ed. 1734. Large quarto. Stiff marbled boards. V. fine.' (5/–). It was not till some thirty years later, when I returned to my books after many years abroad, that I began to examine them systematically with the bibliographies and, on comparing this volume with Griffith, I found mine had an extra leaf at the end. This was the 'Index to the Ethic Epistles', Pope's plan for the whole work, which, according to Spence,[1] 'he annexed to about a dozen copies of the poem and sent as presents to some of his most particular friends. Most of these were afterwards called in again.' My copy turned out to be the only one known. But when I asked Tim about its provenance, he could remember nothing from so long before and could only give me his unselfish congratulations on my good fortune.

It is, however, the critical comments in the lists that bring back most vividly the real Tim – his enthusiasm, his humour and the sheer fun of his collecting. Anyone who knew him will be able to hear his voice again in such quotations as these:

Evans, Abel. *Prae-Existence. A Poem in Imitation of Milton.* 4to. 1740. (2/6)
Splendidly 'Miltonick' in diction – not unlike Sam Wesley's superb parody of Milton 'in the manner of the moderns'.

Trapp, Joseph. *Thoughts upon the Four Last Things: Death; Judgment; Heaven; and Hell.* 2nd ed. Post 8vo. 1748. (1/–)
'Hell' makes quite racy reading.

(Moore, Henry) *A Poem sacred to the Memory of the late P. Doddridge.* 4to. 1st ed. 1752. (1/–)
Even in the cause of salesmanship I can't enthuse much over this. 'Hence the low price', as we say at Q's. Still, if you are covering the whole period, the elegy is a class you mustn't neglect.

The King: a Poem . . . 4to. 1st ed. 1758. (1/–)
A dull poem, but has an amusing and interesting Prefatory Dialogue between the Author and Bookseller. The author says he tried to dedicate the work to 150 different patrons, all of whom refused!

Woodhouse, James, journeyman shoemaker. *Poems on Several Occasions.* The second edition corrected . . . Roy. 8vo. 1766. (3/–)
I have rather a weak spot for these working-class poets, milkwomen, ploughboys and what-not. Woodhouse was a protégé of Shenstone's . . . Is 'the plumy throng' a new one on you for birds?

Graves, Richard. *Euphrosyne; or Amusements on the Road of Life.* 8vo. 1st ed. Frontispiece by Bampfylde. 1776. (2/–)
Do you remember this lovely book? A bit of a wrench [to part with it].

An Invocation to the Genius of Great Britain. 4to 1st ed. 1778. (1/6)
Not unamusing. The author sometimes allows the rhyme to carry away the sense . . . He is very against anything 'continental':

> *Purged be this land from all the reptile race,*
> *Whose manners poison, and whose modes disgrace!*
> *Ill suits with Freedom's sons their boasted* Ton,
> *The light* Cotillion, *or more light* Allemande.

Rogers, Samuel (*not* Memory's Bard). *Poems on Various Occasions.* 2 vols. 8vo. 1st ed. Bath, 1782. (6/6)
A very jolly book, subscribed to by Johnson but not in Williams' list. All the poems are very short, . . . mainly epigrams 'On a favourite Thrush escaping from a beautiful young Lady, about 15, to an old wrinkled Maid of 60', 'On a celebrated Gout Doctor', 'The Female Gallant'. . . Rogers seems to have been the compleat 'occasional' poet and to have had an Impromptu ready for everything.

---

[1] *Anecdotes,* ed. S. W. Singer, 1820, 136–7.

Robert Merry, Mrs. Piozzi, Bertie Greatheed, etc. *The British Album*. 2 vols. 8vo. (3/6)
The choicest flowers of Della Cruscan verse are here gathered together for your delectation.
Mathias, Thomas James. *Runic Odes from the Norse Tongue*. 8vo. New edition. 1790. (2/−)
I don't know if you've ever looked at these odes − I think they are pretty good − much better than
Gray's *odes from the Norse.*
Sonnets to Eminent Men. 1st ed. 4to. 1783. (1/−)
The Sonnets are to several of our old friends and the work ranks as Hayleyiana!
Boyce, Thomas. *Harold. A Tragedy*. 4to. First edition. 1786. (2/6)
Really a poem − at least I trust it was never acted. Very dull indeed!
Sunday. A Poem. 4to. 1st ed. 1790. (1/6)
Much more amusing than its name suggests − the writer had a 'Hail' complex:

> Hail, cleanliness ! thou cheaply-purchased bliss!
> Hail! virtuous influence of Sunday Schools!
> Far from my sight this hallow'd day remove
> The squalid vest, and negligent attire,

and so on, lots of it.
Relph, Josiah. *Poems*. 3rd ed. with improvements. Embellished with picturesque engravings on wood by Mr. T. Bewick. Newcastle, 1799. 8vo. (3/−)
Quite fun. Apart from the very nice Bewick cuts, the poems are rather jolly. I like 'Occasioned by a little Miss's bursting into Tears upon reading the Ballad of the Babes in the Wood.'
Gisborne, Thos. *Walks in a Forest, or Poems descriptive of Scenery & Incidents characteristic of a Forest at Different Seasons of the Year*. 4th ed. 12mo. 1799. (1/6)
I was once thinking of writing Gisborne up − it is rather interesting nature poetry & Romantic themes treated in the decadent classical style of the 1790s. He is not unlike Crabbe in this, the new matter and the old manner and metre.

Finally, from 'Munby's Autumn List No. 11', there is an item which can be roughly dated, since Tim's facetious comment refers to my own mock-18th-century 'didactick' poem *The Pleasures of Inefficiency*, which was published by subscription in June 1936, with a dedication to 'Latimer Munby, Esq.'

(Forsteriana) *The Oeconomy of Happiness*. By E.T. 4to. 1st ed. 1772. (1/6)
In some passages the poet has preceded in a curious way the work of the 20th century poet Mr. Forster − for example, the lines

> Hail, Mediocrity! Thrice happy he
> Who holds thee independent and well knows
> Thy modest worth!

may be said to breathe the very spirit of the later poet's Pleasures of Inefficiency.

I do not know whether the lists of 'Munby Ltd' would now rank as collector's items in themselves. But their value to me is far higher than anything the market could offer − the authentic voice of a much lamented friend.

PHILIP ROBINSON

Recollections of Moving a Library
or, How the Phillipps Collection was brought to London

PLATE I. Thirlestane House, Cheltenham by J. Glover

The fifth and last volume of A. N. L. Munby's Phillipps Studies *was devoted to the dispersal of the collection. It was one of the shortest of that classic work. Having killed off Sir Thomas at the end of Vol. IV the author clearly felt disinclined to linger over a subject compared with which, as he observed in the Preface, 'Hamlet without the Prince of Denmark would be lively'. He described how the Robinson brothers made their first approach to the Phillipps Trustees in December 1944; in September 1945 their offer for the library was accepted and on 19 February 1946 the Court of Chancery gave its consent to the sale. But he devoted only one paragraph to the logistics of moving Bibliotheca Phillippica from Cheltenham to London. In the generation since* Phillipps Studies *was published the humour and vividness of Tim Munby's portrayal have fostered a vigorous growth of interest in the obsessed baronet and his prodigious collection. Readers infected by* virus Middle-Hillensis *can hardly hear enough about them.*

Accounts by the chief participants have survived of some famous literary removals. We are informed of the Florentines' triumphant return along the Arno valley with the Pisan Pandects and of Leone Allacci's convoy of fifty wagons carrying the Palatine Library from Heidelberg to Rome (he suffered more from officious customs officers, he later recalled, than from the marauding bands of thieves and deserters in South Germany). It is sad that we cannot read Thomas Osborne's description of moving the Harleian printed books from Marylebone or James Edwards's of shipping the Pinelli library home from Venice. Philip Robinson's narrative thus belongs to a recognized tradition and fills what for Phillipps enthusiasts has been an aching gap. A.R.A.HOBSON

WHEN in February 1946 the Court set its seal upon our purchase of the Phillipps Collection, I remember a feeling of anti-climax. I personally would have been very willing to relax, but Lionel was made of sterner stuff and would have none of it; he was anxious forthwith to remove the library from Cheltenham and house it under our control in London. I was without difficulty persuaded upon the point, and we started at once upon the arrangements for the removal.

It is perhaps surprising that we should have felt it to be so urgent to secure physical possession of material of which we were already the legal owners; material, moreover, that had proved to be literally unsaleable to anyone but ourselves. It was within our knowledge that the Phillipps Trustees had exhausted every other avenue open to them

PLATE II. The church of Christ the King, Gordon Square by Geoffrey Fletcher

before agreeing to the sale to us; and it was on the record that no library, collector, nor other bookseller, would contemplate it. It is evidence, perhaps, that we were in the grip of an obsession almost as compelling as that which had inspired Sir Thomas. The objection advanced by others to whom the opportunity to purchase had been offered was not the quality of the collection, but its vast size. It had seemed to us a rather odd objection, but we were now about to experience what it meant.

Accommodation in London for the library was not a point we had yet had time to consider, for, as the negotiations had tended to look as if they might conceivably be successful, we became preoccupied with the securing of the purchase money. In one sense, the accommodation position could hardly have been worse. London had not yet recovered from the massive bombing which had erased or damaged so many buildings. But the reverse of the coin was also true. In general, the capital city had not yet fully restored to life and use the many buildings whose normal functions had been in abeyance during the war.

We thought the ideal situation would be in Bloomsbury – near the British Museum, convenient to our premises in Pall Mall, and with rents much lower than the West End of London. It turned out to be an inspired choice. I well remember a bitterly cold Sunday afternoon in March when Marjorie and I decided to wander the streets of Bloomsbury. We chanced, at the corner of Gordon Square, to see a small, faded and almost indecipherable wooden notice board fixed high upon the wall of No. 1 in the square, a large Regency house with, on one side, a delightful classic frieze. It was the house which today has been re-built into the present Warburg Institute. The notice was to the effect that the building was to let; and apply to the University of London.

On the Monday, Lionel inspected and approved of the choice, and we made our application to the University, only to discover that the notice was not intended to be there! It had been overlooked long previously when the owners had revised their views as to the use of the buildings. And then the war had intervened. But the University authorities, in their great kindness, lent a willing ear to our plea for a library in distress, and granted us a short tenancy.

What was truly immense good fortune was that the viewpoint of No. 1 Gordon Square disclosed, almost opposite, a very large and, as it turned out, then almost unused church, the Catholic Apostolic Church. It was a most substantial edifice.[1] Here again, the Trustees of that church were so kind as to listen to our plea in regard to the temporary housing of a great library, and we were able to hire the unused crypt of the building; perhaps 100 feet long by some 30 feet wide by perhaps 12 feet high, and built with all the strength of a monastic building. We owe a great debt of gratitude both to the University of London and to the Trustees of the Catholic Apostolic Church. The church is now as the Church of Christ the King the official 'chapel' of London University. We were to use the crypt for very many years, and we believe that the church's kind act will be recognized in the future as having been a great contribution to the cause of learning.

[1] This church was 'built by R. Brandon (1817–1877), one of the most scholarly and gifted of the earlier Gothic Revivalists . . . and his great church, built of satin stone in 1851–55, though unfinished, (the tower and spire were never completed), is a most marvellous re-creation of Early English style . . .' From the article by Geoffrey Fletcher in *The Daily Telegraph* 17 December 1984, which was accompanied by his drawing of the church, here reproduced with kind permission.

We were now possessed of a large, solid Regency corner house of some four storeys, and an exceedingly large church crypt nearby, and in a highly convenient location. It only remained to effect the elementary restoration and decoration necessary, and here we were assisted by our client and friend, the late C. E. Kenny, the quantity surveyor. Mr Kenny was able to arrange the expeditious putting into order of both sites. I should here mention that Cyril Kenny (whose library was sold in a series of sales) was an enthusiastic collector of the type that would have been appreciated by Sir Thomas Phillipps. Although the *raison d'être* of his collection was allegedly that of a library relating to quantity surveying, he felt able to include under that heading any book, and any manuscript, on any subject whatsoever!

We fitted out the largest of the ground-floor rooms in Gordon Square with rather charming Regency bookcases found in a shop in a neighbouring street. We intended that this room should contain the best manuscripts. Several of the other rooms were shelved in plain deal, and we intended to use in the rest of the house (as in the church crypt) Sir T.P.'s own original box-shelves. Not the least of our acquisitions from nearby Tottenham Court Road were several large, solid (and then almost unsaleable) Victorian mahogany dining tables. These were ideal for the handling of massive quantities of books, and their cannibalization by the 'antique' furniture restorers (which today makes these tables scarce and expensive) had not, at that time, developed.

At Cheltenham, the Phillipps Collection lay stored in the cellars of Thirlestane House, the Regency building on the Bath Road which is now a part of Cheltenham School. It was to this house that Sir Thomas Phillipps moved his library in 1864, when it was becoming impossible to cram more books into his Middle Hill mansion at Broadway. Thirlestane House was very large and splendid. I have been known to so grossly exaggerate as to describe it as having a facade like Buckingham Palace! That is the sort of impression it gives.[2]

When, in 1939, the Ministry of Aircraft Production took over Thirlestane House, the manuscripts and printed books were transferred to cellars which ran the whole length of the building. The job had been very well done. A special effort had been made in regard to what were considered to be the most valuable pieces. These had been put into a separate enclosed enclave, with locked door, the 'Wine Cellar'. It was quite small. On the stone bin shelves therein stood, rank behind rank, the precious manuscripts – in their hundreds. In the same enclosure were also neatly arranged what were considered the most valuable of the printed books, e.g. the first Caxton, a single volume of the grand-folio Audubon, early English books, great incunabula etc., etc. It was a breathtaking assemblage. To us, and I imagine to everybody else, it was, effectively, the Phillipps Collection.

Of the items in the wine cellar there existed lists of the 'Phillipps numbers' so that when the time for removal came, the items could be identified and checked off. Whilst our application was before the Court, we had asked for a glance at the material so as to gauge the storage and removal factors. We were shown only the 'wine cellar', and

[2] See the painting of Thirlestane House by J. Glover (1767–1849) reproduced at the beginning of this article. The artist has clearly received the same impression of the house as I did. Perhaps it was intended to give Sir Thomas the hope that at last he would have a house big enough for his collection.

limited to a very brief period. In the event, both Lionel and I found ourselves at the exit door ahead of our guide. Lionel and I made no comment to each other, but we both knew that our only desire was to see that place shut, locked, and unseen, until (as we fervently hoped) we returned to it as the owners.

Beyond the small, well-lit enclave of the wine cellar stretched the dim undercroft of the great building. Here, stacked pile upon pile, rank upon rank, into the gloom, were the original box-shelves which Sir Thomas had used at Middle Hill and in which he had transferred the books from thence and used again as shelving at Thirlestane House. The excellent firm which had executed the transfer to the cellars had tacked brown paper over the open side of each box. No information was ever supplied as to their contents. Any request for such would have been impossible of performance. Neither we, nor for that matter anyone else, really knew what were the contents of these coffin-shaped boxes. The main cellar was a huge catacomb. It was lit only dimly. Prior to our purchase, we had not even walked to the end of that cellar.[3]

As soon as the house and church crypt in London had been made ready, we confirmed the arrangements for the removal with the transport firm we had selected, Hoults of Newcastle and London. The young men who had originated that now large firm had been our childhood companions in Newcastle, and had transported us to London when we moved to our premises in Pall Mall in 1930 We were successful in enthusing them in regard to a removal which promised to be of a unique nature and scale.

We decided to effect the removal in two parts. Firstly, the contents of the wine cellar – the Collection proper. Then the 'Catlin Gallery', i.e. the collection of some 56 paintings of North American Indians by George Catlin, which was included in our purchase. These removals would be done with the greatest care, every item carefully checked, and the whole arranged at No. 1 Gordon Square before moving on to stage two. The second stage would be the removal of the 'shelf boxes' from the main cellar. This latter would, of course, be essentially a simple job.

Lionel and I decided that he would be in London to receive the material and superintend its installation there; and I would go to Cheltenham to superintend the packing and removal. The removal firm would arrange for an 'unloading team' to assist Lionel in London, and a 'loading team' would be in Cheltenham to assist me. I left for Cheltenham, with my dear Marjorie, and put up at a small hotel almost opposite Thirlestane House.

The contents of the wine cellar were carefully checked off, each item separately wrapped, and packed in tea chests. Everyone, packers included, were impressed with the fact that they were dealing with objects demanding the utmost care. We were emptying Aladdin's Cave! By the end of March, the best manuscripts were at Gordon Square. I returned to London at this stage and assisted Lionel in the marvellous work he was doing at that end. My recollection is that a large proportion of all the wine cellar manuscripts went into the bookcases arranged round what had once been the big drawing-room at

---

[3] Dr Munby (*Phillipps Studies* Vol. 5, page 102) states 'the brothers opened at random a cross-section of the boxes'. This must have been based upon misinformation or upon the assumption that it was what must have happened. In fact no box was examined prior to the purchase. The open area of the 'Wine Cellar' was adequate for our purpose.

Gordon Square, and in the other large reception room across the hall. What rooms they now became!

The printed books in the wine cellar, and the Catlin Gallery, were still to come; and this removal was effected some two weeks later. These also were taken to Gordon Square and arranged in the rooms there. It was the exception to our principle that only manuscripts should be kept in that house. Thus No. 1 Gordon Square, eventually, alas, to be demolished, held for a period a collection not unworthy of its proximity to the British Museum.

In a separate smaller room, we stacked the Catlin Gallery, the collection of original paintings of the North American Indians painted from the life. This collection was eventually, and most appropriately, to find its permanent home at the Gilcrease Foundation at Tulsa, Oklahoma, being acquired by our client (and friend) Thomas Gilcrease, the pure-blooded Red Indian Chief on whose lands oil was found and who conceived the idea of creating a great museum and art gallery of the Indian Nation sited at the geographical centre of the United States.

We were, of course, very conscious of the responsibility of the custody of such material and of the danger of fire and water. Although we had insurance, the responsibility far transcended that. At this stage, our wonderful cataloguer, Ralph Lewis, a middle-aged bachelor of austere tastes, offered to live in the house. It was a noble gesture which relieved Lionel and me enormously. Mr Lewis left his office in Pall Mall and began immediately upon very brief descriptive slips inserted in each manuscript, slips which bore in code his own estimate of what the value might be.

A few weeks later, we decided that having safely removed the 'cream' and established it in London, we should complete the job and bring all the rest to London. There were still several vacant rooms at Gordon Square and the huge empty church crypt, so we could depend upon having plenty of room for arrangement and sorting. In retrospect, how delicious seems such naivety.

Again Marjorie and I booked into our Cheltenham hotel. Messrs Hoults had been warned that we were now going to remove quantity, and we wanted it carried through expeditiously. So the lorries, some with trailers, were arranged to follow one another continuously, and everyone at Cheltenham and at London was keyed up for a massive, simple, straightforward job.

So, one fine morning, the cellar doors of Thirlestane House again were opened and the scene surveyed. It was a daunting sight. The piles of shelf-boxes seemed quite endless. In addition, there were many larger boxes into which the removers had piled masses of charters, miscellaneous papers, and the like. In one dark corner was stacked framed papyri. There was one original Phillipps box of unique shape, being very narrow, about five feet high and with a hinged lid. It contained large rolls, heraldic pedigrees and the like, and maps. It was from this box that there was eventually taken a portolan chart of 1424, which is now famous, and may (after the demise of the Vinland Map) be the earliest known map relating to America.

I judged that it was merely a case of establishing an efficient system. We had the men standing by, and the lorries. As has been mentioned, Lionel and I had decided that manuscripts in all forms, whether codices or historical papers, should go to Gordon

Square; and all printed material to the church crypt. I would, therefore, mark each shelf-box with an 'M' in blue pencil for manuscripts, or a 'P' for printed, and my loading team would put it in the appropriate lorry for the appropriate address. I would have, of course, to glance into each box before making my mark, but that was just a case of ripping a hole in the paper covers.

So two trestles were set up, and the first box placed upon it. I ripped the cover and saw at a glance that it contained manuscripts. Nearly always, it was only a glance that was needed, and only rarely was it necessary to pull out a volume to check. So with my blue pencil, I marked that box 'M'. Two men carried it away, and allowed two other men, waiting with the next box, to place that upon the trestle. We were under way!

Rip – look – mark; rip – look – mark; rip – look – mark . . . How simple. How exhausting. It went on hour after hour with breaks only for meals. Day after day. At intervals, my blue pencil would be renewed or there would be a pause whilst the paper that was piling around me was swept away. And there would be welcome visits from my wife, who would return from searching around the shops of Cheltenham for cigarettes, then in very short supply. These were handed round. Then, once again, rip – look – mark; rip – look – mark. I would hear the lorries approaching and receding outside in a daylight world. It is not surprising that there were occasions when I felt like a pagan priest at a sacrificial altar, as, in that dim light, I stood poised with weapon in hand as my acolytes left and right placed before me and bore away objects of identical size.

The system was not too efficient a one. The bottle-neck was that there was only one individual in the team doing the rip – look – mark, and he was subject to human frailty. In the evenings, Lionel and I talked on the telephone, exchanging our progress accounts. His labours were even more exhausting than mine. He had two places to look after. The astonishing scale of what was happening can best perhaps be appreciated by considering, at this point, the position in London.

As the 'M' (manuscripts) contingents arrived at 1, Gordon Square, the shelf-boxes were stacked against the walls of the rooms, exactly as they had been at Thirlestane House. Steadily, Lionel told me, the rooms became filled. In the event, No. 1 Gordon Square could not absorb all the manuscript material, and a point arrived when 'M' lorries had to be deflected to the church crypt. The 'P' (printed) lorries debouched their contents directly at the church. Down the winding stone stair the boxes were carried, past (believe it or not) a sort of cloister open to the air of Bloomsbury, although beneath ground level, to the heavy oaken door of the crypt.

Lionel had planned the arrangements here with his usual brilliance. As the crypt was so large, he would stack the shelf-boxes up to a convenient 6 or 7 feet on either side of a central channel, and towards the door end of the crypt would leave plenty of room for a sorting space furnished with one or more of our large mahogany tables. The crypt was well lighted. It would be an excellent place in which to sort and work.

But as the lorries continued day after day to shuttle between Cheltenham and London, and as my daily reports gave no hint of any slackening of the stream, Lionel took draconian steps. He saw that we must abandon, *pro tem.*, the question of convenient access. The boxes were now piled up into the very curve of the vaulted roof, and the passage-way blocked in. In such a way he retreated day by day up the crypt, leaving an utterly solid mass behind him. Until at length he and his men arrived at the heavy door, which, most fortunately, opened outwards, and eventually that door was closed upon a huge crypt which had become a solid block. In the passages outside, adjacent to the open cloister, had to be stacked the overflow, and it was considerable.

When the time eventually came to unpack and examine the boxes in the crypt, it took some time (days) to unpick enough boxes out of the mass to get a foothole in that chamber, and very many months to make a central gangway. This gangway was driven to the far end wall of the crypt, and we then proceeded (over the years) to return to the entrance leaving a normal library behind. The shelf-boxes were stacked against the walls, with, at the intervals, wings of shelf-boxes jutting out, rather like Duke Humphrey's Library. And in the centre, boxes were packed to form a long narrow central table. We had, of course, not the slightest idea of the contents of any box before we opened it. All moments were moments of discovery. One box might be a stray from the Slavonic section – or from the Chinese. Or perhaps five or six boxes from the early English section might be found together. One American box might contain some of the volumes of De Bry, whilst the box containing the rest of the set might be many feet (i.e. many months) away.

To return to Cheltenham. The time came when the last lorry was to leave. It was also to carry back my loading team. They spent a long time assisting me to sort through the quantities of packing paper which littered the cellar from end to end. I was very conscious that books or papers might have fallen out of boxes and be hidden. But, in the end, I was satisfied and dismissed my team. And then, after a final very slow walk by myself through the wine cellar and main cellar, stamping upon paper piles and looking into corners, I at last locked the cellar doors behind me.

The light was beginning to fade as I crossed the forecourt to surrender the keys to the porter at his lodge. Although I was very tired and eager for my whisky and soda, I stopped and turned round to contemplate the facade of the huge house. I have wondered since just why I did that. Was it Sir Thomas? After all, it was only a few steps to the porter's lodge, and only a few more to my room in the hotel across the road, where I could have looked at Thirlestane House with my feet up. As I looked up, I realized that my whisky and soda was not yet. Above me was the place from whence the books had come. If in this case nothing, absolutely nothing, had been left behind, it would, I knew, be something unique in our experience of such events. What would I say to Lionel when he asked me: 'I suppose, Philip, you checked through the house?' How many instances we both knew of books and tracts left behind in locked cupboards. I knew I had to go over every inch of that house.

I entered the caretaker's lodge and in handing over the keys I said I would be very grateful if he would walk over the house with me just so I could tell my firm I had done it. The custodian was happy to put me right. 'There's nothing there, Guv. Clean as a whistle.' I assured him I understood that such would be the case and our walk was merely a formality. And I also hinted that I would know how to appreciate the trouble I was giving him. In the end, the custodian agreed and we set off on our tour of Thirlestane House.

It was, as he said, swept clean. We started with the kitchens and the pantries, and moved up to the first floor with its state rooms. Here again, all was empty. Not a cupboard that did not open and was not immaculately swept. Not a stick of furniture anywhere. *Except* one single piece in the shadow at the end of one of the largest rooms. I walked over to it. It was a narrow glass-topped exhibition case, rather dusty internally and externally. It displayed a number of geological specimens, fossils etc. But one of the exhibits was not natural rock. It was an artefact; a barrel-shaped cylinder incised with lettering. I had not seen such an object before, but I had heard of them. I knew it was an ancient clay cylinder. The case was locked.

I called over my companion, and indicated the object. 'That is a book', I said. 'I will have to take it with me.' The custodian looked with astonishment at the madman addressing him. 'That's no book, Guv.' 'Yes, it's a book made long before books as you and I know them.' I explained that my firm had acquired all the books that were here, in any form whatsoever, and this object was, therefore, their property. The custodian demurred a good deal and felt he would have to ask someone about it. 'You go and do that,' I said, 'and I will wait here.' In the end, after further explanations, he was satisfied, produced a key to the case and gave me the cylinder. We then continued our tour of that floor, proceeded up to the next floor, and finally through the attics looking into every cupboard and every stair cavity en route. We saw nothing else. That glass-topped case was the only thing in Thirlestane House.

I parted from the caretaker on good terms, and gratefully made my way back to my hotel. I dropped the cylinder into my suitcase. The last item of the Phillipps Collection to leave Cheltenham would be travelling to London with my shirts.

It was, indeed, an ancient Assyrian clay cylinder and, as it turned out, one of the most famous extant. It was the original cylinder of *c.* 595 BC on which Nebuchadnezzar had recorded his repair of the Tower of Babylon (the 'Tower of Babel') and his completion of the palace whose Hanging Gardens were one of the seven wonders of the ancient world, and where the Hebrew Slaves wept when they remembered Zion.[4]

---

[4] Described and illustrated in our catalogue No. 77 (1948) item No. 127.

DAVID MCKITTERICK

The Young Geoffrey Keynes

THE twenty-fifth of March 1987 would have been Sir Geoffrey Keynes's hundredth birthday. He died so recently, only five years ago, that any centenary celebrations seem premature; but it is not inappropriate this year to recall a little of his youth, and to set on record the beginnings of the career of one of the most influential of all bibliographers. In 1914 he saw published his first book, a bibliography of John Donne. The great bibliography of William Blake (itself the beginning of another literary career in which Geoffrey was no less influential) bears on its title-page the date 1921. In 1922 he reached his thirty-fifth birthday, and thus, according to one of his bibliographical mentors, Charles Sayle of Cambridge University Library, what was arithmetically middle age.[1] For Geoffrey, of course, neither his bibliographical, literary, nor (least of all) his surgical careers were at the half-way point, but the date makes a convenient break.

Geoffrey came up to Pembroke College, Cambridge, from Rugby School in 1906. If one leaves aside such youthful productions as his contributions to the school's Natural History Society *Reports* of 1903–5 on entomology and on the excavation of Roman remains, or the reports in the *Entomologist's Record* of excursions with his father to the continent, then his literary career may be said to have begun with a review of *Tono-Bungay* in the *Cambridge Review* in 1909, and a note on Blake's 'Laughing song' in *Notes and Queries* in 1910. It is of interest, but not particularly relevant to note here, that his first surgical paper appeared only in 1913.[2]

By 1924, the year of *Thomas Browne*, it had become clear to his friends, to reviewers, and to the book trade, that Geoffrey approached each of his bibliographies as a long campaign: he had established a pattern that was to remain for the rest of his life, of collecting an author until he was 'ready' for a bibliography of his chosen subject. He alluded to some of these campaigns himself, in the preface to the bibliography of Sir Thomas Browne for example, where he wrote of its having been 'first projected and the work begun at Cambridge sixteen years ago', or in that to *Evelyn* (1937), where he attributed the book's origins to the early months of the First World War.

For Geoffrey, this necessarily long gestation, a period of research accompanied by a culling of booksellers' catalogues and an ever-increasing correspondence, came to imply also a programme of publication which some, who sought final perfection before being sufficiently satisfied to pass their own books for press, could not approve. His *Donne* (1914)

---

[1] Cf. J. C. T. Oates, 'Charles Edward Sayle' *Trans Cambridge Bibliographical Soc.* 8 (1982), pp. 236–69.

[2] The standard list of Geoffrey's publications is by William LeFanu in *Geoffrey Keynes; tributes on the occasion of his seventieth birthday* (Osler Club, 1961), pp. 27–61.

was the first of four editions; *Blake* was revised piecemeal, but particularly with the help of Edwin Wolf II in 1953; a new edition of *Browne* was published in 1968. This implied a combination of activity with impatience, which Edmund Gosse for one did not entirely appreciate when he reviewed *Browne* in 1924: 'Of all intellectual occupations, bibliography properly conducted is the most leisurely.'[3] It is impossible now to tell whether or not he had his tongue in his cheek. But whatever Gosse's views, Geoffrey learned his bibliographical crafts in a world where the University Press was opposite his own college, and less than ten minutes' walk from his own front door. Printers and publishers were at hand, part of a familiar, almost domestic, business before 1914. A pamphlet could be printed within a few hours, a book published within a few months. The almost continuous rise in book prices through much of his life, and the increasing impossibility of running an operation such as the pre-war University Press, helped also to colour others' assumptions about the propriety of publication in the expectation of further major revision. Stanley Morison was another of Geoffrey's generation who, with easy access to time in the Cambridge composing department, treated the Press's facilities at times almost as others would a secretarial agency's: texts, even printed, could be easily revised. Geoffrey never attained Morison's casualness, and was not in a position to do so; but equally (and paradoxically for one who was so proud in other ways) he never lost the essential humility implied in putting forth a work that he knew would be subject to revision.[4]

Geoffrey was sparing of bibliophilic tales in *The gates of memory*, and deliberately so, in the belief that its readers would find a plethora of them boring or over-boastful. There are plenty of clues to his life as a collector before the First World War, but there is sometimes too little detail. He read Donne with his school contemporary Rupert Brooke; he was introduced to Thomas Browne by Charles Sayle (whose edition of the collected *Works* appeared in 1908) and, later by Sir William Osler;[5] of Blake, to whom we shall also return, he recalled that his first memory was of the plates to *Job* in a shop window. But what of the details?

His first book was published by the Baskerville Club, a society which by 1914 consisted of thirty-seven members. It had been founded by two people in 1903: Arthur Cole of King's[6] and Charles Sayle, like Geoffrey an Old Rugbeian. Sayle was a bachelor approaching forty who after a not wholly successful sally into the literary world had spent four years cataloguing and studying the old library at St John's College before in 1894 he had embarked on what was to have been a union catalogue of pre-1641 English books in all Cambridge libraries. In 1903 he saw published the third volume of what was to prove to be the only part to be completed, that of the University Library. Sayle's work as a bibliographer, now mostly subsumed in *STC* and its revision, is remembered today only by specialists, but in his day he was an influential example and teacher, to W. W. Greg among others. Sayle and Cole (later a successful barrister, and also a

[3] Edmund Gosse in *The Sunday Times*, 17 August 1924.

[4] Geoffrey's own bibliographies of Evelyn (1937) and of John Ray (1951) were both preceded by brief surveys in pamphlet form.

[5] His admiration for the latter was reflected in his edition of Osler's *Selected writings* (Oxford, 1951). Osler's Browne collection is described in *Bibliotheca Osleriana* (2nd ed., 1969), and further references may be found in Harvey Cushing, *The Life of Sir William Osler* (Oxford 1926), I, pp. 501 etc.

[6] Cf. A. N. L. Munby 'Arthur Cole' in *Annual Report of the Council of King's College* (1968), repr. in his *Essays and papers* (1977), pp. 207–15.

distinguished book collector) elected A. T. Bartholomew of the University Library; by the end of the year they had been joined by three members of Trinity: Charles Robertson (who went into the Treasury), G. I. H. Lloyd the economist, and Francis Jenkinson, University Librarian; and by Stephen Gaselee and J. M. Keynes, Geoffrey's elder brother, of King's.[7]

The Club began as a social arrangement, meeting over prolonged breakfasts after the contemporary fashion, to discuss Baskerville, by far the best known of all the Cambridge printers even though he only worked under the University's auspices for a few years.[8] With an ease that now seems extraordinary, the preliminary proofs of the *Handlist* of Baskerville's books were revised at the very first formal meeting, and the volume, recording members' holdings, was published the following summer. Apart however from that handlist, the Club seems to have considered itself as a publishing society almost as an afterthought: nothing about it was added to the rules until 1913, when it was decided, for the first time, that its object should be 'the encouragement of bibliographical studies by publication and otherwise'.[9]

By that time, Geoffrey's bibliography of Donne was well advanced. The Club had expanded to include M. R. James, William Aldis Wright, Henry Jackson and (among the younger members) Cosmo Gordon and W. W. Greg. It had considered various projects, including a catalogue of incunabula in and around Norwich (by A. G. W. Murray), a calendar of and selections from Henry Bradshaw's bibliographical notebooks (by Gaselee), a bibliography of Thomas Gray (by Hilary Jenkinson), and a catalogue of the old library at Cartmel (by Murray, again); but no further book had appeared. It had heard papers on Baskerville by Ralph Straus and on Bodoni by an undergraduate E. P. Goldschmidt, but on (apparently) little or nothing else. From February 1908 until February 1913 the Minute Book records no activity whatever.

It was finally revived in February 1913 at the initiative of Sayle and the secretary Bartholomew, encouraged by another Old Rugbeian undergraduate, Francis Bliss of King's, who died in the war. In a very obvious effort both to recruit the well established and to encourage the young the fifteen nominations included Arundell Esdaile, John Charrington, E. P. Goldschmidt, Norman McLean, Gerald Mander, T. A. Walker and Charles Whibley, as well as Geoffrey. None of these was to have so great an influence on Geoffrey as did the earliest members, and because of the war their part in the Club's affairs was to be minimal; but their election at the same time as Geoffrey is a reminder of the calibre of those among whom he was working.

In view of the extent to which Geoffrey's bibliographies have influenced such work this century, it is of some interest to examine their gestation. The Baskerville Club's Minute Book is a useful starting point. On 26 February 1913 (the day on which he was

---

[7] On Gaselee see the memoir by A. S. F. Gow in *Proc. British Academy* 29 (1943), pp. 441–61; on Keynes see A. N. L. Munby 'John Maynard Keynes: the book collector' *Essays and papers*, pp. 19–26, and D. Scrase and Peter Croft, *Maynard Keynes, collector of pictures, books and manuscripts* (Cambridge, 1983).

[8] Though he was no bibliophile after the manner of most of those mentioned here, it will be recalled that on

going down from Trinity in 1904, Leonard Woolf took among his luggage to Ceylon the Kehl edition (printed in Baskerville's types) of Voltaire. See Leonard Woolf, *Sowing; an autobiography of the years 1880–1904* (London, 1967), p. 202.

[9] The Club's minute book is now Cambridge University Library MS Add. 6673.

elected), Geoffrey offered his work on Donne: the meeting and the election had been prepared carefully, for Bartholomew had already obtained a quotation from the University Press.

After some deliberation and examination of the manuscript of the bibliography, Mr Gaselee moved, that the Council accept Mr Keynes's offer, and that his bibliography of the writings of Dr John Donne be printed as the Club's second publication. Dr Fletcher [W. M. Fletcher, Fellow of Trinity, a physiologist certainly familiar with Geoffrey] seconded the motion, which was carried unanimously. It was further decided that Mr J. M. Keynes and the secretary should confer with the author as to the details of arrangement and production; and that the possibility of shortening some entries should be borne in mind.

What exactly was meant by this is clear from a letter to Geoffrey from Bartholomew, written two days later. Bartholomew had caused the University Press to set a specimen page using his own bibliography of Richard Bentley (1908) as a guide 'as to general style'. Apart from general remarks on page layout, there were also suggestions about the descriptions in Geoffrey's work. 'Rect. & vers. seem not to be liked, though. I personally see no objection. a and b much preferred by the meeting': this was an innovation, in that not only Bartholomew but also his mentor G. J. Gray, and T. J. Wise even in his 1913 bibliography of Coleridge for the London Bibliographical Society were all using 'reverse' in describing one side of a leaf. In Bartholomew's following sentence there may have been the germ of what was to become a long debate: 'It was further suggested that the ms. might be somewhat shortened by leaving out the full titles of certain editions of works which agree exactly with certain other editions of the same work.'

  Having decided on the book, Geoffrey and the Club proceeded together with some caution. Bartholomew was shy of bibliographical formulae, or 'algebra' as he called it, but was alert to write (in a great scribble: he was staying with A. W. Ward, Master of Peterhouse, in Scotland, and was in bed), 'The algebra in the Enclosed wants VERY careful checking . . . The same sort of ambiguity occurs in nearly every entry.' In September, referring probably to the entry for the 1626 *Ignatius his conclave*, he upbraided Geoffrey again:

It is no use being in a fume if you want to be a successful scientific bibliographer! (It may pay in Medicine, but I doubt it.) I disagree with you entirely that G6 'obviously' means that G6b is blank . . .[10]

G6b won. Geoffrey had known Bartholomew even before coming up to Cambridge, and the letter ended with an invitation to walk along Devil's Dyke, near Newmarket, the following week-end; but these were not lessons that Geoffrey learned very easily. By February 1914 the two were discussing the title-page, set finally with a panache entirely lacking in other University Press books of the period. By his own estimate, Geoffrey's additions made in the course of 1913 had added (not subtracted, as the Baskerville Club had intended) one-tenth to the bulk; but despite this, despite the superior paper, and despite the change in format from 'small quarto' (such as the Bentley bibliography) to 'large quarto', the Club felt that it had been overcharged by the Press. Arrangements

  [10] Bartholomew's letters are in Cambridge University Library, Geoffrey Keynes papers Box 8. For Geoffrey's affectionate tribute to Bartholomew see the *Cambridge Review*, 28 April 1933, pp. 348–50.

were made with Quaritch to market the book, and Geoffrey received his first copy at Versailles early in 1915.

The book broke new ground in several ways: most obviously in its large quarto format, which provided ample room for the reproductions of title-pages which became a feature of Geoffrey's bibliographies. The title transcriptions could be idiosyncratic, and not just because of the Baskerville Club's fears as to bulk: although the words, and the spelling, were faithfully copied, no notice was taken of capitalization, black letter, or italic, and ligatures were reproduced only insofar as the University Press's Caslon founts allowed. Long s was used regularly. Even in his nineties, Geoffrey was impatient of quasi-facsimile transcription, and he could rarely be persuaded to indicate line endings with the vertical stroke introduced by Edward Capell in the eighteenth century and used in Cambridge by G. J. Gray as recently as 1907, in his bibliography of Sir Isaac Newton: the Blake bibliography of 1921 was, for Geoffrey, exceptional in this.[11] In a strange way even in 1914 ahead of his time, Geoffrey was beginning to perceive the superiority of illustration over the paraphernalia of quasi-facsimile, but that did not, on this occasion, save him from one *faux pas*. His own copy of the 1625 *First and second anniversaries* was imperfect, so he turned instead to Grierson's recent edition of Donne, and borrowed from the Clarendon Press the modern typographical pastiches of the title-page used there: no comment was made about the deception, which was only fully corrected in the fourth edition of Geoffrey's book.

Subsequently, *Donne* was to be greatly enlarged. Collational formulae were corrected or amended to show unsigned gatherings. More illustrations were gathered in, more copies found and noted, more documents quoted, the introductory remarks to each title rewritten. But essentially the book remained recognizable even in its fourth edition, of 1973. By then the number of books listed as dedicated to Donne had quadrupled, and the celebrated list of works from his library had risen from fourteen to 218: Geoffrey acquired Donne's copy of Bernardino Ochino from Everard Meynell in August 1914 – too late for the proofs. So far, Geoffrey had confined his search to libraries within reach: the British Museum, the Cambridge and Oxford libraries, some but not all of the cathedrals (here his holidays with Cosmo Gordon had been invaluable), and one or two private libraries – notably, apart from his own, that of Edmund Gosse, author of the standard work then available on Donne's life and whose library had been described in a catalogue published in 1893. The only copy of the 1611 *Anatomy of the world* to be

---

[11] Edward Capell, *Prolusiones* (1760). See David Foxon, *Thoughts on the history and future of bibliographical description* (Los Angeles, 1970); Fredson Bowers, *Principles of bibliographical description* (Princeton, 1949), pp. 135–7, and G. T. Tanselle 'Title-page transcription and signature collation reconsidered' *Studies in Bibliography* 38 (1985), pp. 45–81.

For Geoffrey in 1913, the most recent pertinent discussions of bibliographical description would have been Falconer Madan's paper 'On method in bibliography' (*Trans Bibliographical Soc.*) 1 (1893), pp. 91–106, including a report of a discussion at which Madan 'considered that these might be reasonably curtailed (due indication

being given of such curtailment) in the case of books of later periods. The daily cheapening of photography made him hopeful that, in due time, the chief objection to the use of absolute reproduction in facsimile would disappear.' (p. 105). This had been followed in the Bibliographical Society by two major papers: A. W. Pollard and W. W. Greg 'Some points in bibliographical description', and F. Madan 'Degressive bibliography' (*Trans Bibliographical Soc.* 9 (1906–8) pp. 31–65). Geoffrey nowhere mentions these papers in his correspondence with Bartholomew, though he can hardly have been unaware of them.

recorded was that belonging to the Earl of Ellesmere, now in the Huntington. With the exception of a handful of books from the collections of William A. White, Beverley Chew and of Robert Hoe, the last auctioned in New York in 1911, no American library was listed. Though subsequent editions were to be enriched with details of manuscripts and special copies, and a clearer pattern of rarity was to emerge, it is noticeable that in 1914 Geoffrey had established, with the help of Gosse and Grierson before him, the major part of the history of Donne's work as it appeared in print before the end of the seventeenth century.

The reviewers were quick to compliment him and, on occasion, to offer extra titbits. Among the very few to make a serious point was A. W. Pollard, who drew on McKerrow's great 1913 paper on bibliographical evidence[12] (it was almost certainly unknown to Geoffrey, who apparently had yet to become properly acquainted with London bibliographical circles)[13] to point out that the variant states of the 1633 *Juvenilia*, either with or without one of the imprimaturs, were probably the result of stop-press correction. In later editions of his book, Geoffrey himself drew attention to his mistaken attempt to establish an order of priorities among differing copies of the 1633 *Poems* that were the result of the same phenomenon.

Geoffrey's own collection made a respectable showing in the lists of locations. In March 1911 he had bought the first serious book for what was to become one of the best private collections of Donne in the world: a copy of the sermon on Judges V preached in September 1622 (Keynes 14) price 12s 6d from Dobell, then in Charing Cross Road. Within a few months he had the 1648 βιαθανατος and the 1651 *Letters* from P. M. Barnard, a Cambridge graduate with an exceptionally well developed sense for early printed books, then in Tunbridge Wells. The 1627 *Devotions*, from another source, was imperfect, but reasonable enough at five shillings in a contemporary gilt binding. A perfect copy of the 1633 *Poems* was elusive, as Geoffrey chased unsuccessfully after the more interesting copies on the market. Even in 1911 it was an expensive book, when he missed a copy in Newcastle-upon-Tyne for six guineas. The usual price was £10–£15, and in New York the Hoe copy fetched $135. After the war, prices increased noticeably, thanks not least to Geoffrey's own bibliography, and he missed a bargain when, for £15, Francis Edwards offered a copy in exceptional contemporary condition – just the style he most sought. For a long time, Geoffrey had to make do with a gift from his brother of an imperfect copy.[14]

Geoffrey later recalled having been preached to on Donne by Rupert Brooke,[15] who revealed something of his own reading of the poems in a review of Grierson's edition in *The Nation*.[16] In a different vein, Stanley Spencer's painting (now in a private collection)

[12] R. B. McKerrow 'Notes on bibliographical evidence for literary students and editors of English works of the sixteenth and seventeenth centuries' *Trans Bibliographical Soc.* 12 (1914), pp. 211–318. This paper was of course the precursor to *An introduction to bibliography for literary students* (Oxford, 1927).

[13] He was elected to the Bibliographical Society in 1913 (ten years after his brother Maynard), but I have found little evidence of his acquaintance with the Society's most active figures other than the President for 1914, Sir William Osler.

[14] There are very few notes of accession either in Geoffrey's books or in his catalogue of his library *Bibliotheca bibliographici* (1964). The fullest and most reliable source is his own card catalogue of part of the collection, preserved in Cambridge University Library.

[15] Geoffrey Keynes, *The gates of memory* (Oxford, 1981), p. 81.

[16] *The Nation* 15 February 1913.

'John Donne arriving in Heaven', was painted in 1911. Grierson's edition of the poems, the first major new one to appear since Chambers' of 1896, was perfectly timed even if Brooke did find his handling of the love poems priggish. Two years later, a reviewer in *The Spectator* of Geoffrey's bibliography pointed out what had become clear: 'Donne is *par excellence* the poet of the younger poets of to-day, and this offering to his memory will not remain unappreciated.'[17] The bibliography, inspired by Brooke, encouraged by Sayle and formed under the guidance of Bartholomew, thus shows Geoffrey responding to his generation.

But he discovered William Blake quite independently, in 1907 or so, in his second year as an undergraduate:

I was walking along the west-side pavement of Trinity Street and passing the bookshop, now long defunct, of Elijah Johnson, when I happened to raise my eyes to an upper level of his window. There I saw on a shelf two prints which immediately riveted my attention. They were quite unlike anything I had ever seen before, and for me had a quite extraordinary quality, which has held my admiration ever since. It is now impossible exactly to describe what it was in these designs from William Blake's *Illustrations of the Book of Job* that had so great an effect on me.[18]

By the end of 1908 he had begun what in 1921 was to be appear as *A bibliography of William Blake* (a deceptively simple title), though by then, as Geoffrey was later to relate on more than one occasion, it had passed through many vicissitudes. In Cambridge he had allies in his new enthusiasm in a somewhat cautious Sydney Cockerell, Director of the Fitzwilliam Museum (and therefore curator of the Kerrich collection) and, more importantly, in the geneticist William Bateson.[19] By March 1909 Geoffrey had turned into a serious, if overly ambitious, collector. 'I am glad you didn't get the "Satan",' wrote Bateson on 26 March: 'Two in Cambridge would be embarrassing.' Bateson gave Geoffrey a copy of Blair's *Grave* the same year, but facsimiles had usually to suffice: of *The marriage of Heaven and Hell* (John Camden Hotten, 1868), of *The songs of innocence and of experience* (Quaritch, 1893), of *There is no natural religion* and *Poetical sketches* (William Muir, 1886 and 1893), of Thornton's Virgil, edited by Laurence Binyon (1902). The collection that accumulated on the walls and in the shelves and cupboards of an increasingly crowded house was always one of a student, even when it had come to include a great wealth of original materials. It merely moved into another plane with the acquisition in 1913 (not *c.* 1924, as in *Bibliotheca bibliographici*) of an uncoloured copy of the frontispiece to *America*, bought at Hodgson's sale rooms for fifty shillings. Blake's own copy of Winkelmann's *Reflections on the painting and sculpture of the Greeks* (1765) came from Dobell for 3*s* 6*d* in 1914.

[17] *The Spectator* 9 January 1915. Geoffrey was not unique in his quest for Donne's books. In August 1955 he received a letter from S. G. Dunn, of Alveston near Stratford on Avon, who recalled that the 1914 edition of the Donne bibliography listed him as the owner of an inscribed copy: 'I began collecting him early in the century before he became popular & was lucky to get some rather good copies at reasonable prices. Indeed, the most exciting, the sermons with S. T. [Coleridge]. notes cost me 7/6. in 1913 from a catalogue which reached me in a remote valley the other side of Kashmir.' Dunn bequeathed his books to the Bodleian Library.

[18] *The gates of memory* p. 81.

[19] In 1887 the Batesons lived at 8 Harvey Road, and were thus near neighbours of the Keynes family. The best memoir of Bateson is in *William Bateson, F.R.S., his essays & addresses* ed. Beatrice Bateson (Cambridge, 1928): see especially the remarks on his art collections, p. 61.

Geoffrey alluded in *The gates of memory* to Gilchrist and Swinburne, to the work of the Rossettis and to John Sampson's edition of the lyrical poems in the Oxford Standard Authors in 1905. Unknown to him when he saw the *Job* plates in the shop window in 1907, there was already a considerable industry surrounding Blake. 'The crowd of Blake historians increases daily,' wrote Graham Robertson in his introduction to a new edition of Gilchrist in 1906. 'A Book on Blake has taken the place of the Five-act Tragedy in the desk of every aspirant to literary honours.' The Linnell illustrations for *Job* had been exhibited at the Royal Academy in 1894; the Carfax Gallery in London had held major shows in 1904 and in 1906; the Crewe sale in 1903 had released some of the Butts collection on to the market, at prices which seemed bewilderingly high. In America, the Boston Museum of Fine Arts had held a major exhibition in 1891, and the Grolier Club followed in 1905. By 1914, the Earl of Fringal sale in London and the Hoe sales in New York had been interspersed with Joseph Wicksteed's study of *Job* (1910) and Archibald Russell's important account of the engravings (1912): it was Russell, too, who was responsible for the National Gallery exhibition in 1913, and whose 1906 edition of Blake's letters Geoffrey was eventually to displace.

Geoffrey reviewed Wicksteed's book in the *Cambridge Review* in December 1910, but turned for help in his bibliography to Blake's editor, John Sampson. Sampson's principal interests were in Romany literature, but since 1892 he had been the first Librarian of Liverpool University, and among his other interests he had in 1905 produced the first authoritative (even if, as Geoffrey realized, flawed) edition of the poetry. For Geoffrey, he combined authority with what proved to be an unjustified reputation as 'tigerish and unapproachable'.[20] At about the end of 1909 Geoffrey sent off his draft bibliography. Sampson was encouraging but cautious, and replied on 10 February:

> I trust . . . that the enthusiasm which has carried you so far will induce you to bring your work to a happy conclusion. I take it that in its present form it is merely the roughest of drafts and would be considerably re-written and re-arranged before being offered to the public.

Not for the first time, Sampson recalled Henry Bradshaw, the former University Librarian at Cambridge. 'Rember that Bradshaw chose as a motto for himself, and incidentally for other bibliographers "Whatsoever thy hand findeth to do, do it with thy might; for there is no work, nor device, nor knowledge, nor wisdom, in the grave, whither thou goest!"'[21] Several pages of suggestions followed. But unlike Bradshaw, whose natural instinct was to publish nothing until he considered it perfect, and who therefore published very little, Geoffrey pursued his course to a conclusion.

The bibliographical questions surrounding Blake were very different from those of Donne, whom he was pursuing at the same time (and both of whom could only be pursued when Geoffrey's training in medicine and surgery allowed). Few of Blake's lifetime publications had been conventional: *Poetical sketches* in 1783, *The French revolution*,

---

[20] Sir Geoffrey Keynes 'On editing Blake' *English Studies Today* 3 (1964), pp. 137ff., at p. 140. For Sampson, see the notice by Oliver Elton in the *Dictionary of national biography*, though this gives a minimum of attention to his Blakean interests. Geoffrey's letters to Sampson are now in the Sidney Jones Library, University of Liverpool: I am grateful to Michael Perkin for his help with them.

[21] Quoted in the title-page border of Bradshaw's posthumously published *A half-century of notes on the day-book of John Donne* (Cambridge, 1886). See also *The gates of memory* p. 379.

abortively, in 1791, the *Descriptive catalogue* of 1809; and, as Geoffrey came to realize, copies of the *Poetical sketches* themselves differed in that they contained manuscript authorial corrections that were not identical. Of the illuminated books, Sampson had tackled *Songs of innocence and of experience*, but had restricted himself to only about half the number of copies finally unearthed and described by Geoffrey: Sampson's selection from the prophetic books came out only in 1913. Geoffrey was to be the first to examine, or have examined for him, every known surviving copy of these books. To this he eventually added surveys of extant manuscripts, of Blake's engraved work, of engraved work commissioned or designed by others, of plates designed but not engraved by Blake, and of books known to have belonged to him. Whereas, however, in Donne the essence of the bibliography was a search for the common denominator of a printed edition, in Blake the differences between what were ostensibly parts of a common stock were of critical importance. The detailed comparison and examination of different copies of the illuminated books, printed over a long period of time, could be a distraction in the description of conventionally printed editions, and perhaps contributed to the faulty conclusions, and the over-importance attached to press variants, in Donne's *Juvenilia* and 1633 *Poems*, to which I alluded above.

Sampson's remarks in his letter of February 1910 became a year later a full publisher's report to Cambridge University Press, a copy of which Geoffrey preserved and annotated with his own comments.[22] Sampson was frank, and opened

Only in a strangely limited sense can the work be described as a Bibliography of William Blake. It includes descriptions of some MSS. though not of all . . . It includes designs of other artists which merely happen to have been engraved by Blake, while excluding the greater portion of his own artistic work.

At this stage, Geoffrey assumed that Russell, whose work on the plates was published in 1912, would provide for the last; but he was forced to agree wholeheartedly with Sampson's stress on the recording of the locations of copies of the major books:

A very serious omission in Mr. Keynes' bibliography is his failure, in the case of original editions of Blake's works, or of unique or rare reprints, to record the public or private libraries in which copies of these are to be found. But if the Bibliography is to be of any service to the reader this information should certainly be given. Of *Jerusalem* Mr. Keynes says 'this work is usually uncoloured', as though copies in this state might be found on any book-stall. One would like to know precisely how many copies of *Jerusalem*, or of the other *Prophetic Books* are known to Mr. Keynes, and in what public library, or by the courtesy of what private owner these may be consulted.

In view of the care with which Geoffrey eventually recorded individual copies, with their provenances and their current locations, it is not easy now to imagine how much briefer his original intentions were, and how radical an effect Sampson's suggestions were to have on subsequent study.

There was more scope for argument over Sampson's disagreement with Geoffrey's arrangement of his book; but the bibliographical descriptions clearly needed attention:

[22] The report is now in Cambridge University Library, Geoffrey Keynes papers Box 17. Cf. *The gates of memory* pp. 379–80.

Mr. Keynes' descriptions of books show throughout a lack of familiarity with the methods of exact bibliography, and in this regard he might be advised to study the best models . . .

The collations are confusing, and rarely include the quire sequence, which is the only true guide to the completeness of a printed book. Where moreover this has been attempted it is inaccurate. Such an impossible collation as that given of Blake's *Descriptive Catalogue* . . . $A^3.B–F^6.G^3 = 36$ leaves is enough to make Bradshaw turn in his grave. Mr. Keynes can test this for himself by attempting to fold a sheet of paper into 3 leaves! I can only guess that possibly in the copy examined by him, the first and last leaves (perhaps blank) had been removed.

Geoffrey thought the need for a 'quire sequence' 'a matter of opinion', and against Sampson's remark on his collation of the *Descriptive catalogue* noted that he had used 'a perfect copy in original wrappers': this can only have been William Bateson's copy, that nearest to hand.[23] 'It is possible', remarked Geoffrey, 'for leaves to be stuck on with gum.'

As Sampson warmed to his task of evaluation, so Geoffrey gradually realized its value. Against Sampson's 'The "Notes" are one of the weakest parts of Mr. Keynes' Bibliography' he wrote simply 'Alas!' He could also only agree on the need for some practical acquaintance with the technical processes involved – engraving, relief etching, etching and lithography – though he was never to acquire it. By the end he could only respect Sampson's judgements.

The effect of this long report was that Geoffrey revised his plans almost completely, especially with regard to the illuminated books, and now concentrated on the distinctions of individual, precisely located, copies. In October he had a brief questionnaire (see Plate I) printed at the University Press, to be circulated to everyone thought to possess anything relevant. This single quarto leaf set out nine concise questions: on the number of plates, the number of leaves, watermarks, the colour of ink in which the plates were printed, the colouring of the plates, their arrangement and foliation (Ellis and Yeats's edition was to be used for reference here), the nature and date of the binding, the size of the leaves, and the provenance. The information thus gathered was absorbed into the draft; at last in 1914 Geoffrey submitted his revised version, this time to the Clarendon Press at Oxford.

At this point the First World War intervened. 'There will of course be no thought for the present of publishing any Blake bibliography', wrote Geoffrey to Sampson on 12 August. The Delegates of the Oxford press, having, like their counterparts at Cambridge, taken the advice of Sampson, turned the book down – more because the project was unpropitious than because it was inadequate. The news was broken unofficially to Geoffrey by Osler, one of the Delegates, in November.[24] Early in March the following year Geoffrey finally obtained Sampson's verdict: much improved, but not yet perfect.[25]

But perhaps the weakest feature in Mr. Keynes' book is a tendency to lapse into aesthetic criticism or evaluation, which should be fought against by a bibliographer as a Christian fights against sin, or a scientist against sentiment. These feats are not for the likes of us. To say only that a new

[23] This copy is now among Geoffrey's books in Cambridge University Library. Quires *A* and G were printed together, as part of a duodecimo in half-sheets.

[24] Geoffrey to Bartholomew, 1 December 1914.
[25] Sampson sent the report to Cambridge, where it was acknowledged by Geoffrey's father.

List of bibliographical details concerning the engraved books of William Blake :

1. The number of plates.

2. The number of leaves on which the plates are printed.

3. Whether any leaf bears a watermark ; if so, what it is, with special reference to the date.

4. The colour of the ink in which the plates are printed.

5. Whether the plates have been coloured by hand and the characters of such colouring—whether water-colour, opaque pigment, gold-leaf, or a combination of these ; whether thickly or sparingly coloured ; whether the colours are dull or bright.

6. The arrangement of the plates, and whether they have been foliated by Blake. [The arrangement may conveniently be expressed in terms of the facsimile reproductions in the edition of Blake's works edited by Messrs. Ellis and Yeats.]

7. Whether the leaves are bound into a volume ; if so, the character of the binding and its approximate date.

8. The size of the leaf [height × breadth].

9. The history of the book as far as it is known—former owners, sales through which it has passed, etc.

PLATE I. Questionnaire on Blake's illuminated books sent out by Geoffrey Keynes in 1911

section of Blake's most amazing poem – *The Everlasting Gospel* – is 'of considerable interest and importance', is about as adequate as though the same comment were to be made of a retrieved ode of Sappho.[26]

Geoffrey thought the report 'more favourable than I had dared to hope', and was apologetic about his aesthetic criticism. 'It appears I am still guilty in several places of this egregious sin', he wrote to Sampson; 'but the offending passages shall be weeded out before there is any thought of going to press.' 'Indeed', he went on in more serious vein, 'it seems almost fatuous even to think of going to press, sitting here as I am in an ambulance train within sound of the guns. But it is a great relief sometimes to let one's thoughts return to the channels of peacetime. I suppose there will again be a time when bibliography will seem to be a reasonable pursuit.'[27]

[26] Cambridge University Library. Geoffrey Keynes papers Box 17. See also *The gates of memory* pp. 380–2.

[27] Geoffrey to Sampson, 9 March 1915.

For all its disruptions, the War did not stay Geoffrey's enthusiasm as a collector. Book collecting, indeed, became the means of retaining sanity. But it did destroy any hopes that he may once have entertained of his bibliography of Blake being published by the Clarendon Press, which under R. W. Chapman faced the first post-war years in considerable gloom as it contemplated the inflationary effects of the previous few years on a greatly reduced market.[28] The long awaited Linnell sale in March 1918, when Geoffrey was still in France, proved to be unexpectedly productive, in that as a result Geoffrey acquired his first drawings by Blake. But there was no publisher now willing to take on his work. He appealed without success at a meeting of the Blake Society on 23 September 1919, and then, exactly a month later, found unexpected help. He met William Ivins, of the Metropolitan Museum of New York, at the Cambridge home of the Darwin family, and a little later received an enquiry from him:

Have you made any arrangements about printing it yet? I mentioned it at a meeting of the Grolier Club Council recently and several of the members asked me to find out from you whether you would care to let the Club have it for publication and if so what your ideas about quids pro quo &c might be.[29]

There most of the bibliographical tale ends. With great generosity, the Grolier Club gave Geoffrey virtually a free hand in the design and manufacture of one of the most magnificently produced bibliographies ever to have been published. Printing was begun in November 1920 at the Chiswick Press under Charles Jacobi, who could handle both the letterpress and the collotype illustrations, on a special making of Hodgkinson's paper from Wookey Hole, and illustrated with collotypes, some of them in colour. The presswork was finished in November 1921, and Geoffrey signed his name in his own copy in February 1922. The decision to print in England was not taken lightly. But Geoffrey could always be persuasive, and even in 1920 was alert to the dollar-sterling rate. The printed page was modelled, with some adjustment, on that in his *Donne*: it is both slightly larger and considerably more complicated. The estimates were alarming: four collotypes in full colour were to cost £200 ($728), and they were eventually printed in up to fourteen colours in the desire to reproduce the originals as exactly as possible: even this was inadequate for two of Geoffrey's initial choices, which he was therefore forced to abandon. The frontispiece (the British Museum's 'Glad Day') was one of the substitutes.[30]

Geoffrey's own relations with the Grolier Club, from that first meeting with Ivins, were generally cordial through all the inevitably protracted negotiations conducted through the media of committee and surface mail. His principal contact with the Club was with Ruth Granniss, and whatever the Club's private fears may have been, they were not reflected in her letters. Henry Watson Kent at least was one of the more cautious when it became clear in 1921 that Geoffrey was determined to replace the Club's usual

[28] Peter Sutcliffe *The Oxford University Press; an informal history* (Oxford, 1978), p. 190.

[29] Cambridge University Library. Geoffrey Keynes papers Box 19.

[30] I am grateful to the Grolier Club and to Mr Robert Nikirk for permission to examine and quote from papers relating to this project. Geoffrey's own annotated proofs of his bibliography of Blake are in Cambridge University Library, Keynes M.5.4.

device on the title page with Cumberland's visiting card: 'He seems polite, but not convincing.'

Much more patience was required when the book was finished. Unwittingly, the Chiswick Press violated American copyright law in printing (without reference to the Grolier Club) a notice of the Club's claim to copyright on the verso of the title-page. Copies were impounded by the New York Customs, and released only when the offending leaf had been reprinted in England with no such claim: as a result, copies in the American market differed from the twenty-five retained by Geoffrey for presentation in England.

Geoffrey released his copies in February. Club members received theirs only in April, six or more weeks after the book had been reviewed in the *Times Literary Supplement* in London. The price to members was $50, and a decision to raise the price almost immediately to $75 naturally drew criticism from some members, who thought it improperly commercial in such a club. In fact, the book was a great bargain, having cost far more than that to produce. It was a bibliographical extravaganza that would have been impossible without the very large subsidy provided by the Club. The Clarendon Press could never have afforded to put such a book on the market at such a price; but more seriously, the general market was alienated at least temporarily. At Quaritch, E. H. Dring thought that a retail price of £25 would be too much (he would be buying copies at $100, or £21): 'Speaking from a commercial point of view, I do not think it is worth $100.'

Geoffrey dedicated the book to one of his Cambridge mentors, William Bateson, and paid particular tribute not only to Sampson, but also to various collectors. In America, Miss Henrietta C. Bartlett, librarian to the Brooklyn collector William A. White, had been invaluable in unearthing copies (her annotated copy of the 1919 Grolier exhibition catalogue is among Geoffrey's papers). But by 1921 Geoffrey was also in touch with S. Foster Damon, who described the arrival of the book at Harvard on 27 May 1922:

This morning I saw Dr. Winship of the Widener Library opening a large volume from the Grolier club. 'What is that?' said I carelessly. 'Oh!' he cried, 'this is the Keynes bibliography at last!' 'Is it! Excuse me, sir.' So I grabbed it up and ran away with it. The chase was exciting, but I am a younger man than he; and when I knew I was safe, I examined the tome at leisure.

Oh! glory! glory! glory! glory! What a book! I suppose it is rather difficult to speak to you now. How jealous your poor brother must be![31]

Bateson rewarded Geoffrey with his own copy of the 1809 *Descriptive catalogue*, once thought to be the only one still in original wrappers and the same one over which he had disagreed with Sampson back in 1911. That spring, too, Geoffrey reached his thirty-fifth birthday, and so by Sayle's standards the beginning of the second half of his life. Donne and Blake had dominated the years before the war, and on them Geoffrey cut his bibliographical teeth. He summed up many of his difficulties, at least in general terms, in the preface to *Blake*:

It is difficult for an amateur bibliographer to arrive quickly at a standard form for his entries, particularly when, as in the present case, it has to be frequently changed to suit the varying nature of the material.

[31] Cambridge University Library. Geoffrey Keynes papers Box 17.

A professional might say the same. I have already touched on the distinction necessary in approaching these two very different subjects, Donne and Blake, bibliographically. Both were to absorb Geoffrey to the end of his life. The Blake collection was begun in 1908, the Donne in 1911. Of his other preoccupations from these early years, apart from moderns such as Aubrey Beardsley, H. G. Wells, Hilaire Belloc, A. E. Housman and Henry James, Sir Thomas Browne has already been mentioned. The first book by Thomas Fuller to arrive seems to have been *The holy state* (1642) in 1910; but he began to pay serious attention to Fuller only in 1916, the year in which he also tackled Evelyn, Jane Austen, William Wordsworth and Samuel Butler.

In October 1914 he wrote only of Blake and Donne. With the deaths of some of his closest friends in 1915 (Rupert Brooke's, the best known, was but one in a sequence of such blows), he became noticeably depressed; Bartholomew especially, with Sayle's help tried to distract him. Booksellers' catalogues arrived only irregularly in France, and the acquisition in November 1915 of Drayton's 1630 *Poems* was so much of a triumph that it made him think of attempting a bibliography of Drayton. By the end of the following February however, he was set on Evelyn, and in a brief few days of leave had scoured the London shops. The *Handlist* of Evelyn's books, compiled jointly by Geoffrey and by Bartholomew and printed in an edition of twenty-five copies only, reached him in France in August. Though ostensibly confined to copies in three public collections, the British Museum, the Bodleian and Cambridge University Library, in fact, by a series of asterisks, it indicated also what the two compilers owned themselves. It was a working document, provided with plenty of space for annotation and endowed with no bibliographical information apart from imprints (where known) and formats. In effect, it was a shopping list, for which Bartholomew acted as Geoffrey's agent.

Geoffrey's army pay gave him a new freedom to buy books. 'When I come back, with my 24/– a day and no expenses, I shall be unprecedentedly rich. Books will be cheap, and I shall have a wonderful haul of Donnes and Blakes, everybody else being too poor to buy.'[32] Even long before the war, with relatively little spare money, he had preferred books in contemporary condition to those that had been rebound; after the war, many of the inferior copies of books bought in the previous fifteen or so years were to be sold off at Sotheby's, as better copies were found. As he accumulated his Evelyn collection in 1916, and thus, from France, was obliged to express his preferences to Bartholomew in writing, he emphasized repeatedly how much he preferred generally to wait for a good copy, rather than buy an inferior one immediately. Bindings by Bedford or Zaehnsdorf held no attractions when on a seventeenth-century book. Instead, when necessary, he had his books repaired as conservatively as possible, in Cambridge. For the local binding firm of Gray's he had a lasting respect, even fifty years later.

The consequences of this emphasis, wherever practicable, on contemporary condition, are to be seen in his shelves now, and became more pronounced as he explored Sir Thomas Browne and John Evelyn, or later authors such as Hazlitt or Jane Austen. Not everyone even in Cambridge understood this perfectly. Considering the reverence popularly accorded to the market stall run by Gustave David, and the extent to which those

---

[32] Geoffrey to Bartholomew, 18 October 1914.

PLATE 11. Gustave David's bookstall in Cambridge Market, *c.* 1910

before Geoffrey – his brother, E. P. Goldschmidt, Charles Whibley and a host of Cambridge dons and undergraduates – are known to have relied on David, it is surprising to find how few of the books in Geoffrey's library at the end of his life can be shown to have been bought from this traditional treasure trove.[33] There were, of course, major finds, such as the manuscript miscellany of Donne's poems now in the University Library.[34] But generally speaking the books bought there, and still in Geoffrey's collection, were not by authors to whom he gave most attention as a bibliographer. The eighteenth-century novelists, or Samuel Johnson and his circle, were more frequent than those with whom I have here been principally concerned. The Baskervilles from this

[33] Cf. *David of Cambridge; some appreciations* (Cambridge, 1937). Sir William Nicholson's drawing of David, reproduced as a frontispiece, has been recently acquired by the Fitzwilliam Museum.
[34] MS Add. 5778.

source were by no means the most important, though on the other hand Geoffrey's collections of both Pickering imprints and of Thomas Bewick prospered here. It would be
unfair to ascribe to Geoffrey any long-held opinion solely on the basis of that held in
France in April 1916, but it is one supported by evidence now on the shelves of the
University Library: 'David *never* knows when a copy is a decent one or not; or at any rate
doesn't exercise any sort of judgement.'[35]

Having formed his priorities as to condition, Geoffrey then developed them only
gradually. Although within a very short time he was usually to abandon the practice, for
a time in about 1917 he fell into the habit of buying books in seventeenth-century calf
and having their spines lettered in gilt – straight on to the leather, rather than on a patch.
Examples of this are now to be seen especially among the Donnes and Brownes.
Bartholomew, more sensitive to condition, protested, and so received a diatribe from
Geoffrey, who reminded him that even Bartholomew's place of work, the University
Library, was not without sin:

I am prepared to defend my lettering of old sheep at the point of the bayonet. It seems to me only
reasonable to give the deare olde thinges a distinguishing mark, so that one can pick them off the
shelves without difficulty. If you've only got six of course there's no necessity. But then I'm buying books now 'on rather a large scale' (to quote your measured phrase . . .); and surely I have the
precedent of the ULC to justify me. It surprises me to find you, the Eminently Reasonable, the
Scorner of bibliographical affectation, up against me in this matter. Now if I had red and green
labels plastered all over them, or tore out the leaves and pissed on them a Rivière, you'd have
some reason . . . There's more to say than I can manage in a letter.[36]

Bartholomew won, and in 1918 preserved in Geoffrey's copy of Browne's *Pseudodoxia
epidemica* (1669) its owner's note of instructions sent off from France to Gray's in
Cambridge. The volume, bound in seventeenth-century calf, needed to be rebacked, so
even Bartholomew's criticisms might on this occasion have been muted; but the further
instruction was wholly admirable for the occasion: 'No end papers or other additions
will be wanted.'[37]

In 1921 many of the best parts of Geoffrey's collections, even of authors in whom he
had so far specialized, were still to come. The Dobell manuscript of Donne's poems, for
which he knew Dobell to have paid only six shillings, was priced at £100 in 1916; it was a
tempting but unattainable prospect, and went to Harvard: the no less desirable
Leconfield manuscript was to cost Geoffrey precisely the same in 1928. In the Browne
collection, Sotheby's had provided Elizabeth Lyttelton's presentation copy to the dedicatee, the Earl of Buchan, of *Christian morals* (1716), and Dobell had produced her own
commonplace book.[38] The sale of the residue of Browne's nineteenth-century editor
Simon Wilkin's library in October 1921 was to produce more. The Draycott House sale
in the following month offered books in just the kind of condition which Geoffrey most
valued – by Donne, Fuller, and, later, Bartholin, Henry King and Rabelais. A little later,

---

[35] Geoffrey to Bartholomew, 5 April 1916. His later
remarks (9 March 1917) were more balanced: 'David is
hopeless in some ways; but what can one do? We owe him
far too much ever to be really cross at him'.

[36] Geoffrey to Bartholomew, 9 March 1917.

[37] Cambridge University Library Keynes B.6.23.

[38] Edited by Geoffrey as *The commonplace book of
Elizabeth Lyttleton, daughter of Sir Thomas Browne*
(Cambridge, 1919): the book was designed by Bruce
Rogers.

the sale of the library of the seventeenth-century Daniel Fleming was to provide the trade with stock for Geoffrey's shelves for decades. For Geoffrey, bibliography and bibliophily had become inseparable. He regarded his collection as a working library, and went about his collecting with the same systematic attention that he did his work as a surgeon. Of the great author collections by which he became best known – many of them associated with his standard bibliographies – most of William Harvey was collected fairly rapidly between 1924 and 1928, a couple of years after his Oxford monograph on blood transfusion and in time for the tercentenary celebrations of *De motu cordis* in 1928; Hazlitt and Jane Austen had been started by 1921; Henry King was begun in 1924; William Cowper in 1927; Boyle in 1929; Timothie Bright in 1931; Francis Bacon in 1932; Thomas Hooke in about 1936. George Berkeley, though begun in the early 1930s, was mostly assembled after the Second World War, necessarily in the steps of his brother Maynard.

With the publication in 1914 of *John Donne*, Keynes became an authority; with *Blake* in 1921 he confirmed and enlarged his position in a startling way. Though he relished the attention to production that societies and small publishers could pay to his books (the Nonesuch Press, with which he was to become so deeply involved, was ideal in this), it is noticeable that thereafter he usually found little difficulty in persuading ordinary publishers to take on his work. In the book trade, his exploits in the antiquarian shops became subjects for the gossip columns even in 1917, as the London trade gathered itself to face his quest for John Evelyn.[39] At its lowest level, his task was not only a bibliographic one: it also charted rarity in a reliable way, often for the first time. When he began, there was little available apart from Lowndes and *Book prices current*. The *Short-title catalogue* appeared only in 1926, Wing not until 1945–51. Keynes numbers were being quoted by London booksellers in 1921, first by Leighton (whose catalogues at the time were compiled with notable bibliographic care), then, gradually, by Myers of High Holborn, Birrell and Garnett, Dobell and Francis Edwards. In 1913 Geoffrey had acquired his copy of Donne's *XXVI sermons* with the 'at the charge of Dr. Donne' imprint in a job lot at the Dowden sale. In 1930, Dobell, of whom Geoffrey had by then been a regular customer for about two decades, offered a copy of the same issue, price £25: 'This third volume of Dr Donne's Sermons is an exceedingly rare book. It occurs with three different imprints. THE ONLY OTHER COPY KNOWN WITH THE ABOVE IMPRINT IS THAT IN THE POSSESSION OF DR. G. L. KEYNES.' No wonder that Geoffrey had to face the wrath of the trade over his mistaken ordering of the first two editions of *Religio medici*, on which he retracted in 1952.[40]

His bibliographies became required reading, for librarians as well as for book collectors and booksellers. For their respective subjects they became the mainstays of desiderata lists. When the history of this century's institutional collecting is finally written, it

[39] 'Donne (pronounced Dun) is the chief literary revival of this century; and Geoffrey Keynes . . . has been instrumental in gingering-up the market for his first editions. Within a year or two the Donne quartos jumped from five to fifteen pounds, and all the booksellers seemed to be alert for fine copies – generally, one discovered, at the behest of the same young customer, Geoffrey Keynes.

The other day a bookish friend told me that the world of dealers was suddenly bestirring itself about John Evelyn, the diarist. Quaritch and all his understudies are searching out and advertising for his rarer pieces. Then I heard the reason: G. Keynes again!' (*Sketch* 10 January 1917).

[40] Sir Geoffrey Keynes 'Religio Bibliographici', preface to *Bibliotheca bibliographici* (London, 1964).

will have to address itself to the degree in which its priorities were formed by the existence of major author or subject bibliographies. In that respect, Geoffrey's influence on twentieth-century librarianship, particularly in the United States (and therefore, via accessions policies, on scholarship) has yet to be measured. In March 1929 George P. Winship, then Assistant Librarian at Harvard, thought it not inappropriate to add a postscript at the end of a letter in which he corrected earlier misinformation on an edition of Donne. Harvard had just greatly benefited by the estate of William A. White, through his daughter Mrs White Emerson: 'In all, we get 291 "STC" titles from Mr. White's collection, giving us in all 3717 S.T.C. numbers, well over 14 per cent.'

Geoffrey's own library is generally acknowledged to be one of the finest of its kind collected this century. Blake's paintings, drawings, separate engravings and illuminated books have mostly joined those of R. E. Kerrich, T. H. Riches and W. Graham Robertson in the Fitzwilliam Museum. Most of the rest of his library is kept, as a collection, in Cambridge University Library. Its great value is not only as a remarkable collection of collections, nor even as a library deliberately collected with an eye to contemporary condition; but also as the collection from which was constructed some of this century's most significant bibliographical and editorial work. Geoffrey's edition of Blake appeared in 1925, of Thomas Browne in 1928–31, and of Rupert Brooke in 1946, while his various bibliographies have become touchstones for other editorial projects, especially for the seventeenth century. These bibliographies were constructed primarily from copies of books in Cambridge University Library (Geoffrey's most convenient research library) and from his own shelves. Despite the acknowledged importance of author bibliographies not only in literary studies, but also in the study of the book either as an artefact or as an object capable of provoking strikingly different perceptions, curiously little attention has so far been paid to the history of bibliographical description. For the twentieth century at least, Geoffrey's library would be an ideal place in which to begin. At his centenary, however, it is appropriate to recall Geoffrey in his youth, rather than in his influence. He had learned his methods from Sayle, Bartholomew and Sampson, with the help of other friends such as Cosmo Gordon and Sir William Osler: in many ways, it was a curiously provincial training. He knew himself to be in the van, certainly better in the end than T. J. Wise, in whose bibliography of Wordsworth published in 1916 he found a 'finished pattern of how not to make a bibliography'.[41] On a visit to Wise in 1917 he found the talk of his host's enlarged prostate gland and aunt's cancer merely irritating, and he came away in feline mood to write to Bartholomew:

It's interesting to observe other peoples methods, and of course little podgy Mr Wise . . . is reckoned one of the Princes of the Cosmos Bibliographicus; but I fancy that's reckoning in terms of bullion rather than of competence isn't it?[42]

How far Geoffrey had come since that first hesitating approach to another authority, John Sampson, in 1910. His bibliography of Blake was still undergoing revision; and although he had tackled one author from the hand-press period he had yet to begin serious work on those after about 1800: Jane Austen, Hazlitt and, abortively, Thomas Love

---

[41] Geoffrey to Bartholomew, 29 July 1917.   [42] Ibid.

Peacock. They in turn were to present entirely different bibliographical questions, relating to paper, to bindings, to printing, and to the North American trade. So far these were questions of which he had barely thought.

In conclusion, it is appropriate to return to the Baskerville Club, which went into another hibernation during the War, having elected (certainly at Geoffrey's instigation) Sir William Osler in November 1914. At its next meeting, on 15 November 1921, it had before it for election S. C. Roberts of Pembroke (later Secretary to the Press Syndics, and Master of his college), A. F. Scholfield of Trinity (later University Librarian), Owen Morshead of Magdalene (later Royal Librarian), Percy Babington of St John's, and the late E. J. Dingwall, of Pembroke. Three months later it held what was to prove to be its final meeting; and having exerted its independence by declining to send a formal message of congratulation to the new Oxford Bibliographical Society it considered a possible third publication. Of the nine proposed, nothing was to come immediately of a new edition of Gunning's reminiscences of early nineteenth-century Cambridge, or of a new census of Baskervilles. Charles Sayle's suggestion, 'Illustrations of bindings in Cambridge libraries', became in 1928 G. D. Hobson's invaluable survey, and Babington's proposed bibliography of J. A. Symonds was published in London in 1925. The other proposals were Geoffrey's: unpublished letters by Sir Thomas Browne, a bibliography of Jane Austen, a revised edition of the Evelyn handlist, a 'select Pickering bibliography', and a supplement to Donne. He cannot have known that by the time he had completed all these tasks not only would the Club be extinct, but that he would also have seen through the press bibliographies of Sir Thomas Browne, William Harvey, William Hazlitt, George Herbert and Henry King, quite apart from editions of Browne and of Harvey, and a dozen books by or about William Blake.

B. H. BRESLAUER

Martin Bodmer Remembered

An Essay in Autobiography
Addressed to the Friends of Bodmeriana on 13 October, 1986

REMEMBERING to-day, in the very edifice which houses his life's achievement, my relations with Martin Bodmer, the greatest, the most universal book collector of his time, I am stirred by emotions which by no means spring from professional pride alone, however gratifying it is to a dealer, motivated by more than purely commercial interests, to have gained the confidence of a great collector and to have contributed to a celebrated library. I am moved by the recollection of a man who was one of the most fascinating of the many remarkable personalities in various walks of life it has been my good fortune to encounter in a fairly long life, and a relationship that ripened into mutual understanding to a degree for which the word friendship may not be too strong a term, however formal it outwardly remained.

My connection with the Bibliotheca Bodmeriana – it received this designation only in 1951 – spanned a whole lifetime, as Martin Bodmer himself stated in a memorable letter from which I shall be quoting at greater length. Indeed, it was an inherited one. I am not certain when exactly my father, Martin Breslauer, started dealing with him directly, but I know that Bodmer acquired from him through intermediaries important works from the library of the Princes of Stolberg-Wernigerode, of which my father successively bought large sections from about 1930–1931 onwards. In the early stages of his collecting career, Dr Bodmer wished to preserve a certain anonymity, working with and through a few dealers who had gained his confidence. By 1935 when I entered my father's firm in Berlin, this confidence had been established between the two M.B.s, and some of the greatest rarities of classical German literature from the library of Gotthilf Weisstein and from the Lessing Collection formed by General Lessing, a collateral descendent of Gotthold Ephraim Lessing, recent acquisitions of my father's, had found their way directly to Zurich.

It was at that time that my father, almost too late, began to realize that the Hitler regime was going to be more than an ugly dream from which Germany would soon awake, and that he had to face the almost unthinkable: to leave, at the age of almost sixty-five, the country of his birth. Although his international reputation and the assistance of English friends and colleagues soon secured for him and his family the British Government's permit to settle in London, the task of realizing his assets – the condition imposed upon the intending emigrant before the Nazi Government let him go, stripped of most if not all of his possessions – proved to be extremely difficult. The biggest problem in this respect was his private library of 21,000 volumes, a unique *instrument de travail* on all aspects of the history and bibliography of the printed book and on the works of the *peintres-graveurs*, the result of thirty years' collecting. A special feature of this library I may mention: many of the volumes had been beautifully bound in richly gilt half-morocco bindings in all the colours of the rainbow, with morocco lettering pieces in contrasting hues. This extraordinary library was well-known, and my father was afraid the Nazi Government would confiscate it if he asked for permission to take it with him to England. Even if there had been time to sell it piecemeal, his overriding wish was to see what he considered his life's work preserved as a whole. Martin Bodmer came to the rescue, realizing after some hesitation that my father's library would provide a splendid scholarly apparatus for his own. However, there were certain sections which he thought would not serve his purpose and were therefore split off, such as the 450 volumes on bookbindings, the vast collection of library catalogues, the 2,000 volumes on artists, etc. In all, he acquired about 15,000 volumes, the largest single accession the Bodmeriana ever received, and one of its largest single components to the present day, in spite of subsequent sales. The fate of the remaining 6,000 volumes can be quickly told: the German Government allowed my father to take them with him, having been declared by kindly and courageous colleagues to be the valueless remainder of a once great collection, but not before it had taxed away, on the shabbiest of pretexts, the entire sum which Martin Bodmer had paid for the bulk of the library. A few hundred works of it would today realize more than the original purchase price – such were the abysmal market conditions of those years.

In a way, Martin Bodmer had bought a pig in a poke. There was no complete catalogue of the library, only a resumé of the sections of which it was composed, and a list of the most important works. The establishment of a catalogue was therefore an urgent need. To me then fell the task of laying the foundations of a card index which Dr Bodmer's librarian was then to complete – an onerous task for a young man of twenty. How worthy I showed myself of the confidence placed in me I dare not contemplate. But the two periods of three months each which I spent in Zurich in the spring and autumn of 1938 were among the happiest of my youth, overshadowed as it had been by the gathering clouds of political persecution, by emigration and the struggle, shared with an elderly father, to establish a new existence in alien surroundings during a period of world-wide economic depression.

My temporary employer had me established in a small boarding house near the 'Enge' railway station of Zurich. Several of my fellow lodgers with whom I shared my meals in the somewhat dingy dining-room were young unmarried members of the Zurich City Theatre orchestra whose table talk was mainly concerned with the music they performed, with gossip about their colleagues, and with the outside engagements that sometimes came their way. In their rooms they often practised on their instruments. I especially remember the first oboist of the orchestra who endlessly rehearsed passages from Mozart's quartet for that instrument. It is the only piece of Mozart's compositions which I positively learned to hate. Periodically I received from the hands of Dr Bodmer's secretary the pocket money agreed upon. If it proved to be inadequate and had to be supplemented with subsidies from home, this was mainly due to my extravagance, for not infrequently I spurned the somewhat monotonous fare offered at the 'pension Enge', and lunched or dined out. I also went to the opera and to theatres, and visited the cafés frequented by intellectuals, many of them refugees, who appeared to form mutually exclusive cliques which I was far too shy to make contact with. But I greatly improved my French, as I had made the acquaintance of a charming young French girl, from Lyon, I believe, who was attending a Pensionat for girls, but had to be back every night by seven o'clock which left me free to sample, very occasionally, the rather innocent night life of Zurich which closed down at eleven o'clock or midnight, being under the thumb of the all-powerful *Frauenvereine*, the Women's Leagues.

Every morning I presented myself at the former school house in the Bederstrasse, at the foot of the Freudenberg and adjoining the Bodmer estate. Bodmer had only recently acquired this large house to serve as his library, and the furnishing of it had not yet been completed. My father's library had been put up in the reconstructed basement of the house, and there I worked. Often Bodmer would descend from the upper regions, and for a short while talk to me about my work, about his latest acquisitions, about his aims in forming his library, about literature, and about the events of the day. I especially remember one on which he arrived in a state of great agitation. 'Have you heard', he asked me, 'the Germans have marched into Austria. This is horrible – it could also happen to us here!'

These conversations were a great experience to me, and I looked forward to them keenly, as they illumined my somewhat lonely task underground. But occasionally, I confess, I would abandon my duties – not that Dr Bodmer would have minded – and steal upstairs, looking at the long rows of books, pull out a volume here and there, read a poem, a short story, an essay, and return, refreshed in spirit, to my cataloguing work.

But the most vividly remembered of these conversations was my very first, when I presented myself on arrival in Zurich at the great house with its Grecian portico. I was led through several large rooms hung with splendid pictures. Tea was served in his study. It was the first time I had ever met him. I was both impressed by and in immediate sympathy with this patrician with the face of an intellectual whose features, so animated in conversation, were already then, in repose, beginning to assume the ascetic contours which the years were to etch more deeply upon it. He at once gave me a *tour d'horizon* of his collection. He already owned the Gutenberg Bible and the four Shakespeare Folios, but regretted having been unable to acquire the Codex Sinaiticus, of which he had been given the first refusal. The price originally demanded had been a quarter of a million pounds. 'I could not', he said, 'divert so large a sum from my fortune to a single purchase. But', he added with a note of regret that amazed me, 'in the end the Russians accepted £120,000. Perhaps I made the same mistake as my father who collected paintings. He had an opportunity to buy the Dürer now in Berlin' – was it the Madonna with the Bullfinch? I never asked him – 'but as the price exceeded the limit he had set himself for a single picture, he let it pass.'

In my youthful enthusiasm, I came away from this first encounter with the idea that I had not only talked to a great collector, but perhaps also to a creative writer. I only mention it, because it conveys the impression of intellectuality which I felt surrounded him. As far as I know, all his writing was confined to the exposition of the concept, literary, historical and if you want, philosophical, that underlay his collecting activities, in books, speeches, and personal correspondence. Hardly more than a year before his death he wrote me that he was busily working on a book which he described as 'a rather interesting synthesis of human civilization (*Kultur*), with the collection – indirectly – as background'. I wonder, how far he got with this work. One sometimes had the impression that it was not he who owned his library, but that it was the library that possessed him.

While working in Zurich I also had one of my first independent successes as a bookseller. Martin Bodmer had told me that he did not yet own a Shakespeare Quarto. Shortly before leaving for my second stint at the library, I spent a weekend in Brighton. On the promenade I ran into Gabriel Wells, the American bookseller, who specialized in early English literature. Could he offer me any Shakespeare Quartos? A week later, on his cabled instruction, there arrived from his New York office a whole list of Quartos, mainly of late date, but among them the second edition of *The Merry Wives of Windsor*, 1619. My father was appalled: Wells was bound to know Bodmer; as it turned out he didn't. Bodmer bought it, his first Shakespeare Quarto (Plate I). In 1947 he reproduced its title page in 'Eine Bibliothek der Weltliteratur', the first full exposition of his aims as a collector.

If I have dwelt, perhaps at excessive length, on these early encounters with Martin Bodmer, it is because they formed, I believe, the foundation of a relationship that came to fruition much later, in fact only during the last eight years of his life. The war had interposed a long hiatus in our connection. My father had died in 1940, victim of an air attack on London. I myself returned, in 1945, from war service to take over the conduct of a firm whose base had been further depleted, after the losses sustained in Germany, by the intervening years. It took a long time to reconstruct and expand it. From time to time Bodmer would order one or the other item from my catalogues to fill minor gaps, but I had few major contributions to his library to make. All the same, there were some fine autograph poems by German authors, such as Mörike, Grillparzer, Fontane, Keller, Conrad Ferdinand Meyer, an unpublished song by Debussy, 'Il dort encore' (Plate II), the complete and hitherto lost autograph MS of the second canto of Lamartine's unfinished long poem 'Les Visions' [on thirty pages], the beginning of a homily by Aelfric, a precious fragment of an eleventh-century MS in Anglo-Saxon, and a magnificent Turkish sixteenth-century calligraphic manuscript Koran, a scroll ten meters long, to be carried in the shaft of the battle standard, in front of the Turkish armies. A rather curious story attaches to a monumental cuneiform inscription in Assyrian, *c.* 885–860 BC, from the palace of Ashur-Nasir-Pal, commemorating his conquests. Originally, Bodmer had ordered it in 1951. Alas, it arrived in Geneva broken in two, and was forthwith returned. For ten years the two thick stone slabs served as a foot-rest to my secretary. I then heard of an excellent restorer of antique artefacts, and after ascertaining that there was no loss to the text, had the two pieces joined together by him. I then offered it again in a catalogue, and again Bodmer ordered it, this time keeping it for good. Among the printed books he acquired from me at that time, I remember with pleasure one of the rarest of all Molière first editions, and of French seventeenth century literature in general, 'Les Plaisirs de l'Isle Enchantée', 1664, the only complete copy recorded (Plate III).

A

Moſt pleaſant and ex-
cellent conceited Comedy,
of Sir Iohn Falſtaffe, and the
merry VViues of VVindſor.

VVith the ſwaggering vaine of Ancient Piſtoll, and Corporall Nym.

VVritten by W. SHAKESPEARE.

Printed for *Arthur Iohnſon,* 1619.

PLATE I. Shakespeare *The Merry Wives of Windsor* 1619 (second quarto).
Bibliotheca Bodmeriana

But the first really outstanding contribution I was able to make to the Bodmeriana happened in 1963. It was an autograph sonnet by Michel Angelo, followed on the same page by a letter of dedication to Vittoria Colonna (Plate IV). I had bought it from the collection of Prince Ginori Conti in Florence, after it had been refused as too expensive by some of the foremost European and American dealers, but it was even then a bargain for both the immediate buyer and the ultimate owner. It is certainly one of the most spectacular and moving literary autographs to have passed through my hands and owned today, I can claim with some justification, by the Bodmeriana. Martin Bodmer was immediately fascinated, but there were difficulties, as he explained in his letter of

PLATE 11. Debussy, autograph of 'Il dort encore'. Bibliotheca Bodmeriana

26 January 1963, a characteristic specimen of his epistolary style: 'This is in itself a splendid object which would wonderfully fit into the frame of my collection', he wrote, 'I therefore know how to appreciate your kindness in giving me the first refusal of it. But I find myself in a very special situation. In the course of the last years I have bought rather too much, and as the stock exchange has been low since last April, I have been waiting for it to recover, and in the meantime have allowed my overdraft to increase. It now exceeds seven figures, and I have yet to pay out large amounts due within the next few months, the largest among them being taxes. I must therefore weigh each purchase with fine scales, if it can be considered at all. In this special case, I ought to say that I am saturated with Michel Angelo, however grotesque that may sound. But last summer I

PLATE III. Molière *Les plaisirs de l'isle enchantée* 1664. Bibliotheca Bodmeriana

acquired at Sotheby's the famous drawing "Christ before Pilate" which on the verso also contains a sonnet, or rather a draft of one. As for the last thirty years I have owned a Michel Angelo drawing, this would appear to be all that one could wish for. And yet I am not saying no to your offer, but would ask you to reserve the item for me. Perhaps I can bring myself to part again with the very expensive leaf, and in that case your autograph would be welcome. In the meantime I shall take soundings, as there appears to be an amateur for it.' The amateur proved to be Count Antoine Seilern, the famous drawing collector in London who had been the underbidder at the sale. He took over the drawing at cost price – more than six times the price I was asking for my leaf. This transaction had a rather dramatic epilogue. I had decided to hand over this marvellous autograph to Dr Bodmer personally, stopping off in Geneva on my way to Italy. The night before my departure I gave a farewell party in its honour. It turned out to be a rather splendid affair, attended by appreciative connoisseurs and members of the London *beau monde*. Next morning, afraid that through my absentmindedness I might lose a briefcase, I placed the sonnet in my large suitcase – those were the days when thefts of registered luggage were unheard-of. After the Geneva-bound plane had been in the air for a few minutes, it suddenly made a sweep of almost a hundred-and-eighty degrees. A steward, white as a sheet, announced we were returning to London for an emergency landing, and that, as

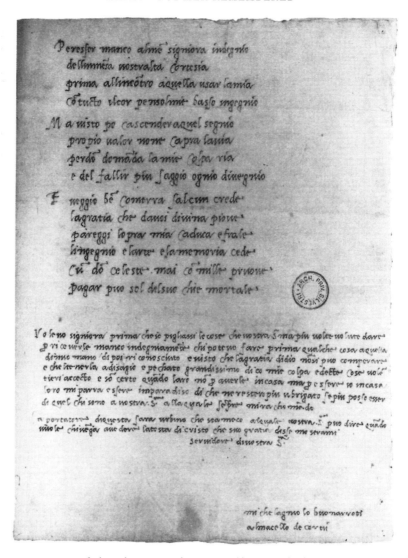

PLATE IV. Michelangelo, autograph sonnet and letter. Bibliotheca Bodmeriana

soon as the aircraft stopped, we must tear open the emergency windows and jump, as there was danger of an explosion. We touched down, racing past batteries of drawn-up fire-engines and ambulances, and came to a halt, but found that if we jumped on to the runway, we would break all the bones in our bodies. Painfully slowly, the passengers escaped down a single emergency chute. As I was finally standing at some distance from the plane which might at any moment blow up, with the Michelangelo sonnet in its belly, I considered: what was of greater importance – my own survival or that of the unique autograph? In the event, nothing happened, and we were loaded, with our luggage, on to a replacement aircraft. When I arrived, hours late, at the Grand Cologny and excitedly related my adventure, Bodmer calmly smiled, and simply said: 'I wondered what had happened to you.'

This was the first time he received me in his private house, and not in the library. He had appeared to make a clear distinction between his private and social life, and his business contacts as a collector. Perhaps his rubbing shoulders with a large variety of people at the international bibliophiles' congresses was now mellowing his reserve. In Zurich, with a single exception, he had only seen me in the old school house. There, a little scene had occurred which still sticks in my memory I had had the temerity to ask for a small increase in my pocket money. I forget now whether or not he granted it – in any case, he appeared not very pleased, and politely pointed out that my pocket money was larger than the salary of his secretary. Only his gardeners were paid more, as they were unionized. That put me firmly in my place. It was not until 1959, at the first International Bibliophiles' Congress in Munich, that Bodmer introduced me to his wife. She was to become, on various occasions, my delightful hostess at the Grand Cologny, and I learned to appreciate her poise and quiet sense of humour. After Bodmer's death I repeatedly visited her, now a somewhat lonely figure in the big house, or dined with her in town. But for a long time I thought of myself, in my purely social contact with Bodmer, as a kind of Charles Swann whom Marcel's family never invited to their formal dinner parties, unaware of his position outside their own circle. I confess that I have always been keenly interested in the social scene around me and its infinite nuances.

The Michel Angelo transaction marked the beginning of that close collaboration between Martin Bodmer and myself to which I have already alluded. Our correspondence became so lively that it was at times 'absolutely raining letters', as he put it. If during the last year or two there were fewer, this was due to the modern enemy of letter writing: the telephone. He typed all his letters himself, and no doubt found this was increasingly taxing his strength. I wish I had kept notes of these conversations, some of them lasting for a whole hour – an expense which I gladly bore, for he never telephoned me. On occasion we would quote Goethe at each other, and other German poets, but of course, he knew much more by heart than I. He liked to be informed as soon as possible of the results of the sales for which he had given me commissions. If my efforts had been successful, he would say: 'I congratulate you' – as if the favourable result had been entirely due to me. On one occasion I got my congratulations in first. In July, 1970, a unique English poetical autograph was coming up at Sotheby's in London, but at a very inauspicious moment, as I had just spent half a million marks in Hamburg at the Schocken sale on his behalf – more of this anon. It was the only surviving autograph of a poem by John Donne, his verse epistle to Lady Carey. It was said it might fetch as much as forty or fifty thousand pounds. I pointed out that, since autographs by Shakespeare did not exist, Donne was the next best thing. After the Hamburg bloodletting, as he called it, Bodmer found himself *hors de combat*. I pleaded with him to have at least a try, as one can never predict what might happen at a sale. Audibly weakening, he suggested a bid of £15,000. This appeared to me too low to have a chance. 'Let's try it at £17,000, then.' I asked whether I might go up to £21,000 – these auctions before an auction were not infrequent features of our discussions. 'Why 21,000?' he asked. 'Because it's always advisable at sales to go one bid above a round figure.' 'Twenty-one thousand, then, but, please, no more.' The poem was knocked down to me at £23,000. At that figure, incidentally, I would have gladly bought it for stock, but if a dealer accepts a commission, he must have no regrets foregoing his own interest. I congratulated him, a little sententiously, on having added to his collection the most important English poetical autograph of the Elizabethan age. 'May I ask how much I had to pay for it?' he inquired. 'Only £2,000 more than we had anticipated.' 'I congratulate you', he said. Alas, the British authorities refused it an export licence, and this once pristine leaf is now in the Bodleian Library, permanently disfigured by an ugly library stamp.

Re-reading his letters after the lapse of so many years, I am again delighted by their charm, their style, his unfailing courtesy and consideration. My detailed recommendations of books and manuscripts were always 'interessant' or 'liebenswürdig'. His refusals, of course too frequent for my liking, were never simply a 'no', but reasoned explanations of his motives. I may add that his 'no's' were not always final: not infrequently, on second thoughts, he purchased what he had first refused. Conversely, he would explain at length why an object would be an essential addition to his collection.

I am touched how, in his letters, he commented on my professional successes which, to no small degree, were, in the beginning at least, also due to his continued confidence and support. On the publication of my Catalogue 101, he wrote me on Christmas Day, 1969 – I am quoting his words not from vanity, but as an example of his generosity of spirit: 'Your catalogue has just arrived ... It is really magnificent, and I congratulate you on this extraordinary achievement by which you make a name for yourself in the world of important antiquarian bookdealers – or, more correctly, worthily continue the illustrious traditions of your house.' This for me, from such a quarter, was an accolade indeed.

In his letters, there were constant references to his finances; needless to say, they were always precarious, and the stock exchange was in chronic, even scandalous, ill health. I once reminded him that Swiss bank shares had risen by 20 per cent the previous year. 'If that weren't the case', he replied, 'I should have to put a bullet through my head at once.' For some time there was talk about his 'Wiese' – his meadow – which, if sold, would bring financial relief. I was mystified: how could the sale of a mere meadow, situated, I imagined, on the gentle slope of some idyllic Swiss valley, have such results? One day, the meadow had been sold. It was, I heard later, an important piece of real estate. But financial lamentations continued. However, when it came to the crunch, when something of real importance turned up, he never hesitated, and funds were always available. In retrospect I assume that he did not only spend income, but also capital. If this assumption is correct, one can only conclude that it has been a wonderful investment, much better than any stocks and shares, and any number of very large 'Wiesen'.

There were, however, in Martin Bodmer's letters and conversations references to acquisitions of a nature that, I confess, disturbed me – assuredly not because they competed for his purse and attention. I mean his increasing preoccupation with antique artefacts, works of art, and even the earliest remains of life on earth. Of course, a collector is under no obligation to justify his choices, save to himself, and my rôle was only that of an agent, but I was sufficiently convinced of his design for a 'Library of World Literature', to wonder whether he was extending it backward into the inchoate, and sideways into human achievements that had little or nothing to do with literature as such. Was he, in fact, creating a kind of *Musée de l'Homme*? After his death I received his article – was this the work he had told me he was working on? – published, strangely enough, in 'Image, Photo-Documentation Médicale Roche'. It is a far cry from his work of 1947 – world literature is now only part of a much larger, all-embracing historical scheme. It cannot be my task to examine, much less to criticize, the final evolution of his ideas. I only wish to record briefly my occasional involvement with it which, strangely enough, remained unsuccessful in each instance. But it is interesting also on account of the large sums which Bodmer was willing to invest in the extension of his original plan. In 1969 and 1970, I had to bid on his behalf on two marvellous old-master drawings offered at Sotheby's. One was Dürer's water-colour of a stag-beetle, now in the Getty Museum, the other was Rembrandt's red-chalk drawing of a bearded man seated in an armchair. Each realized almost £60,000, a large sum in those days, but on each I was out-bid by Alain Delon, the French film actor who after the first sale told me he would have to make a new film in order to earn the purchase price. I was more successful with a large gouache on vellum of the building of the Tower of Babel, by Jacob van der Ulft, Bodmer's very last purchase from me. After his death Mrs Bodmer asked me whether I would like to take it back. I did, indeed, and it still hangs on a wall in my apartment, one of many cherished reminders of him. But I must also briefly tell the story of the Ichthyosaurus. Bodmer had bought it at Sotheby's, bidding directly through the auctioneers. But, as it turned out, he could not quite do without me, and had to ask for my help: since he had always bought through dealers at Sotheby's, his name was unknown there, so that I had to vouch for him and arrange for the transport of the enormously long and heavy fossil. Had he asked me to have a look at it beforehand, I could have warned him. I first saw it stretched out on the floor of the subterranean gallery connecting the two library pavillions, occupying a good part of its length. It was far too large an object to be exhibited. The next time I was there, it had disappeared, and I do not know its ultimate fate.

My rôle as Martin Bodmer's representative at auction sales came about almost by accident. For some years his agent in England had been Heinrich Eisemann, a dealer originally from Frankfurt, a colourful, even fascinating personality. His handsome, bearded features were of so oriental a cast that we called him among ourselves 'The Assyrian'. He acted almost exclusively as a middleman, buying and selling on commission which earned him another sobriquet, that of 'Mr Ten Per Cent'. Although he had never published a single catalogue in his life, he was by word of mouth known to, and dealt with, many of the most important collectors of his day. His orthodox piety was proverbial, and appeared to impress also devout believers in a faith different from his own. He held himself incommunicado, refused to transact any business or make even indirectly a profit on the Sabbath or other feast-days for which he would always hurry home to his numerous family, however far away he might be. 'I am', he used to proclaim, 'the servant of my clients, but at home I am king' – a confession that would leave my father speechless. He was a strange mixture of humility, flamboyance and pride. I believe Bodmer was fascinated by him, but it was not easy to imagine the kind of conversations that took place between these two very different personalities, one so exuberant, the other so reticent. Poor Eisemann, after the death of his wife, went into a sad decline, and began losing his memory. Modern medicine would probably diagnose his final descent into

PLATE V. Mozart, autograph of the string quartet in C (K.593). Bibliotheca Bodmeriana

senility as 'Alzheimer's Syndrome'. Bodmer was forced to look for another agent, and found him in me. Eisemann's fate saddened me, as I had known him almost as long as I could remember, and I was very conscious of the fact that my good fortune was, however indirectly, the result of his misfortunes. It was thus, about 1965, that I came into even closer contact with Martin Bodmer.

It would be impossible, within the framework of this talk, to give an even half-way comprehensive account of the books, manuscripts and autographs which Martin Bodmer acquired from and through me in the course of these years. Before mentioning a few of those which appear to me to be most outstanding, I hope I will not bore you with the account of two acquisitions which provided the greatest excitement and pleasure. The story of the first of them is rather involved. In 1969, the firm of Stargardt in Marburg offered for sale by auction one of the few complete autograph musical manuscripts of an important work by Mozart remaining in private hands, the magical string quintet in C, Köchel No. 593, written on 39 pages, one year before his death (Plate V). Strangely enough, Bodmer at first did not at all want to buy it for his own collection, since he already possessed a twenty-page long autograph MS by Mozart, his youthful string quartet in F, composed at the age of seventeen. He only wanted to buy the quintet, in order to offer it in exchange for a literary autograph he had coveted for a long time,

Nietzsche's 'Birth of Tragedy', in the magnificent autograph collection of Stefan Zweig which, after his and his second wife's double suicide, had been inherited by a member of her family. I had known his wife Miss Altmann, a tallish, thin slightly *exalté* spinster by no means in the first flush of youth, quite well, as she had been the secretary of Heinrich Eisemann who supplied Zweig, during his rather lonely and unhappy though very comfortable exile in London, not only with autographs but also with a wife – a story that would be absurd, if it had not ended so tragically. Through Eisemann, there had been previous contacts between Bodmer and the heiress, and he therefore knew that she and her husband were more interested in the musical, than in the German literary autographs in the Zweig Collection, but beyond this knowledge he had no assurance that they might enter upon the transaction he had in mind. I therefore suggested that he should buy and keep the quintet, and offer in exchange the quartet which I was convinced to be able to sell at a price in proportion to what we might have to pay for the larger and more important autograph, should the intended deal fall through. Martin Bodmer agreed, and I set off for Marburg, with an ample bid in my pocket. The atmosphere was electric; several people asked me the silly and futile question whether I had come to buy the Mozart. Of course, I pretended to a complete lack of interest. The autograph was knocked down to me at the extremely reasonable figure of 168,000 marks. But there was a sudden movement at the back of the room. The auctioneer announced that there had been an objection, and that he had overlooked a bid – he must therefore put up the item again. I protested. He referred me to the conditions of sale which allowed him, in case of dispute, to re-offer a number, and he re-opened the bidding. There was one bid from the back, and the Mozart was finally adjudicated to me for 170,000. During the interval my friend, the auctioneer, came up to me in a state of great excitement: the foreign underbidder who knew no German, had thought the last bid had been 270,000 marks, and had therefore stopped bidding. 'You would never have got the Mozart, if the lady had not made a mistake', my friend said. 'Who tells you that?', I replied, 'I would have gone on bidding'. He visibly paled. What had happened, I later learned, was this: a well-known overseas collector, too economically minded to pay a commission to his usual representative, had sent his daughter to bid for him. Not knowing German, she had hired a student as interpreter, a Frenchman whose German was not perfect either. Thus Bodmer got the Mozart at a bargain price. But the hoped-for exchange of autographs never materialized, and the quartet has since found a permanent home in the former Prussian State Library in West Berlin, the munificent present of the late Georg Henle, while the quintet remains in the Bodmeriana.

The other acquisition, or rather group of acquisitions, with one stroke enriched the Bodmeriana's already uniquely extensive holdings of the relics of the poet who, above all others, was nearest to Martin Bodmer's heart and thought: Goethe. In June 1970, Ernst Hauswedell in Hamburg was going to offer for auction the splendid collection of Goethe autographs formed by the late Salman Schocken. The two most exciting items were Goethe's notebook in which he had entered in chronological order some of the most important events of his life, in preparation for his autobiography, 'Dichtung und Wahrheit', and three pages from 'Faust'; there were also nine autograph poems, among them three for the 'Westöstlicher Divan', and four unknown lines for 'Faust', unrecognized by the compiler of the catalogue, to which I alerted Bodmer. As I was afraid that the absurdly low price estimates might raise false hopes – as indeed they did in the beginning, for they amounted to only about a 120,000 marks for all the items that Martin Bodmer felt were absolutely essential to him – I flew to Geneva. During our lengthy discussion, including, of course, one of our pre-auction auctions, we drew up a battle plan. The first choice was, needless to say, the notebook, the pages from 'Faust', and at least one or two of the 'Divan' poems; everything else was left to me. He sent me on my way with the plea: 'Please don't spend more than half a million'. As it turned out, double that amount would not have been enough to secure everything of interest to him. The first item offered was the notebook, estimated at 60,000. I abandoned it at 460,000 marks, not only because I should have spent the entire amount at my disposal on this one item – I had decided to buy everything else at my own risk – but I thought the price unjustified. The buyer told me afterwards that, for personal reasons, he had been prepared to go up to any amount. This sometimes happens at sales. I then proceeded to buy everything of importance: the 'Faust' pages, estimated at 10,000, for 180,000, and seven of the nine poems. Bodmer was delighted, and did not regret the loss of the notebook. 'I congratulate you', he said, and rang off. There was one item which I kept and own to the present day: Goethe's printed list of his autograph collection – he was one of the first to collect autographs – entitled 'Autographa', one of the few copies known with his autograph signature and date.

Through me Bodmer added another half a dozen important poems – he would generally pass over the numerous occasional verses mainly addressed to ladies and exalted personages – to this collection of Goethe autographs, the largest ever assembled in private hands. I repeatedly asked him to show it to me, but he never did. His reticence in this respect was extraordinary: he would freely talk about his possessions, but would never produce them, apart from those exhibited in the showcases of the library.

Other autographs which I contributed to the Bodmeriana range from the Renaissance to recent times, from Lorenzo de' Medici, Machiavelli, Erasmus and Hutten to Schiller, Hugo Wolf (the composition of a poem by Heine), to Herzel (an inscribed copy of the first edition of 'Judenstaat'), and James Joyce.

Among medieval MSS, there were three dating from the ninth century: a Mainz Canons of the Council of Aix-la-Chapelle of 815 (Plate VI), a pocket-size North-Eastern French Augustine, Retractiones, and the Homiliary of Paulus Diaconus from Lake Constance which was later sold to Kraus. From the 13th century there were the Chanson d'Aspremont, one of the *chansons de geste* of the Charlemagne cycle, written in England (it was a miracle that it obtained an export licence), a superbly illuminated Bolognese MS, Azo's Summa in Codicem, a chronicle roll written and illuminated in England, Peter of Poitier's Compendium Historiae, and another beautifully illuminated MS, a Latin Psalter for the Diocese of Constance. Also remarkable is a 14th-century Dioscorides, De Materia Medica, written in Aragon, and four outstanding Italian 15th- and early 16th-century humanistic MSS of Polybius, Propertius and Cassiodorus, the last written and magnificently bound for Leo X (Plate VII), and an unknown 15th-century translation into Italian of Augustine's City of God. Among richly illustrated Persian MSS, I mention Jami's Divan, dated Shiraz in 1497 of our era, the same poet's

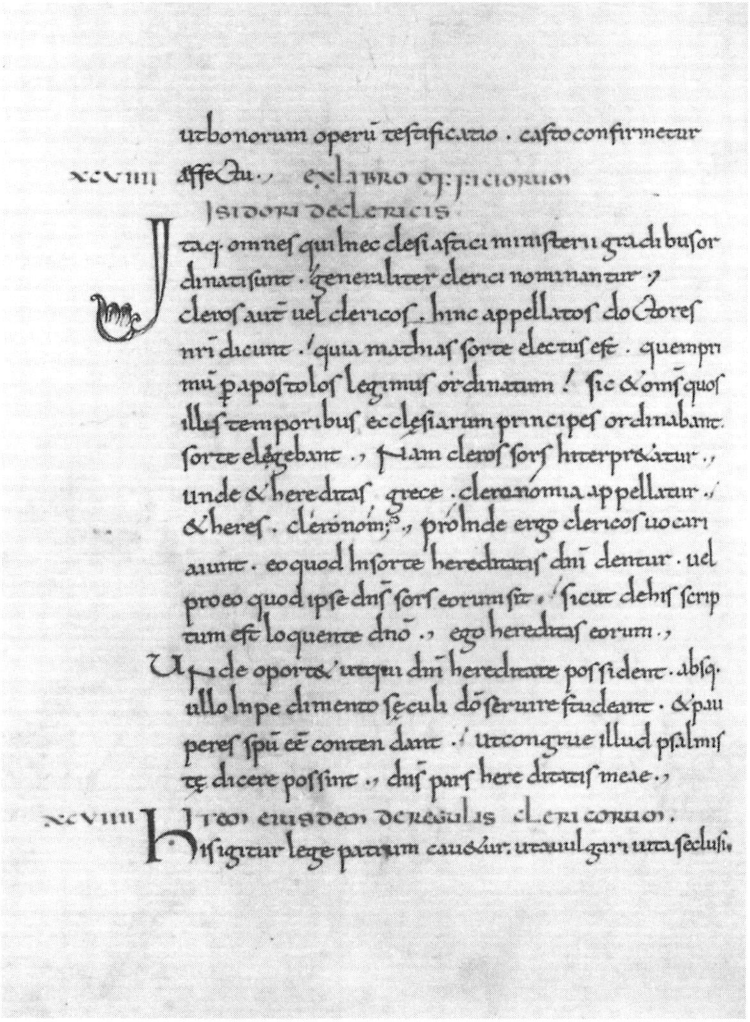

PLATE VI. Canons of the Council of Aix-la-Chapelle, 9th century. Bibliotheca Bodmeriana

Salaman u Absal (Solomon and Absalom), written and illuminated at Khurasan, *c.* 1580 (Plate VIII), and another notable Shiraz MS, dated 1516, of the Khamsa of Nizami. My study, and acquisitions, during repeated visits to the Orient, of Persian and Turkish illuminated MSS, from which especially the Bavarian State Library and the Metropolitan Museum of Art profited, also enabled me to advise Bodmer in this field.

Over the years, all these acquisitions represented, as can be readily imagined, very considerable investments, but were even exceeded by the sum unsuccessfully ventured — if that is the right expression. For as I have shown by a few examples, defeats in the salerooms were by no means the exception, but became more frequent in a rapidly rising market, with the corollary that more and more of those items I did manage to secure for

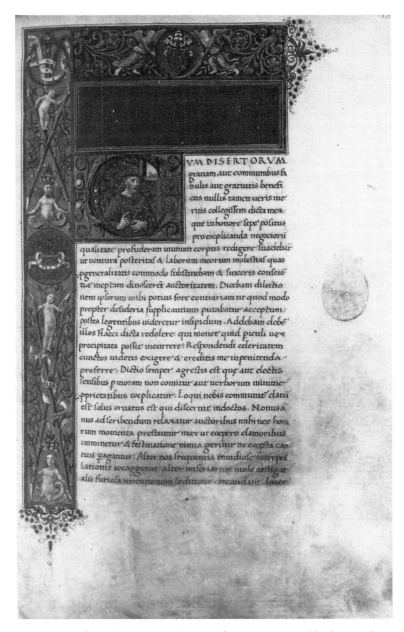

PLATE VII. Cassiodorus, 'Institutiones', written for Pope Leo X. Bibliotheca Bodmeriana

the Bodmeriana were the most favourable purchases in which I ceded my own interest against the purely nominal fee. But I happily continued with an arrangement which had been so important to me in a less affluent period, and which, in any case, no longer represented a substantial portion of my total activities.

I mentioned, *en passant* the name of Hans Peter Kraus, my colleague, friend and fore-

PLATE VIII. Jami, 'Divan', Shiraz, 1497. Bibliotheca Bodmeriana

most competitor. Since this discourse is exclusively concerned with my personal memories of Martin Bodmer, this is not the place to discuss the transaction, of which I heard only after his death, between him and Kraus in 1970. It was to create the capital fund required to sustain the 'Fondation Martin Bodmer'. Through Kraus's memoirs it has become public knowledge (in fact there were two disposals, the second posthumously); his account of it makes amusing and instructive reading. Both Bodmer and Kraus were right: the one wished to realize a very large sum at once, the other wanted to get as much as possible of its equivalent in books and manuscripts; both succeeded admirably. Whether it could have been done better in another way remains an open – and idle – question. The matter only concerns me in as far as my father's former library became a victim: many works were sold from it, without my having been given a first chance of re-acquiring them. I should have been prepared to pay almost any price for them. But I now fully understand: the problem was an embarrassing one – how much to ask, or accept, for something that thirty-five years ago had cost next to nothing. That problem was elegantly avoided.

We have only to look around us in these two graceful buildings in order to realize that Bodmer's *cris de coeur* 'Kraus, you are destroying my library' and 'You have succeeded in denuding me', as recorded by that memorialist, were fortunately half-humourous exaggerations. The haemorrhage was not mortal, and the Bodmeriana remains one of the great European private libraries of all times.

The last times I saw Martin Bodmer were just before Christmas 1970 and early in February of the following year, on my way to Senegal, and on my return journey. As these flights began and ended in Geneva, I used these opportunities to call on him. I noted in my diary, alas too sporadically kept, that he looked desperately ill, but was optimistic that he would get better again: he even asked me to let him know how I liked Dakar – perhaps he might go there himself one day. Five or six weeks later, his mood had changed. 'You are speaking to someone', I remember him saying with grim humour, 'who is already half underneath the turf.' On the evening of 22 March, I received the telegram announcing his death. I attended the impressive ceremony at St Pierre, filled with a vast congregation. As I was standing, afterwards, with Mr and Mrs Frederick Adams, in front of the Cathedral, Mrs Bodmer, seated in her car, saw me and let me know that she wished me to attend the reception at Le Grand Cologny. We joined the cortège following the hearse to the small churchyard at Cologny. In the cool air and darkening light of that March afternoon the short commitment, in its wonderful simplicity, was even more moving than the solemn pomp in the Cathedral. At the Grand Cologny Alice Bodmer received us with admirable grace and composure. I had the impression that the Adamses and I were the only guests who were not members of the Bodmer and Navil families.

In thanking me for my congratulations on his seventieth birthday, Martin Bodmer wrote me: 'Your connection with the Bodmeriana goes indeed back a full lifespan, and this is of much greater weight to-day, in these precipitously changing times, than ever before. It often seems as if one had lived several lives, and thus the unswerving occupation with Humanioria is certainly not the most dynamic activity, but it is nonetheless, the best one can do. For the future, as for to-day, it is doubtless still meaningful and ennobling. Let us therefore continue with this task, and, each in his own way, go on contributing to the transmitted edifice of true culture.'

These words, and the summons they contain, are as valid today as they were almost twenty years ago when they were written, indeed as long as his life's work continues to be preserved and is made to fulfil the purposes for which it was created.

B. J. ENRIGHT

'I Collect and I Preserve'
Richard Rawlinson, 1690–1755, and Eighteenth-Century Book Collecting[1]

RICHARD RAWLINSON chose the unusual motto 'I Collect and I Preserve' for his non-juring episcopal seal, while his armorial bookplate proclaimed 'Sunt Antiquissima Quaeque Optima'. The manuscript and book collections he left to the Bodleian Library in 1755 make it possible to trace his collecting activities during the first half of the eighteenth century. In these he reveals the sort of collector he was, illustrating some of the timeless characteristics of book collectors, their trials and tribulations as well as their triumphs, and in particular the controversial issue concerning the question of final disposal or institutional deposit of collections.

Rawlinson would undoubtedly have been pleased to have figured in a Grasmere Book Collectors' Weekend, as the Rawlinson family hailed from Grizedale, near Hawkshead. As early as 1592, one of his forebears bequeathed money towards the purchase of a dictionary for the School at Hawkshead while his grandfather, Daniel, who made his fortune in the London wine trade and became a friend of Pepys, always proudly recalled the family origins. He rebuilt Hawkshead School, providing funds for a writing master and for sending a poor boy every fifth year to University. Not only did he present books to the School library, but he persuaded no less than seventy-five of his friends to do the same. It is hardly surprising to find his grandson, Richard Rawlinson, following him in this tradition nor is it necessary to look far for the stimulus for his urge to collect. The example, as well as the resources to follow it, had been provided by his family.

Surprisingly little attention has been given to Richard Rawlinson, whose bequest to the Bodleian was the largest collection it had ever received and one which took the Library over 150 years to catalogue.[2] The number of references to Rawlinson manuscripts in scholarly works seemed to demand more substantial biographical information than appeared in Macray's *Dictionary of National Biography* entry and in the anecdotal accounts which frequently confused him with his brother, Thomas, or his Saxonist cousin, Christopher, and emphasized his economies and the curious provisions of his

---

[1] Paper given at the Wordsworth Trust Book Collectors' Colloquium, Grasmere, January 1987, based on my D.Phil. thesis in the Bodleian Library (MS. D.Phil.d.1786). All references to MSS are to Bodleian collections, unless otherwise stated.

[2] W. D. Macray, *Annals of the Bodleian Library*, 2nd ed., Oxford, 1890, pp. 231–51; I. G. Philip, *The Bodleian Library in the seventeenth and eighteenth centuries*, Oxford, 1983, pp. 94–8.

will. He tended to be dismissed as 'crotchety', 'a bit of a crank' and 'seldom out of a quarrel' – characteristics not uncommon among book collectors – but also 'as quintessential an antiquary as may be conceived'.

One of Rawlinson's contemporaries, John Wesley, who was persuaded by friends to visit the newly-established British Museum, was impressed by what he saw, but he had a fundamental reservation and queried: 'What account would a man give to the Judge of the quick and the dead for a life spent in collecting all these?' It would be vain to pretend that much of Rawlinson's life was not devoted to transcribing manuscripts in a scrawling, unattractive hand or to sorting the mountains of paper which filled the attics of London House where he lodged. Probably he regretted having to spend his life in the somewhat uncongenial atmosphere of the early eighteenth century – like George Hickes, a fellow nonjuror, he was to some extent an exile of his own generation – for at no time did he express appreciation of the political, social or cultural developments in which that age took pride and for which it is now generally remembered. He yearned nostalgically for the golden era of his youth when family prestige and fortunes had been at their height. The constant struggle against debts and disappointments to which he was condemned accounted not only for his eccentric economies but also for much of his petulance and vindictiveness. He gloried in being in a state of passive resistance to all that the progressive age of enlightenment stood for. In politics he was an uncompromising Jacobite, in religion a nonjuror – unwilling to swear allegiance to William III and his successors – and his zeal for the study of antiquity was sustained by the fear that it, too, was a lost cause and on the decline. Quite apart from any shyness – he described himself as 'one who loves too well Obscurity' – he had good reasons to avoid notoriety and to seek concealment in the Jacobite and nonjuring backwaters of the eighteenth century. His eagerness to cover his tracks (is secrecy, one might ask, a common characteristic of book collectors?) adds interest to the detective quest for biographical information.

It is, in fact, the tension between the individual and the age which makes Rawlinson's life particularly worthy of study. D. C. Douglas, in that outstanding work *English Scholars*, noted the curious dwindling of interest in antiquarian studies after about 1730 which produced what Stuart Piggott recently called 'an age of second-rate scholarship', a time of 'intellectual doldrums'.[3] Thomas Hearne lamented: 'There is every day a visible decay of Learning for which reason I must lessen the number of copies I print'. The movement of historical scholarship declined in the secular atmosphere of the age of enlightenment when the earlier motives of enquiry were disdained and when elegance was rated above research and interpretation above discovery.

Rawlinson, however, refused to move with the times. Despised, insulted and occasionally caricatured, he stubbornly declined to submit or even to compromise. He was determined that the scholarly traditions of the late seventeenth century in which he had been brought up should not perish or become, as he said, the 'Prey of Time'. The past was generally regarded as the source of ammunition for waging contemporary controversies – an early example where the possession of records enabled the owner to be, if he was so inclined, somewhat economical with the truth! Rawlinson, as a committed

[3] D. C. Douglas, *English Scholars 1660–1730*, 2nd ed., 1951, p. 27; S. Piggott, 'Antiquarian studies' in *The History* of the University of Oxford, Vol. v, *The Eighteenth Century*, Oxford, 1986, p. 766.

Jacobite and nonjuror, realized that there was always a risk, if his political and religious aspirations were to triumph, of a repetition of the civil wars of the previous century with all the damage they did to antiquarian records. He lamented not only by what he described as 'the Injury of Time' but 'by the more injurious and sacrilegious Hands of Trimphant Rebellion'. Hence his emphasis on preservation as well as on collecting.

'In short, this Study', Rawlinson wrote of Antiquity, 'is at a very low ebb, and we must provide for Posterity without regard to the ungrateful Age.'[4] Here lies the claim to be remembered of one who, as he humbly described himself, 'had little more than an Affection for Antiquities'. Undaunted by the lack of success which his own research and publications encountered, in spite of the rebuffs of friends, family and fortune, he devoted himself ceaselessly not merely to accumulating vast collections but also to preserving them permanently from destruction. In this way, he hoped he would provide a link between the great era of English antiquarian scholarship and a future age which, unlike his own, might appreciate and attempt to emulate its achievement. This was his purpose: how did he set about the task, how were his collections built up, how successful was he in overcoming obstacles in the way of their preservation?

Rawlinson's father was knighted by James II, became Master of the Vintners' Company, and Lord Mayor of London in 1705. He was determined to give his sons the education which he himself lacked. Richard followed his elder brother, Thomas, that 'Leviathan of Book Collectors' (the Tom Folio of *The Tatler*), to Eton and St John's College, Oxford. In many ways, Richard's life was a completion and fulfilment of his elder brother's unrealized hopes. Thomas's influence on Richard's collecting and antiquarian interests was crucial. Apart from giving him access to his extensive library, Thomas introduced Richard to the London bookshops, took him to book auctions, showed him how to collate books (marking them 'C & P'),[5] and encouraged him to travel in England and abroad to collect books and inscriptions. Thomas also introduced Richard to fellow antiquaries and bibliophiles, including the redoubtable Thomas Hearne in whose diaries the growth of Richard's collecting activities at Oxford can be followed. Richard's college accounts include frequent bills for binding, lettering and the purchasing of books and pamphlets (especially topographical items) as well as portraits of the Pretender and of Dr Sacheverell. He even attempted to follow Hearne's example and published anonymously a short life of his Oxford hero – the antiquary, Anthony Wood. His years at Oxford as a privileged gentleman commoner clearly gave him scope to develop his antiquarian collecting enthusiasms. He regarded them as a halcyon time. He always spoke of St John's as 'his beloved college' ('Animo Semper Joannensis'). Far away in Padua in 1725 he wrote: 'I must not forget my dearest Oxford . . . God grant I may be ever able in some measure to show my gratitude.'[6]

The years between 1712 and 1719, after he came down from Oxford, were spent travelling throughout England and publishing works based on his brother's and his own topographical and historical collections. It is curious to find Rawlinson in close

[4] MS.Ballard 2, f. 48ᵛ, 11 Aug. 1739.
[5] Richard's 'bold black scrawl' (S. de Ricci, *English Collectors of Books and Manuscripts*, 1930, p. 46) is readily distinguished from Thomas's collation mark. See J. B.

Oldham, *Shrewsbury School Library Bindings*, Oxford, 1943, p. 104. Examples appear in the Bodleian printed book collection 4° Rawl. 53, 55, 97, 101.
[6] MS.Rawl.D.1186, p. 2397, 29 Nov. 1725.

PLATE I
Richard Rawlinson
(1690–1755)

co-operation with the notorious publisher, Edmund Curll, renowned for his less respectable non-antiquarian publications and his clashes with Pope. But together they made an extensive antiquarian tour of Oxfordshire and Curll's notes are not only characteristically lively but enable the precise route of the tour to be identified.[7] Richard had been encouraged by Hearne to compile a collection of the most important inscriptions throughout England and he launched into this project with relentless thoroughness,

[7] See B. J. Enright, 'A proposed history of Oxfordshire 1715–1720', *Oxoniensisa*, XVI (1951), pp. 57–78.

even visiting a stonemason's shop to copy instructions from monuments which had not yet been erected. He also took the opportunity of adding to his library, and complained bitterly on a visit to the family property near Hawkshead about the 'absence of a book-seller in the handsome town of Kendal'. He published anonymously a spate of the lives and works of English antiquaries of the sixteenth and seventeenth centuries (later grouped together by Curll into the series *Anglia Illustrata*) to which he added new inscriptions and appendixes as original documents from his own or his brother's collections. The books themselves are now collectors' items fetching handsome prices. He illustrated them with copperplate prints of seals and coins, often showing both obverse and reverse. To secure materials for the histories of Oxfordshire and Middlesex, Rawlinson used the device of circulating questionnaires – printed 'Quaeries' or 'Blanks' as they were known – for local clergymen and antiquaries to complete. In 1720, he published *The English Topographer*, an extensive survey of topographical manuscripts and books in public and private hands, providing a summary of his earlier labours and perhaps his most useful published work. It was certainly the most comprehensive survey until Richard Gough's *British Topography* of 1768. His antiquarian work did not prevent him from becoming a Governor of the Bridewell and Bethlem Hospitals, a Fellow of the Royal Society, a nonjuring priest and a Doctor of Civil Law at Oxford – a distinction of which he was very proud and had the seal engraved for a new bookplate.

It was natural for Richard to follow the example of his elder brother in travelling on the continent between 1719 and 1726 to search for books and manuscripts as well as for inscriptions of those of his countrymen who had not had the good fortune to die at home, a Grand Tour with something of a difference. There was another reason for travelling abroad which he did not care to advertise. Hearne was convinced that Rawlinson had been on a sort of a pilgrimage, first to the Jacobite Court at St Germain and later to that in Rome to establish links and to seek royal approval for nonjuring consecrations. It is clear that Rawlinson considered getting to Rome in time for the birth of the Young Pretender in 1720 to be a particular triumph.

Rawlinson's remorseless searches through Continental bookshops and libraries can be followed in his travel diaries. He recorded how a monk in a monastery in Northern Italy spoke to him 'of many old M.S.S. in their Library, very valuable, as also of many of the old Editions of first impressions of books, which he, ignorant as he was, said were some printed in 1440, before the art was discovered or so much as known'.[8] Exploring the catacombs in Rome, his collecting met with a reverse: 'myself too curiously taking up a bone, I was reprimanded and told that to carry it off was excommunication', while on another occasion he sadly noted: 'I lost my silk purse out of my pocket while I was looking over some books at a shop in the Corso'.[9] Braving the threats of shipwreck and of the Barbary pirates, he travelled as far as Sicily and Malta, not commonly visited by English travellers. One monastic library in Sicily he considered as 'perhaps the only collection in this part of the world which has escaped my countrymen's money'. In Malta, he secured an audience with the Grand Master who failed to realize that Rawlinson was the criminal for whom a reward had been offered since it was he who, in his collecting zeal, had

[8] MSS.D.1180–7, p. 134.   [9] *Ibid.*, p. 2019.

PLATE II. Print from the original copperplate of the frontispiece of the English translation of Gracian de Antisco, *Galateo Espagnol*, London, 1640. (Now Rawl. copperplate g.221)

removed a Papal Bull (condemning a heretical historical work by Giannone) which had been nailed to the door of the Cathedral.[10]

Large quantities of books were acquired – a manuscript list includes over 2000 titles – and there are frequent entries in the diaries describing their despatch 'embaled in a box' and consigned to London by English merchants. Rawlinson was gratified to find that no tax was charged for an export licence at the Customs House at Naples: 'No country but England knows a tax on learning. The doctrine of Naples broached by the Emperor Charles V is Libri sint liberi, and that in a country fertile of taxes', adding 'this I speak to the Honour of Naples who, ignorant enough as they are, encourage learning'.[11] The vast collections, not only of books but also of coins, medals, seals and marbles, the recollections of the magnificent libraries he had visited and the friendly relations he had established with foreign scholars, had a profound influence on his later interests and career. Rawlinson was intensely proud of his travels and of his linguistic skills, and never let his friends forget that he had seen the 'shores of the Mediterranean'.

[10] *Ibid.*, pp. 1918–19, 9 Jan. 1724. The document is now in the Bodleian Library, together with Rawlinson's reprint. Vet.A4.c.79.

[11] MS.D. 1180–7, p. 599.

Undoubtedly, Richard would have liked to have remained abroad, as did his younger brother and travelling companion, Constantine. The situation following the death of his elder brother, Thomas, in 1725, which had forced his return, was far worse than he expected. 'Such hardships as have happened in your family', wrote a friend 'are scarce to be paralleled.' Thomas Rawlinson, in his search after bibliographical rarities, had accumulated vast debts and neglected the family estates. After losing money in the South Sea Bubble speculations, he had been forced to sell part of his library and he had ruined himself completely by marrying his servant, who had come with a not very attractive reputation from a nearby coffee-house. There were rumours that she had even poisoned her husband. Before he died Thomas, in desperation, tried to break the entail on the family properties, had ordered all his books to be sold, and died £10,000 in debt.

Richard naturally resented his brother's efforts to undermine what he called 'Hereditary Right'. He immediately challenged the 'barbarously-framed will', but fearing the delay and cost of a legal contest – Hearne proclaimed to him what seems to be an eternal truth, 'If things come to the lawyers, God knows where there will be an end' – Rawlinson came to terms with his brother's widow who had by then remarried. He took over the administration of his brother's will and undertook to organize the sale by auction of Thomas's library in order to settle his debts. The agreement required Richard to keep detailed accounts and the ledger costing 3s 0d, now a manuscript in St John's College Library, allows us to study the day-to-day organization of ten large book auctions during which over 50,000 books and manuscripts were sold between 1726 and 1733.[12]

Here lies the explanation of the puzzle why Richard, himself a dedicated book collector, had to dispose of his brother's magnificent collections – the quintessence of cruelty for a bibliophile. It also explains why he, to all appearances in charge of the auctions, was forced to buy at the actual sales in competition with other collectors and creditors. The reason for the urgency which led to the release of so many books on to the market in such a short space of time also becomes clear: it was only when the library had been sold that Rawlinson could begin to control the family properties when the troublesome interference of Thomas's wife and her grasping husband could be eliminated. It was hardly surprising that Rawlinson was put off marriage which, he considered, 'spoiled the Antiquary'.

Overall, Rawlinson was very disappointed by the sum realized from the sales. Hearne wrote, sympathizing: 'The booksellers and others are in a combination against you' and he added scathingly that 'people are in love with good Binding more than good Reading'. Yet many of Thomas's books were imperfect as the somewhat surprising entries in the accounts for reprinting missing pages indicate. Inevitably, the disposal of such a large collection and so many duplicates produced a 'glut' of books on the market. Rawlinson was concerned about a commission of £50 from France for one rarity: 'I hope England will not lose such a treasure but I can't well afford to be a master of it'. He was determined to minimize the damage caused by the dispersal of the library by commissioning copperplate engravings of 'some specimens of several hands in the most ancient, fair

---

[12] For a full account see B. J. Enright, 'The later auction sales of Thomas Rawlinson's Library, 1727–1734', *The Library*, 5th series, xi (1956), 23–49, 103–13.

and best manuscripts' from his brother's library. He obtained expert help in compiling the auction catalogue of Thomas's manuscripts 'in whose description I have been as particular as possible that it may be of use to posterity, if they can discover into whose possession any article may come'. As a curiosity, he reprinted the catalogue of Thomas's collection of paintings, inserting the price each item fetched and chose an appropriate motto for the title-page of one of the catalogues 'Qui non credit, eras credat'.

Rawlinson realized that unless he could re-establish the family fortunes he would be unable to build the large collections he desired. Furthermore, unless he could break the entail of the family properties, any collections which he might make would be likely to be dispersed on his death. The bitter experience of dealing with his brother's problems was never forgotten. Thomas Baker warned him: 'Your brother's case ought to be a caution to us all not to engage too deep' and the experience accounts for his uncompromising determination in dealing with the feckless and intractable members of his own family as well as with his farm tenants and agents. It was to be a long and difficult struggle. By 1749 he was completely free from debt and his title to the family estates was secure.

Even the proportion of Rawlinson's collections in the Bodleian makes it difficult to identify his interests with any precision. Macray indicated the particular value of the manuscripts for topography, biography, heraldry and seventeenth-century history but he referred to the 'omnigenous' character of the collection which included everything from early copies of the Classics and Fathers to the most recent log books of sailors' voyages. Rawlinson was referred to by contemporaries as 'a Universal Collector' who liked 'without breach of the Tenth Commandment' to make 'collections as perfect as possible'. He maintained that his books were 'the pleasure, I may almost say, the only pleasure of my life'.[13] The diversity of his collections can in part be explained by the varied interests of his many friends whom he liked to satisfy by loans, but mainly by his determination to provide for posterity's needs when interest in historical studies might have revived, for from the outset Rawlinson schemed to ensure that his collections would be safely preserved in institutional hands.

There was a yet more urgent reason for Rawlinson's anxiety to hoard. The waste-paper monger of the eighteenth century was a common enough figure for Hogarth to record in his cartoons crying 'Waste Paper for Shops'. Pope referred to the popular, undignified use of learned tomes

> Twelve of ample size
> Redeem'd from tapers and defrauded pyes[14]

Rawlinson's salvaging zeal was almost as remorseless as that of his model, Anthony Wood who, it was indelicately reported, 'used to rake in the Oxford Boghouses for papers thinking to find something of scandal'. Rawlinson described to a friend how calamity had befallen a work attacking the nonjurors, 'A book which I believe has grown scarce, not for its value, but like some others, the Impression has supplied the Pye Shops and Trunk Makers for some time'. He recorded joyfully his acquisition of some Sancroft

[13] MS.Ballard 2, f. 75ᵛ, 13 Dec. 1740.
[14] *Dunciad*, I, line 156. For Rawlinson's salvaging activities see B. J. Enright, 'Rawlinson and the chandlers', *Bodleian Library Record*, IV, 4 (1953), pp. 216–27.

manuscripts from Mr Fletcher, bookseller in the Turl at Oxford, 'these, like many other papers, were retrieved from wast at little more than weight price'. In 1739 he described how Sir John Cooke's manuscripts 'were sold by his nephew's widow to support pyes, currants, sugar etc., and I redeemed as many as came to 12s at 3d per pound, which I intend to digest and bind up'. Two years later he 'rescued from the grocers and chandlers a parcel of papers once the property of Compton and Robinson, successively Bps of London' and after discovering some papers of Archbishop Wake in a chandlers he remarked: 'This is unpardonable in his executors, as all his MSS were left to Christ Church. But quaere whether these did not fall into some servant's hands who was ordered to burn them'. Relatives were likewise to blame, in his view, when he retrieved papers belonging to Mr Orme, a nonjuring clergyman which 'by the neglect of his widow had fallen into a Presbyterian bookbinders hands'. Perhaps his most significant triumph in his battle with the chandlers came in 1749 when he 'redeemed from the shop-keepers' nearly a hundred volumes of papers formerly belonging to Samuel Pepys, a nonjuror and frequent visitor to the Mitre Tavern kept by Richard's grandfather, Daniel.

The problem with Rawlinson's collections is not so much why an item came into his possession but rather how and when. Former ownership meant much to eighteenth-century collectors. Rawlinson himself thought it odd that Bishop Tanner should bind manuscripts up 'and leave no memorandum of how he came by them'.[15] His own collections appeared to have been kept in blocks as they were acquired, together with the relevant list or a marked auction catalogue. These sale catalogues Rawlinson treasured and his extensive collection covering the first half of the eighteenth century is now in the Bodleian. Instead of Cottonian busts of Roman Emperors, Rawlinson seems to have used portraits of former owners, noting a print of Michael Maittaire 'to go along with Mr Mattaire's manuscripts and to be hung over them'. A source of many items in his collections can be identified by the auction labels on volumes which have escaped over-vigorous rebinding.

Rawlinson was a well-known figure in the salerooms, receiving advance proof copies of sale catalogues, and executing commissions for friends. He was to be found at most of the main auctions of the 1730s, purchasing items from the libraries of Peter le Neve, Thomas Atterbury, Thomas Grainger and Christopher Rawlinson. He secured fifty manuscripts in 1740 from Lord Halifax's sale, noting that the Library 'was garbled by Ld Sunderland, and was never improved by his late Nephew, who delighted in nothing but Horseracing, Cocking, Turd, Turnips, and Mob Elections'.[16] At the sale of the library of Edward Harley, second Earl of Oxford who died in 1741, Rawlinson bought five manu-scripts which were accidentally disposed of with the printed books. He considered Harley to be a 'dog-in-the-manger', and heartily distrusted Thomas Osborne, book-seller in charge of the sales, suspecting that he would blend 'his own large stock with them, sub larva Comitis'.[17] As he considered the prices extravagant, he decided not to give himself 'the trouble and fatigue of a three mile's walk only to be mortified, tho' Lent be the proper Season'.[18] But temptation must have triumphed, for he admitted 'I saw the books before the opening of the sale, and a beautiful sight it was but [I] have not

[15] MS.Ballard 2, f. 268, 24 Jul. 1753.
[16] MS.Eng.th.c.35, pp. 6, 28 Mar. 1740.
[17] MS.Ballard 2, f. 119ᵛ, [23 Oct.] 1742.
[18] Ibid., f. 123 26 Mar. 1743.

laid out one liard'.[19] It was not to be long, however, before he relented and was to be found buying 'many of the late Ld Oxford's books now selling under real or fictitious names' adding later, 'the Booksellers all cry out ruin by his Auctions, and indeed it seems now the worst trade in the Kingdom'.[20]

In 1747 he purchased many fine Irish manuscripts (formerly belonging to Sir James Ware) at the sale of the Library of the Duke of Chandos. Some appear to have been acquired outside the saleroom,[21] a practice in which Rawlinson appears to have been particularly skilled. He even approached Daniel Perkins who 'had the chief Management of the MS Catalogue of the Library' to find out whether his purchases were genuine, only to be told that the compiler of the 'hurried' catalogue 'Laboured every Day from Morning to Night without either eating or drinking' but that the auctioneer had 'altered and mangled it' out of all recognition.[22] Rawlinson wrote to Bodley's Librarian about the books in the library of Conyers Middleton, sold in 1751, which he considered 'mostly curious, not numerous, as he, like yourself, had the use of a public Library, and rose to high sums; tho' many he bought when with me at Rome, Florence &c were purchased easy enough . . . I don't hear much of Oxford Commissions which I the more wonder at, as such as the present Collection does not often come up'.[23] In 1754 he wrote to a friend promising to obtain a sale catalogue of the Library of Samuel Gale 'and intend to take the prices they go at for your Collection'.[24] Later in the year at the sale of Lord Coleraine's library, he rejoiced 'that the affair of MSS. is much fallen into my Hands, and they scarce fetch the velom, so that I have but few rivals and I made some valuable purchases'.[25] The last auction he attended, the library of the eminent Dr Richard Mead, symbolically marked the end of a period in the history of English booksales when rarities could be obtained relatively cheaply. Rawlinson noted sadly that 'in general, the Articles . . . went beyond my Purse, at monstrous Rates'.[26]

Rawlinson realized that he could often obtain better terms when dealing with book collectors or their executors direct and so pre-empt the sale room. In 1737 he captured some of Ashmole's papers (including some Dugdale items) in this way.[27] One of his most important acquisitions, the manuscripts and annotated printed books of Thomas Hearne were also bought privately. Rawlinson was delighted at his success, writing to Bodley's Librarian that they might 'even hereafter come to Bodley . . . but at present they are not so ripened by 14 years, as to bear inspection, as he was very free on Men and things'[28] including, incidentally, some very critical remarks about Rawlinson himself. In 1751 he negotiated successfully with the bookseller, Fletcher Gyles, for the purchase of the Thurloe State Papers which had been discovered during building work at Lincoln's Inn hidden in a ceiling. Many of the manuscripts, which undoubtedly constitute the chief authority for the history of the Protectorate, had not been printed by Birch in 1742.[29]

Having been secretly consecrated a nonjuring bishop in 1728, Rawlinson was in a par-

---

[19] Ibid., f. 129 [18 May 1743].

[20] Ibid., f. 161, 16 Oct. 1744.

[21] MS note in Rawlinson's copy of the Sale Catalogue. Bodleian shelfmark Mus.Bibl.III.8°.44, facing p. 173.

[22] MS.Rawl.D.811, ff. 1, 5ᵛ, 25 Aug., 8 Nov. 1747.

[23] MS.Rawl.C.989, f. 164ᵛ, 14 Mar. 1751.

[24] MS.Ballard 2, f. 226, 30 Jan. 1754

[25] MS.Ballard 2, f. 253 16 Mar. 1755.

[26] British Library Add.MS.5833, f. 185, 12 Mar. 1755.

[27] MS.Ballard 2, f. 16ᵛ.

[28] MS.Bodl.Add.A 64, f. 259, 1 Feb. 1749.

[29] MS note by Rawlinson at the beginning of MS.Rawl.A.68.

ticularly favourable position for securing the papers of his nonjuring colleagues. He considered it vital to prevent records from falling into hostile hands as well as to capture documents which could furnish ammunition in future controversies. One friend commented humorously that Rawlinson could hardly wait for nonjurors to die before he pounced on their papers. Overton, the authority on the nonjurors, praised him as one who 'in common gratitude should never be forgotten by those who take an interest in the nonjurors, for more than any other man he has supplied original, contemporary and trustworthy information'.[30] Rawlinson's success in collecting original materials on the history of Jacobitism and of freemasonry meets similar praise.

Rawlinson followed the example of Wood and Hearne in transcribing those items which he could not acquire. Over 200 volumes of such transcripts in his hand survive, some of which he left to St John's College fearing that the originals in the Bodleian might be tampered with. His projects concerning Eton, Oxford and nonjuring biographies often provide authoritative bibliographical identification based on the completion of printed questionnaires by contemporary authors themselves.

After the completion of the sale of Thomas Rawlinson's library in 1734, Richard established himself in London House, formerly the Bishop of London's residence where Thomas had originally lodged and which was close to the bookshops of Little Britain. A friend visiting him there in 1742 found 'such a confusion of Books and MSSs that there was no end in viewing of them. It would have took me up a twelve months time to have gone through with them and in short I looked into very few of them [no] more than what he shewed me in a transient prospect for he has no conveniences to sitt down to see or write out any thing for he does not spend much time in his Chamber, but only to take his Breakfast for I went 3 or 4 times before I could be admitted for he gets up into the uppermost Rooms and there is no making him hear at the Door you enter into'.[31] Seven years later George Vertue, the painter, reported a similar disarray: 'I saw his great collections of manuscripts, many finely-illuminated writings, and innumerable printed books, pamphlets &c., many in confused heaps on the floors, stools, tables, and shelves; and many marbles, pictures bronzes, stones, prints &c. All the great rooms in this house filled with them in presses, and also more rooms in the garrets'.[32] Rawlinson admitted that he was obliged to return loans speedily as they 'would with difficulty be kept safe amongst my indigested heap' but his own, almost daily, loans to friends speak well for his familiarity with his collections. Condemning idleness in others, Rawlinson did nor spare himself, declaring: 'I labour hard every day to sett my books in order, which costs me much patience and sweat'.[33]

Rawlinson established ownership of items once acquired by means of one of series of bookplates inserted by a library clerk or an amanuensis. Rawlinson took an active part in the organization of his collections: 'The better to preserve letters, and strengthen them, I putt all sizes first by dates, and then each within a single sheet of paper, and with these praecautions and strong Cloths, it is to be hoped they will be of no use to Chandlers &c the sad fate of many valuables.'[34] While he did not believe in lavish binding, it was odd

[30] J. H. Overton, *The Non-jurors*, 1902, p. 318.
[31] MS.Ballard 41, f. 222ᵛ, 13 Nov. 1724.
[32] *Notes & Queries*, II, xii (1861), 83, 17 Jun. 1749.
[33] MS.Carte 103, f. 579ᵛ, 10 Jul. 1736.
[34] MS.Ballard 2, f. 149, 28 Apr. 1744.

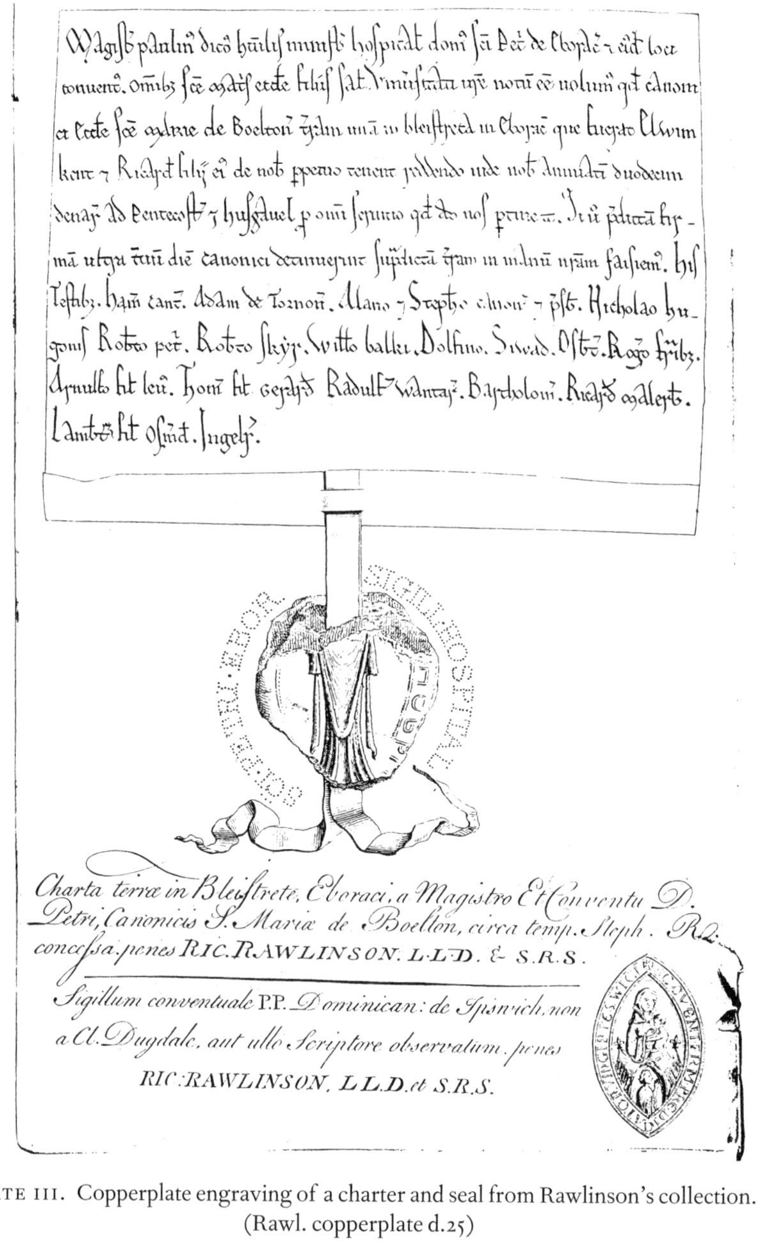

PLATE III. Copperplate engraving of a charter and seal from Rawlinson's collection.
(Rawl. copperplate d.25)

to find someone who was so careful to preserve documents commending the use of 'a strong bind of old parchment leases' as covers.[35] He was essentially practical in recognizing that in all collections 'there must necessarily be a quantity of rubbish', adding later 'I am digesting and putting together my M.S.S. and I'm gleaning my large collection in order to contract my compass, and throw out a great quantity of Chaff, for we

[35] MS.Ballard 2, f. 181, 3 Aug. 1748.

collectors are insensibly overwhelmed with learned paper and dust'.[36] Rawlinson constantly worked on his collections, collating books, foliating manuscripts, inserting names of former owners, identifying authors and handwriting. He was particularly alert to alterations in the texts of books when he discovered that what he termed 'an uncastrated manuscript' was 'somewhat different from the print'.[37]

Rawlinson clearly considered printing to be one of the most effective ways of preserving the contents of manuscripts. In collecting printed books, he looked particularly for those bearing manuscript annotations. Among his intended bequest at the Bodleian he drew attention in his will to those of his books printed on vellum or silk, as well as such 'as shall appear to have therein any manuscript additions, or explanatory enlightening or controversial notes either by myself or any other person or persons whatsoever' and ordered them to be placed amongst his 'other manuscripts'. He considered that such books would be likely to be of great use for new editions. Rawlinson's close contacts with printers and publishers, editing for Curll, commissioning reprints from Bettenham and Bowyer, placed him in an advantageous position for obtaining printers' copies and corrected proof sheets. His use of the printing press as a preservation medium can be seen in his private printing of nonjuring consecration instruments and in the facsimile reprint of Laud's Star Chamber speech of 1637 with Archbishop Williams's notes inserted in the margin. Rawlinson considered copperplate engraving, using the rolling press, an excellent device to preserve and publicize, writing about one curiosity 'I shall be glad to be a purchaser, and that only in order to multiply it by the Engraver's Tool'.[38] Prints reproducing items from his collections of charters and seals were often exhibited and distributed at meetings at the Society of Antiquaries. In leaving his copperplate collections to the Bodleian Library 'to be by them worked off into one volume and the impressions to be sold for their use and benefit' he hoped: 'I flatter myself it will be a good ticket to them'[39] and it is pleasant to report that the Bodleian has recently begun to circulate reprints. Rawlinson collected sets of old copperplates including a frontispiece of a short title catalogue item,[40] while another had a significant role in the reconstruction of Colonial Williamsburg.

Book collectors in the eighteenth century seldom specialized and in addition to books and manuscripts Rawlinson had an insatiable appetite for coins, seals, paintings, marbles, bronzes, busts and other curiosities which defied classification. Skeletons later bequeathed to the Company of Surgeons kept guard over a collection of childrens' samplers, described ingenuously by Rawlinson as 'the work of learned ladies'. It is not surprising that Rawlinson stipulated that a prize for the essay founded in his memory was to be a gold medal engraved with the words 'Antiquam exquirite matrem'.

'It is a pleasant thought', De Ricci remarked, 'to discover how public-spirited English book-collectors have been in the course of the last four centuries . . . personal vanity, the mainspring of collecting, has continually given way to local and national pride'.[41] In one of his sermons Rawlinson condemned 'this fatal desire of the good opinion of the world

---

[36] MS.Ballard 2, f. 134, 12 Jul. 1743.
[37] MS.Rawl.A.318.
[38] MS.Ballard 2, f. 215, 20 Dec. 1751.
[39] MS.Ballard 2, f. 260, 11 May 1754.

[40] Gracian de Antisco: *Galateo Espagnol*, 1640, from Rawl. copperplate g.221.
[41] *English Collectors*, p. 193.

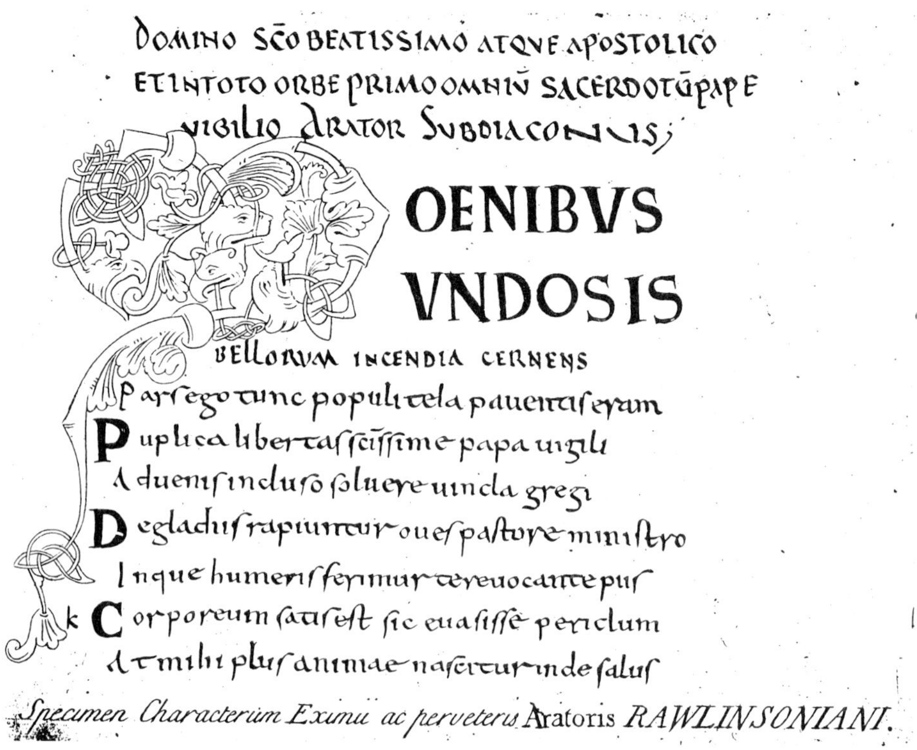

DOMINO SĒO BEATISSIMŌ ATQVE APOSTOLICŌ
ETINTOTO ORBE PRIMO OMNIŪ SACERDOTŪPAPE
VIGILIO ARATOR SVBDIACONVIS;

OENIBVS
VNDOSIS

BELLORVM INCENDIA CERNENS

P arrego tunc populi tela pauentaseram
P uplica libertas sciissime papa vigili
A duens induso soluere uincla gregi
D egladis rapiuntur oues pastore ministro
I nque humeris ferimur terevocante pus
k C orporeum satis est sic euasisse periclum
A t mihi plus animae nascitur inde salus

Specimen Characterum Eximii ac perveteris Aratoris *RAWLINSONIANI.*

PLATE IV. Copperplate engraving of a page from MS. Rawl. *c* 570 (Rawl. copperplate f.90)

. . . aimed at even by those who write books and preach against it'.[42] Yet he could not fail to be flattered when a friend sought permission to dedicate a book to him as one 'like to prove the Best Mecaenas in England'.[43] Far from being selfishly possessive or mean, Rawlinson was determined that his collection should have the greatest possible influence on contemporary scholarship. He told a nonjuring congregation that 'all the abilities and perfections we have are given to us at that end that we might advantage others by communicating our gifts unto them'.[44] Never was an exhortation more zealously put into practice than by its author. A wide circle of friends benefited from the loans of curiosities, while gifts of rarities were presented to institutions and individuals as a way of encouraging them to collect. Rawlinson was classed as one of the 'great Patrons' of the age who 'obliged all Lovers of Antiquities'.[45] His liberality left Thomas Baker, 'the Ornament of Cambridge' lost for words with nothing to add 'but what I am sure I ought to desire, that you will hold your hand, not plunder your own Study, by filling mine'.[46] Isaiah Tucker of Bristol spoke for many in praising Rawlinson for 'a communicative Disposition, which is not always to be found in those who have amassed such vast Treasures together'.[47]

---

[42] MS.Rawl.E.217, f. 354.
[43] MS.Rawl.J.fol.2, f. 43, 31 Oct. 1743.
[44] MS.Rawl.E.218, f. 135.

[45] MS.Rawl.B.268, f. 115.
[46] MS.Rawl.H.30, f. 181.
[47] MS.Rawl.H.114*, f. 323.

While after 1730 Rawlinson, for a variety of reasons, ceased to publish, he eagerly assisted authors with original manuscripts following Thomas's example whom he described as 'more useful in supplying materials for others to work upon and collecting than any attempt to finish ought'. He contributed so much to a new edition of Bacon's works and of Bale's Chronicle, that he was thought to be the real editor. Francis Peck was not disappointed when he approached Rawlinson for help with a book 'to set the Affair of the Restoration (hitherto so dark a Matter) in its true and just Light from unquestionable Authorities',[48] while Thomas Carte was told 'if any thing turns up for your use any way be assured you . . . shall not be forgot'.[49] While Rawlinson was critical of the way authors abused the device of subscriptions, as he said to 'midwife out their brats', his name figures frequently in contemporary subscription lists and he is second only to Mead in the subscription ratings for the first half of the eighteenth century.

Rawlinson was eager to support learned institutions. Cambridge University rejected his overtures but from the Bodleian, 'that sanctuary of use and curiosity',[50] the Librarian graciously agreed to 'accept whatever you shall think proper to bestow'.[51] Rawlinson found the meetings of the Royal Society 'for the most part out of the way of my studies';[52] he considered their affairs were in 'such an unsettled state, occasioned by Parties, that Learning is not regarded among them, but Party and private Interest sway all, so that Things are deplorable'.[53] The Society of Antiquaries was more to his taste, and scarcely a meeting passed without his putting on show some curiosity. He actively supported the Society's programme of commissioning prints of antiquities engraved by George Vertue. He became interested in the internal organization of the Society, taking the chair at meetings and campaigning for the election of his friends. It is significant that during the 1740s Rawlinson failed to make his annual visits to Oxford. In 1749, at a meeting of the Society of Antiquaries, he recommended 'that it was high time to think of obtaining a charter, and of removing from a tavern to a place where they could be secure of what they already had'.[54] Rawlinson was clearly beginning to think of the Society as a possible resting place for his collections, where they would be respected and safely preserved.

As early as 1726, Hearne had told Rawlinson: 'You have a most noble Collection, such as is exceeded by few and is very much for your Reputation. You are much in the right to settle it so that it may not be separated, tho' 'tis a pretty difficult matter to do so.'[55] By 1749 Rawlinson felt that time was running short: the choice of the future home where his collections would be kept intact became a matter of such urgency and importance as to eclipse all other considerations. He grew alarmed when the Bishop of London sought Parliamentary permission to sell London House: 'As I can find no one place to contain my effects, I begin to think of being an eye witness of the disposal of the largest part of them'[56] but the threat passed. While Rawlinson never wavered in his determination to show his gratitude to what he termed 'his Mother, Oxford', he had some doubts whether

[48] *Ibid.*, f. 251.
[49] MS.Carte 103, f. 579ᵛ.
[50] MS.Rawl.H.31, f. 444, 19 Jul. 1744.
[51] MS.Rawl.H.29, f. 317, 12 May [1729].
[52] MS.Rawl.H.30, f. 47.
[53] T. Hearne, *Remarks and Collections*, x, 402, 3 Apr.

1731.
[54] *The Family Memoirs of the Rev. William Stukeley* (Surtees Society, vol. 76) Durham, 1883, ii, 367.
[55] T. Hearne, *Remarks and Collections*, ix, 199, 2 Sept., Oct. 1726.
[56] MS.Ballard 2, f. 185ᵛ, 1 Apr. 1749.

to include his book and manuscript collections among his other intended benefactions. He had confided to Hearne: 'It would be a torment, in another state, to know the ill usage posthumous papers meet with; by nothing has mankind more suffered, than by the vanity or avarice of those who have come after them; Was it not an injustice this procedure would induce a Man to burn all his papers and deprive an ungrateful world of any benefit they might receive from them'.[57] Rawlinson feared that the Universities might even become 'a morsel for some future Henry. The monasteries little thought of such a fate as we do now'.[58] Even if Oxford survived, there seemed at times little interest in antiquarian studies there. He feared that his manuscripts might lie as neglected as his memory – indeed their very safety might be threatened if 'Party, Fury' broke out at the University. For the future of manuscripts imposed heavy responsibilities and he warned a friend 'Dispose of your Treasure so as, to be faithfully preserved the Advantage of a better Age than the present'.[59]

During the last five years of his life Rawlinson watched closely the reactions of the University and of the Society of Antiquaries. A rebuff from one sent him over to the other. Like an eligible lady with a valuable dowry, he waited to be wooed. It was largely through the patience and tact of Bodley's Librarian, Humphrey Owen, that Oxford's suit was successful. Owen's bibliothecal behaviour could be regarded as a model for any librarian dealing with demanding benefactors for he succeeded in retaining Rawlinson's favour without surrendering his own independence. In 1750 Rawlinson endowed an Anglo-Saxon Lectureship at Oxford. While he confessed that he was 'not very conversant with the Saxon tongue',[60] he hoped to re-establish that 'profluvium of Saxonists' he had known in his youth. But he grew irritated at the University's delay in altering the statutes of the Ashmolean Museum which he considered hindered access to the manuscript collections there. He issued a thinly-disguised warning to Bodley's Librarian: 'It is with much reluctance that I am not so diligent for Bodley as I am inclined to be. I should be sorry to turn the stream another way',[61] adding the following year 'I have sent nothing for some time, and I shall hold my hand until the affair of the Museum is settled'.[62] A bout of illness perhaps accounted for some of his irritability and obstinacy. He complained about the lack of news from Oxford, loftily maintaining that 'no body is less captious than my self, and will take a rebuke, when he deserves it'.[63]

Fortunately Oxford responded and changed the rules which had been in Rawlinson's view lucrative for the benefit of the keeper of the Ashmolean. Rawlinson was jubilant and recalled, some years later, that 'these alterations were passed at my desire and are such as were calculated to make the place more easy of access and less expensive, and this I add without vanity, that I have always studied the benefit of the publick, and encouraged it, when it lay in my power'.[64] Meanwhile, at the Society of Antiquaries, he supported a motion that 'several Persons would give them considerable Donations for their Future Encouragement to proceed in their said Studies if it were made a Body Corporate

---

[57] MS.Rawl.H.27c, f. 140ᵛ, postmark 18 Jan. [1732?].

[58] MS.Ballard 2, f. 26, 15 Aug. 1738.

[59] MS.Ballard 2, f. 223ᵛ, 23 Jan. 1754. Cf. 'Happy is he who is wise enough to keep his Library within narrow limits, and rich enough to leave it . . . out of the category of realisable assets.' W. C. Hazlitt, *The Book Collector*, 1904, p. 87.

[60] MS.Ballard 2, f. 15, 14 Jan. 1737.

[61] MS.Rawl.C.989, f. 157, [28 Dec.] 1750

[62] MS.Ballard 40, f. 62, 26 Mar. 1751.

[63] MS.Don.d.90, f. 22, 9 Aug. 1751

[64] British Library Add.MS.6211, f. 55, 12 Jun. 1754.

and capable of holding the same in Perpetuity which at present they are not, being only a Voluntary Society'.[65] Towards the end of 1751 Rawlinson learnt that the Society's Charter had received royal approval and that he had been elected to the Council of the Society. He arranged for the Charter to be printed, including a special vellum copy for himself, and also presented the nucleus of a working library to the Society as well as an insurance policy covering their possessions for seven years.

It was at this point, June 1752, that Rawlinson made his will. Not surprisingly, after the controversies over Thomas's will, Richard was punctilious to the point of eccentricity. His will was loaded with conditions and was to be printed at the Bookseller's expense 'in order to perpetuate the same, and be a check upon all concerned, as well as to be a direction to them'. His possessions were divided between St John's College, The Bodleian Library and the Society of Antiquaries. He visited Oxford and found the air and 'Sir Thomas Bodley's conversation' very agreeable. He was reported to be 'buried alive in the Bodleian' which he recalled 'has as yet escaped Gothic fury, and has been well preserved together. May it be so to the end of Time'.[66] St John's College allowed him to have his old chambers for a 'Ware house' where he felt his collections would be 'safer than in private hands'.[67]

Back in London at the Society of Antiquaries, Rawlinson began to meet opposition. He found that the majority had grown tired of copperplate engravings, preferring to use the printing press and 'a la mode the Royal Society print some account of our Transactions'.[68] Far more objectionable was a proposal for the election of Richard Blacow, that arch enemy of the Old Jacobite Interest who had been active in securing the conviction of Jacobites in the 1747 Oxford disturbances. Political bitterness was at its height during the 1754 election, described as the greatest trial of strength between the friends of the Pretender and those of the Hanoverian succession since the '15 and '45 Rebellions, and Rawlinson's enemies successfully engineered his being dropped from the Society's Council. He reacted immediately. It had become, he wrote 'a Society of Faction' and he signed a codicil to his will on the Society's premises cancelling all his 'generous intentions towards them, and indeed I shall exclude them or their successors from receiving any benefit by what I design for Alma Mater, so that the being a member of the Royal or Antiquarys Societys shall be a disqualification to enjoy any benefit from me. Such ingratitude . . . deserves publishment, to more than the third generation.'[69]

In June 1754 he felt that 'the discharge the Antiquaries have given me will hasten me to Oxford'[70] where he spoke of his joy to walk twice a day in the fields beyond Worcester College and the restorative effects of a drop of brandy or rum since he was suffering from ill health again. He began to make arrangements for his own tomb, preferring not to leave it to Executors 'for that sort of gentry have generally paid little regard to items of that nature in last wills, nor is a Man the nearer enjoying it for seeing it'.[71] He secured a faculty to make a vault in the North West end of St Giles's Church, Oxford, where he went on All Souls Day and noted 'I placd these Coyns in the North wall, wrapt in lead

---

[65] Society of Antiquaries Minute Books, vi, p. 89, 14 Mar. 1751.
[66] MS.Ballard 2, f. 271, 21 May 1754.
[67] St John's College Muniment, R298, 29 Dec. 1752.

[68] MS.Ballard 2, f. 220, 12 Jan. 1754.
[69] MS.Ballard 2, f. 257, Eve of St George's Day, 1754.
[70] MS.Ballard 2, f. 273, 18 Jun. 1754.
[71] St John's College Muniment, R269, f. 34.

PLATE V
A selection of
Rawlinson's
bookplates

222

and wax 6 feet high . . . in the presence of Mr John Townsend [the mason] and saw them walled up securely'.[72]

Rawlinson's old enemy, Blacow, the Editor of the *Evening Advertiser* greeted Rawlinson's reappearance in London by printing a notice that 'Our old friend, the *Nonjuring Bishop is returned to town, from assisting the old interests* and showing his teeth . . . in Oxford'.[73] He went on to condemn Rawlinson as 'a *mitred nonjuror*' who 'calumniates the Government, and becomes a nuisance and a common disturber of every subordinate Society he finds admittance into – unless they be distinguished for faction like his own'.[74] Rawlinson quickly retaliated by publishing a report in the London *Evening Post* about the loss of some important papers which had been presented to the Society of Antiquaries, and reflecting adversely on the reputation of some of the members.[75] Declining health forced him to desist from baiting the Society. Still concerned about the future safe custody of his manuscripts and unwilling 'to leave the event to providence'[76] he made a fourth and final codicil to his will ordering the Bodleian to keep certain manuscripts locked up in 'red Russian leather trunks' until seven years after his death. He was resigned, as he wrote to a friend, that his own unfinished projects would have to be trusted to some future editors: 'As I follow you in years, and in my Grand Climacterick, I must leave them to Posterity to find them in Bodley . . . Sic vos non vovis'.[77]

His last notes complained about the high prices of the Mead booksales and recorded the purchase of a view of Oxford. The death on 6 April 1755 of the 'ingenious and learned' Dr Rawlinson was reported in *Jackson's Oxford Journal* followed by some complimentary verses in which 'Candidus' lamented 'great Rawlinson's no more'. A week later the same journal announced the arrival from London of the remains of Richard Rawlinson: 'His Body was interred in a new Vault lately made by the Doctor's own Directions in the North Isle of St Giles's Church; and his Heart inclosed in a Silver Vase was deposited according to the Directions of his Will, in the Chapel of St John's College in this University.'

The bestowal of his heart into the safe keeping of St John's College in a black marble urn inscribed 'Ubi thesaurus, Ibi cor' and of his body to St Giles in his beloved Oxford were, for Rawlinson, acts of true symbolism. But monuments alone, as none knew better than Rawlinson himself, were but poor things to preserve the memory of the collector and antiquary. The lasting memorial – his collections – the summary of his hopes and of his achievements, had been safely preserved and were destined to take their place in the Bodleian. In writing the obituary of Thomas Baker, one of his closest friends, Rawlinson had composed his own when he said that he 'tho' dead, in his Virtues and Collections will live as long as Time shall endure'.[78]

---

[72] MS.Rawl.J.8°.16, f. 15ᵛ, 2 Nov. 1754.
[73] Nichols, *Literary Anecdotes*, ix, 619, 19 Nov. 1754.
[74] *Ibid.*, ix, 618.
[75] Society of Antiquaries Minute Books, vii, p. 168,

1 Dec. 1754.
[76] MS.Ballard 2, f. 271, 21 May 1754.
[77] British Library Add.MS.5833, f. 184ᵛ, 12 Mar. 1755.
[78] MS.Rawl.J.fol.8, f. 8, 8 Jul. 1740.

A. I. DOYLE

John Cosin (1595–1672) as a Library Maker[1]

O N 20 September 1669 John Cosin as Bishop of Durham issued his charter of foundation for the Episcopal Library adjoining his Castle and the courts of his palatine government in that city. Like many such documents the charter was by no means the beginning, or even the conclusion, but only the culmination of the work of creating an institution with its own home and endowments. The building had apparently been erected, and was being decorated, by 19 September in the previous year, 1668,[2] and Cosin's own collection of books had been installed during the summer of 1669, but the catalogues were still being compiled, more books procured, bindings stamped with the Bishop's arms, and the small adjacent room constructed, in 1671,[3] and some if not all of these were unfinished when he died on 15 January 1672. According to his will and a list of his various benefactions the building had cost £500 and the books £2000 'and the care of above five and fifty yeares together'.[4]

Fifty-five years before he wrote or dictated those words, in December 1616 Cosin, as a Cambridge bachelor aged twenty-one, had recently become secretary and librarian to John Overall, then Bishop of Lichfield and subsequently of Norwich, to whose memory Cosin bequeathed a monument in the latter Cathedral which continues to testify to his discipleship.[5] Neither Cosin's theology nor his scholarship can have been wholly owing to Overall's influence, but from that time he evidently dated his deepened awareness of the value of a substantial collection of the instruments of learning: 'Non minima pars eruditionis est bonos nosse libros' is the motto (thought to be derived from Joseph Scaliger) he had carved over the main entrance of the library at Durham.[6]

Cosin himself had been born at Norwich, on 30 November 1595, the eldest son of a tradesman there. It is relevant that the first public city library in England independent of a church or school, though still clerical in character, was established at Norwich in 1608, two years before Cosin went up to Gonville and Caius College, Cambridge, at the age of fourteen. In the late sixteenth and early seventeenth century several towns got endowed libraries under one form of management or another, with bishops and clergy among the

---

[1] This article is based on part of a lecture given in Cosin's Library, Durham, in celebration of its tercentenary, 1969.

[2] The Correspondence of Miles Stapylton, ed. J. C. Hodgson, Northumbrian Documents, Surtees Society 131 (Durham, 1918), p. 185.

[3] The Correspondence of John Cosin, ed. G. Ornsby, II, Surtees Soc. 55 (Durham, 1872), 268–71, 273–5, 277–8, 280, 283, 287, 291.

[4] Correspondence of John Cosin, II, 171, 295; cf. 301.

[5] P. H. Osmond, A Life of John Cosin (London, 1913), p. 11; in his will dated 1671 but with a codicil saying that it had been paid for already: Correspondence, II, 308.

[6] W. Hutchinson, The History and Antiquities of the County Palatine of Durham, 1 (Newcastle upon Tyne, 1785), 533: a misquotation in fact closer to the probable source, Coniectanea in M. T. Varronem de Lingua Latina, in the edition of Varro's Opera (Geneva, 1581), p. 5.

chief benefactors, for instance Toby Matthew in his home town of Bristol in 1613 and Samuel Harsnett, his successor as Archbishop of York, at Colchester in 1631.[7]

Cosin's first six years at Cambridge may have been in a period of comparative quiet after the controversies of Elizabeth's reign, but theologians of Calvinist sympathies were still highly placed and influential, both in the university and the Church of England at large. Overall, as Regius Professor of Divinity and Dean of St Paul's, had been one of the leaders of a reaction, though the articles of the Canterbury Convocation of 1606 did not go far enough towards the divine right of kings to satisfy James I. His collection of books must have been sizeable for Cosin to have been called his librarian, but it does not survive identifiably in any quantity, so far as I know. Cosin's Library however contains the original copy of the Convocation articles signed by Overall[8] and also Masius's edition of Joshua (Antwerp, 1574) with an inscription to Overall by Richard Thomson on his leaving Cambridge in 1592.[9] Thomson (who had been born in Holland) was, according to the opposite party, the introducer of Arminianism into England. He was later with Overall on one of the committees for the Authorized Version of the Bible, published in 1611, which ended the long predominance of the Geneva translation.

Arminius himself had died in 1609, in 1610 the Remonstrance against severer Calvinist doctrine was addressed by his followers to the States of Holland, and in 1613 (the year of Richard Thomson's death) their leader Hugo Grotius visited England to solicit support in the complicated religio-political struggle. Overall and Lancelot Andrewes were two of the most sympathetic divines with whom he conferred and he continued to correspond with Overall after his return home, particularly concerning Thomson's writings and the question of predestination. In 1617, when Cosin had become Overall's secretary, Grotius sent the manuscript of his work *De imperio summarum potestatum circa sacra* for Overall's and Andrewes' criticism. One of Cosin's first known letters is that sending the text back to Grotius at Paris in 1621, shortly after his escape, hidden in a basket of books, from a two years' imprisonment in the Netherlands, during which Overall had died.[10] Cosin's Library contains many of Grotius's works, notably the anonymous tract *Disquisitio an Pelagiana sint ea dogmata quae nunc sub eo nomine traducuntur* (Paris, 1622), with Cosin's inscription that it was given him by the author;[11] and his portrait is one of a trio (with Erasmus and Scaliger) in a set painted for the Library on Cosin's instructions in 1668–69.

After Overall's death Cosin returned to Cambridge as Fellow of Caius from 1620 to 1624, but managed to combine it with the post of chaplain to Richard Neile, Bishop of Durham, spending much of his time with the circle of churchmen and courtiers based on Durham House in the Strand. It was on Neile's nomination that in 1624 he was given the tenth stall in the Durham Cathedral Chapter. In 1625 he also got the rectories of Elwick and Brancepeth in county Durham as a result of William Laud's influence with Charles I's favourite the Duke of Buckingham, and the Archdeaconry of the East Riding by the

---

[7] T. Kelly, *Early Public Libraries* (London, 1966), pp. 71, 74.

[8] Cosin MS. B.I.11; published from a transcript by William Sancroft in 1690.

[9] A.III.11 There is another book of Overall's in Cosin's Library and at least one from Cosin at Peterhouse.

[10] *Praestantium ac Eruditorum Virorum Epistolae Ecclesiasticae*, 2nd ed. [by] C. Hartsoeker & P. a Limborch (Amsterdam, 1684), pp. 659–60.

[11] S.IV.3/2.

resignation of Marmaduke Blakiston, a fellow-canon of Durham whose daughter Frances he married in 1626. Among Cosin's books is one given to him by Laud when Bishop of St David's (1621–26),[12] and the fullest edition of Francis Bacon's *Essays* (1625) in a contemporary embroidered binding with a portrait of Charles on one cover and what perhaps was taken for Buckingham on the other;[13] and a painting of the latter is one of three statesmen apparently done for Cosin after 1660 which now hang above the gallery in his Library. On the accession of Charles in 1625 he had become further involved in the court. The King's own copy of the Coronation Service is in Cosin's handwriting,'[14] and when something was requested to rival Henrietta Maria's popish prayerbooks for her Anglican ladies-in-waiting, Cosin compiled the *Collection of Private Devotions*, published anonymously in 1627 and largely drawn from earlier sources.[15] It is plain that by this time he was widely read in theological and liturgical literature of mediaeval and Catholic as well as Orthodox origins, and many of the books of the sort in the Library must have been acquired in this period, as his annotations and other markings can confirm.

Four editions of the *Devotions* within the year or dated 1627[16] were accompanied by a storm of Puritan pamphleteering and parliamentary protest, led by William Prynne, and it may not be accidental that by the summer of 1628 Cosin seems to have decided to settle in his Durham rectories and prebend, though not to be a compromising or idle pluralist.[17] Within a few weeks of his arrival a new Act of the Dean and Chapter for the reform and restoration of their library, and a new register of donations thereto, were both drawn up in his hand and little doubt by his zeal.[18] From 1628 to 1635 all the gifts to the Chapter Library are recorded in his writing, mostly of money, and it is likely that he was in effect the librarian, at least until 1633–34 when Elias Smith, minor canon, was first paid as keeper of the books, an office he performed most faithfully (with an enforced break) until 1676.[19] Cosin was still making entries in the donations register in 1639 and 1642, in the former year a record of thirty volumes given by himself, in addition to more

[12] B.V.24, P. Palacios de Salazar, *Enarrationes in Evangelium secundum Matthaeum* (Venice, 1581).

[13] S.R. 6.A.32 (Cosin Y.IV.6). The embroidery is virtually identical with that on the copy given to the Bodleian Library after the Duke's death with his portrait on both covers, under ducal crowns: cf. C. Davenport, *English Embroidered Bindings* (London, 1899), pp. 76–7; *Fine Bindings from Oxford Libraries 1500–1700* (Oxford, 1968), no. 173. The Cosin portraits are indistinguishable, but are surmounted with royal crowns, except that the one on the front cover has been obliterated.

[14] St John's College, Cambridge, MS. L.12, pp. 1–51 at least; annotated by Laud. MS. L.16 may also be from Cosin's hand, p. 69 at least. Cf. *The Coronation of Charles I*, ed. C. Wordsworth, Henry Bradshaw Society 2 (London, 1892).

[15] *Correspondence*, I, Surtees Soc. 52 (Durham, 1869), pp. 284–5; *A Collection of Private Devotions*, ed. P. G. Stanwood & D. O'Connor (Oxford, 1967).

[16] L. W. Hanson, 'John Cosin's *Collection of Private Devotions*, 1627', *The Library*, 5th series, 13 (1958),

282–92.

[17] J. G. Hoffman, 'John Cosin's cure of souls: parish priest at Brancepeth and Elwick, County Durham', *Durham University Journal*, 17 (1978), 73–83; 'Another side of "Thorough": John Cosin and administration, discipline and finance in the Church of England, 1624–44', *Albion* 13 (1981), 347–63.

[18] *Correspondence*, I, 142–4; Durham Cathedral Library MSS A.IV.32 and Hunter 11, no. 20: the former the fair copy, the latter the draft with large cancellations and alterations, all in Cosin's hand, though signed by Dean Hunt.

[19] H. D. Hughes, A *History of Durham Cathedral Library* (Durham, 1925), p. 108; D. R. S. Pearson, 'Elias Smith, Durham Cathedral Librarian 1633–1676', *Library History*, 8 (1989), 65–73, discusses the claim of Isaac Gilpin, made library keeper by the parliamentary commissioners in 1645, to have been instrumental in saving the books from the Scottish prisoners after the battle of Dunbar, traditionally credited to Smith.

than twenty in the two preceding years.[20] The list includes items of various dates and on various subjects, predominantly theological but not of narrow interest: for instance, William Lyndwood's *Provinciale* (Paris, 1501), the first editions of Cuthbert Tunstall's *De arte supputandi* (London, 1522) and Marsilius of Padua's *Defensor pacis* [Basle 1522], Bishop Pilkington of Durham's copy of the first edition of Polydore Vergil's *Anglicae historiae libri XXVI* (Basle, 1534), and William Chillingworth's *Religion of Protestants a Safe Way to Salvation* (London, 1638). Although some may have been got specifically for the Chapter Library, and Cosin was buying books for it before this,[21] it looks as if he had already a large enough personal collection to be able to dispose of some (hardly just duplicates, however), especially after his appointment as Master of Peterhouse, Cambridge, in 1635, where he could expect to find what he might want more easily.

As Chapter Treasurer in 1627–28, Receiver in 1631–32 and Treasurer again in 1633–34 he showed similar diligence, especially in the checking of the Magnum Repertorium of the medieval monastic muniments and its augmentation.[22] The copious copying of old and modern music for services in the 1630s is almost certainly another result of his energy, for the contents of the choir-books now in the Chapter Library are closely interrelated with those at Peterhouse dating from his Mastership.[23] It was just a week after his revival of the Chapter Library in 1628 that he was subjected to the first of the attacks on his innovations in Cathedral services by Peter Smart, only quelled after three years by the exercise of royal prerogative and the support of Laud and Neile, now respectively Archbishops of Canterbury and York.[24] The peak of Cosin's career at Durham came with Charles I's visit in 1633, for which he was obviously the master mind, receiving as one reward a royal order for the removal of tenements from the Cathedral churchyard and the mayoral pew from the choir;[25] I wonder also when he got the copy of Hertzfelder's illustrated account of the abbey church of SS Ulrich and Afra, Augsburg (1627) in extra-gilt morocco with the king's arms, presumably a presentation to or by the latter.[26]

After Cosin's appointment to Peterhouse he continued to hold his Durham benefices, and to return for his statutory periods of residence (with occasional dispensations) up to and after the Scottish invasion and the onset of the Civil War. Meanwhile he soon made up in Cambridge for any books he had left in Durham. Any ancient library is like an archaeological site on which the levels of accumulation and the artefacts deposited can be studied chronologically and morphologically. The annotations and bindings of the books, as well as their contents, imprints and dates, may afford evidence of when, how

[20] MS. A.IV.32, f. 9r: listed by Smith in his catalogue, MS. B.IV.47, and later copied into A.IV.32 by Thomas Rud.

[21] Durham University Library, Mickleton & Spearman MS. 91, f. 62r, is a list in Cosin's hand of books 'taken of Mr Whitakers for Durham Library Febr. 4. 1634': printed by D. Pearson, *Book Trade Bills and Vouchers from Durham Cathedral Library, 1634–1740*, History of the Book Trade in the North [Working Papers] 45 (Newcastle upon Tyne, 1986), p. 1.

[22] Cf. J. G. Hoffman, 'John Cosin, Prebendary of Durham Cathedral and Dean of Peterborough, 1624–43', *Durham University Journal*, 78 (1985), 1–10.

[23] A. Hughes, *Catalogue of the Musical Manuscripts at Peterhouse, Cambridge* (Cambridge, 1953), pp. x–xiii, xv–xvii; G. B. Crosby, 'Durham Cathedral's liturgical musical manuscripts, c. 1620–c. 1640', *Durham University Journal* 66 (1973), 40–51; *A Catalogue of Durham Cathedral Music Manuscripts* (Oxford, 1986).

[24] *Correspondence*, I, 144–221 I; J. G. Hoffman, 'The Arminian and the Iconoclast: the dispute between John Cosin and Peter Smart', *Historical Magazine of the Protestant Episcopal Church* 48 (1979), 274–301.

[25] *Correspondence*, I, 212–17.

[26] +GACA.C27H (Cosin R III.15).

PLATE 1. John Cosin as Bishop of Durham
(portrait in Cosin's Library)

and why the collection was built up, although it is liable to misinterpretation if not seen in a wider context than as a single case. Many of the books in Cosin's Library, and some in the Chapter Library, are still in distinctive binding styles, simple or elaborate, of Cambridge in the 1620s and 1630s.[27] Some also have notes of the cost of the contents and

[27] Cf. G. D. Hobson, *Bindings in Cambridge Libraries* (Cambridge, 1929), pl. XLIII–VI; D. Pearson, 'Cambridge bindings in Cosin's Library, Durham', in *Six* *Centuries of the Provincial Book Trade in Britain*, ed. P. Isaac (Winchester, 1990), pp. 41–60

binding in a small neat script which Cosin does not seem to have used after about 1640, no doubt because of deteriorating sight, and many are sealed (to pursue the archaeological analogy) by shelf-marks of the Peterhouse library, into which his books left there during his foreign exile, 1644–60, were temporarily absorbed, such as his first folio of Shakespeare (1623) which he may well have acquired before the second folio came out in 1632.[28]

It was under Cosin's mastership that the Peterhouse library was furnished with new bookcases, at the same time as his embellishments of his predecessor Matthew Wren's new chapel were exciting comparable hostility to that met by Cosin's innovations at Durham.[29] In 1639, as Vice-Chancellor, he added a screen in the University Church and revived his murdered patron the Duke of Buckingham's plans (when Chancellor) for a new University Library and Senate House.[30] But the collection of funds, to which Bishop Morton of Durham had promised £600, was curtailed by the Scottish seizure of the Bishopric and Cathedral estates, and in the same month as Cosin was made Dean of Peterborough (partly in compensation for his losses) the Long Parliament began and with it Peter Smart's and his party's revenge, culminating in Cosin's expulsion from the Mastership and Deanery in March 1644, after he had sent the college plate to the King's mint at York. As it was only nine months later that Laud was put to death it is not surprising that Cosin had by then fled to France.

Although the new Master and Fellows installed by Parliament at Peterhouse placed Cosin's books, after begging them back from Parliamentary sequestration, in the college library and added its shelf-marks, at first they indicated the origin, if not ownership, in the borrowing register.[31] In 1649 Cosin's only son and namesake entered the college as an undergraduate, taking his degree in 1652, and some of his books from that period survive in his father's collection, so he presumably took them with him to Paris, where the elder Cosin had settled as chaplain to the Anglican members of the households of Henrietta Maria and Sir Richard Browne, the King's ambassador there. The younger Cosin's conversion to Catholicism soon after his arrival (and we may remember that Richard Crashaw had been at Peterhouse from 1636 to 1643) must have strengthened the Protestant reaction in his feelings which is evident henceforward. The mental pressure on the English exiles, especially after Charles I's execution in 1649, must have been very strong.[32] Cosin's distress was accompanied, at least for a time, by shortage of money and in 1651 he began negotiations with John Evelyn, Richard Browne's son-in-law, for the sale of part of his library still in England, through his daughter Mary there, but, fortunately for Durham, they eventually fell through, because the price offered (£300) was

[28] A. I. Doyle, 'The Cosin First Folio', *Durham University Journal* 56 (1964), p. 85.

[29] T. A. Walker, *Peterhouse* (Cambridge, 1935), pp. 55–9; J. G. Hoffman, 'The Puritan revolution and the "Beauty of Holiness" at Cambridge: the case of John Cosin Master of Peterhouse and Vice-Chancellor of the University', *Proceedings of the Cambridge Antiquarian Society* 72 (1984), 93–105.

[30] *Correspondence*, II, 283–4; J. C. T. Oates, *Cambridge University Library: a History*, I (Cambridge, 1986), 164–71, 397.

[31] They were returned by the Earl of Manchester in 1644 when a catalogue was to be made, presumably that which remains at Peterhouse of about 1050 volumes, arranged alphabetically within format, individually valued, to a total of £247 10s.; forty-odd more items are listed by another hand as wanting in the catalogue. Peterhouse MS. 403 is the borrowing register, c. 1645; MS. 401 reversed is a register c. 1657–8 not mentioning Cosin. Cf. Walker pp. 132–5.

[32] *Correspondence*, I, 282–5; Osmond, chapter V.

thought inadequate.[33] At the Evelyn library auctions in 1977 Cosin's Library acquired an edition of Grotius *De veritate religionis Christianae* (Paris, 1640) with an inscription of gift from Cosin to Evelyn at Paris in 1650.[34]

It is hardly surprising that Cosin (who was very precise about particular prices and on reserving some books which he had made annotations in) began with what funds he had to build up a fresh and substantial collection in France, reflecting this new environment but also including books from England. An early refugee like himself was Thomas Hobbes to whom in 1646, when he was gravely ill, Cosin ministered.[35] Cosin's Library has a large paper copy of the genuine first edition of *Leviathan* (London, 1651), for which the author corrected the proofs and dated the preface from Paris; and also the rare variant of the second edition of *De Cive* (Amsterdam, 1647).[36] Neither has an inscription, and they are both now in post-Restoration bindings, but pencil marks characteristic of Cosin before that time appear in the margins of the latter book, particularly where Hobbes says that only a few copies have been printed for friends, and in the portions about religion. During his sixteen years in France Cosin's talents were engaged not only in ministering to his co-religionists but also in counsel and debate supporting Anglican positions against Roman ones, which resulted in his most lengthy works – *A Scholastical History of the Canon of Holy Scripture* (London, 1657) and the posthumously published *Historia Transubstantiationis Papalis* (London, 1676) – in addition to various shorter treatises[37] and much of his second series of notes on the Book of Common Prayer.[38] Each of these employed a wealth of exact citation of theological and historical sources of various kinds, nearly 400 in the *Scholastical History*, some of which the nineteenth-century Oxford editor could not obtain, so one may wonder how Cosin did, in the penury and hostility he complained of.[39] It is likely that he had access to some scholarly French libraries – the Bibliothèque du Roi, the Bibliotheca Thuana or at the Reformed church of Charenton; the Bibliothèque Mazarine, not long founded, was in temporary sequestration and partial sale in the middle years (1649–52) of his stay in Paris.[40]

As time went on friends in England and Holland sent him some of his own books and money to buy more, while English and French acquaintances gave him their publications. This is one way by which the Durham collection comes to have a high proportion of French printing, of which 585 items are actually in that language, mostly seventeenth-century theological pamphlets, many from provincial and Protestant presses, and about

[33] £300: J. Evelyn, *Diary*, ed. W. Bray & H. B. Wheatley, III (London, 1906), 451; ed. E. S. de Beer, III (Oxford, 1955), 62, 636. In 1654 Cosin's daughter Mary got an order for the delivery of the books at Peterhouse for the benefit of his children, but it was evidently not carried out: *Calendar of State Papers Domestic, 1654* (London, 1880), p.302.

[34] I.VI.41: Christie's auction, 30 Nov. 1977, lot 676.

[35] Osmond, p. 121.

[36] T.I.1 and T.V.47; H. Warrender, 'The early Latin version of Thomas Hobbes's De Cive', *The Library*, 6th series, 2 (1980), 45–6, is unaware of the Cosin copy.

[37] Osmond, pp. 115–20; G. J. Cuming, *The Anglicanism of John Cosin* (Durham Cathedral Lecture, 1975).

[38] S.R. 5.F.9 (Cosin C.I.1)' *B.C.P.* (London, 1636),

with interleaving like no. 2338–40 found in Paris books of 1643–8 by E. Heawood, *Watermarks Mainly of the 17th and 18th Centuries* (Hilversum, 1950); cf. *The Works of John Cosin*, ed. J. Stevenson et al., V (Oxford, 1855), xviii–xix.

[39] *Works*, III (1849), iii.

[40] The royal library, though more open to scholars from 1642, had only 1329 printed items in this period, and that of the Reformed church at Charenton only 1534 by 1685, while Cardinal Richelieu had 6135 titles in 1643, the De Thou family in 1653 perhaps 7500 volumes and Mazarin had 13,000 in 1654 and over 20,000 by 1660: *Histoire des bibliothèques françaises: les bibliothèques sous l'Ancien Régime*, ed. C. Jolly (Paris, 1988), pp. 82, 107, 129, 188.

eighty of these with acknowledged authors are not in the catalogue of the Bibliothèque Nationale, besides differing editions, and an as yet to be ascertained number of the anonyma.[41] There is a parallel with the collection of continental books made in Holland at the same period by Michael Honywood, whom Cosin must have known in Cambridge in the 1630s, and which was bequeathed to Lincoln Cathedral Library, although the overlap between them is not great, and the only one comparable in respect of French items in the British Isles is probably that left by Elie Bouhéreau to Archbishop Marsh's Library, Dublin, though formed later in the century.[42]

In the course of his exile Cosin, who had long had only one good eye for reading, developed cataracts on both which hindered him for the rest of his life and impaired his handwriting; but neither this nor the expense seems to have deterred him, in his middle and later years abroad, from employing a Parisian bookbinder or two to put a fair number of his books in covers of morocco, calf or sheep elaborately gold-tooled on the spines and boards in the pointillé style, like that of many of Browne's and Evelyn's books, and in his correspondence with Edward Hyde, Charles II's chief minister, then in Holland, shortly before their return to England in 1660, he discusses taking the binder and his *doreur* with them, to demonstrate and teach their superior techniques.[43] This does not seem to have happened, however, and the great flowering of the art in England in subsequent years, of which there are only a few examples in Cosin's Library (the two finest, from Samuel Mearne's workshop, given by Cosin's successor as Bishop of Durham, Nathaniel Crewe) may have been owing to other agents.[44] A portrait of Hyde as Earl of Clarendon painted for Cosin hangs in the gallery of his Library.

In June 1660 Cosin came back to England, recovering his mastership at Cambridge, the deanery at Peterborough, canonry and rectories in Durham, only to be elevated to the bishopric by the end of the year. One week after his consecration, on 11 December, the library-keeper of Peterhouse checked and delivered to Cosin's successor as Master there 1174 of his books, with a note of three the borrowers had not yet restored, two of them lost under a previous keeper. A couple of months later the master was writing to ask Cosin that £100 owing to him by the College might be spent on the library 'for your Lordship's books being taken out of the Lybrary and divers of Dr Perne's books being lost, unlesse we can get some new books to supply the vacuum, I shall not know what to answer the visitors'[45] – an argument well calculated for one whose own visitation enquiries had been and would be searching on the provision of books, in church, college or cathedral. Whether at once or over the next few years I am not certain but later Cosin

[41] D. Ramage, 'Cosin's French books', *The Durham Philobiblon*, 2 pt 8 (1964), 57–63, pt 9–10 (1969), 65; E. Dubois, 'La bibliothèque de l'évêque Cosin à Durham et sa collection de livres français de théologie et de spiritualité protestantes des XVIe et XVIIe siècles', *Bulletin de la Société de l'Histoire du Protestantisme Français*, 1982, 175–88.

[42] N. Linnell, 'Michael Honywood and Lincoln Cathedral Library', *The Library*, 6th series, 5 (1983), 126–39; N.J. D. White, *A Catalogue of Books in the French Language, Printed in or before A.D. 1715, remaining in Archbishop Marsh's Library* (Dublin, 1918).

[43] Bodleian Library, *Clarendon State Papers*, IV (Oxford, 1932), 652–3, 668. For Browne's and Evelyn's bindings see Christie's auction catalogues, 30 Nov.–1 Dec. 1977. Richard Steward refers to Dr Cosin's bookbinder at Paris in February 1648/9: Durham Univ. Lib. Cosin Letterbook Ia, no. 53.

[44] H. M. Nixon, *English Restoration Bookbindings* (London, 1974), nos 14–15; *Five Centuries of English Bookbinding* (London, 1978), no. 37.

[45] *Correspondence*, II, 13–14: Peterborough Cathedral Library MS. 20, ff. 111, 116, 123 (the last not in *Corr.*).

could boast that he had in all given Peterhouse '1831 volumes of good bookes, fairely and well bound; which cost him about £300', and a number of them which can be identified have evidence that they came from his own collection and were not just purchased for that purpose.[46] Any he did not leave at Peterhouse then, which must have been the majority of his pre-war acquisitions, and presumably those from France, were gradually moved north, some perhaps to Durham Castle but most to the long gallery at Auckland Palace.[47] William Sancroft and George Davenport, who had sent him money and books when he was abroad and were now his chaplains, the one a canon of the Cathedral and the other Rector of St Mary-le-Bow, Durham (at that time in fact a ruin), were engaged respectively in listing and receiving consignments as late as June 1662.[48]

It was Sancroft who in the meantime had been acting as Cosin's secretary at the Savoy conference on the Book of Common Prayer, for which the bishop's learning, his long-made notes and probably portions of his library were called into service. In the so-called Durham Book (actually a folio edition of 1619)[49] it is Cosin's own hand which makes the majority of the proposed amendments of the text and rubrics, but Sancroft's which notes that not all the most significant were eventually accepted by the other bishops after the collapse of the conference, where Cosin in other regards was thought to have been nearer the non-conformist members, perhaps as a result of his French experiences. But following the Act of Uniformity he showed no hesitation in ejecting the non-conforming ministers of his diocese and in persecuting other sectaries, notably the Quakers who had established themselves during the interregnum. In 1657 George Fox had recorded in his journal how he did his best to discourage the starters of the university college founded at Durham in place of the Cathedral Chapter, and which the jealousy of Oxford and Cambridge soon helped to kill. Another of his encounters was with Sir Henry Vane at Raby Castle, where each of the two enthusiasts thought the other mad.[50] In 1622 Cosin caused not a little annoyance at Westminster when, reviving the regalian rights of a ruler of the Palatinate, he seized Sir Henry's goods after his attainder and execution as a regicide:[51] Cosin's Library contains a copy of Milton's Latin defence of Charles I's execution (London, 1651) presented to Vane as President of the Council of State by the printer William Dugard, who had surreptitiously produced for the other side the so-called King's Book, *Eikon Basilike* (1649), and, having been discovered, had to turn his coat in order to save his skin.[52] A smaller book is a volume of Quaker tracts seized by one of the Bishop's officers in 1663 from a meeting at Haughton-le-Skerne, when a scare about a dissenting rebellion was at its height.[53] In August of the previous year amongst some Quakers imprisoned in Durham gaol (the old North Gate) was John Langstaffe of Bishop Auckland, one of the earliest members of the Society of Friends in

[46] *Correspondence*, II, 173. Peterhouse MS. 408, a catalogue of its library (1686?) has notes of donors including Cosin, but hardly reaching that total.

[47] *Correspondence*, II, 27.

[48] Letter of Davenport to Sancroft, 16 June 1662: Bodleian Library, Oxford, Tanner MS. 48, no. 12.

[49] *The Durham Book: Being the First Draft of the Revision of the Book of Common Prayer in 1661*, ed. G. J. Cuming (London, 1961).

[50] G. F. Nuttall, 'George Fox and the rise of Quakerism in the Bishoprick', *Durham University Journal*, 36 (1943–4), 94–7.

[51] S. L. Greenslade, 'An inventory of Raby Castle 1662', *Transactions of the Architectural & Archaeological Society of Durham and Northumberland*, 10 (1946–54), 205–10.

[52] K.III.15: D Ramage, 'Dugard, Milton and Vane', *The Durham Philobiblon*, I pt 8 (1953), 55–6

[53] N.V.12: J. Perrot, *A Visitation of Love*, and fourteen others by him (1660–1).

the area.[54] He was a builder and stonemason who had been employed by Sir Arthur Hesilrigge, the Commonwealth man from London who had bought Durham and Auckland Castles, to pull down and replace the latter by a modern mansion. Yet by 2 January 1663 Cosin was agreeing with Langstaffe to demolish Hesilrigge's house and to restore the palace, as part of the great programme of repairs and improvements there and in Durham begun in that year, largely recorded in his papers added later to the Library.[55] Langstaffe was one of a number of local contractors and craftsmen whom Cosin engaged for these works, together with a couple of foreign artisans, and there is no evidence in the agreements, plans and letters of any other single mind directing and designing, not merely the general conceptions but even the decorative details, than that of Cosin himself or possibly his steward Edward Arden. It has been surmised that Langstaffe's commissions were intended to convert him from his Quakerism, but the records of his persistence and of his usefulness to the Bishop are equally clear. It was he who was employed for Cosin's house at Brafferton (N. Yorks) where some of his books were kept, for rebuilding the Durham County Court on the west side of Palace Green and the schools on the east side as Cosin's almshouses, and for the new construction of the Episcopal Library next to the Exchequer, though in the last case he may have sub-contracted some of the work to Christopher Scurrey, a freeman of Durham, in order to avoid the opposition of the city guilds, despite the traditional exclusion of the peninsula (the outer bailey of the Castle) from their jurisdiction.[56]

We do not know what the Library replaced but it was probably part of the Castle stabling or outhouses. It was made to abut on the fifteenth-century Exchequer and Chancery Court building, no doubt for economy but also to be accessible by the Bishop and his officers more easily, and it was for long regarded as part of the Castle. For its purpose the shape was more of an innovation than may now be obvious, and its appearance from the outside must have been less clumsy before a low-pitched roof hidden by battlements was replaced by the present steep roof behind higher solid parapets in the nineteenth century.[57] A rectangular hall 52 feet in length east to west, 30 in width north to south, and 26 high, stands on the edge of the bishops' garden at the west end, with one large five-light window taking up most of that wall, while at the east to Palace Green the entrance doorway is surmounted by a round arched broken pediment framing Cosin's arms and the Library's motto, with a three-light window above it and two of the same size in the upper half of the south wall, and none (because of the Exchequer) on the north. Inside the door a small porch (with a painted inscription) and shelving along the lower half of the walls except, originally, under the west window and for a doorway to the smaller room and a fireplace in the north wall. This new model of wall shelving had been introduced to England on a large scale in the Arts End of the Bodleian at Oxford earlier in the seventeenth century but Cosin's was possibly the first substantial English

[54] G. B. Longstaff, *The Langstaffs of Teesdale and Weardale*, rev. ed. (London, 1926), pp. 52–95; J. W. Steel, *Early Friends in the North* (London, 1905), pp. 3, 19, 31; Durham Cathedral Library, Surtees MS. 47, p. 387.

[55] J. Raine, *A Brief Historical Account of the Episcopal Castle or Palace of Auckland* (Durham, 1852), pp. 103–4; *Correspondence*, II, 356–83.

[56] W. H. D. Longstaffe, 'Is the Cathedral within the city of Durham?', *Archaeologia Aeliana*, 2nd series, 2 (1858), 207–8, 213–14.

[57] A bird's-eye drawing from the Cathedral tower by Cuthbert Bede (pseud., i.e. Edward Bradley), dated 1846, now in the Castle, shows the old roof and parapets.

library to have been designed wholly on that principle and there can be little doubt that he had been influenced by what he saw in France, especially by the original building of the Bibliothèque Mazarine in Paris, and the general change to shelving books with spine decoration and titling outwards.[58] But as in his own portrait hanging in the Library a shelf of books is still shown with the fore-edges outwards, so in the collection there are some which bear written fore-edge labels which suggest that not all were at first turned the new way.[59] Yet more of the bindings had spine titles from earlier in the century, from both Cambridge and France, and it was Cosin's declared wish (not far realized in his lifetime) to have his arms stamped on every spine.

What are now single bookcases between double ones were originally meant to be open seats for readers with their backs to the wall under the existing canopies with Cosin's eagle crest and swags, but they had to be converted with shelving even in the founder's lifetime, from underestimate or extra provision of books.[60] The present bookcase doors with diamond wire grilles are thought to be a later addition, since they hide the only lettering now to be seen, at the top of one case (class I, 'Reformati'), and the earlier paintwork was a matt buff, not the varnished false graining which now covers the doors, frames and canopies. The scheme of three portraits on an oblong canvas above each double case, representing authors in the class shelved below (or intended to be, as not all may have been completed)[61] had various antecedents in England (especially the Bodleian) and abroad,[62] but again the particular design may be attributable to Cosin himself. The portraits were executed by a painter from the Low Countries, Jan Baptist van Eersell, who had already done decoration in Durham and Auckland castles and who was meant to do the inscription in gilt capitals in the porch of the Library. The models for his heads were black and white engravings in books of the collection, notably a fine folio by André Thevet, *Pourtraits des hommes illustres* (Paris, 1584), where marks of paint are visible on some pages, and frontispieces in the authors' works.[63] Despite Cosin's constant chiding (conducted from a distance, in London, through his agents in Durham) van Eersell seems never to have finished the scheme for the main hall nor to have done what was planned for the small adjacent room, where in 1961–62 Mr D. G. Ramage, then University and Cosin's Librarian, supplied the omission imaginatively by his own hands.[64]

Although the Arts and Selden Ends of the Bodleian and the Mazarine had integral galleries from their erection there is no evidence that Cosin intended to have one, apart from the height of the hall. It was only in 1834 that the present gallery was built to accom-

[58] Cf. A. Hobson, 'English library buildings of the 17th and 18th century', *Wolfenbütteler Forschungen*, 2 (Bremen, 1977), 63–74; P. Gasnault, 'Cardinal Mazarin's library', *The Connoisseur*, 204 (1980), 202–7; *Histoire des bibliothèques françaises*, I, 135–45.

[59] Some on folios which must have lain flat, perhaps in his private library, but some on smaller books including publications of 1667 and 1669.

[60] Cosin Letterbook 5, no. 19, 29 Oct. 1668 (not in *Corr.*).

[61] D. Ramage, 'Portraits in Cosin's Library', *Trans. Archit. & Archaeol. Soc. of Durham & Northumberland*, 11

(1958–65), 65–74; in 1982 a list was found in the university archives of the placing in 1836, with additional names of three groups of three which must have been lost when a memorial fireplace was installed in 1845.

[62] A. Masson, *Le Décor des bibliothèques du moyen âge à la Révolution* (Geneva, 1972); *The Pictorial Catalogue: Mural Decoration in Libraries* (Oxford, 1981).

[63] T.I.21.

[64] D. Ramage, 'Portrait heads for Cosin's Library', *Trans. Archit. & Archaeol. Soc. of Durham & Northumberland*, 11 (1958–65), 461–4.

modate the first books of the newly-founded University and spectators of its congregations held on the floor. The wall-space previously may have been used for one of two sets of full-length portraits of post-Reformation English bishops, together with Charles I, of which the other set was probably for the Castle, where both were subsequently kept, matching in style and dress the portraits of Cosin and his successor Crewe which now hang on the east wall.[65] The choice of subjects and the manner of execution suggest that it was Cosin who had one or both sets painted, as also the half-lengths of other Anglican bishops and statesmen of the sixteenth and seventeenth centuries which used to hang in the Castle but since 1968 have been placed above the gallery bookcases.[66]

We do not know when Cosin first formed a plan of building and endowing an Episcopal Library in Durham, in which he may have been influenced by that at Rouen as well as earlier English ecclesiastical instances. In October 1664 he made his last recorded gifts to the Cathedral Library,[67] to which he also paid a lot of attention at his visitation in 1665,[68] but there is at least one other book there which from its Peterhouse shelfmark must have come from his collection after 1660.[69] Though not so easy to identify as his earlier acquisitions, additions must have been made to his books in this period, from references in his letters. Once his new venture was settled his enthusiasm for enriching and embellishing it was unflagging, if dependent for accomplishment on his agents, Miles Stapylton and George Davenport, minutely directed and harried in letters from the Bishop in London, where he was now for much of his time. New and second-hand books to be procured there were to be paid for out of fines for renewal of leases by tenants of the Bishoprick, or gifts of books were to be exacted in lieu.[70] Hugh Hutchinson, the Durham bookbinder, was to bring his blocking-press into the Library to stamp the Bishop's arms on every spine.[71] Cosin enjoined regular fortnightly or monthly wiping of the books in front of the fire, to prevent or remove mildew; the roof was already leaking in its first winter,[72] as it did in following centuries to the sad damage of not a few books, which might have been rescued by prompt action on his advice.

By his charter of 1669 he endowed the Library with an annual income of £20 from the manor of Great Hilton and other lands at Carleton still to be bought by him, out of which the library keeper was to receive £13 6s 8d as his stipend with the remainder for the maintenance of the building, providing fires, and buying and binding books.[73] Miles Stapylton, the Bishop's Auditor, was nominated as the first keeper, and after his death another official or Auditor should enter into a bond of £100 in the Palatine Chancery that he would diligently look after the Library and its books, not only those already listed in

[65] The other remains of both sets are in store, except for one of Laud now in the Deanery, Gloucester; all listed by J. Ingamells, *The English Episcopal Portrait 1559–1835* (Guildford, 1981).

[66] Also in Ingamells; those of Toby Matthew and James Ussher, mentioned by him as missing, have now been found.

[67] Durham Cathedral Library MS. A.IV.32, f. 91v.

[68] *Correspondence*, II, 113.

[69] Durham Cathedral Library P.IV.25, G. Paleotti, *De bono senectutis* (Venice, 1598), a text also in Cosin's Library.

[70] Whiting, pp. 21–2.

[71] *Ibid.*, 26–7.

[72] *Ibid.*, 23.

[73] The original is missing, but, perhaps because it was already lost, an exemplification was made (from the Palatine Court of Pleas record) in 1675, when the keepership seems to have been in dispute: Durham University Library Hogg MS. 2, ff. 1–2; Mickleton & Spearman MS. 91, f. 169, is another copy, certified 1696, from the original exemplification (now lost).

an alphabetical catalogue signed by Cosin on 9 May 1669 (not now extant) but also any subsequently given and placed there; and that he would observe the rules also signed by Cosin (now also lost), hung by the chimney. The Archdeacons of Durham and Northumberland were to be visitors, making an annual inspection about Christmas in person or by prudent deputies, not only of the fabric but also of the state and number of the books, which the keeper was bound to repair or replace. Except for its reliance on economic stability this was all fairly farsighted; but its safeguards seem to have been not always respected after Cosin's death and the regime more than once had to be reformed. In his last few years various friends and local people (such as Richard Baddeley, James Mickleton and Robert Shafto) made gifts, and George Davenport, who had not only received Cosin's books in 1662 but also moved them into the Library in 1669, gave a number of substantial printed books and his valuable collection of seventy medieval manuscripts which he had assembled over fifteen years and most of which he had rebound by Hugh Hutchinson.[74]

This is not the place to narrate the later history, acquisitions and losses of the Library, which was founded to be a public one for the ancient county and diocese of Durham (but is still sometimes confused with the Dean and Chapter's),[75] except to say that since the creation of the University of Durham in 1832 it has been administered in conjunction with its library and since 1937 has been in the legal trusteeship of the University.[76] So the founder's purposes are protected and promoted better, we hope, than his original arrangements could ensure.

The total stock of printed volumes is now 4400, containing 5457 editions, of which more than three-quarters came from Cosin or in his time, which, especially if you add the books he gave to the Cathedral and Peterhouse libraries, made his personal collection one of the larger of the era in England.[77] There are seventy-seven volumes of medieval manuscripts, of which only five belonged to Cosin himself, the most notable of the latter being the leading copy of the history of the church of Durham and its predecessors by the monk Symeon, 1104 × 9, which had left the Cathedral Library before Cosin acquired it and entered his own name in the list of bishops; an early thirteenth-century Benedictional of French origin which had been Archbishop Cranmer's; and a unique late fourteenth-century English Lollard dialogue between a knight and a clerk interleaved with a modernized version intended for publication by William Crashaw (hammer of papists yet father of the poet Richard) with a dedication to King James I, from whom, or his son, Cosin could have got it.[78] There are twenty-one volumes of post-medieval manuscripts, apart from those of his letters and other documents, records of the Library, and antiquarian collections acquired later; they include some of his own writings and of people whom he knew, such as John Overall and Daniel Tilenus, the Huguenot theologian.[79]

---

[74] A. I. Doyle, 'Hugh Hutchinson bookbinder of Durham c. 1662 or 1665–95', THE BOOK COLLECTOR 24 (1975), 25–32.

[75] E.g. by Linnell (n. 42 above).

[76] *University of Durham Calendar 1938–39* (Newcastle, 1938), pp. 80–1, 92–3.

[77] Having over 1000 volumes before the Civil War and

4000–5000 after the Restoration: cf. D. J. McKitterick, *The Library of Sir Thomas Knyvett of Ashwellthorpe c. 1539–1618* (Cambridge, 1978), pp. 1–2.

[78] See the catalogue by Thomas Rud c. 1720 in *Catalogi Veteres Ecclesiae Cathedralis Dunelmensis* [ed. J. Raine], Surtees Society 7 (Durham, 1838), pp. 136–84.

[79] *Ibid*, pp. 184–91.

Returning to the printed books, only eight are incunabula.[80] Durham may lament that Cosin gave his copy of the second printed Bible [Mainz or Bamberg c. 1458], to Peterhouse, if only its second volume. There is a copy of Nicholas Statham's *Abridgement of English cases in law French* printed at Rouen 1490, for Richard Pynson in London, with spaces provided and used for contemporaneous manuscript addenda; the Nuremberg Chronicle 1493 with two leaves of the German edition instead of the Latin; and a *Pontificale Romanum* 1497 collated by Cosin with that of Pope Clement VIII, 1596. There are 632 sixteenth-century European items, including the first edition of More's *Utopia* (Louvain, 1516), in a contemporary foreign blind-stamped binding; the *Mirabilis Liber* (Paris [c. 1520]), a Latin and French compilation of prophecies which was imitated by Rabelais, in a blind panel binding in which fragments of an otherwise unknown printing of the York *Horae* were found;[81] a volume of astronomical and mathematical works of Stoeffler (Tübingen, 1514) and Apianus (Ingolstadt, 1533) with the editio princeps of Archimedes (Basle, 1544), in a blind panel binding probably from Belgium, this a gift of 1668; the fête-book of Philip of Spain's reception at Antwerp, 1550; the second edition of Vesalius's Anatomy (Basle, 1555); a presentation copy of Heinrich Bullinger's *De origine erroris* (Zurich, 1568), in red vellum with gilt gauffered edges; the first edition of Etienne Pasquier's *Des recherches de la France*, book I (Paris, 1560); and one of only two or three known copies of the first issue of Petrus Plancius's map of the British Isles ([Antwerp?], 1592).[82]

There are 541 items within the scope of the British Short Title Catalogue up to 1640, in both editions of which many are cited under the siglum DUR3. There is the massive *Graunde Abbregement* of Sir Anthony Fitzherbert printed by John Rastell and Wynkyn de Worde, 1516; the second version of More's book against Luther printed by Pynson 1523; and the *Myrroure of Oure Lady*, a commentary on the office of the nuns of Syon Abbey, printed by Richard Fawkes, 1530. There is a first edition of the Book of Common Prayer of 1549, and early ones of that of 1552 and the Communion Order of 1548.[83] *Ane compendious tractive conforme to the scripturis, ressoun, and authoritie*, by Quintin Kennedy, opponent of John Knox (Edinburgh, 1558), is one of five known copies and the only one in an English library.[84] *An earnest complaint of divers vain wicked and abused exercises, practised on the Saboth day*, by Humphrey Roberts (London, 1572), is one of two known copies, with the title-leaf lacking in the BL copy, and two other items in the same volume of Puritan tracts are each known in only two other copies.[85] From a now broken-up volume of pamphlets about the second Virginia plantation, 1609–11, comes R. Rich's doggerel verse *News from Virginia, or the lost flock triumpahnt* (1611), believed to be a source for Shakespeare's *Tempest*, one of four known copies.[86] Cosin's copy of the First Folio of Shakespeare (1623) we can make a good claim to be the only one in continuous possession of one library from the time of its publication to the present day, since the Bodleian sold its own (after getting the Third Folio in 1664) and only bought it

[80] E. V. Stocks, 'Incunabula' [in Durham], *Durham University Journal*, 21 (1913–18), 472–4; 22 (1918–22), 21–3, 57–9.

[81] RSTC 16101.8.

[82] R. W. Shirley, *Early Printed Maps of the British Isles*, I (London, 1973), no. 171.

[83] RSTC 16267, 16281.5 (variant), 16457.

[84] RSTC 14932.

[85] RSTC 21090, 11694, 15431.

[86] RSTC 21005.

back in this century.[87] On the second issue of James I's English works (1616–23), in what is probably a standard presentation calf binding with the royal arms and thistles gilt Cosin has made early notes, one mentioning an unnamed Oxford professor who spoke abusively of the King and yet preached his funeral sermon in the University Church.[88] Cosin also annotated Donne's *Eighty Sermons* (1640), from which he used phrases in one of his own sermons in Paris during his exile.[89]

There are 841 items within the scope of Wing's STC 1641–1700, many standard books, but not as many pamphlets perhaps as if Cosin had remained in England from 1644 to 1660, quite a number nonetheless; one is the first edition of Milton's *Tetrachordon* (1645), which is of extra interest since Cosin as bishop occasioned criticism for supporting a bill of divorce.

As already said, there are 585 items in French, mostly seventeenth century, of which eighty by acknowledged authors are not in the Bibliothèque Nationale, Paris, while it has not yet been possible to check for more than a few of the anonyma, of which the catalogue is only now gradually being published on microfiche. Altogether there are 2400 items published abroad in the seventeenth century, about two-thirds, that is, of Cosin's contribution, and if we deduct those in French the remainder, about 1800, half of his, are overwhelmingly in Latin, Greek or Hebrew, and few in the last two unaccompanied by the first. There is a handful in Italian, in some of which Cosin and his son have left signs of learning it, and there are some bilingual and polyglot dictionaries, phrasebooks and grammars. The Latin works include a wider range of subjects than might be expected, such as science and archaeology, though they are strongest in theology and liturgy. As specimen notabilia may be mentioned Kepler's *Tabulae Rudolphinae* (Ulm, 1627) and the anonymous proscribed first edition (second state) of Spinoza's *Tractatus theologico-politicus* (Hamburg [Amsterdam], 1670). The importance of the collection however lies not so much in first, rare and fine editions as in its depth and breadth. In one class, canon law, out of 150 items twenty-five are not found in any form in the British Library and a further twenty-five not in the same edition. And as already indicated, the types of binding are of great interest, not least the number of books, chiefly of the smaller formats in what may be best called cartonnages, as they are probably French, sewn in unpressed and uncut (some still unopened) sheets in pulpy pasteboard buff or orange covers with yapp edges, flat spines and manuscript titles, some certainly by Cosin's hand. They and other items in original condition afford invaluable evidence for physical bibliography. The separate sources of the collection are another large topic which has been only touched on above.

In recent years a British Library grant has enabled the whole library to be recatalogued to modern standards, with record of provenance and binding, besides imprints, on the automated system developed by Dr David Shaw at Canterbury, which is producing handsome hard copy and also the possibility of on-line access and searching.

In conclusion it should be added that Bishop Cosin's Library is only one, and not the largest, of the special collections of Durham University Library, which, together with

[87] D. M. Rogers, *The Bodleian Library and its Treasures, 1320–1700* (Nuffield, 1991), p. 78, no. 64.

[88] +ELCB.C16J (Cosin K.II.13).
[89] Cosin C.II. 5.

those of the Cathedral and Ushaw College Libraries, make the city one of the more important British centres for the study of older books.[90]

PLATE II. Interior of Cosin's Library, looking to the south-east

[90] *A Directory of Rare Book and Special Collections in the United Kingdom and the Republic of Ireland*, ed. M. I. Williams (London, 1985), pp. 59–64.

CHRISTOPHER DE HAMEL

Chester Beatty and the Phillipps Manuscripts

T HE first time I saw Anthony Hobson was when as a student I came to watch a
Phillipps sale at Sotheby's in 1972. He knew my late uncle and I met him again
in Salisbury and Oxford. Three years later he took me on at Sotheby's to help
with the final Phillipps sales, and together we compiled the catalogues for 1975–6: 'a baptism by fire', muttered Peter Croft, as the first cache of Phillipps manuscripts was
unloaded on to my new desk. Once, and only once, Anthony Hobson took me to the
house in Park Road in Barnet where the Phillipps manuscripts were still in the Middle
Hill boxes in which they had been moved down into Thirlestaine House in Cheltenham
in 1863 and in which, after Sir Thomas Phillipps' death in 1872 they passed eventually to
his grandson Thomas Fitzroy Fenwick and in 1946 to Lionel and Philip Robinson.

If to have been the architect of the last generation of Phillipps sales was Anthony
Hobson's greatest achievement at Sotheby's, these were by no means the only great dis-
persals of his time. There were those of Hely-Hutchinson, Sydney Cockerell, Dyson
Perrins, Major Abbey and Chester Beatty, among many others, the latter forming a second instalment, as it were, of the sales in 1932–3 masterminded by Geofrey Hobson.
Among the reference books at Sotheby's is a little loose-leaf notebook presumably left
behind after one of the Chester Beatty sales, and inspection shows it to comprise the
notes kept by Alfred Chester Beatty during his visits to the Phillipps Collection in
Cheltenham in 1920–5. In the same way as Anthony Hobson must have worked with a
connoisseur's eye through and through the Phillipps boxes in the 1960s and 70s, sorting
and sifting the superb from the frankly negligible, so Chester Beatty was confronting the
same task in the year that Anthony Hobson was born.

There are two recent books on Sir Alfred Chester Beatty (1875–1968). A. J. Wilson's
The Life and Times of Sir Alfred Chester Beatty (1985) chronicles his extraordinary life as
a mining engineer from the gun-wearing prospector in Colorado to the chairman of
Selection Trust in London with mining interests in Africa, the Balkans, and Russia. It
hardly mentions book collecting. Brian Kennedy's *Alfred Chester Beatty and Ireland,
1950–1968, A Study in Cultural Politics* (1988) covers the period when the library was
already mostly formed and documents the setting up and donation of the magnificent
Chester Beatty Library of oriental manuscripts and works of art in Dublin. A study of
Chester Beatty as a collector has still to be written and would be an extraordinarily interesting undertaking. His visits to the Phillipps collection are recounted in A. N. L. Munby,
Phillipps Studies, V (1960), pp. 71–5, to which I owe most of the chronology which is
very absent in the little notebook at Sotheby's.

The booklet comprises 152 pages of lined paper, punched as for a ring folder but held together with string, written throughout in pencil, mostly in Chester Beatty's hand. The pages are not tied in their original order. Altogether Chester Beatty made notes on 148 Phillipps manuscripts which he considered buying, and he actually acquired fifty-two of them. It was by far his largest single source of western manuscripts. Of those he saw and rejected, at least twenty were finally sold by Anthony Hobson half a century later and we can compare their descriptions.

Chester Beatty first came to visit Thirlestaine House on 14 December 1921. Few private collectors at this time were allowed access to the Phillipps manuscripts which were jealously guarded by Fitzroy Fenwick who had firm ideas of the commercial value of his manuscripts and was suspicious of booksellers and rogues. According to Munby, he had initially approached Chester Beatty for advice about possible sales to an American institution and in the ensuing correspondence the collector expressed interest in making purchases himself. Chester Beatty was, by all accounts, a man of great genial charm and bluff good humour. One of his purchases on his first visit was the Walsingham Bible which Fitzroy Fenwick had specifically put aside as not for sale, and so the charm began to work early. Chester Beatty looked at many manuscripts, writing brief descriptions and comments – 'condition rather poor'; 'writing poor, illumination fine'; 'Don't care for this although writing is fine' (one's heart bleeds at the lost opportunity for this was the supreme romanesque Gundulf Bible from Rochester); 'Nothing to get excited over' (this the great Dante later in Kraus's *Monumenta* catalogue, 1974, no. 32, at $450,000); 'Miniatures interesting, a little on the crude side but OK if price right' (a single miniature from this Bible was lot 10 at Sotheby's, 18 June 1991, and Chester Beatty's comment is quite right), 'Good writing, Scribe has signed it, Not an important book' ('a good regular upright humanistic hand . . . an interesting treatise', wrote Anthony Hobson in the Phillipps sale of 1973, lot 605); 'worth having if price reasonable'; and so on. Evidently the first impression was of slight disappointment, and the condition of many Phillipps manuscripts held against them. This was still the great problem in the 1970s. When he had made his comments, Chester Beatty wrote 'Price' and left a space. Then later Fitzroy Fenwick came round and named a figure which Chester Beatty entered in darker pencil, and marked 'B' (bought) if the asking-price was lower than the collector's evaluation or 'R' (rejected or returned or refused) if the price was higher.

Then there are two pages of neat lists in the notebook, 'The following books have been purchased subject to the approval of the court from the Philipps Collection' (like all of us – once – he mis-spelled Phillipps and corrected it) and there follows a list of twenty-six Phillipps numbers and prices. Munby tells that the books were collected from Thirlestaine House on 31 December 1920. These first purchases were as follows:

Phillipps MS. 125, bought for £480. Gratian, Decretum, s.xiii/xiv, W.MS.66, still in Chester Beatty Library, Dublin.

Phillipps MS. 240, bought for £125. Cicero. Orationes Novem, s.xv, W.MS.125, Chester Beatty sale 1968, lot 28, £4800.

Phillipps MS. 250, bought for £115. Petrarch, Trionfi, s.xv, W.MS.99 (number later reassigned).

Phillipps MS. 385, bought for £155. Suetonius, s.xii, W.MS.33, Chester Beatty sale 1932, lot 9, £150, now B.L. Egerton MS. 3055.

Phillipps MS. 437, bought for £4 Lotharius, De Miseria Humanae Conditionis, s.xiii, ceded in 1936 to Dr A. S. Yahuda.

Phillipps MS. 447, bought for £135. Bible, s.xiii, W.MS.57, Chester Beatty sale 1969, lot 51, £6000.

Phillipps MS. 934, bought for £270. Gregory on Ezechiel, s.xi/xii, W.MS.18, Chester Beatty sale 1968, lot 4, £10,000; Abbey sale 1978, lot 2976, £22,000.

Phillipps MS. 1092, bought for £250. Bede on Luke, s.xii, W.MS. 31, Chester Beatty sale 1932, lot 7, £150, now Harvard fMS.Typ.202.

Phillipps MS. 2165=21787 [numbered twice], bought for £1500. Gospels, s.ix, W.MS.9, sold by Mrs Beatty 1952, now Morgan M.862.

Phillipps MS. 2251, bought for £225. Columella, De Re Rustica, s.xv, W.MS.102, Chester Beatty sale 1932, lot 28, £560; Hornby/Abbey sale 1975, lot 2962, £18,000.

Phillipps MS. 2506, bought for £490. Bible volume, s.xiii/xiv, W.MS.173, Chester Beatty sale 1969, lot 57, £2000, now broken up.

Phillipps MS.3009, bought for £250. Quintilian, De Institutione Oratoria, s.xv, W.MS.120, Chester Beatty sale 1969, lot 60, £18,000; Sotheby's, 13 July 1977, lot 58, £11,000.

Phillipps MS. 3010, bought for £500. Livy, De Secundo Bello Punico, s.xv, W.MS.112 (number later reassigned), Chester Beatty sale 1933, lot 59, £440, now New York Public Library Spencer MS. 27.

Phillipps MS. 3339, bought for £330. Justinian, Codex, s.xiii/xiv, W.MS.67, Chester Beatty sale 1932, lot 17, £600; Hornby/Abbey sale, 1974, lot 2917, £25,000.

Phillipps MS. 3344, bought for £285. Job glossed, s.xii, W.MS.29, still in Chester Beatty Library, Dublin.

Phillipps MS. 3535, bought for £360. St Trond Lectionary, s.xii, W.MS.23, Chester Beatty sale 1933, lot 41, £330; Eric Millar, sold in 1957 to Morgan Library, now M.883.

Phillipps MS. 3674, bought for £230. Gregory, Dialogi, s.x, W.MS.16, Chester Beatty sale 1933, lot 39, £250.

Phillipps MS. 4259, bought for £2000, Bible in 4 volumes, s.xiii, W.MS.54, Chester Beatty sale 1932, lot 13, £600, now Boston Public Library MS. 1532.

Phillipps MS. 4597, bought for £250. Peter Lombard on the Psalms, s.xii, W.MS.32, Chester Beatty sale 1932, lot 8, £260.

Phillipps MS. 4600, bought for £190. Augustine, De Civitate Dei, s.xiii/xiv, W.MS.68, Chester Beatty sale 1933, lot 51, £120.

Phillipps MS. 4769, bought for £2000. Walsingham Bible, s.xii, W.MS. 22, still in Chester Beatty Library, Dublin.

Phillipps MS. 6972, bought for £400. Hyginus, De Sideribus, s.xv, W.MS.114 (number later reassigned), Chester Beatty sale 1933, lot 60, £580, now New York Public Library Spencer MS. 28.

Phillipps MS. 12283, bought for £285. Lactantius, De Divinis Institutionibus, s.xv, W.MS.104 (number later reassigned), Chester Beatty sale 1933, lot 57, £160, now Harvard MS.Typ.143 H.

Phillipps MS. 12348, bought for £800. Stavelot Gospels, s.x/xi, W.MS.17, still in Chester Beatty Library, Dublin.

Phillipps MS. 17364, bought for £40. Josephus fragment (3 fols.), s.xii.

Phillipps MS. 21948, bought for £285. Minor Prophets glossed, s.xii, W.MS.24, Chester Beatty sale 1933, lot 42, £560; Hornby/Abbey sale 1974, lot 2906, £42,000, now Morgan M.962.

This is a major haul of manuscripts, and includes books from the romanesque abbeys of Gladbach, St Trond, Stavelot, Anchin, and Walsingham, and from the libraries of

Cardinal Bessarion and Matthias Corvinus. There is the thirteenth-century Bible perhaps signed by Oderisi da Gubbio (although the signature was not noticed until Andreas Mayor found it in 1969) and the most unusual Limoges manuscript of St Gregory signed by Petrus del Casta, *c.* 1100. The total price came to £11,954, a sum neatly worked out by Chester Beatty in his notebook. Fenwick's prices were high for their time, and of the thirteen which had to be re-sold fifteen years later, Chester Beatty made a loss on seven, especially on the 4-volume thirteenth-century Bible bought for £2000 and sold for £600. It is one of several large late thirteenth-century illustrated manuscripts here, with prickly French gothic illumination so fashionable in the Yates Thompson era, and doubtless their crisp lapis and azurite blues and sparkling burnished gold appealed strongly to the mining engineer and gold prospector who had been collecting mineral specimens since his schooldays. In fact, the image of Chester Beatty poking around for treasure amongst the dross of the Phillipps midden is very much that of the prospector. On this occasion he rejected several very early manuscripts, which is where the real gold of the Phillipps library lay. He did buy the Stavelot Gospels but really only as a bargain: 'Incomplete and damaged, Was apparently never finished, Worth having if price OK', and wrote his biggest 'B' of all when Fitzroy Fenwick named a figure of £800. He turned down the Carolingian Homilies (Phillipps 6659) at £185 – 'condition rather poor' – and Phillipps 4558 – 'Very early IX Century, crude Irish influence, Condition fair to poor' – which it is a shame to have lost for another £800. He dismissed completely Phillipps 6446 as 'Russian, OK if reasonable, otherwise not', returning it at £500; this was the medieval Glagolithic Missal from Yugoslavia, one of Phillipps's own favourite manuscripts and 'of utmost rarity . . . entirely unpublished', as Anthony Hobson wrote in the Phillipps sale of 1966.

But Chester Beatty the miner took away his specimens, and sought advice from manuscript historians, and he must have come to realize that although the Phillipps mine was not an easy one to quarry, it held pieces which already in the 1920s could be found nowhere else. He had bought the twelfth-century Mostyn Gospels at Sotheby's that summer and it cost £2250, which must have made the Phillipps prices look less outrageous. He went back over his notebook adding and underlining '*See again*' beside, for example, Phillipps 1329 (seventh- to eighth-century uncial leaves now at Yale) and Phillipps 2829, the twelfth-century Paterius which he had first dismissed as 'Simply writing' and which Anthony Hobson was to describe more justly in 1965 as 'an early and handsomely written manuscript, in a medieval binding and in very sound original condition, of a scarce text'. But throughout 1921–2 Chester Beatty was occupied with establishing diamond mines in the Gold Coast and in Sierra Leone, and Mrs Fenwick's illness and death in 1922 made access to the Phillipps collection inappropriate, and Chester Beatty's second visit to Cheltenham was delayed until 21 February 1923. 'It gives me the greatest pleasure to let such an enthusiast as yourself see some of the fine works of art that happen to be in my possession', Fenwick told him in his letter of invitation. Chester Beatty's notebook gives detailed comments on at least twenty-five manuscripts seen on this occasion.

He enjoyed Phillipps 1047, the thirteenth-century Roman du Saint Graal (now in the Bodmer Library), '129 miniatures, most of them in first class condition' (actually there are 167), and asked for a Bestiary ('The drawings of the beasts and animals in the margins are quite good but the writing is atrocious – Not interested') and an Ovid ('Early XIII French or English, Glossed in careful fine writing, Good clean condition, Quite an attractive book, One or two letters in blue and red' – it was recently in the Abbey sale, 1989, lot 3011) and his notes on Phillipps 2164 are dated 23rd February and fill a whole page: 'Virgil, XV Century, French, Studied this book again, This is one of Mr. T.F.F.'s important books, There are 18 miniatures ½ page, 4 of these are later very poor about 1600, The other 14 are fine each miniature is divided in 4, Date about 1470, A very fine book of a poor period, Infinitely prefer the Duc de Berri book EB just bought for me for £1500 . . .', and so on. EB is Edith Beatty, his second wife whom he married in 1913, and the Duc de Berry book is presumably the *Histoire Ancienne* with seventy-eight miniatures, *c*. 1375, which Mrs Beatty bought from Quaritch that year for her husband, now in the Schøyen Collection in Oslo (its association with the Duc de Berry is ultimately elusive but the two demonstrably Berry books in the Chester Beatty library had been bought in the Yates Thompson sale three years earlier, neither for £1500). On another page Chester Beatty comments in similar style on Phillipps MS. 116, 'miniatures follow the style of the Duc de Berry but they are dreadfully decadent': the rejected book was the 3-volume Livy which was lot 594 in the Phillipps sale of 1973. The Sotheby catalogue referred to 'the type associated with the library of Charles V' but Anthony Hobson confessed to me afterwards that he thought the book decidedly second-rate. 'Don't care for this', Chester Beatty had added too.

The notes on these manuscripts have Chester Beatty's idea of prices in a facile code, which can be solved by noting which of Fenwick's prices resulted in a sale. A is 100, B is 200, C is 300, and so on, quite simply to H as 900. There are also the letters 'DCFI' beside rejected books, apparently a tactful way of noting (in case Fenwick should see the notebook) something like 'Don't Care For It'. A fifteenth-century Ptolemy, for example, is marked thus, and so is a French Missal of about 1440. Although he called the fifteenth century a 'poor period', we see Chester Beatty struggling with the very early manuscripts. 'Good early book', he noted of Phillipps 6659 but (how easy to envisage) 'Very dusty'. Of Phillipps MS. 10190, he records reassuringly, 'Dr. Low [*sic*] who assigns this to Tours IX Century is the Paleographer at Oxford'. That was good enough authority (later on another page he jots down E. A. Lowe's address). Chester Beatty's purchases in February 1923 amounted to £2470, and they were:

Phillipps MS. 1036, bought for £395. Gratian, Decretum, s.xii, from Cîteaux, W.MS.46, Chester Beatty sale 1968, lot 11, £4000, now Walters W. 777.

Phillipps MS. 3383, bought for £165. Aristotle, De Celo, etc., s.xiii, W.MS.65, Chester Beatty sale 1968, lot 15, £5800.

Phillipps MS. 6546, bought for £250. Canons of Aix-la-Chapelle, s.ix, from Nonantola, W.MS.12, Chester Beatty sale 1968, lot 3, £14,000, now Rome, Bibl.Vitt.Eman.cod.1348.

Phillipps MS. 8400, bought for £880. Homiliary, s.viii/ix, from Ottobeuren, W.MS.2, Chester Beatty sale 1933, lot 34, £680, now Rome, Bibl.Vitt.Eman.cod.1190.

Phillipps MS. 10190, bought for £500. Capitulary of Ansegisus, s.ix, W.MS.11, Chester Beatty sale 1932, lot 3, bought in at £260; Chester Beatty sale 1969, lot 40, £24,000, now Yale, Beinecke MS.413.

Phillipps MS. 12262, bought for £280. Bede on the Canonical Epistles and Apcolypse, s.ix, from Nonantola, W.MS.7, Chester Beatty sale 1968, lot 1, £17,000, now Rome, Bibl.Vitt.Eman.cod.1347.

Two more were added soon after:

Phillipps MS.389, bought probably for £450. Canons of Aix-la-Chapelle, s.ix, W.MS.13, Chester Beatty sale 1969, lot 39, £19,000, now Bodmer cod.68.

Phillipps MS. 390, bought probably for £400. Collectio Dionysio-Hadriana, s.x, W.MS.14, Chester Beatty sale 1969, lot 41, £12,000, now Princeton, Scheide Library.

In 1924 Chester Beatty and Eric Millar conceived their plan to publish a vast catalogue of the western manuscripts in the Chester Beatty Collection, to be arranged chronologically. When the first volume appeared two years later, seventeen of the eighteen earliest manuscripts were revealed to be Phillipps purchases. The notebook too betrays increasing anxiety to fill in the sequence of very early books. Under the heading 'Important Mss. ACB', Chester Beatty made notes to himself: 'Be sure and look up very early fragments' and (ever hopeful) 'How about Irish Mss – discuss with Fenwick', and, on another page, 'How about Hebrew VI Century'. He tried several times to buy the uncial leaves which were later in the Lansburgh collection and are now at Yale, Phillipps MS. 1329: 'worth getting, F would not put a price on these'; he saw them a second time, but the final time he asked for them they were lost in the library. The third visit to Cheltenham took place in July 1924. The first book he examined was the Bede from Dore Abbey ('a good book worth buying not very valuable') followed by five eighth-century manuscripts and three fragments. There are two pages of sums and lists marked with ticks and question marks, headed 'Mss. Taken to London'. The eventual purchases totalled £5105 and were:

Phillipps MS. 3075, bought for £275. Eutropius, Historiae Romanorum, s.ix/x, from Nonantola, W.MS.15, Chester Beatty sale 1933, lot 38, £220, now Oslo, Schøyen Collection MS.50.

Phillipps MS. 3897, bought for £600. Flores Historiarum, s.xiii/xiv, W.MS.70, Chester Beatty sale 1968, lot 18, £6000, now London, Mr J. Paul Getty jr.

Phillipps MS. 4448, bought for £285. Missal fragment, s.xiii, W.MS.58, Chester Beatty sale 1969, lot 52, £4000, now Oxford, Lincoln College MS. 149.

Phillipps MS. 12200, bought for £675. Bede, De Temporum Ratione, s.xiii/xiv, W.MS.59, Chester Beatty sale 1933, lot 49, £270, now B.L. Egerton MS.3088.

Phillipps MS. 12260, bought for £750. Epistola Datiani, s.viii/ix, from Nonantola, W.MS.4, Chester Beatty sale 1932, lot 2, £760, now Rome, Bibl.Vitt.Eman.cod.1006.

Phillipps MS. 12261, bought for £850. Augustine, De Vera Religione, etc., s.viii, from Nonantola, W.MS.3, Chester Beatty sale 1933, lot 35, withdrawn, now B.L. Add.MS.43460.

Phillipps MS. 12263, bought for £850. Eugippius, excerpts from St Augustine, s.viii/ix, from Nonantola, W.MS.6, Chester Beatty sale 1933, lot 36, £390, now Rome, Bibl.Vitt.Eman. cod.Sessor.590.

Phillipps MS. 12264, bought for £800. Augustine, Sermones, s.viii, from Nonantola, W.MS.5, Chester Beatty sale 1969, lot 38, £48,000, now Rome, Bibl.Vitt.Eman.cod.1357.

Phillipps MS. 36275, bought for £20. Bede fragment, s.viii, W.MS.1, Chester Beatty sale 1932, lot 1, £48, now Morgan M.826.

Notable among this purchase are five manuscripts from the ancient abbey of Nonantola, diocese of Modena, rejoining two more from the same monastery which Chester Beatty had acquired the previous year. Books from this source were still emerging when Anthony Hobson was cataloguing Phillipps manuscripts in the 1960s and 70s. Phillipps himself had listed them as coming from Fossa Nuova, but, although Monsignor Ruysschaert first published their true origin as recently as 1955, E. A. Lowe had suspected as much in the 1920s and Chester Beatty must have been told of this for he recorded in the notebook 'The books come from the Monastery of Nonantola in North Italy'.

Chester Beatty always claimed that he was no scholar and that he bought simply on personal choice. One sees here, however, self-taught observations – 'Like Mss. in B.M.', 'The scribe does pictures during the century of this Mss. – XII', 'Seems much later and a good part of middle missing', and so on. Three pages list titles of reference books. Once he adds, 'Check out study after getting price'; and having declined the Glagolithic manuscript, as recounted above, he relented as far as to note 'See the Glagolitic Evangelia at the British Museum, compare with the one in the Phillipps Collection'. Curious, in view of the supreme importance of his oriental collections later, is Chester Beatty's lack of serious interest in non-western manuscripts in the Phillipps library. He wrote 'See Armenian Book again' in February 1923, probably Phillipps MS. 15364 which he did see again ('Interesting date XV Cent? Did not care to sell'), but he did not press the point, and bought it thirty years later from Messrs Robinson. 'See damaged Akbar book', he wrote, but there is no further reference. It may be the slightly imperfect manuscript of Nasiri, Phillipps MS. 6959, which made £48,000 in the Phillipps sale in 1974, lot 684. He did, however, look carefully through the Warren Hastings album of Mughal miniatures, Phillipps MS. 14170. It had been assembled for Hastings around 1775 and had been bought by Phillipps at the dispersal of the Hastings library in 1853. Its forty miniatures were sold separately when it finally re-emerged in the Phillipps sale in 1968, lots 367–406. Chester Beatty had looked at all forty and graded the quality of each one by one, reckoning fifteen as 'Poor', twenty-two as 'Fair' or 'Fine', and three as 'Very Very Fine'. Compare with Anthony Hobson's selection of plates for the 1974 Sotheby catalogue. Fifteen of the Warren Hastings lots were illustrated with half-page plates or none at all, twenty-one were illustrated with full-page black-and-white plates, and four were illustrated with colour plates. With only one exception, therefore, the judgments of Hobson and Beatty exactly correspond fifty years apart.

On their assessment of bindings, Chester Beatty and Anthony Hobson would not have agreed. 'Simply a binding', wrote Chester Beatty of the renaissance Cicero which Hobson described in the Hely Hutchinson sale in 1956, lot 219, 'A BEAUTIFUL HUMANISTIC MANUSCRIPT, COMPLETE AND IN FINE CONDITION' (his capitals). 'Binding of no interest', he wrote of another. He evidently liked his bindings to be gothic and northern. 'Fine Binding Pig Skin', he observed of a fifteenth-century Mainz binding, with 'Show Ede' (his wife). 'Fine old binding, Mss not of much value', he noted of the tenth-century Liesborn Gospels with its distinctly odd and much later carved wooden cover. The book is important – Fenwick priced it at £900 but Chester Beatty valued it privately at £250 – but it went instead to Rosenbach and re-emerged in the Doheny sale, 1987, lot 139, £380,000, and it is now in the Schøyen Collection, MS. 40.

Chester Beatty evidently had no real interest in the texts of manuscripts, except as a means to distinguish one book from another. The comments are on condition – often disappointing – and on the quality of the script and illumination: 'Very fine quality miniatures – poor writing' of one book, and 'remarkably fine writing – no important first page – simply writing' of another, but 'Simply Calligraphy – Not of much value' of a third. There are many judgments like this. 'Very attractive book but I have some finer', he noted of a renaissance Caesar, valuing it at £250 compared with Fitzroy Fenwick's £425; and of another: 'Clean and fairly attractive French XV Century but not top notch quality DCFI'.

The notes give an evocative sense of Chester Beatty rummaging and Fitzroy Fenwick prowling round behind him, giving prices (Chester Beatty notes indignantly if the prices have risen between visits), or declining to name figures at all. 'Do not believe he cares to sell it', noted Beatty wistfully of the Boucicaut Master Livy which Hobson catalogued in 1965. There are tantalizing glimpses of where books were shelved at Thirlestaine House: five of them 'in Mr. Fenwick's Study in small bookcase', a little sketch map with an arrow between two book shelves and a little cross marking the location of the ninth-century Bede from Nonantola, a note of the St Trond Lectionary as being 'Top shelf ', and of the uncial leaves misplaced somewhere in that vast library: 'Can't find – lost pro tem'.

An intriguing list copied twice is headed 'Order in which Mr. F. places Mss' and itemizes telegraphically Fitzroy Fenwick's idea of his most precious books: 1. *Book of the Chase* [Phillipps MS. 10298, the Gaston de Foix recently acquired by the Morgan Library in the bequest of Clara Peck]; 2. *Statius* [Phillipps MS. 1798, see below]; 3. *Medici XV Century* [Phillipps MS. 2163, the Scriptores Historiae Augustae now in the State Library of Victoria, Melbourne]; 4. *Vergil French XV* [Phillipps MS. 2164, now at Harvard]; 5. *Lancelot* [probably Phillipps MS. 130, now at Yale]; 6. *Cretensis* [Phillipps MS. 3502, see below]; 7. *Liber Precum* [Phillipps MS. 4790, the Breviary of Ferdinand of Aragon sold in the Phillipps sale of 1969, lot 476]; 8. *Cité de Dieu, 1 Vol.* [Phillipps MS. 4417, now in the Walters Art Gallery]; 9. *Livy* [perhaps Phillipps MS.266 or 2924]; 10. *Vergil Italy* [Phillipps MS. 3506, now in the Bodmer Foundation]; 11. *Caesars (12) Bourdich.* [Phillipps MS. 1940, sale 1946, lot 28a]; 12. *Aesop Greek* [Phillipps MS. 23609, now in the New York Public Library]; 13. *Ferdinand, Italy XV* [Phillipps MS. 6640, see below]; 14. *Greek Gospels* [perhaps Phillipps MS. 3886, now in the J. Paul Getty Museum]; and 15. *Cité de Dieu 4 Vol.* [Phillipps MS. 4359, now at Yale]. Chester Beatty apparently never saw no. 1, the Gaston de Foix. No. 2 he described as 'a beautiful book . . . of uniformly high grade – The book is not for sale except at a high price £3000–£5000'. No. 3 he called 'A De Luxe Book – Fit for any museum' valued by Fenwick at £3/4000 and by Beatty at £1200. No. 4 he thought 'a remarkably fine book . . . Not for sale? Will take £5000 – too high'. No. 5 was also priced at £5000: 'Too high – not interested'. So the notes continue, every time a reference to one of these books occurs. '1st Visit talked about £5000' for no. 6. He considered no. 7: 'Does not care to sell same but if he did would probably want a price far in excess of its value – Would be glad to have book at a moderate price . . .'.

Altogether, Chester Beatty looked carefully at eleven of the fifteen books on Fitzroy Fenwick's top list, and agreed with the evaluations of none of them. It must have been bitterly frustrating, and he was wise to use his resources for the very early manuscripts and to leave the most luxurious late manuscripts to the taste and diplomatic negotiation of his wife.

Edith Beatty came to play a very important role in the building of the collection of western art, and she used to tease her husband that he had no artistic taste at all. She accompanied him to Thirlestaine House from the first visit and Fitzroy Fenwick described her as charming. The note 'Show Ede' occurs often beside Chester Beatty's jottings on illuminated manuscripts. He sought her opinion of the three-volume illustrated French Livy, cited above, adding afterwards and initialling his own, 'Dont care for this ACB'; and it stayed in the Phillipps collection until 1973. The opinion swung the other way when they looked at MS. 4417, the *Cité de Dieu* by the Boucicaut workshop: 'Ede did not like', and so they did not buy that either.

Towards the end of the notebook the handwriting changes from Chester Beatty's rather flamboyant backward sloping hand to a smaller forward-slanting cursive. This must be Edith Beatty's hand. She presumably secretly borrowed the notebook. The tale of her clandestine visit to Thirlestaine House in November 1925 is charmingly recounted by Munby. She pretended to him that she was visiting the races in Cheltenham when her real purpose was to go shopping in the Phillipps Collection for a spectacular birthday and Christmas present for her husband. The notebook in fact includes three short lists of race horses in her hand, but Mr Rowan Moore assures me that these are well-known runners on the flat whereas the Cheltenham races are hurdles. Munby quotes her letter of thanks to Fitzroy Fenwick on her return to London: 'Needless to say on my arrival I was *bombarded* with questions – "Had I seen any books – if so which?" etc. etc. To which I replied "I spent the whole evening with the *Book of the Chase*" mentally hoping the Lord would forgive me . . .'. That one book, as far as one can tell from her lists full of crossings-out, she did not see at all, but she did buy three from Fitzroy Fenwick's select list of top manuscripts, including his no. 2 and no. 6, the former with breathtaking grisaille miniatures attributed to Altichiero, and the latter written by Sanvito for Cardinal Francesco Gonzaga. Her November evening yielded eight magnificent manuscripts, the last (as it happened) that the Chester Beattys secured from Fitzroy Fenwick. They were:

Phillipps MS. 134=3948 [numbered twice], bought for £450. Liber de Naturis Rerum, s.xiv/xv, W.MS.80, Chester Beatty sale 1932, lot 21, bought-in at £460, and still in the Chester Beatty Library, Dublin.

Phillipps MS. 137, bought for £550. Lactantius, De Divinis Institutionibus, s.xv, W.MS.110 (number later reassigned), Chester Beatty sale 1933, lot 58, £250, now J. Paul Getty Museum, MS.Ludwig XI.1.

Phillipps MS. 1798, bought for £7000. Statius, Thebaid, s.xiv, W.MS.76, still in the Chester Beatty Library, Dublin.

Phillipps MS.3502, bought for £7000. Dictys Cretensis, De Bello Troiano, s.xv, W.MS.122, still in the Chester Beatty Library, Dublin.

Phillipps MS. 6640, bought for £3000. Francesco Barbaro, Epistolae, s.xv, from the Aragonese royal library, W.MS.113, still in the Chester Beatty Library, Dublin.

Phillipps MS. 6659, bought for £300. Paul the Deacon, Homiliary, s.ix, W.MS.110, Chester Beatty sale 1968, lot 2, £14,000, now Bodmer cod. 128.

Phillipps MS. 7084, bought for £2000. Pontanus, Opera, s.xv, made for Duke Alfonso of Calabria, W.MS.108, still in the Chester Beatty Library, Dublin.

Phillipps MS. 12269, bought for £1500. Augustine, De Civitate Dei, s.xi/xii, W.MS.43, still in the Chester Beatty Library, Dublin.

The total spent that night by Edith Beatty was £21,800. This, one need hardly stress, was in 1925. Had such a princely choice of books ever before been conferred as a surprise present on a bibliophile? 'I know in my soul I will not be strongminded enough to keep the books until Xmas, so when they arrive I will give him one a day, reserving the two *great ones* for Xmas and birthday', wrote Mrs Beatty. With the image of the Sanvito on the birthday morning, we salute the birthday of Anthony Hobson, in whom the Phillipps manuscripts and the Italian renaissance found their supreme champion.

ARNOLD HUNT

A Study in Bibliomania
Charles Henry Hartshorne and Richard Heber

THIS is the story of the meteoric bibliographical career of Charles Henry Hartshorne. It must be admitted that the human interest of the story outweighs the bibliographical, for this is a story of a young, inexperienced and inadequate scholar, whose early works, 'The Book Rarities in the University of Cambridge' (1829) and 'Ancient Metrical Tales' (1829) are scarcely consulted today. But that is not the end of the matter. For the story also casts a flood of light on that small world of scholars and bibliophiles at work in the 1820s, and on that larger world of English upper-class society to which they all belonged. While it cannot match the sustained illumination of A. N. L. Munby's 'Phillipps Studies', it can – more securely perhaps, than that study of an eccentric, obsessive individual – locate the phenomenon of bibliomania in its social context.

Charles Henry Hartshorne was born in Shropshire on the 17th of March, 1802, and educated at Shrewsbury School. In January 1821 he entered St John's College, Cambridge, as a pensioner, and came into residence in October. His father was dead, but his family was well connected in Shropshire society, and several friends were willing to offer him patronage and fatherly advice. The letters that he received from one such friend, Sir James Allen Park, a distinguished judge described by his biographer in the *DNB* as 'sound, fair, and sensible, a little irascible, but highly esteemed',[1] paint a picture of Hartshorne with which we will become familiar.

Another thing you really must guard against, and that is bibliomaniasm. This caution arises from your introduction to Mr Dibdin. When you have finished your acquaintance with the *inside* of Books, if ever that can be, it will be time enough for you, provided you have the means without injury to yourself or your family, to indulge in collecting curious and expensive editions. But when you have not those means, *over indulgence* in this respect becomes *a vice*.[2]

Book collecting was suddenly in vogue. The mania had reached Cambridge; among Arthur Pendennis's friends, as readers of Thackeray will recall, is young Wormall, who runs up bills 'with Parkton, the great bookseller, for Aldine editions, black-letter folios, and richly illuminated Missals of the XVI. Century'. (Thackeray went up to Trinity in 1826, the year after Hartshorne graduated.) Park found it necessary to redouble his warnings. On an allowance of £130 and an exhibition of £90 a year, it is necessary to

[1] Though among lawyers his reputation as a 'starched and pedantic person' survived into the present century, along with the proverb 'as empty as Judge Park's wig when the head is in it'. 'The Pollock-Holmes Letters' (ed. Mark DeWolfe Howe, Cambridge, 1942), vol. 1, p. 151.

[2] Park to Hartshorne, 16 August 1821: Hartshorne papers, Northamptonshire Record Office (N.R.O.) X7227 album E no. 48.

'practise the strictest economy . . . Surely you cannot with any propriety give Dinner or Supper parties – nor even breakfast parties . . . but if you do any thing, it ought *not to exceed* a breakfast party'. Book collecting was out of the question. 'What I most dread in you, is the passion for Books.'[3]

Little of Hartshorne's correspondence survives for his first two years at Cambridge. The earlier letter that I have found is addressed to David Laing, the Scottish antiquary and publisher, and dated 24 January 1822. It describes the Pepysian Library, which Hartshorne had visited in October 1821, 'as early as I could', and to which Laing was now planning a visit. Hartshorne praises the early English books in the collection – 'about fifteen Caxtons in the most marvellous preservation, some fine W. de Wordes and Pynsons, a magnificent and matchless Lydgate on vellum' – but singles out Pepys's collection of ballads as 'perhaps the most valuable thing in the Library'. Though this is not a distinction which Hartshorne would have recognized, it is fair to say that the tone of the letter is that of the connoisseur rather than the scholar. 'I am very much given to the collecting of black letter books myself, otherwise I should not have taken so much interest in the Pepysian Library.'[4]

Hartshorne's source of inspiration is not far to seek. He had fallen under the spell of Thomas Frognall Dibdin. By April 1823, and probably before, he had met Dibdin in person, as a stray note in the Bodleian Library reveals:

> My dear Sir
>   Let nothing prevent your meeting me at Lord Spencer's on Monday at 3 o'Clock
> – and walking with me to Kensington to mutton, at 5.
>   In haste
>   T. F. Dibdin[5]

Dibdin had taken his education in hand, dispensing in his letters a heady mixture of antiquarian scholarship and unabashed bibliomania. Hartshorne was set to work compiling a list of the Caxtons in the Pepysian Library, and searching for Aldine editions on vellum in the University and college libraries. Meanwhile Dibdin was counselling him that 'The Aldine taste is a good and elegant one' and (in a letter addressed to 'My dear Pupil') presenting him with a copy of his 'Library Companion', 'deliciously, soberly, chastely, and classically girted, in a dark green morocco surtout' by Charles Lewis.[6]

This was not quite the piece of generosity it might seem: the book was a gift, but Hartshorne had to pay for the binding. Still, Hartshorne received a most generous tribute in the pages of the 'Library Companion' itself: 'this young thorough-bred bibliomaniacal Racer (who, I predict, will win all the cups and sweepstakes that he starts for) is just now occupied in the weaving of a *Golden Garland of Early English Poetry*,' composed of pieces little known, or, for the greater part, wholly unknown. Take a specimen, musewooing Reader' – and Dibdin went on to record some of the editions of early poetry printed by Wynkyn de Worde that Hartshorne had discovered in the Pepysian Library.[7]

---

[3] Park to Hartshorne, 16 October 1821, 5 November 1822: N.R.O. X7227 album E no. 51, 59.

[4] Hartshorne to Laing, 24 January 1822; Edinburgh University Library (E.U.L.) La.IV.17.

[5] Dibdin to Hartshorne, [April 5 1823]: Bodleian Library, Oxford, Ms. Eng. lett. d.456 f.13.

[6] Dibdin to Hartshorne, 13 March 1823, 11 December 1824: N.R.O. X7225 album B nos. 49, 51.

[7] Dibdin, 'Library Companion' (2nd edition, 1825), pp. 672–3.

PLATE I. Charles Henry Hartshorne with his wife Frances and eldest son Charles, painted in 1831 by Paul Falkoner Poole.
Reproduced by kind permission of the owner, Mr Hugh Wyatt.

Hartshorne was gratified but a little embarrassed. He did indeed intend to publish an edition of metrical romances, but, as he explained to Dawson Turner, 'they will not be published with the whimsical title my friend Dibdin has said that they would, neither will the two volumes contain such second rate pieces as he has precociously led the public to imagine.' This was a little unfair, as it was the very title that Hartshorne himself had proposed in a letter to Francis Douce. But it was not the first time that Hartshorne had found Dibdin's attentions unwelcome: in 1821, fired with enthusiasm for his young protégé, Dibdin had offered to put him up for election to the Society of Antiquaries, a suggestion which Hartshorne had had the good sense to decline. 'I approve very much, my dear Charles', wrote Park, 'that you refused Mr Dibdin's offer to make you a fellow of the Antiquarian Society – kindly intended no doubt on his part, but very absurd to so young a Man, and to whom, in a pecuniary view it would have been inconvenient.'[8]

[8] Hartshorne to Turner, 28 November 1824: Trinity College, Cambridge (T.C.C.) O.13.28.
   Hartshorne to Douce, 7 June 1823; Bodleian Ms. Douce d.24 f.165.
   Park to Hartshorne, 26 September 1821: N.R.O. X7227 album E no. 30.

Hartshorne could afford to distance himself from Dibdin because he had another patron, and a far more influential one: Richard Heber. Indeed, it was probably Heber who had introduced him to Dibdin. It was inevitable that Hartshorne and Heber should have met, for Heber was not only a celebrated book collector, assiduous in his attendance at bookshops and auction-rooms, liberal in his assistance to scholars, but also a wealthy landowner with large estates in Hartshorne's native county of Shropshire. He was also MP for the University of Oxford, a man of considerable influence, and one who was prepared to exercise that influence on behalf of his scholarly friends. In April 1822 Philip Bliss sought his help in obtaining a post at the British Museum. Having ascertained that there were no other strong candidates, Heber began work on the Trustees. He secured the support of Lord Spencer; he mentioned Bliss's name 'during a friendly chat' with the Speaker of the House of Commons; and he promised Bliss that, if necessary, he would 'testify my sense of your merits and claims' when he next met the Archbishop of Canterbury.[9]

Small wonder, then, that Hartshorne's friends and relations should have urged the young man to recommend himself to Heber. While he was still at school, Hartshorne, 'being advised to cultivate the acquaintance of Mr Heber by every means in his power . . . addressed to Mr Heber a copy of Latin verses, with the elegance of which Mr Heber was so much charmed, that he invited the young man to his house'. Or so it was later recalled; although it is clear from Park's letters that the Latin verses did not achieve their object unaided. In June 1821, Park regrets that Hartshorne's approaches to Heber should have received no response, but advises him to go to Shrewsbury at the next assizes 'to pay your respects' to Heber in person. In July Hartshorne visits Heber's house at Hodnet for four or five days. By September Park is expressing his satisfaction that Heber should have 'taken so kindly' to Hartshorne.[10] Whether it was Hartshorne's Latin verses or his person that charmed Heber, there is no doubt that the two were soon firm friends. By October, when Hartshorne went up to Cambridge, he was corresponding regularly with Heber about classical reading and book collecting. He spent Christmas of 1823 in Oxford 'with my friend Mr Heber' visiting the Bodleian and the college libraries and being fêted by academic society, dining with (among others) the Vice Chancellor and the heads of Brasenose, Magdalen, New College and St Mary Hall.[11] For the first time, Park's regular fulminations against the perils of book collecting begin to betray a softening of tone:

What is perfectly innocent, nay perhaps praiseworthy in Mr Heber, would be highly criminal in you – *fine impressions, large paper, wide margins*, do not suit every man's pocket. And yet, *you rogue*, you have lately *outdone Heber himself*, for I have lately seen his name down as a subscriber to the Common edition – while my *dear extravagant* C.H.H. is put down for a large Paper copy of Blakeway's Shrewsbury.[12]

We catch a glimpse of Hartshorne in the letters of another St John's man, Charles Brooke, to the Oxford antiquary Philip Bliss, a friend of the Brooke family who took a

[9] Heber to Bliss, 6 April 1822: British Library (B.L.) Add. Ms. 34568 f.449–50.
[10] Park to Hartshorne, 29 June, 26 September 1821: N.R.O. X7227 album E nos. 41, 50.
Cobbetts Weekly Register vol. 64 no. 5 (Saturday 27 October 1827), p. 268.
[11] Hartshorne to John Roberts, 1 January 1824: St John's College, Cambridge.
[12] Park to Hartshorne, 2 July 1822: N.R.O. X7227 album E no. 56.

kindly interest in the young man's progress. Brooke was the model 'reading man': having entered St John's as a sizar, he transformed his position by obtaining a College scholarship, and later graduated 23rd wrangler on his way to a distinguished scientific and surgical career. He was anxious to assure Bliss that the financial security of his scholarship would not lead him into frivolous pursuits. 'With regard to the occupation of my time; I am up ¼ before 5, read till 7, go to chapel; lecture at 8, breakfast at 9; lecture at 10; a pupil at 11 (N.B. gratuitous), and by instructing him, I keep up a recollection of the lower, while I am myself reading the higher branches of Mathematics; – this I have found of great service; lecture at 12; read from 1 to 3, walk till 4, which is my dinner hour; chapel at ½ p.5; tea at ½ p.6 and then read (if at home) for the remainder of the evening . . . I never play at any thing except chess; and occasionally a rubber of Whist, not exceeding shilling points . . . I have never been drunk since I have been in Cambridge, and *tipsy* only once.' He was, in his own words, 'a decidedly steady man'. Bliss offered to introduce him to Hartshorne; the two had met during Hartshorne's visit to Oxford the previous Christmas, and Hartshorne had delightedly reported that 'the excellent Dr Bliss' deserved to rank above Wood, Leland and Hearne. But Brooke had already heard of Hartshorne, and was not at all anxious to meet him. Hartshorne was not a reading man, and therefore 'quite out of my line'. Brooke's circle of friends, though small, 'is composed *entirely* of men who are, like myself, disposed to make the most of their time.' In any case, Cambridge etiquette forbade a freshman to call unannounced upon a third-year man.[13] Bliss must have passed the gist of these remarks on to Hartshorne, who called upon Brooke a week later. The meeting was a great success. 'My dear Dr Bliss' (wrote Brooke in his next letter),

Since I last wrote to you, your friend Hartshorne has called on me, and has been exceedingly civil; I find him to be a very different sort of man from what I had understood him to be, and I am very much obliged to you for the introduction.

I find he is devoting all his time to classics, consequently he stands very low in the examinations, which are almost entirely mathematical; therefore I had, prima facie, set him down as an idle man; but I find the case to be quite the contrary.[14]

Hartshorne conforms to another Cambridge stereotype, that of the classic irked by the severely mathematical character of the university curriculum. 'The useless and besotted pursuits of this University', he sternly informed Francis Douce, 'but barely raise the men in power a degree above savages, and literature has little to expect from Cambridge so long as Mathematics are the *only* path, to honor and preferment.' His reading, according to a letter of March 1824, was almost exclusively classical, with a few exceptions such as Wynkyn de Worde's edition of the Gesta Romanorum, Ritson's collection of metrical romances and John Dunlop's new 'History of Roman Literature'.[15] The Gesta Romanorum must have been the unique copy in the library of St John's College, dated [*c.* 1510] by STC. The previous term, he had been occupied in writing an article on the Latin academic plays acted at Cambridge in the seventeenth century. This

[13] Brooke to Bliss, 28 February 1824: B.L. Add. Ms. 34569 f.16–17.
[14] Brooke to Bliss, 8 March 1824: B.L. Add. Ms. 34569 f. 21–22.

[15] Hartshorne to Douce, 26 February 1825; Bodleian Ms. Douce d.25 f.36–37.
Hartshorne to Bliss, 11 March 1824: B.L. Add. Ms. 34569 f.21–22.

was published in the *Retrospective Review* in 1825, with an introduction in which Hartshorne warmly defends antiquarian research against the 'all-pervading spirit of illiberality' that exalts one subject at the expense of all others – evidently another attack on the University curriculum. The article cites an impressive range of authorities, including manuscripts in the University Library, Trinity, Emmanuel, St John's, King's, Queens', and the University Registry, but also betrays signs of carelessness. Some of the mistakes are printer's errors: in a letter to Douce, Hartshorne complained that the article had been 'printed without my corrections', and also drew attention to such misprints as 'Oxford' for 'Cambridge'. But other mistakes are undoubtedly the author's, such as the statement that Joseph Simons's 'Zeno', a Jesuit play, had been performed at Cambridge in 1631. This error survived for very nearly a century: it was repeated by F. G. Fleay in 1891 and laid to rest only in 1923, when G. C. Moore Smith showed that it rested on a misunderstanding of the words 'anno 1631 acta' (which probably refer to Douai) in the University Library manuscript of the play. In short, Hartshorne's work proves to be thoroughly unreliable – though a charitable critic might retort that it also proves to have been a century ahead of its time in its choice of Latin academic drama as a subject worth studying.[16]

This combination of wide learning and shallow scholarship was a foretaste of Hartshorne's later work. As Thomas Kerrich, University Librarian, lamented to Douce in May 1824:

Mr Hartshorne is playing the fool sadly, and very often in my house. We see a great deal of him, for I like him, and lament he will not study in a wider, and *consecutive* manner – His ears are open to every thing. He gathers up little bits of knowledge and information of all sorts ('as Pigeons Pease') which are all separate and repulsive among them selves, and he will be in the end as useless a Composition as Mithridate or Theriaea.[17]

Hartshorne's extra-curricular activities were coming to occupy more and more of his time. When the Cambridge term ended, he went to London and stayed with Heber for two months, visiting libraries and book auctions; the pair 'fatigued me sadly the other day', Douce told Kerrich, 'with a long and unconscionable visit.' It was mid-August before he returned home to Shropshire, and, once there, he was 'in daily expectation of a summons' from Heber, either to travel north to visit Sir Walter Scott, or to travel to Germany to attend the Meerman sale. But Heber was delayed in London. When the summons finally arrived, there was only time for a trip to town and 'another fortnight's visit to Mr Heber' before Hartshorne returned to Cambridge, two days in time to satisfy the residence requirements necessary for his degree. In December he wrote in jaunty Dibdinese to tell Bliss that, with his final examinations only a month away, he would be unable to spend Christmas in Oxford that year 'albeit my heart

---

[16] 'The Latin Plays acted before the University of Cambridge', *Retrospective Review* vol. 12 (1825), pp. 1–42.
Hartshorne to Douce, 5 August 1825: Bodleian Ms. Douce d.25 f.101–102.
F. G. Fleay, 'A Biographical Chronicle of the English

Drama' (1891) vol. 2, p. 249. G. C. Moore Smith, 'College Plays performed in the University of Cambridge' (Cambridge, 1923), p. 96.
[17] Kerrich to Douce, 5 May 1824: Bodleian Ms. Douce d.36 f.130.

yearneth moche so to doe'.[18] Meanwhile Kerrich's letters to Douce were becoming increasingly anguished:

Pray Heaven nobody may meddle with poor Peppercorn at present or *interrupt his Studies*. I fear he has been wretchedly idle during the whole summer, and has thrown away his precious time on frivolous people, and frivolous pursuits. It is *now* the *very Crisis of his Fate*: in 3 weeks he must go into the Senate house, and *according to his appearance* in the Examination there, will his Character be *irrevocably* fix'd, for the *whole of his future Life*. If a man be disgraced at his Degree, it *never can be recover'd* – and if he should only *stand low*, it will always be remember'd by the rest of the men who will take their degrees with him, and who will be dispersed all over the Kingdom: they, you may be sure, will not fail to tell it – they will affect to look down upon him, and always speak of him with contempt.[19]

Hartshorne went into the Senate House on 17 January 1825. On the publication of the class lists he wrote to tell his friends that he had emerged with what he called 'a very good share of credit'. 'I am glad to learn', wrote Douce to Kerrich, that Hartshorne 'went triumphantly through his college ordeal.' 'No he did not', wrote Kerrich indignantly in the margin of Douce's letter. He wrote back to set Douce right.

Poor Peppercorn *got* his Degree – and that *was all*. Nothing triumphant: even Honours quite out of his reach. I like the young man, and wish he had done better. I really think he might.[20]

There is no evidence to suggest that Hartshorne gave the matter any further thought. He turned instead to 'subjects much more profitable, and infinitely more pleasant'. By the middle of February he had obtained a grace of the Senate, backed by two bonds from his friend Samuel Fennell of Queens' College, to borrow two manuscripts of Middle English poetry from the University Library. 'I have vigorously begun transcribing from one of them', he told Douce. In addition to this 'I have other schemes; the one nearest to me at present is that of making a good and perfect *text* to Chaucer's *Minor* Poems: I include in the *Minor* Poems every thing, except the Canterbury Tales.' And did Douce have any information on early English liturgical printing? 'I also wish to know, every thing that can be known, relating to the various Missalia and Calendaria'. 'Young Hart that can scamper as fast as you can', was Douce's private comment, wry but admiring, in the margin of one of Hartshorne's letters. No wonder that Hartshorne, advanced on such an ambitious editorial programme, had regarded his university examinations as relatively unimportant. Even Kerrich surrendered to Hartshorne's enthusiasm, though with bad grace: 'It does not so much signify, now he has got his Degree: his time is not now so precious.'[21]

---

[18] Douce to Kerrich, 23 June 1824: Corpus Christi College, Cambridge (C.C.C.) Ms 607 f.96.

Hartshorne to Turner, 28 November 1824: T.C.C. O.13.28.

Hartshorne to Laing, 10 May 1824: E.U.L. La.IV.17.

Hartshorne to Bliss, 14 December 1824: B.L. Add. Ms. 34569 f.147–48.

[19] Kerrich to Douce, 23 December 1824: Bodleian Ms. Douce d.36 f.276.

[20] Hartshorne to Turner, 24 April 1825: T.C.C.

O.13.29 no. 67.

Douce to Kerrich, 3 February 1825: C.C.C. Ms. 607 f.138.

Kerrich to Douce, 18 February 1825: Bodleian Ms. Douce d.36 f.280.

[21] Hartshorne to Douce, 20 February, 26 February 1825: Bodleian Ms. Douce d.25 f.34–37. Douce's note: *ibid.*, f.49.

Kerrich to Douce, 18 February 1825: Bodleian Ms. Douce d.36 f.280.

Besides these and many other short-lived interests, two more serious and sustained projects claimed Hartshorne's attention. The first was a survey of the rare books in the University and principal college libraries, which would eventually be published as 'The Book Rarities in the University of Cambridge' in 1829. In the preface to that book, Hartshorne states that most of his research was done in 1825, but it is clear from his correspondence that he was collecting material long before he took his degree, though with no plan of publication. His time at Cambridge coincided with a sudden revival of interest in the college libraries. The transcription of Pepys's diary in 1822, and its publication in 1825, excited much interest and attracted attention to the treasures of the Pepysian Library. Hartshorne visited the Library in October 1821 and drew up a summary description of its contents which was then circulated to Dibdin, Heber and Douce. This attracted Dibdin to Cambridge in October 1823, when he visited the University Library and the Pepysian. Dibdin was collecting material for his 'Library Companion', though he may also have made discreet enquiries about the possibility of negotiating a sale of some of the early printed books; on his return visit the following year, accompanied by Joseph Haslewood, he informed Lord Spencer that 'I "sighed and looked in vain" over the second Caxton's Chaucer – heartily wishing it a more *civilised* place of abode'. In the 'Library Companion' he speculates about the price that a copy of this book, the second edition of the 'Canterbury Tales', might fetch 'were it now submitted to sale'.[22]

Again, Hartshorne led the way in surveying St John's library, of which he had compiled a twenty-two page description by May 1823. Dibdin seems to have paid a flying visit ('A glorious Chasse! for about an hour!') in October, and a second visit, with Hartshorne acting as cicerone, in November 1824. It was not the first time Dibdin had been to Trinity: he had already been shown a few of the manuscripts, though not the printed books. But again Hartshorne had got there first, having visited the Capell collection in June 1823 and found the library 'bending under venerable dust, and slumbering in an almost unbroken repose'. Hartshorne was indeed a pioneer, at least in his own generation; the antiquaries of the late eighteenth century – Richard Farmer, William Cole, William Herbert – had long since passed away, and on Dibdin's first visit to the library of St John's, he noted that 'The Gentlemen of the College, who accompanied me, and who were Senior Members of it, saw these Curiosities for the *first* time.'[23]

In 1825, with time on his hands, Hartshorne took up his notes again and began to visit the rest of the college libraries. He gained access to Jacob Bryant's books in King's College – not a difficult task, as the books (having been donated in 1804) were laid out on the floor of the side-chapels, where Dibdin came across them unexpectedly in October 1825 while attending evensong. He also paid shorter visits to Queens' (the 'most disordered' library in the University), Corpus Christi and Pembroke (where he found 'nothing remarkable' except for two books: Ortelius's *album amicorum* and an edition of Homer), all of which received brief mention in footnotes to the 'Book Rarities'. By this time Hartshorne had made up his mind to publish his notes, in the form of 'a little book,

[22] Dibdin to Spencer, 22 October 1824: B.L. Althorp G.335 (unfoliated).
[23] Dibdin to Spencer, 21 November 1824: B.L. Althorp G.335.

Dibdin, 'Horae Bibliographicae Cantabrigienses', published in facsimile with an introduction by Renato Rabaiotti (Oak Knoll Books, New Castle, 1989), p. 68.

containing a list of all the printed curiosities in the University', a decision which Dibdin heartily approved:

There can be no doubt but that the volume will *disappear* as rapidly as the morning mist tho' of somewhat more substantial materials. Get an engraving by way of frontispiece. Call ye tome

Bibliographical Flowers
Collected in the *Gardens* of the Colleges of St John, Magdalen &c. &c. In the University of Cambridge

or

A Nosegay for a Roxburgher;

or

Bibliographical Flowers
&c. &c.

Let Harding and Triphook publish it. The *latter* is the better title, and worth a rouleau of 20 sovereigns for the success of your Work. Let it be a genteel, *taking*, crown 8vo. or 450 pages: with copies on l.p. 4to. to suit the *Roxburghe books*.[24]

The eventual title, though less picturesque, was more apt: for Hartshorne's attentions were devoted exclusively to books and exclusively to rarities. In his account of Trinity Library, having whetted the reader's appetite with an allusion to 'manuscripts written by the immortal Newton, and Milton, and Barrow', he then states rather baldly that 'As it does not fall in with the author's plans to give a notice of Manuscripts, he must pass over this most fertile and inviting field without further remark'. As for rarities, no bibliophile could have been more discriminating. Hartshorne made it clear in a letter to Douce that the main attraction of many of the books in the Pepysian Library was not their contents but their rarity: 'my heart beats high on thinking on them: but what most delights me, is that, I meet with books entirely unknown to Herbert, Ames, and Dibdin'. Although this principle might be considered admirably suited to descriptive bibliography, it is possible to take it to extremes. Those extremes Hartshorne had already explored. 'Caxtons', he told Douce, 'I consider nothing unless they are unique, because they are books met with in all our College Libraries, and tomes of common occurrence: as so with the W. de Wordes, and early Classics.'[25]

Hartshorne applied the same principle to his second major project, an edition of Middle English poetry 'printed from M.S.S. unpublished, and unique copies only'. This had begun quite modestly, as a plan to reprint two poems, 'The justes of May' (Wynkyn de Worde, 1507? STC 3543) and 'The epitaffe of the most noble and valyaunt Jasper late duke of Beddeforde' (Richard Pynson, 1496. STC 14477), which Hartshorne had discovered in the Pepysian Library in May 1823. 'These are unnoticed by all bibliographers', he exulted. 'Mr Dibdin never heard of them – Mr Douce too is in equal ignorance – no one in fact knows of them.' (The Pepysian copies are in fact unique.) Hartshorne proposed to reprint them, together with an introduction, notes and glossary, with David

---

[24] Dibdin to Spencer, 20 october 1825: B.L. Althorp G.335.

Hartshorne, 'Book Rarities', pp. 192, 245–6, 266.

Hartshorne to Douce, 10 May 1825: Bodleian Ms. Douce d.25 f.65–66.

Dibdin to Hartshorne, 21 May 1825: N.R.O. X7225 album B no. 58.

[25] 'Book Rarities', pp. 278–9.

Hartshorne to Douce, 7 June 1823: Bodleian Ms. Douce d.24 f.164.

Laing as his publisher. In his excitement he could not make up his mind whether the book was to be a bestseller or a rare and limited edition. 'I think the book will sell, in fact I am sure it will – we will print no more than enough to cover the expences, and gain a trifling profit, which we will divide – it shall be a rare book, and only to be found in the cabinets of the curious.'[26] Laing was encouraging, though perhaps less so than Hartshorne had hoped. He agreed to take a share of the edition, but advised Hartshorne to find a London publisher, as 'to London we would have to look for the disposal of at least two thirds of the impression.' He warned Hartshorne against making the book too much of a collectors' item. 'For my own part, except in some very peculiar cases, I am almost sick to death of reprints in black-letter – and the publick too, I believe, are not so readily tempted with them now, as formerly.'[27]

These plans came to nothing. 'The Master of Magdalene with true monkish feeling told me he did not wish to have any thing transcribed from the Pepysian', Hartshorne informed Laing. But by this time the work had grown in Hartshorne's imagination from an edition of one or two poems to a collection of all the unpublished Middle English poetry he could find. This would be 'one of the most curious and valuable collections in existence . . . My notes I may say without vanity will be very curious, to the purpose, and display great research.' He may also have intended it to be a companion volume to the 'Book Rarities', as most of his transcripts were taken from manuscripts in Cambridge libraries. The most important of these was the unique manuscript of the alliterative poem 'William and the Werwolf' or 'William of Palerne' in King's College (James 13). Jacob Bryant had made use of it in 1781 to support the authenticity of the Rowley poems, but (probably to spare Bryant's reputation) no other scholar was permitted to examine it until 1825, when Hartshorne, through the intercession of Henry Drury, former fellow of King's and member of the Roxburghe Club, secured permission to make a transcript.[28] He copied the first 560 lines but characteristically failed to complete his transcript before turning to other things. From February 1825 he was occupied in transcribing University Library Mss Ff.1.6 and Ff.5.48, the two volumes which Fennell had borrowed on his behalf. A few scholars had seen these manuscripts before him – Ritson knew of the manuscript of 'Sir Degrevant' in Ff.1.6, but did not print it, while Robert Jamieson had printed 'Robyn Hode and the Munke' from Ff.5.48 in his 'Popular Ballads and Songs' (1806) – but most of the contents had never been published. Douce, however, took a dim view of some of the 'hitherto unknown' poems which Hartshorne eagerly described to him:

No. VI. 'Tale of a King and a Knight'. This is a bad clue to so many tales of Kings and Knights.
   IX.   'Tale of Shepherd' I suppose like the many stories of kings who take shelter in cottages while hunting. I could quote a dozen of them, all imitations of one original.

But as one who wished every manuscript he edited to be 'unique', Hartshorne was not prepared to acknowledge the wisdom of collating one manuscript with another. The only work he took the trouble to collate, apart from a few poems which appeared in both

[26] Hartshorne to Laing, 8 May 1823: E.U.L., La.IV.17.
[27] Laing to Hartshorne, 14 May, 4 July 1823: N.R.O. X7225 album B nos. 74, 72.
[28] Hartshorne to Laing, 10 May 1824: E.U.L. La.IV.17. 'William and the Werwolf', ed. Madden (Roxburghe Club, 1832), pp. i–ii.

University Library manuscripts, was 'Piers of Fulham', transcribed from Trinity Ms. R.3.19 and collated for him by Philip Bliss with a Bodleian manuscript, probably Rawlinson C.86.[29]

An indication of Hartshorne's high spirits at this time is given by a small book produced in an edition of twenty copies, with the title 'A Geyfte ffor the Neue Yere: or, A playne, pleasaunte, and profytable Pathe = waie to the BLACK LETTRE Paradyse. Dedycated on a Red Lettre Daie to all braue Boke = buying Biblyomanes, by a Black Lettre Byblyophyle.' It bore the imprint 'Explicit Feliciter. Emprynted ouer the grete Gate = waie off Saincte Jhonnes Colledge, Cambridge, by me Westonne Hattfelde, anno MDCCCXXV.' and is small enough to have been printed on a portable press in Hartshorne's own college rooms, A1, First Court, which were indeed over the East Gate.[30] If the two-colour printing (red and black, naturally enough) caused any difficulty to its amateur printer, there is no sign of this in the surviving copies. Hartshorne distributed it to his friends at New Year 1825, together with a single sheet containing his sole excursion into poetry, entitled 'Carmina Cornucervinia'. The opening lines are sufficient to convey the flavour:

SUM menne yn shoppes offten loke
To ffynde an erly prented BOKE;
Thei liken best, as ich han herd,
One by CAXTON or DE WORDE.

Douce acknowledged his copy with a note of thanks. 'The "carmina" I imagine to be a trial piece as a candidate for the office of *Poeta Laureatus* to the Roxburghian fraternity. It will secure your election.' This was a shrewd comment. Of those known to have received copies, most, with the exception of Douce, Thomas Amyot and Dawson Turner, were members of the Roxburghe Club: Henry Drury, George Hibbert (one of two copies on vellum), J. H. Markland, and (we may assume) Dibdin and Heber. The previous year Hartshorne had received the unprecedented privilege of an introduction, as a guest, to a meeting of the Roxburghe Club. 'The day passed in the usual manner', Dibdin reported to Lord Spencer, adding unnecessarily, 'and with considerable hilarity.' Hartshorne was admitted towards the end of the evening, in time for the toasts. Joseph Haslewood takes up the story:

Here the record might have been closed were it not from a circumstance occurring not warranted by precedent and which *may* have a result neither intended or thought of by all parties concerned. At about half past ten, when our mirth seemed near its highest noon, after a short introductory speech from the V.P. [Dibdin] and seconded by Mr Heber (rehearsed before our door opened, by these members) there was admitted to the honour of a sitting that truly bibliomaniacal spirit Mr Charles Hartshorne. – It is enough here to record the irregularity and hope nothing serious to the abrogation of the Club shall arise from this unexpected breach of privilege.

---

[29] Arthur Johnston, 'Enchanted Ground: the study of medieval romance in the eighteenth century' (1964), appendix 2.

Douce to Hartshorne, 8 March 1825: N.R.O. X7225 album A.

Hartshorne's transcript of 'Piers of Fulham': Bodleian Ms. Add. a.60.

[30] G. C. Moore Smith, 'Lists of Past Occupants of Rooms in St John's College' (Cambridge, 1895), p. 4.

The formal proceedings ended at midnight, and most members, including Dibdin, stayed until one o'clock, but Heber, Hartshorne, Haslewood and a few others remained, drinking red wine and curaçoa, until four.[31] Who could doubt that Hartshorne, 'that truly bibliomaniacal spirit', would be elected to the honour of membership next time a vacancy occurred?

But Hartshorne's literary interests were now to take him much further afield. Several years previously Heber had introduced him to Frederick North, fifth earl of Guilford. Lord Guilford, like Heber, was a bachelor, free to devote much of his time to Continental travel and much of his wealth to book collecting and other literary pursuits. In the summer of 1825 he invited Hartshorne to accompany him to Corfu, which was then a British protectorate, to assist him in his cherished project, the establishment of an Ionian University on the island. As a classical scholar and a bibliophile, Hartshorne was an obvious choice, for the aim of the Ionian University was to further the cause of Greek nationalism, not least by the creation of a library of books and manuscripts to reintro-duce Greeks to their ancient culture. After Lord Guilford's death in 1827 the library was returned to England to be sold, and the flow of investment from the North family estates to the Ionian University abruptly ceased. But that lay in the future, and Hartshorne, unaware of the library's imminent dispersal, was to be employed to buy books from the Greek mainland on Lord Guilford's behalf. On his own, Hartshorne could not possibly have afforded to travel so far afield, and it is likely that he had financial support from Lord Guilford, although some of his travelling expenses were paid by his cousin Charles Guest. His friends and relations were naturally in favour of 'so advantageous an offer'. 'Nobody would think of declining such an opportunity', wrote Kerrich. There was much to see in Europe, especially in Italy; as for the Near East, 'I confess I never have perceived any men much the wiser for their visit to Greece or Athens: however it is some credit to a man, to have been there.' 'At all events', he promised Hartshorne, 'we shall always rejoice to hear of your success: more particularly should there by any prospects of it's tending ultimately to promote your interest, and tend to preferment.'[32]

Hartshorne planned to accompany Lord Guilford across the Continent to Italy, thence by steamship to Corfu, to spend the winter of 1825–6 there, then to make a tour of Asia Minor, taking in Smyrna, Ephesus, Constantinople and Athens, and then to return to Corfu in June before making his way back to England. Lord Guilford apparently hoped that Hartshorne might be persuaded to settle permanently at Corfu. 'Lord Guilford would wish me at Corfu', wrote Hartshorne to Charles Guest in 1826, as he left the island, 'which would not answer my wishes or my future prospects.' To Lord Guilford himself he had written that 'I hope some good luck will throw me into a Government office, or a place in the British Museum.'[33]

Hartshorne was not relying on good luck alone. Frederic Madden was also making

---

[31] Douce to Hartshorne, 8 March 1825: N.R.O. X7225 album A.

Dibdin to Spencer, 21 June 1824: B.L. Althorp G. 335.

'The Roxburghe Revels' (Edinburgh, 1837), pp. 37–8.

[32] Kerrich to Hartshorne, 4 September 1825: N.R.O. X7226 album C no. 89.

Hartshorne's affidavit in the case of R. v Shackell:

Public Record Office (P.R.O.) KB 1/49/73.

[33] Hartshorne to Guest, Lucca 17 July 1826: N.R.O. X7225 album B no. 24.

Hartshorne to Guilford, 4 December 1824: Kent Archives Office, Maidstone (K.A.O.), North family papers, U471 C78.

stealthy moves to obtain an appointment at the Museum, and on 17 January 1826 recorded in his diary that 'a very strong party' headed by a Mr Tyndale, one of the trustees of the Museum, Richard Heber and Josiah Forshall, sublibrarian at the Museum, were seeking to obtain the appointment for Hartshorne and 'intend to move Heaven and Earth to carry their point'. This was a blow to Madden, though he remained cautiously optimistic. 'Mr Petrie tells me I have nothing to fear from Mr Hartshorne yet, and as great changes are to take place in the establishment of the Museum, we may probably *both* be appointed.'[34] Once again Heber's patronage promised to prove decisive. Sir James Allen Park, writing to Hartshorne in 1825 before his departure for the Continent, evidently thought as much.

I should also like to know, whether Heber has done or said any thing about your future course. It is a great pleasure to me to see how that good man has taken to you: for it not only proves his goodness of heart, but your worth, otherwise so good and clever, and I will add so discerning a man would hardly have taken to you in the manner he has.

On that encouraging note, Hartshorne left England, relying on his friend Thomas Amyot to keep 'a good look out on the King's Library for me'.[35]

Hartshorne never wrote an extended account of his foreign travels – a projected article on the Ionian University in the *Quarterly Review* seems to have been forestalled by Lord Guilford's death; or perhaps it was one of his many uncompleted projects. But an unsigned review which he contributed to the *Edinburgh Review* in July 1840 recalls something of his experiences fifteen years before.

We are not unaware of, neither are we disposed to underrate, the obstacles that exist in travelling through this country [Asia Minor]. Its deserted state often places the bare necessities of life out of the traveller's reach; and the ignorance of its inhabitants leads them to watch all his movements with prejudice and suspicion. We know that it is not merely needful to possess a temper imperturbable as that of the Turks – one little liable to be ruffled by accidents – but also to unite with it a constitution that has long been disciplined by temperance, and made capable of bearing excessive fatigue ... Yet we have also experienced that these varied difficulties are speedily lightened, if not indeed entirely forgotten, amid the lofty associations which the magnificence of the country arouses.[36]

Hartshorne's support for Greek nationalism was decidedly lukewarm: he was in favour of Greek independence 'because it is always a glorious thing when a nation strives to be free', but found little to admire in the Greek character. 'The most experience I have had individually, and the more most people have had, who have seen the two contending powers, makes me say without the slightest hesitation, that the more you see of the Greeks, the more you dislike their character. They are fawning, graceless, and hypocritical...' The only reason for the success of the Greek rebellion, in Hartshorne's opinion, was that 'bad as the Greeks are in point of discipline, the Turks are worse'. Nevertheless,

---

[34] Madden's journal, Tuesday 17 January 1826: Bodleian Ms. Eng. hist. c.146 f.358–9.
[35] Park to Hartshorne, 12 February 1825: N.R.O. X7227 album E no. 71.
Hartshorne to Guest, 17 July 1826: N.R.O. X7225 album B no. 24.

[36] Unsigned review of Charles Fellowes, 'A Journal written during an excursion in Asia Minor', *Edinburgh Review*, July 1840, p. 396, identified as by Hartshorne in W. E. Houghton, ed., 'The Wellesley Index to Victorian Periodicals' (1966), vol. 1, p. 488.

he was greatly impressed by the University, and had nothing but praise for Corfu. It was, he assured Kerrich, 'the most beautiful island . . . I have ever seen. I should compare it to an unique copy of a book on vellum.'[37]

About his literary pursuits in Corfu there are scattered remarks in his letters and in the 'Book Rarities'. Corfu contained a library for the use of the British garrison, 9000 volumes in the University library, and over 3000 manuscripts ('properly arranged and bound', Hartshorne thought, the total might reach 4000) in Lord Guilford's collection. The strength of the collection lay in its assemblage of Italian state papers, augmented by transcripts of documents in Italian libraries, many of them relating to affairs in England. Most of these were bought by Sir Thomas Phillipps at the Guilford sale, along with many single items of importance, including a large number of Italian humanist manuscripts. Hartshorne singled out a fourteenth-century manuscript of Livy in Italian, 'exquisitely written and illuminated', as 'the most beautiful of the manuscripts'. A large part of the collection was bought *en bloc* from the Abbé Parigi when Hartshorne and Lord Guilford were in Florence in 1826, notable the Vettori family archive, including a series of letters concerning Aldus Manutius the younger which Hartshorne later published in the 'Book Rarities'.[38]

After his departure for Constantinople in 1826 Hartshorne bought 'eighteen very delightful Modern Greek M.S.S.' for the collection, in circumstances which he later described in the 'Book Rarities': 'At the breaking out of the Greek revolution, many of the principal families residing in and near Constantinople had their property confiscated: their books and manuscripts were all sold by weight to a Jew who dwelt in the Validi Khan, from whom the author had the satisfaction of purchasing some curious specimens of modern Greek Literature.' These may have included some of the manuscripts which subsequently passed into the Phillipps collection and were sold again in 1968: a political satire on the Ottoman Empire, Michael Perdikaris's poem 'Diomedias' and Jakovakis Rizos Neroulos's tragedy 'Aspasia'. More significantly, Hartshorne seems to have approached some of the Greek monasteries in search of manuscripts for the Guilford collection. He preceded Robert Curzon, whose first trip to the Near East was in 1833–4. In the 'Book Rarities' Hartshorne states only that in the spring of 1826 he 'tried in vain to procure' a copy of the Greek Anthology 'from the celebrated library in the Isle of Patmos', but Curzon noted in 1837 that Lord Guilford had been successful in acquiring a manuscript of Josephus from Mount Athos.[39]

This was some consolation for the fact that Hartshorne's travelling arrangements had been upset by the outbreak of the war. He was unable to visit Athens, and had to remain

---

[37] Hartshorne to [?Henry] Wollaston, Corfu May 1826 (copy), and to Kerrich, Corfu 12 November 1825: N.R.O. X7225 album B nos. 9, 26.

[38] Hartshorne to Amyot, 1 June 1826 (copy): N.R.O. X7225 album B no. 28. The Vettori papers passed into Heber's collection, and at the Heber sale in 1836 were divided between the BM (Add. 10263–10281) and Phillipps; see the article 'Phillipps and Italy' in THE BOOK COLLECTOR, vol. 17 no. 4 (1968).

[39] Hartshorne to Guilford, Zante 13 April 1826: K.A.O. U471 C78.

'Book Rarities', pp. 188–90, 372, 385. A. N. L. Munby, 'Phillipps Studies', vol. 3 (1954), pp. 56, 172.

'Catalogue of the Extraordinary, Curious, and Extensive Collection of Manuscripts of the late Lord Guilford' (Evans, 8–13 December 1830). Frederic Madden's annotated copy of the catalogue is in the Munby collection (Munby c.138) in Cambridge University Library. *Bibliotheca Phillippica* new series, part 4 (25 June 1968) includes many Guilford manuscripts.

at Constantinople for five weeks; as he left, the Turkish fleet was preparing to sail, and on the way to Zante his ship passed the Greek fleet stationed off Missolonghi. He arrived back at Corfu to discover that his mail had been forwarded to Smyrna. This minor inconvenience was to have momentous consequences, as it meant that until further letters reached him at Lucca in August 1826 he remained ignorant of events in England. What he read in those letters sent him hastening home at top speed.

When Hartshorne set out from England, in Lord Guilford's company, at the beginning of September 1825 he had been unaware that Heber had left England a month before. On reaching Calais he had been surprised to find a letter from Heber waiting for him, dated 'Calais 3rd August 1825'. 'I am at present rambling in the Netherlands', Heber wrote to Lord Spencer in October, 'and intend proceeding at Germany.' This was nothing out of the ordinary: his friends knew that he was a regular visitor to the Continent and that his reports of his movements tended, as Dibdin put it, to be 'vague and unstable'.[40]

Heber did not mention, however, that a month previously he had written to the Vice Chancellor expressing his determination not to stand again as MP for the University of Oxford. His aim, he wrote, was 'to save the University all unnecessary trouble and ferment', an aim which was not realized: his friends in Oxford were taken completely by surprise, and had some difficulty in finding a candidate to succeed him. To Philip Bliss Heber wrote more candidly about the reasons for his decision:

To say the truth, I am tired of late hours, and long speeches, and tho' proud, as it deserves, of the honour from which I descend, am impatient, and have been, for some time, to be the master of my own time and pursuits.

I am at present making an agreeable ramble on the Continent.[41]

But was there perhaps another reason? It had been rumoured that Heber had suffered, like so many others, in the financial panic of 1824–5. Heber certainly had financial problems, though of longer standing. In 1821 some of his Shropshire estates were mortgaged for £9000 to an aristocratic consortium consisting of the Marquis of Buckingham, the Earl of Mansfield, Earl Cathcart and Earl Stanhope.[42] It is not clear whether Heber needed the money for his book-buying or for alterations to Hodnet Hall. But whatever the explanation, this could hardly be the reason for his resignation, as William Cobbett sardonically pointed out. For 'to a man in pecuniary distress the honourable, honourable House is the most comfortable of all possible things: no bailiff, or bailiff's follower, can lay his vulgar hand upon his shoulder . . . no unreasonable tradesman, be he butcher, baker, brewer or vintner, can incommode him, any more than if he were rolling about amongst bags of gold'. Nor was Heber in any danger of losing his seat, for the members of the University demanded little from their MP. 'One little thing, and that a very little one, indeed, would have been necessary to Mr Heber: he must have been at Oxford at the time of his re-election: he must have been *in England* at that time, or must have produced very satisfactory reasons for his absence, or else the pride of his constituents would have

---

[40] Hartshorne's affidavit, P.R.O. KB 1/49/73. Heber to Spencer, 17 October 1825: B.L. Althorp G.140.

Dibdin to Spencer, 29 July 1824: B.L. Althorp G.335.

[41] Heber to the Vice-Chancellor, Antwerp 15 September 1825 (copy) and to Bliss, 15 September 1825 (copy): Bodleian Ms. Eng. misc. c.406 f.111, 99.

[42] Heber-Percy muniments, Hodnet Hall, Box 1/13 a–c. I am indebted for this reference to Miss Marian Roberts, who is compiling a catalogue of the muniments.

been touched.'[43] Cobbett's conclusion followed with devastating logic. If Heber had no reason to wish to give up his seat, he must have had a very good reason to wish to be out of the country.

Rumours of a homosexual relationship between Heber and Hartshorne were in circulation as early as June 1824, at the time of the Roxburghe Club dinner to which Heber had introduced his young protégé. 'The scandalous chronicle reports strange things respecting the connection between the Member for Oxford and that young Bibliomaniac', Dibdin told Lord Spencer, 'but I apprehend it to be merely scandal.'[44] How widely the rumour was known at that time, there is no way of telling. Heber's departure does not seem to have excited open speculation for some time. But by January 1826 his resignation was public knowledge, and the speed with which the rumour then spread suggests that many people regarded the resignation as confirming what had already been suspected. In February, Thomas Amyot wrote to Bliss, fishing none too subtly for information: 'What a sudden and singular step our friend Heber has taken! I am told that you are one of the *very few* friends with whom he communicated on the subject.' In March, Dibdin learned from several members of the Roxburghe Club that 'some very ugly conclusions were being drawn' and urged Lord Spencer to write to Heber to request his return.[45] On 16 April, the bookseller Henry Foss discussed the matter with Henry Crabb Robinson; Robinson was inclined to disbelieve the report, but his remarks show all too clearly how prevalent the gossip had become:

On our walk home H:F. mentioned the report which Southern had mentioned to me before concerning [*in shorthand*: Heber] which is sufficiently spread to render his return from the Continent necessary. Amyot says that he is quite satisfied of the groundlessness of the report And that it cannot be traced to any authority whatever. And this much is at least true that it is precisely on this subject that the very worst of rumours might arise out of the most insignificant of idle remarks – No body knows why – keeps abroad – It is quite unaccountable – his friends say nothing – So says A to B – have you asks B to C very gravely heard why – keeps away? Dreadful surmises – Broke? asks C. No worse than that but it is not to be mentioned. Shocking whispers! ergo says C to D – I hope there is nothing in it, for I thought him a sensible man and excellent Companion – And so the whisper runs down to Z comes back again and crosses and jostles And unless some one gives himself the trouble to write to the subject of these reports and he comes home he is blasted in reputation for ever.[46]

On 5 May Dr Bandinel, Bodley's Librarian, showed Madden a letter from the publisher Joseph Harding which stated that Heber had been requested, in writing, to return to England, and had made no reply. In his journal Madden did not trouble to conceal his satisfaction. 'All interest therefore he might have possessed with regard to the Museum, in opposition to my views, is now at an end, and I have nothing in future to fear from that quarter.'[47] Two days later the rumour finally appeared in print, in the Tory scandal-sheet

[43] *Cobbett's Weekly Register*, Saturday 27 October 1827, pp. 262–4.

[44] Dibdin to Spencer, 21 June 1824: B.L. Althorp G.335.

[45] Amyot to Bliss, 9 February 1826: B.L. Add. 34569 f.283–4.

Dibdin to Spencer, 11 March 1826: B.L. Althorp G.335.

[46] Robinson's diary, volume 12 f.33b (16 April 1826): Dr Williams's Library, London. For the shorthand see R. Travers Herford's notes, Dr Williams's Library Ms. H.C.R. (II.) 31.i.

[47] Madden's journal, 5 May 1826: Bodleian Ms. Eng. hist. c.146 f.411.

John Bull. Heber, though a Tory, was suspected of liberal tendencies on the question of Catholic emancipation (this, it was said, was why he never spoke in Parliament) and in January *John Bull* had welcomed his resignation with the comment that a man with no oratorical skills was plainly unsuited to be the representative of a 'Protestant University'. The paper now inserted a brief paragraph which would have meant little to a reader not already in the know:

Mr Heber, the late Member for Oxford University, will not return to this country for some time – the backwardness of the season renders the Continent more congenial to some constitutions.

A week later it added a slightly broader hint:

Mr Heber's complaint, for which he is recommended to travel, is said to have been produced by an over addiction to *Hartshorn.*[48]

Any hopes that this might at last induce Heber to return home were dashed when Dibdin received a letter from him at the end of May. Heber alludes to the rumours, almost in passing, at the very end of the letter, and there is no mention of a return to England. Dibdin told Bliss tersely: 'it does not satisfy me'.

As to myself the strange and unfounded rumours, which have got, [I know not how *deleted*] by some means, into circulation, have surprized most certainly, and annoyed me – How they originated or obtained circulation and credit, I am at a loss to conceive. However, I have a stout and a light heart, buoyant spirits, kind friends, and what is best, a conscience void of offence. Yrs ever, my dear Dibdin, with every kind wish RH.[49]

There are signs that Heber's friends were now preparing to abandon him. Lord Spencer and Thomas Grenville 'think it all over with him!' wrote Dibdin to Bliss a few days later. 'The whole matter resolves itself thus. If *all* his friends say his *appearance alone* – and in the most *marked* manner – can save him, and he chuses *not* to come: – there can be but *one* alternative.'

The news did not reach Sir Walter Scott until 25 June. Scott had been one of the original sponsors of *John Bull* at the time of Queen Caroline's trial in 1820, but if he had seen the newspaper reports he had evidently failed to understand them. Scott and Heber were close friends, so the shock was great. 'God, God whom shall we trust! Here is learning, wit, gaiety of temper, high station in society and compleat reception every where all at once debased and lost by such a degrading bestiality. Our passions are wild beasts. God grant us power to muzzle them.' No one was safe. Scott reflected with horror that he might easily have allowed his own son to visit the Continent in Heber's company. The more circumstantial account in Scott's journal for 10 July adds a detail of which I have found no corroboration. 'His life was compromised but for the exertions of [Henry] Hobhouse under Secretary of State who detected a warrant for his trial passing through the [Home] office.'[50] In the absence of supporting evidence (which may yet come to light

---

[48] *John Bull* 29 January 1826, p. 37; 7 May 1826, p. 150; 14 May 1826, p. 158. On Heber's politics see R. H. Cholmondeley, ed., 'The Heber Letters' (1950).

[49] Heber to Dibdin, Mechlin 17 May 1826: letter in the collection of Arthur Freeman.

[50] Scott, *Letters*, ed. H. J. C. Grierson (1936), vol. 10, pp. 68, 73.

Scott, *Journal*, ed. W. E. K. Anderson (Oxford, 1972), p. 170.

among the Home Office records) I am inclined to regard this as apocryphal, though significant in that it shows the dimensions of the rumour at this time. Hartshorne, it must be remembered, still knew nothing of all this. On 2 August Dibdin received a letter from him which made it '*quite clear*', he told Lord Spencer, 'that the writer is wholly ignorant of what has been said in these parts concerning his character'.[51] He wrote an urgent reply, and it was this letter which brought Hartshorne scurrying home.

Hartshorne arrived in England on 3 September. He convened a meeting of his friends and, on their advice, wrote to Heber at Brussels imploring him to return home. 'I entreat you my dear Sir who are equally innocent of so horrid an imputation to come home instantly and by your presence and what other means you think advisable join me in convincing the world of its falshood previously to taking any legal measures which will better originate with you than with me . . . I write to you in as good spirits as these horrid reports will allow me to possess, they have made me extremely miserable but a clear conscience has supported me as it will do you.'[52] Copies of this letter were circulated among his friends, including Dibdin, Hibbert, Sir Francis Freeling and Thomas Amyot. Considering it advisable 'to shew himself as openly as possible', Hartshorne then left London in order to visit his friends in Cambridge and family in Shropshire. In his absence, Freeling and Amyot were deputed to open Heber's reply when it arrived at the Athenaeum: an arrangement born not only of convenience but also of legal caution. In the event of a lawsuit it might be necessary to show that there had been no secret communication or collusion between Heber and Hartshorne. The precaution suggests that Hartshorne already considered it likely that Heber would not return to England.

Heber's reply was dated 17 September 1826. This important document requires lengthy quotation, as Heber's fullest justification of his actions. The original does not survive – it is probably no accident that both sides of the Heber/Hartshorne correspondence have been lost – but copies were widely circulated. There is a transcript in Hartshorne's hand among Lord Guilford's papers, and another in an unidentified hand among Sir Walter Scott's papers.[53]

My dear Hartshorne,

Had I for a moment conceived my presence in London necessary to clear your character, I would not have waited for a summons to bring me over. But I am firmly convinced on the contrary that we shall accomplish our common object most effectually by *independent firing* – each fighting his battle in his own way, and consulting his reputation in the manner in which he thinks best. In fact, I, who am quitting, and you who are entering, public life, may fairly be allowed to take separate grounds, and adopt different weapons of defence. Your future professional, and other prospects make it advisable to set yourself straight with the opinion of the world as speedily as possible. I may be permitted to entertain sentiments of mortified pride, and of confidence in past character – both of which have a tendency to produce contempt for calumny, indifference to the arbitrium popullike, and stubbornness in adhering to my own judgement. Accordingly I shall proceed as if nothing had happened, and shall come home in my own good time, whether it be sooner or later.

[51] Dibdin to Spencer, 4 August 1826: B.L. Althorp G.335.
[52] Hartshorne to Heber, 8 September 1826, quoted in full in P.R.O. KB 1/49/73.
[53] National Library of Scotland MS. 891 f.66–67. K.A.O. U471 C78.

Heber assumed that Hartshorne would pursue an action for libel against *John Bull*, and offered financial support 'if the *sinews of war* are *wanting*'. He declared that the charges against Hartshorne had given him more uneasiness than the charges against himself, an ambiguous statement which may have been the closest Heber could come to an apology, knowing as he did that his words would be read by many eyes: an indication, in other words, that whatever the truth about his own private life, Hartshorne had not been involved. 'Farewell my dear Charles', the letter concludes. 'Yours under much and deep affliction faithfully Richard Heber.'

This letter is remarkable for how little it gives away. Together with Heber's consistent refusal to respond directly to the accusations against him, it may even be regarded as a necessarily tacit plea of privacy; pamphlets arguing for homosexual rights, on the grounds that sexual activities between consenting partners are the responsibility of the individual, not of the state, were in circulation on the Continent during the French Revolution, and may have been known to Heber.[54] But to Heber's friends it was an unsatisfactory, even evasive reply. Dibdin believed it showed a 'melancholy perversion of all sound reasoning' and pointed out the logical flaw: 'whatever applies to Hartshorne, does, from Heber's own shewing, apply with tenfold force to Himself. As to feelings of 'mortified pride' &c. who has the Complainant to blame but *Himself*? – for who ever took so much pains to kick down, with his *own* foot, that fabric of reputation, which his friends, in placing him in the seat of Oxford, were so assiduous and so anxious in rearing?'[55] It is clear that Dibdin and his friends were extremely shaken by the whole affair – and with good reason. Much of the humour of Dibdin's bibliomaniacal writings, with their 'raptures', their 'ecstasies' and their 'stiff and magnificent' vellum incunabula, rests in the parade of *double entendre* – a style we would now describe as camp. Insiders could treat it as a deliciously naughty joke: Hartshorne's 'Geyfte ffor the Neue Yere' pretends (Dibdin would have handled the joke more subtly) that the true book-lover has no time to spare for girls: 'hy promysede a Boke to a Ladie, and greuiovsly forget it', 'hy saide he wold mete soome fayre Ladyis: & was sore afrayde, & whant qvite another waie', 'hy sayd a Boke off Grolyeres loked ffayre as a ladie'. I stress this point because Dibdin's modern admirers tend to avoid it. But even suspicious outsiders like Sir James Allen Park were perfectly well aware of it, though uncertain whether or not to treat it as a joke: in their eyes bibliomania was a 'lust', a 'passion', a 'vice'. The Heber scandal turned the joke into frightful reality. Not surprisingly, Heber's absence from the Roxburghe Club dinner in June 1826 cast a shadow over the proceedings. Dibdin observed that 'not a syllable' was said of Heber all evening. Haslewood hoped that the affair 'may remain unintelligible beyond our circle'.[56]

Here, indeed, lay the dilemma: should Hartshorne prosecute, or should he let the matter die down without further publicity? Among his friends, his reputation was intact; in Kerrich's view, he had 'nothing to do but be quiet'. As he himself admitted, he had the satisfaction of knowing that his side of the story was being put about by Bliss, Drury and

[54] Wayne Dynes, 'Privacy, Sexual Orientation and the Self-Sovereignty of the Individual: Continental Theories 1762–1908', *Gay Books Bulletin* (New York), vol. 1 no. 6 (Fall 1981), pp. 20–3.

[55] Dibdin to Spencer, 26 September 1826: B.L. Althorp G.335.

[56] Dibdin to Bliss, 7 June 1826: B.L. Add. 34569 f.328. 'The Roxburghe Revels', p. 43.

Copleston in Oxford, 'by Dibdin, Lodge, Kerrich and numbers of others, in Cambridge', by Sir James Allen Park among his legal colleagues, and by 'some of our leading Athenaeum members in the first political circles'.[57]

This influential support was not all for the sake of a young man scarcely out of university. It is not without significance that practically all of Hartshorne's friends in London – Amyot, Dibdin, Hibbert, Inglis, Markland, Turner – as well as Hartshorne himself, were members of the Athenaeum. Heber had been an active member of the founding committee when the club was established in 1824, and if one glances down the list of original members, all the lines of his friendship and patronage seem to come together. Many members were book collectors (Lord Spencer and E. V. Utterson as well as the names above); many were either Whigs or (like Robert Peel and Heber himself) on the liberal wing of the Tory party; some were personal friends of Heber, like Sir Walter Scott; some were Shropshire worthies, like Hartshorne's old headmaster Dr Butler of Shrewsbury. Henry Crabb Robinson's diaries show how smoothly a man who moved in the right literary circles could be drawn into Heber's orbit. Robinson was proposed for membership of the Athenaeum by Heber, at Amyot's suggestion, in 1824 ('My becoming a member was an epoch in my life'); in April 1825 he can be found visiting Dibdin's house in the company of Amyot, Heber, Dawson Turner and Charles König of the British Museum.[58] Bibliophiles, then as now, tended to hunt in packs. The result was that an extremely powerful party could be mustered in Hartshorne's defence, with the Athenaeum as its principal base; three public dinners were held there in the course of 1826 to rally Hartshorne's supporters. But it was Heber, not Hartshorne, with which that party was most closely associated. There was a widely-held opinion that Heber's interests would not be served by the publicity of a court case, and that Hartshorne should let the matter die down quietly. Amyot stated firmly: 'It is high time for him to pursue steadily the prospects of his future life, and I think he may now do so without danger of further calumny.'[59]

Despite this, Hartshorne was determined to go ahead with the prosecution of *John Bull*. 'Nothing satisfies my relations, at least those I have seen, but *law*, and nothing else will satisfy me.'[60] He knew the peculiar horror that homosexuality aroused: in his first year at Cambridge he would have witnessed the disgrace of the unfortunate Mr Thomas Jephson, fellow of St John's, who was apprehended with his trousers down, in the company of a young man from the gravel pits, in a ditch at the edge of the cricket ground on the Cherry Hinton road. Jephson's claim that he had climbed into the ditch in order to relieve himself was received with scepticism. 'The walls were placarded, the public

---

[57] Kerrich to Douce, 7 November 1826: Bodleian Ms. Douce d.36 f.317.

Hartshorne to James Lusignan, 26 September 1826: K.A.O. U471 C78.

[58] List of original members conveniently printed in Michael Faraday, *Correspondence* (ed. Frank James, 1990), vol. 1, pp. 341–5. Robinson, 'Diary, Reminiscences, and Correspondence', ed. Thomas Sadler (1869), vol. 2, p. 275. Robinson's diary, vol. 9 f.78b (25 April 1825) and reminiscences, vol. 2, p. 401: Dr Williams's Library. Reprinted with omissions in Edith J. Morley, ed., 'Henry Crabb Robinson on Books and their Writers', vol. 1 (1938), p. 319. For another account of the visit to Dibdin, see Turner's letter to Hartshorne, 27 May 1825: N.R.O. X7225 album B no. 109.

[59] Hartshorne to Guilford, 24 December 1826: K.A.O. U471 C78.

Amyot to Turner, 23 December 1826: T.C.C. O.13.31 no. 160.

[60] Hartshorne to Guilford, 18 October 1826: K.A.O. U471 C78.

houses of Cambridge and the neighbouring market towns were constantly filled with parties hostilely canvassing his case; and cheap publications issued from the press, in which his guilt was assumed as past all question.'[61] In this light it is easy to understand Hartshorne's fear of leaving the matter unsettled:

Though in the eyes of every reasonable person, it must be evident that the steps I have taken have been most open, and such as to tell them I had no cause for fear. But yet others may say, 'Why did Mr Hartshorne stop in the middle? it looks suspicious' there is no means to tell them the reason, and so I may live with the suspicion of these people upon me, to whom I never could have an opportunity of explaining why I had so acted.

He made it clear that he had seen nothing of Heber since the latter's departure for the Continent, 'and yet', as he told David Laing, 'some good natured people have said we left together, and were living together.'[62]

Hartshorne chose to seek a criminal information in the Court of King's Bench, instead of pursuing a civil action. This was in some respects a surprising choice, as it meant that even in the event of a verdict in his favour he could not be awarded costs. 'Poor H. will have I fear a heavy account with his lawyers', wrote Douce to Kerrich. 'It is a pity it had not been an action for *damages* as was the advice of several of us and then he would have been indemnified as to expence. I could', he continued, referring to the saga of his long and tedious action in Chancery to recover the Nollekens legacy, 'dilate largely on these absurd niceties and quibbles of the law which wants much correction as to simplicity of proceeding.' ('No doubt you could', was Kerrich's sour annotation.) Douce was right to forecast heavy expenses for Hartshorne. At the beginning of the trial Hartshorne had estimated the eventual costs at £200, and feared he would have to borrow money in order to pay it. In the end his expenses, including the cost of residing in London, came to £450.[63]

Why then did Hartshorne pursue the action in the criminal courts? One reason was probably the notorious willingness of the judiciary to grant criminal informations against the press. Hartshorne's counsel had not finished speaking when he was interrupted by one of the judges with the words 'Whatever determination a jury will come to, *we* think this a most fit case for granting a criminal information', and a rule was immediately granted.[64] This, in a case which Hartshorne's lawyer had initially feared would not be strong enough to take to court! The paragraph was libellous – that was clear – but who was responsible? *John Bull*'s publisher, Edward Shackell, stated that the paragraph had been sent to the printing office 'among various miscellaneous communications' by an unknown person, and printed without alteration. The word *hartshorn* had been put in italics because it had been underlined in the copy – normal printing-house practice. The possibility of making a case against Shackell, let alone against the paper's editor,

[61] 'The Case of Mr Thomas Jephson' [Cambridge, 1823], p. 36. see also R. F. Scott, 'Admissions [to St John's College, Cambridge]', part 4 (1931), p. 332.

[62] Hartshorne to Turner, 22 December 1826: T.C.C. O.13.31 no. 159.
Hartshorne to Laing, 24 October 1826: E.U.L. La.IV.17.

[63] Douce to Kerrich, 5 November 1827: C.C.C. MS. 607 f.210.
Hartshorne to Turner, 22 December 1826 and 19 November 1827: T.C.C.O.13.31 no. 159 and O.14.1 no. 117.

[64] Hartshorne to Guilford, 24 December 1826: K.A.O. U471 C78.

Theodore Hook, seemed remote. If so, as Hartshorne admitted, 'I am left in a very awkward predicament.' It was fortunate for him that the Bench was so sympathetic to prosecutions for criminal libel.[65]

But there was another reason for Hartshorne and his friends to prefer a criminal action. At this time, before the passing of the Libel Act of 1843, truth was no defence to criminal libel, though it was always a defence to a civil action.[66] This meant that *John Bull* had no reason to seek to substantiate its allegations by bringing before the court evidence about Heber's private life. Indeed, the paper withdrew them at once, with no attempt at a justification. No sooner had a criminal rule been granted than the paper printed a long statement offering Hartshorne a 'full, ample, and unambiguous explanation and atonement for an inadvertent injury'.[67] Hartshorne regarded this not only as a vindication of himself (which it certainly was) but also as a vindication of Heber.

It can only be said that Hartshorne's awareness of irony was not acute. It is true that *John Bull* declared its 'utter disbelief' of the allegations against Heber, but it then added the entirely gratuitous information that Heber was travelling on the Continent under an assumed name ('in order to avoid the imposition to which his celebrity as a book collector would lay him open were he known'). The statement ended on a brazenly sarcastic note:

… we believe him [Heber] as innocent of that, which it now seems by the affidavits in this case to infer he had been guilty, as WE were of the real meaning of the piece of information, when we inserted it.

This was a clear signal that the allegations about Heber would continue, though by innuendo and suggestion rather than in open court. As time passed and Heber remained on the Continent, it became increasingly difficult for his friends to rebut those allegations. Dibdin's opinion was that Hartshorne had been injured not only by *John Bull* but also 'by the shuffling conduct of his professed Patron'. When the case finally came to court in November 1827, and Dibdin was called to the Guildhall to give evidence, his only fear was that the defence might question him about Heber. 'Denman … who knows my feelings and opinions about the *other* party, may elicit something from me in X examination, to give an apparent colouring of justification to what was said in regard to him.'[68] His anxiety was unnecessary. Instead of conducting *John Bull*'s defence on the grounds that the defendant was aware of the allegations, believed them to be true and published them in the public interest (a line of argument which William Cobbett, in a long editorial published after the end of the trial, believed the defence should have adopted) it was claimed that the defendant knew nothing of the rumours and had published the offending paragraphs in all innocence, unaware that they contained any hidden meaning. The reference to the 'backwardness of the season', it was suggested, might merely have been an allusion to Heber's 'backward and lukewarm' views on the subject of Catholic

---

[65] Hartshorne to Turner, 4 March 1827: T.C.C. O.13.32 no. 52.
Shackell's affidavit: P.R.O. KB 1/49/172.
Hartshorne to Laing, 24 October 1826: E.U.L. La.IV.17.
[66] See J. R. Spencer, 'The Press and the Reform of Criminal Libel' in P. R. Glazebrook, ed., 'Reshaping the Criminal Law: essays in honour of Glanville Williams' (1978), pp. 266–86.
[67] *John Bull*, 10 December 1826, p. 396.
[68] Dibdin to Spencer, 24 September 1827, 17 October 1827: B.L. Althorp G.336.

emancipation. These were the tactics of desperation, although the alleged innuendo in 'the backwardness of the season' was not a subject on which the prosecution cared to dwell.[69] (One is reminded of the *Lady Chatterley* trial and the prosecution's reluctance to cite passages referring to sodomy.) Cobbett was of the opinion that the innuendo was scarcely detectable and that the defence would have been better advised not to have mentioned the matter. Even in a trial which hinged on allegations of homosexual practice, homosexuality remained an unmentionable subject. The same taboo applied to private letters: one of Douce's letters to Kerrich comments 'I could say more about another person but perhaps it is best to be silent here. We might hereafter talk over the matter . . .' after which he advises Kerrich to put the letter into the fire.[70] In such a climate of opinion it was inevitable that the Heber affair would never be satisfactorily resolved.

To no one's surprise the jury, without leaving the courtroom, returned a verdict of guilty, and John *Bull*'s publisher, Edward Shackell, was fined £500. By *Bull*'s standards this was not an unusually heavy fine, and as the paper was reckoned to make a profit of £4000 a year after libel costs had been deducted, it was not an especially damaging blow; nor did it affect the editor, Theodore Hook ('the reptile Hook', as Hartshorne called him), who was always careful to ensure that his connection with the paper could not be proved.[71] But for Hartshorne the verdict was an unqualified victory. The defence counsel, as Cobbett observed, had 'painted him out as a sort of angel of light', and the crown prosecutor declared that 'I never saw a gentleman who conducted himself with more propriety than Mr Hartshorne throughout these proceedings, or whose innocence has been more clearly established'. He wrote soberly to Dawson Turner after the conclusion of the trial:

The clouds have all blown over, and I feel myself (though still deeply wounded) to be a better man than I should have been, if I had never experienced the roughness of adversity.[72]

By this time his future was settled. His hopes of a post in the civil service or the British Museum had been dashed by Heber's fall from grace. Instead he had chosen a clerical career, though perhaps with some dissatisfaction, to judge from his description of the wearisome search for a curacy. 'I have been making enquiries in all directions for a curacy, but without a dawn of success, so hopeless indeed have been my endeavours, that I am nearly reduced to think I am seeking after what is unattainable.' In August 1827 Dr Forester, a family friend, came to his rescue and gave him a title for orders upon the parish of Benthall, Shropshire, adjoining his native Broseley. He was accordingly ordained deacon on 9 September 1827, and priest on 3 August 1828.[73] On 10 December 1828 he was married to Frances Margaretta Kerrich. It was an advantageous match. Thomas Kerrich had died earlier in the year, and his daughter now came into possession

[69] *Cobbett's Weekly Register*, Saturday 27 October 1827, pp. 274–6.

The Examiner (Sunday 26 November 1826, p. 765) renders the paragraph: 'Mr Heber, the late Member for Oxford University, will not return to England this season.'

[70] 'No.' writes Kerrich in the margin. Douce to Kerrich, 9 November 1826: C.C.C. Ms. 607 f.184.

[71] H. R. Fox Bourne, 'English Newspapers' (1887), vol. 2, pp. 5–10.

[72] *The Examiner*, Sunday 25 November 1827, p. 745.

Hartshorne to Turner, 15 January 1829: T.C.C. O.14.3 no. 9.

[73] Hartshorne to Martin Routh, 14 April 1827: Magdalen College, Oxford, MS 475 (iii.) no. 15.

Hartshorne to Turner, 14 August 1827: T.C.C. O.14.1 no. 44.

of a substantial fortune (part of the Nollekens legacy of which Douce and Kerrich had been joint beneficiaries): £11,500 invested in the three-per-cents, to which was added a further £10,000 when Mrs Kerrich died in 1835. Hartshorne now had a career, a comfortable income, and soon a family: Charles Kerrich Hartshorne, the first of fourteen children, of whom all but four lived to adulthood, was born in October 1829.[74]

The demands of literature no longer seemed so pressing. Still, Hartshorne continued to work fitfully on the preparation of his two books for publication. By May 1827 he had almost finished preparing his work on Cambridge libraries for the press, in the optimistic hope that it would be published by the summer; and in July Longmans issued a prospectus announcing the forthcoming publication, in November, of 'Bibliographica Cantabrigiensia; or Remarks upon the most valuable and curious Book-Rarities in the University of Cambridge'. Douce, who had formed accurate surmises about the completeness of the work, objected to the title 'because it indicates a general account of Cambridge libraries', and suggested a more fanciful Dibdinian title. 'Typographical flowers excerpted from the Cambridge libraries'? 'A typographical nosegay of Cambridge curiosities'? This inspired Hartshorne to another suggestion: 'Bibliographical Flowers from a Garden of Cambridge rarities'. Dawson Turner had more serious objections to the prospectus: it did not include Hartshorne's name (though this may have been a calculated decision to avoid publicity during the trial) and it did not mention a price. Hartshorne admitted that the latter was an 'important point' but put the blame on the publishers, who had issued the prospectus 'without my knowledge or sanction'. Turner agreed with Douce that the work should be aimed at a more general readership:

You will do well to add the embellishment of art to your publication, tho' at the necessary consequence of augmenting its price: You will then attract a considerable number of purchasers, in addition to the mere bibliographers, who are also, in general, men of a certain degree of property and of leisure, such as like to please their eyes as well as instruct their minds; and I would suggest to you whether, in this first publication, it might not be desirable to take a leaf from a book of a Reverend Doctor, and pledge yourself that the plates shall be destroyed and the book never be reprinted.

Hartshorne preferred to hope that the book might go into a second edition.[75] He agreed, however, about the desirability of illustrations, and had already commissioned two of his Cambridge friends and contemporaries, Albert Way and William Thornton, to produce two full page plates and a number of head- and tailpieces. The slightly incoherent nature of the book is well brought out by the fact that most of the illustrations are taken from illuminated manuscripts in Cambridge libraries, which the text, of course, entirely ignores.

---

[74] Hartshorne's marriage settlement is in the University Library, Cambridge (U.L.C.), University Archives, Prem. II.18 (1). I am indebted for this reference to Dr E. S. Leedham-Green.

For a family tree, see Albert Hartshorne, 'Notes on the Postlethwayts of Millom', *Transactions of the Cumberland and Westmorland Antiquarian and Archaeological Society*, vol. 10 (1889), pp. 244–52.

[75] Douce to Hartshorne, 10 May 1827: N.R.O. X7225 album A.

Turner to Hartshorne, 14 July 1827: N.R.O. X7225 album B no. 112.

Hartshorne to Turner, 14 August 1827: T.C.C. O.14.1 no. 44.

It has been unkindly suggested that the illustrations are the most valuable part of the book. Thus Brunet describes the book as 'Livre curieux, mais d'un intérêt local; il est orné de vignettes gravées en bois, la plupart tres-jolies.' Cambridge men have usually been more generous in their assessment of the work. It was a principal stimulus to J. O. Halliwell in his researches in the college libraries as an undergraduate in the 1840s, and his 'Manuscript Rarities of the University of Cambridge' (1841) echoes the title of Hartshorne's book. Samuel Sandars filled his copy with marginal and interleaved notes to form what he evidently hoped would be the basis for a union catalogue of Cambridge incunabula.[76] But the work is disorganized and frequently inaccurate. Hartshorne transfers a copy of Caxton's edition of 'Reynard the Fox' (1489; a unique copy which he conflates with a description of the 1481 edition) from the Pepysian to the University Library, and a copy of Coverdale's New Testament (1538; dated by Hartshorne 1539) from King's to St John's. Books are confidently and incorrectly identified: a Latin Bible in the University Library printed at Paris in 1475–6 is described, despite the clear evidence of the colophon, as 'Biblia Latina, Vulgatae versionis. Two volumes folio. Moguntiae, 1462.' An Elizabethan edition of Malory's 'Morte d'Arthur' (1578) in the University Library is correctly identified in one of Hartshorne's letters to Douce but then, in the 'Book Rarities', put down as Caxton's edition of 1485. From these examples it is possible to reconstruct Hartshorne's unfortunate habit of supplementing an incomplete description in his own notes with a more detailed description (often of another copy) in a printed source such as 'Bibliotheca Spenceriana'. Henry Bradshaw's copy contains the exasperated note 'Why will people print catalogues from rough notes wh. they do not verify?' and Bradshaw's annotations, though they correct some of Hartshorne's more glaring errors, are sparing; he was aware that the work was simply too inaccurate to serve as the basis for a future catalogue.[77] Thus Hartshorne's work was out of date within his own lifetime. Nevertheless, it is worth quoting the more sympathetic verdict of another Cambridge bibliographer, Charles Sayle, who was under no illusions about Hartshorne's accuracy, but who also knew how little studied the college libraries had been since Hartshorne's time and how little known they still remained.

That work, admirably conceived, would have been a monumental work had not its author been compelled to prepare in haste what should only have been compiled at leisure. As it is, it still remains the only book on the bibliographical collections in the University as a whole, and it is much to be desired that a new edition of it should be undertaken.[78]

The preparation of 'Ancient Metrical Tales' was plagued by even more difficulties. Hartshorne had originally anticipated a two-volume edition. After he left Cambridge he had fewer opportunities to collect material, and the two volumes shrank to one. It shrank still further as Hartshorne discovered that several of his poems had already been printed in other collections, and in August 1828 he sent an urgent appeal to Douce. The printing of the volume had 'proceeded as far as the sixteenth sheet, and all my M.S. is exhausted.' Could Douce supply any more material 'from your own treasures'? Douce could not. And so the book appeared with a number of minor pieces bringing up the rear, including

[76] Sandars's copy: U.L.C. SSS.49.4.
[77] Bradshaw's copy: U.L.C. Adv.c.77.30.

[78] Charles Sayle, 'Annals of Cambridge University Library' (Cambridge, 1916), p, vi.

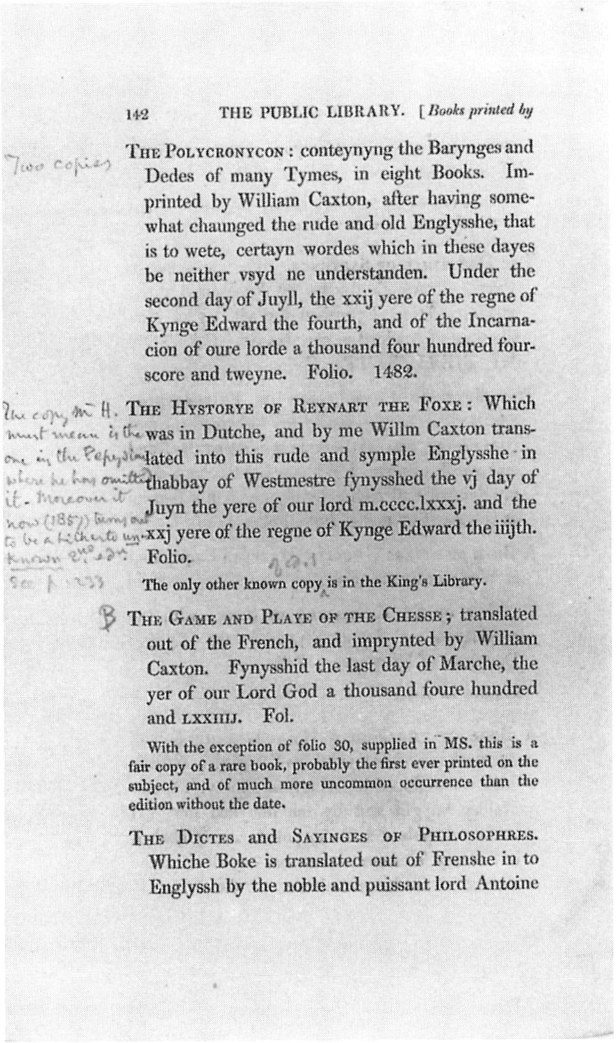

142   THE PUBLIC LIBRARY. [*Books printed by*

Two copies

THE POLYCRONYCON : conteynyng the Barynges and
Dedes of many Tymes, in eight Books. Im-
printed by William Caxton, after having somewhat chaunged the rude and old Englysshe, that
is to wete, certayn wordes which in these dayes
be neither vsyd ne understanden. Under the
second day of Juyll, the xxij yere of the regne of
Kynge Edward the fourth, and of the Incarna-
cion of oure lorde a thousand four hundred four-
score and tweyne. Folio. 1482.

The copy in H. THE HYSTORYE OF REYNART THE FOXE : Which
must mean is the was in Dutche, and by me Willm Caxton trans-
one in the Pepys lated into this rude and symple Englysshe in
where he has omitted thabbay of Westmestre fynysshed the vj day of
it. Moreover it Juyn the yere of our lord m.cccc.lxxxj. and the
now (1857) turns out xxj yere of the regne of Kynge Edward the iiijth.
to be a distinct un- Folio.
known ed^n ... 1833
    The only other known copy is in the King's Library.

ℬ THE GAME AND PLAYE OF THE CHESSE; translated
out of the French, and imprynted by William
Caxton. Fynysshid the last day of Marche, the
yer of our Lord God a thousand foure hundred
and LXXIIIJ. Fol.

With the exception of folio 30, supplied in MS. this is a
fair copy of a rare book, probably the first ever printed on the
subject, and of much more uncommon occurrence than the
edition without the date.

THE DICTES and SAYINGES OF PHILOSOPHRES.
Whiche Boke is translated out of Frenshe in to
Englyssh by the noble and puissant lord Antoine

PLATE II. A page from 'The Book Rarities in the University of Cambridge', with Henry Bradshaw's annotations distinguishing, for the first time, Caxton's two editions of 'Reynard the Fox'. (University Library, Cambridge, Adv.c.77.30, reproduced by permission of the Syndics.)

one, 'The Kyng and the Hermit', reprinted without apology from Brydges and Haslewood's 'British Bibliographer' (1814).[79] Hartshorne admits in the preface that the book is incomplete, 'sent forth in a smaller size' than originally intended, due to 'every probability of a still longer delay if the Editor's earlier plans are adhered to'. He cannot have been satisfied with the result. It is a miscellaneous collection of poems, some religious, some secular, mostly late medieval (with at least one, 'Doctour Doubble Ale', as late as the sixteenth century), ranging in length from short to very short. There is hardly any editorial commentary; the special features of 'William and the Werwolf', by far the oldest and the longest work in the volume, are left for the reader to discover. 'Ancient

[79] Hartshorne to Douce, 11 August 1828: Ms. Douce d.26 f.136–7. Sir Egerton Brydges and Joseph Haslewood, eds., 'The British Bibliographer', vol. 4 (1814), p. 81.

Metrical Tales' remains the only printed text of many of the poems – it is, for example, cited in STC as the only modern edition of 'A tale of King Edward and the Shepherd', printed by Hartshorne from Ms Ff.5.48 ('written in the 15th century') but now known in a single, fragmentary copy of an early sixteenth-century edition printed by Wynkyn de Worde (STC 7502.5), a discovery which would have pleased Hartshorne. But its textual inaccuracies make it a highly unreliable authority.

The book exists in two states, the second with an additional four-leaf gathering containing 'The Demaundes Joyous' reprinted from the unique copy of Wynkyn de Worde's edition in the University Library. 'I only wish that to fall into the hands of Collectors', Hartshorne explained to Laing, 'there being in it such an unusual degree of freedom of wit, that I feared to let my name appear as a divine, with it.' Presumably Hartshorne had in mind passages such as '¶ Demaunde. Which is the moost cleynlyest lefe among all other leues. ¶. it is holly leues, for noo body wyll not wype his arse with them.' The presence of this 'curious collection of charades', as Hartshorne delicately described it, in 'Ancient Metrical Tales' is in any case a little incongruous, as it is neither in verse nor printed from manuscript. Douce pointed out the incongruity in a letter to Hartshorne shortly before the book's publication. 'I presume you are aware that the "Demaundes joyous" have been printed by W. de Worde or Pynson, and that it is a translation from the French. No matter, it will bear reprinting.'[80] But by this time Hartshorne was in too much of a hurry to get the book published and off his hands to worry about its internal consistency.

'Ancient Metrical Tales' was published at the beginning of 1829. Sir Walter Scott, who had received a copy from David Laing, noted the diversity of the contents with some perplexity. 'I glanced over some metrical romances published by Hartshorne, several of which have not seen the light. They are considerably curious, but I was surprised to see them mingled with *Blanchefleur and Flores* and one or two others which might have been spared. There is no great display of notes or prolegomena, and there is, moreover, no glossary. But the work is well edited.'[81] His view of Hartshorne's editorial competence was not widely shared. When the publisher William Pickering wrote to Hartshorne in December 1829 he did not mince matters:

The Ancient Metrical Tales have not gone off as they ought, I do not believe 150 copies out of the 500 printed have been sold – and the general impression is that they are incorrectly printed – Those Individuals who are tolerable judges state this – One would have reviewed it, but he could not upon carefully going over, or he would have done [me *deleted*] the work injury – I have just now a letter before me of which the following is an extract. 'It is to be regretted that Mr Hartshorne has paid so little attention to the correction of errors of the press (assuming them to be such) and that he has permitted the volume to appear before the public without having bestowed a little more pains upon it. In the fragment I have mentioned (William and the Werwolf) I have detected what I conceive to be above 50 errors and I think he has permitted a hiatus in the MS to pass unnoticed – viz at p.277 'And scythe' &c. is spoken by the daughter who continues the speech, tho' the father evidently commences it, there is probably a whole folio wanting, or it may be transposed in the binding.'

[80] Hartshorne to Laing, 14 January 1829: E.U.L. La.IV.17. Douce to Hartshorne, 23 August 1828: N.R.O.   X7725 album A. 'Book Rarities', p. 159.   [81] Scott, *Journal* (Edinburgh, 1890), vol. 2, p. 237.

'Inaccuracy destroys the fair reputation of an Editor', Pickering reminded Hartshorne mildly, 'and also the hopes and expectations of a poor publisher.'[82] The reluctant reviewer was Frederic Madden, whose copy of 'Ancient Metrical Tales', now in the British Library, contains the resounding testimonial: 'This is the *worst* edited volume of Old English Poetry I ever met with.' Madden received his subscription copy from Pickering on "January, and described it in his journal as 'a volume, which might have been made exceedingly curious, had common pains been bestowed on it. As it now appears, without Glossary, or Notes (for those to *Piers of Fulham* deserve not the name) and printed so incorrectly from the MSS. it is of little value.'[83]

Madden was himself to edit 'William and the Werwolf' for the Roxburghe Club in 1832, a volume which marks a new epoch in the scholarly editing of early texts. Madden sought to produce a faithful facsimile of the original, preserving contractions and leaving punctuation unaltered; Hartshorne, by contrast, added his own punctuation freely, and silently introduced conjectural readings. There is no way of distinguishing lacunae in the manuscript sources from passages which Hartshorne had been unable to decipher, as asterisks are used for both. Once again, Hartshorne's work represents an unsystematic, discursive approach to scholarship that was already becoming old-fashioned. He himself agreed that the work was incomplete without a glossary – he did not admit to the errors in the text – but blamed Pickering for its absence. 'I always intended to give one, but latterly I was so much hurried by him to publish, *he* could not wait, "as 50 copies were to be delivered to the Booksellers at New Years day" and as *I* was furnishing my house, and correcting sheets for the Book Rarities, it was obliged to come out in the present state.'[84]

The publication of the 'Book Rarities' in December 1829 marks the virtual end of Hartshorne's bibliographical career. He was now curate of Little Wenlock, Shropshire, where he was to remain until 1836; and his remoteness from London, from which proof sheets had to be sent to him in instalments, was one of the causes of the long delay in the book's publication, although Hartshorne, with more justification this time, preferred to blame Longmans for their 'extraordinary slowness'. His plans for further literary publications – a second collection of metrical romances, an edition of Walter de Mapes, an annotated edition of English Popular Tales, 'a complete edition of Skelton's works in two volumes' – did not bear fruit. As he admitted to Douce, they would require 'a residence in town . . . in the Royal Library or Museum', and although Hartshorne never lost hope of such a job he never received one.[85] In February 1845 he wrote to the Master of Trinity, William Whewell, expressing interest in the post of College Librarian, recently vacated by the resignation of James Ind Smith, but Whewell replied that although 'I should be happy to see you our Librarian' he could not lend his support to an outside candidate against a fellow of the College. Whewell's letter was cordial but firmly discouraging. The successful candidate, George Brimley, though not a fellow of Trinity, was a recent graduate who had competed twice, without success, in the fellowship

[82] Pickering to Hartshorne, 23 December 1829: N.R.O. X7225 album B no. 83.

[83] Madden's annotated copy: B.L. C.62.b.29. Madden's diary, Bodleian Ms. Eng. hiss. c.147 f.107.

[84] Hartshorne to Turner, 14 January 1829: T.C.C. O.14.3 no. 9.

[85] Hartshorne to Douce, 8 May 1827, 11 August 1828: Bodleian Ms. Douce d.26 f.32–33, 136–37.

examination.[86] His appointment in June 1845 ended what was probably Hartshorne's last chance of a career as a scholar-librarian – a career which he would almost certainly have preferred to that of a parish priest, and which he would almost certainly have achieved had it not been for the Heber affair. Throughout his life he was a prolific author of books and articles on local antiquities, but (with the exception of an edition of Fulke's 'Defence of the sincere and true translations of the Holy Scriptures' produced for the Parker Society in 1843) he never returned to the literary pursuits with which he had hoped to make his name. Hartshorne's failure to obtain a university post is a perfect illustration of the widening division between the amateur antiquarian and the professional academic.[87] The gap was perceptibly wider in the 1840s than it had been in the 1820s, when Madden and Hartshorne, despite their fundamentally different approaches, inhabited the same world – the world of the gentleman scholar – and competed on equal terms for the same jobs.

The Heber affair was no nine days' wonder. While Heber remained on the Continent, his old acquaintances in England speculated endlessly about his motives. In January 1830 John Payne, of the booksellers Payne and Foss, regaled Dibdin with an account of his recent meeting with Heber in Louvain. Heber was 'as gay, chatty, and amusing as ever!' wrote Dibdin to Lord Spencer.

He enquired after *all* his old *Roxburgh* friends, told John Payne that he had purchased a library of 12,000 volumes at Nuremberg – *all* printed in *the fifteenth century*! – and concluded by saying he should be in *England* as soon as *himself*. Meanwhile (to complete, if possible, the bizarrerie of his character) a civil law suit, for £2000, has been carried on against him, and he is, at this moment, *actually outlawed*![88]

Dibdin, it is clear, did not seriously believe that Heber would dare to return to England. Heber's arrival in England in the autumn of the following year thus came as a great surprise, and by no means an agreeable one. As Alexander Dyce reported to his brother-clergyman and fellow-antiquary John Mitford in September 1831:

Among the marvels of the present day, the bursting out of the volcano, &c. &c., the most marvellous is Heber's return to England! When I first heard it, I could not have been more startled by the intelligence that the Cholera was in London. I understand that his former friends and acquaintances have kept aloof; and it was reported that the members of the Athenaeum, on the event of his appearing there, were to receive him with the most marked coldness.

But Dyce was prepared to resume contact.

Finding that he had been asking Rodd sundry questions about me, I wrote to him forthwith, requesting the loan of a MS. poem by Skelton (who now occupies all my thoughts) and received the next day the most civil answer possible, informing me that it should be sent to Gray's Inn as soon as he returned from the country (whither he is going immediately) and that it would afford

---

[86] Whewell to Hartshorne, 19 February 1845: N.R.O. X7227, E600.

Robert Sinker, 'Biographical Notes on the Librarians of Trinity College' (Cambridge Antiquarian Society, 1897), pp. 69–70.

[87] See Philippa Levine, 'The Amateur and the Professional: antiquarians, historians and archaeologists in Victorian England 1838–1888' (Cambridge, 1986), p. 73.

[88] Dibdin to Spencer, 9 January 1830: B.L. Althorp G.336.

him the greatest satisfaction to contribute, as far as lay in his power, to the success of any of my undertakings. I have now nearly made up my mind that such an obliging gentleman could not be guilty of any thing atrocious.[89]

Heber's readiness to make his collections available thus provided the passport for his readmission into the community of gentleman scholars. He continued to frequent the salerooms, and Dibdin informed Lord Spencer in 1832 that he was 'now spoken to by most people'. Hartshorne even considered applying to him in 1831 when the living of Hodnet, which was in his gift, fell vacant, but thought better of it. Heber, however, was becoming increasingly reclusive in his habits, and by the end of 1832 the gout in his feet had left him practically bedridden. The 'severe cold on the chest' of which he complains in a letter of December 1832 was probably a symptom of the lung disorder, perhaps emphysema, which killed him nine months later. 'Heber's departure was rather a surprize to me', wrote Spencer to Dibdin, 'though I had heard that he looked very ill. What a strange life has his been! What is to become of the Books ?'[90]

Most of Heber's obituaries said little about the scandal. The *Gentleman's Magazine* treated it obliquely:

In the year 1831 he returned to England, but, alas! not into the society which he had left; living, with the exception of his visits to the auction-rooms and booksellers' shops, entirely secluded among his books at Pimlico or Hodnet.

The *Annual Register* repeated this passage, but with a significant addition. 'In the year 1831, he returned to England, but not into the society which he had left; for rumours had been in circulation degrading to his moral character.' It is surprising to find this alteration in what is otherwise a heavily condensed version of the obituary in the *Gentleman's Magazine*. I am tempted to conjecture that the *Annual Register*'s version derives directly from the author's manuscript, and that the extra clause was not added to the *Annual Register* but struck out from the *Gentleman's Magazine*. Be that as it may, other journals were not so reticent. Shortly after Heber's death, the *Morning Chronicle* published several articles in his defence. It was maintained that the scandal had been a 'diabolical method of raising a cry against poor Heber for not supporting his furious Anti-Catholic constituents at Oxford'. Heber's silence on the matter was treated as hyper-sensitivity: 'Shrinking from the notoriety which prosecution would obtain for him ... he adopted the unwise resolution of taking no notice of the imputation.'[91] Some of Heber's friends were evidently determined to clear his name. Some, it seems, considered that the libel case had been a betrayal. Much later, 'Don Leon: a Poem by the late Lord Byron', a scandalous but generally sympathetic account of homosexuality in high society, expressed this view. Though it implies that Heber was unjustly accused, the poem goes on to insinuate a

---

[89] Dyce to Mitford, 28 September 1831: Victoria and Albert Museum, 86.Y.100 (14).

[90] Park to Hartshorne, 3 March 1831: N.R.O. X7227 album E no. 91.
Heber to his sister Mary, 13 December 1832: Bodleian Ms. Eng. lett. d.204 f.94.
Spencer to Dibdin, 6 October 1833: Houghton Library,

Harvard, Ms. Eng. 1177.1 (4).

[91] *Gentleman's Magazine* January 1834, p. 108, and *Annual Register . . . of the* Year *1833* (1834), p. 246. *Morning Chronicle*, Thursday 24 October and Saturday 26 October 1833. Bliss continued to believe in Heber's innocence: Dibdin to Spencer, 4 November 1827: B.L. Althorp G.336.

scandalous connection between Heber's flight to the Continent and the subsequent suicide of his 'intimate friend' James Stanhope.

> Then friends shall shun him, and a venal press
> Shall seal in blackest types his wretchedness.
> Whilst some false lawyer, whom he called his friend,
> To damn his name his arguments shall lend.
> Shall take a brief to make his shame more clear,
> And drop his venom in a jury's ear.
> But had that tongue with earnest friendship glowed,
> His words had lighted, not increased the load;
> Had poured a balmy unguent on his sore,
> And chased mendacious slander from his door.
> So uncorked hartshorn, when its odour flies
> Forth from the phial, almost blinds the eyes;
> But, if the stopper is replaced with care,
> The scent diffused evaporates in air.[92]

The scandal was not forgotten. After the sale of Heber's library, it was rumoured that
Dibdin had discovered, and destroyed, a copy of Rochester's 'Sodom' among Heber's
books. But Heber himself was not forgotten by his friends. Many years later, in 1854, the
nonagenarian Dr Routh remembered him and spoke of him to a visitor a few days before
his death.[93] It is not recorded that he spoke of the scandal, but Routh's recollections testify to the fascination that the enigmatic character of Heber continued to exert over his
friends. Even after the details of the scandal had been forgotten, Heber was remembered,
passing into common currency as the archetype of the bibliomaniac, a man whose passion for books was a manifestation of a deeper abnormality – a concept of bibliomania
which remains current even today.[94]

Hartshorne died suddenly in March 1865, at the age of sixty-two. The following
August his books were sold at Sotheby's, and the follies and extravagances of his youth
– 'Bibliotheca Spenceriana' in blue morocco, Owen and Blakeway's 'History of
Shrewsbury' on large paper, and the author's own annotated and extra-illustrated copy
of the 'Book Rarities' – were exposed for sale alongside the historical and genealogical
reading of his more sober middle age. His books narrowly escaped the fire at Sotheby's
premises on 29 June 1865 – early reports stated that the collection had been completely
destroyed – but the destruction caused by the fire, which reduced the Offor library to
charred fragments, may explain why Hartshorne's books were sold as 'a portion' of his
library, while the fact that the books were sold 'not subject to return' on account of
water-staining may explain the low prices they fetched. The highest prices were made by
the sets of standard county histories like Eyton's 'Antiquities of Shropshire' (£11.5.0);

[92] 'Don Leon; A Poem by the late Lord Byron'
(London, 1866), p. 34. See also Louis Crompton, 'Byron
and Greek Love: Homophobia in 19th-century England'
(1985), pp. 352, 358.
[93] William A. Jackson, 'An Annotated List of the
Publications of the Reverend Thomas Frognall Dibdin'
(Cambridge, Mass., 1965), p. 51.

R. D. Middleton, 'Dr Routh' (1938), pp. 266–7.
[94] For Heber's posthumous reputation, see
Chambers's 'Book of Days', vol. 2 (1864), pp. 645–6. For
a humorous account of bibliomania as a pathological condition, see W. D. M. Paton, 'Bibliomania: a clinical case-
study' in THE BOOK COLLECTOR, vol. 37 no. 2 (1988).

the author's copy of the 'Book Rarities' went to Willis and Sotheran for £6.15.0. The wood-blocks for the 'Book Rarities' came up for auction probably from a trade source, at a miscellaneous sale at Hodgson's on 17–19 April 1866, and made £3.[95] It was a melancholy end to Hartshorne's scholarly labours, and a far cry from their confident beginning.

Less than a year before his death, however, Hartshorne had received an unexpected reminder of his past, when he was informed of his election to the Roxburghe Club.[96] Did he permit his mind to dwell for a moment on Douce's prophecy forty years before, on the friends of his youth, on Cambridge and its book rarities in the high noon of bibliomania? The irony is perfect. But Hartshorne's sense of irony, as I have suggested, was never very strong.

NOTES ON HARTSHORNE'S EARLY PUBLICATIONS

1. A Geyfte ffor the Neue Yere: or, A playne, plesaunte, and profytable Pathe = waie to the BLACK LETTRE Paradyse. [Title to second part:] Crumbes off conceyte to cache Black Lettre Boke = Louers: or, A Rare and Racie Repaste ffor a real Roxburgher. [Issued with:] Carmina Cornucervinia.
Three copies have been located:
   1. St John's College, Cambridge, A.3.83. Inscribed 'Henrico.Drury.Socio.Roxburgensis. Societatis.huncae.libellum.D.D.D.Carolus. Henricus. Hartshorne. only 20 copies printed.' Bound in later 19th-century morocco, gilt, with the bookplate of William Bell Scott.
   2. Bodleian Library, Oxford, Douce H.6. Inscribed 'To Francis Douce Esqr,. F.A.S. from C. H. Hartshorne. only 20 copies printed.' Bound in paper-covered boards (orange with gold chevrons), probably not contemporary, with Douce's bookplate laid down on front pastedown.
   3. British Library, 1080.a.42. Uninscribed.
   Other recipients included Dawson Turner, Thomas Amyot, and J. H. Markland. George Hibbert states (letter to Hartshorne, 29 January 1825, N.R.O. X7226 album C no. 85) that he received a copy 'with much pleasure and gratitude and being somewhat unreasonably ambitious of possessing Copies on Vellum I am most thankful that you have thought me worthy of "one out of the two".'

2. Ancient Metrical Tales: Printed Chiefly from Original Sources. Edited by the Rev. Charles Henry Hartshorne, M.A. 'Adeo sanctum est vetus omne poema.' London: William Pickering. MDCCCXXIX.
   1a. Ordinary copies. Published February 1829, at 12s. (*English Catalogue*)
   Primary binding of red glazed cloth with paper spine label 'ANCIENT | METRICAL | TALES. | EDITED BY | HARTSHORNE.' A copy in the University of British Columbia (Colbeck Collection PR10 K6 P5 1829) is bound in dark green pebble-grain cloth. Martin Routh's copy (University of Durham R XXIV.F.27) is bound in grey boards.
   The following presentation copies are known:

[95] *Notes and Queries*, 3rd series, vol. 8, p. 85. Hodgson's sale: copy in B.L. S. C. Hodgson, 1866.
[96] Clive Bigham, 'The Roxburghe Club: its history and its members, 1812–1927' (Roxburghe Club, Oxford, 1928), p. 68.

    1. Private collection, Cambridge. Inscribed 'To William Thornton Esqr. with the kind regards of the Editor.'

    2. Florida State University, Shaw Collection. Inscribed 'To Charles Guest Esqr. with the affectionate regards of his relation, The Editor. Little Wenlock Jany. 24. 1829.'

1b. Some copies have an additional four-leaf gathering, usually bound at the end of the book, with the heading 'THE DEMAUNDES JOYOUS.' and the imprint 'REPRINTED BY THOMAS WHITE, | JOHNSON'S COURT, | MDCCCXXIX.' The following ordinary copies contain it:

    1. Bodleian Library, Oxford, Douce P.176. Contemporary half calf, red marbled boards, spine gilt with title 'ANCIENT | METRICAL | TALES | ED. BY | HARTSHORNE.' This is listed in Douce's notebook of 'Lib. donat.' (Ms. Douce e.70) as a presentation copy from Hartshorne, but the entry is crossed out.

    2. Case Western Reserve University, Cleveland, Ohio. Inscribed 'T. Willement Esqr. With the publisher's kind regards.' Bound in modern cloth. The recipient is probably Thomas Willement (1786–1871), heraldic artist.

2. 'Large paper' (i.e. fine paper) copies. Twelve were printed, each with a limitation statement signed by Pickering on the front free endpaper. Of these the following have been located:

    no. 1. Cleveland Public Library, Cleveland, Ohio. Limitation statement removed when volume was rebound in 1960s.

    no. 6. Pickering and Chatto, London. Bound in blue glazed cloth.

    no. 9. Huntington Library, California. Bound in later morocco; from the library of Robert Hoe.

    Out of series. British Library, 11621.c.21. Bound in contemporary dark blue morocco, spine gilt and divided into six compartments with the title 'ANCIENT | METRI-CAL | TALES | HARTSHORNE' and at the foot 'LONDON 1829'.

    Of these copies, the British Library and Cleveland Public Library copies contain 'The Demaundes Joyous'.

    One large paper copy was presented by Hartshorne to David Laing (Hartshorne to Laing, 14 January 1829, E.U.L. La.IV.17).

3. The Book Rarities in the University of Cambridge. Illustrated by Original Letters, and Notes, Biographical, Literary, and Antiquarian. By the Rev. C. H. Hartshorne, M.A. London: Printed for Longman, Rees, Orme, Brown, and Green, Paternoster-Row; and J. and J. J. Deighton, Cambridge. 1829.

    1. Prospectus. 'In November, 1827, will be published, in one volume, octavo, Bibliographica Cantabrigiensia; or, Remarks upon the most valuable and curious Book-Rarities in the University of Cambridge. Illustrated by original letters, and notes biographical, literary, and antiquarian . . . A few copies will be printed on Large Paper to match "Bibliotheca Spenceriana," &c. for Subscribers only, who are requested to send their Names as early as possible to the publishers, Messrs. Longman, Rees, Orme, Brown, & Green, Paternoster-Row, London; or Messrs. Deighton, Cambridge.'

    Printed on the first recto of a bifolium; watermark 'CANSELL 1825'. Copies recorded:

    1. Sent by Hartshorne to Dawson Turner, 3 July 1827. Trinity College, Cambridge, O.14.1 no. 1.

    2. Sent by Hartshorne to Philip Bliss, 27 June 1827. British Library Add. Ms. 34569 f.436.

    2. Ordinary copies. Published December 1829, at 31s.6d. (*English Catalogue*) Primary binding of blue glazed cloth, yellow paper label 'THE | BOOK RARITIES | IN | THE UNIVERSITY | OF | 𝕮𝖆𝖒𝖇𝖗𝖎𝖉𝖌𝖊 | BY THE REV. | C. H. HARTSHORNE.' Copies located:

1. Florida State University.
2. Reference collection, Pepysian Library, Magdalene College, Cambridge.

The following copies are bound in variant cloth bindings:

1. University Library, Cambridge, Adv.c.77.30 (Henry Bradshaw's copy). Dark blue cloth, with a blind-stamped centre- and cornerpiece design, spine title 'HARTSHORNE'S | BOOK RARITIES | OF | CAMBRIDGE.' in gilt, yellow endpapers.
2. Glasgow University Library. Dark green cloth, spine with six compartments separated by blind-stamped double bands, with the title 'BOOK | RARITIES | | HARTSHORNE' in gilt in the second compartment.

Most surviving copies are bound in contemporary half calf or morocco, or in a modern binding. One presentation copy is recorded:

1. Yale University, Beinecke Library. Inscribed 'To Francis Danby Esq. With the best wishes of the Author.'

3. Large paper copies. Lowndes gives the price as £2.12.6, but a copy in Glasgow University Library (Ewing Collection) contains a receipt made out to 'The Honorable Mr. Baron Bolland. London Dec 4 1829. 1 Hartshorne's Book Rarities of the University of Cambridge. *Large paper* 3/13/6 *Subscriber's Copy*'. Primary binding as for ordinary copies, but approximately 27 cm. tall, compared to 22 cm. for an ordinary copy. Copies located:

1. University Library, Cambridge, SSS.28.20. (Ticket of F. Westley, Friar St., Shoemaker Row, near Doctors Commons.)
2. Lehigh University, Bethlehem, Pennsylvania.
3. Durham University Library, R.LXXIII.B5 (Martin Routh's copy). 'Mr Justice Park has sent me eleven excellent subscribers for l.p. His Royal Highness the Duke of Sussex, and Lord Spencer have transmitted me their names through their respective Librarians. I have not yet received the list from Longmans and Deightons, or exerted myself at all in Cambridge where there may be much to be done after the vacation. My own list counts hard upon thirty names for l.p. amongst which I beg to thank you for yours.' (Hartshorne to Dawson Turner, August 14 1827, Trinity College, Cambridge, o.14.1 no. 44.)

The book is listed in Deighton's catalogue of 'Books Published' (?1835) at £1.11.6, and in Deighton's catalogue of 'Works Published' (?1838) at 10s.6d. (See U.L.C. Cam.c.836.24 for copies of these catalogues.)

ACKNOWLEDGEMENTS

I should like to thank the libraries mentioned herein, for their assistance in answering queries and for their permission to publish extracts from manuscripts in their possession. I should particularly like to thank the staff of the Northamptonshire Record Office. I am also grateful to Dr Eric Glasgow, for drawing my attention to the material in the Kent Archives Office at Maidstone; to Mr Jeremy Maule, for reading this article in draft and making many suggestions for its improvement; and to Dr John Pickles, for placing his own notes on Hartshorne at my disposal.

PETER BEAL

'My Books are the Great Joy of My Life'
Sir William Boothby, Seventeenth-Century Bibliophile

T HE discovery in 1994 of four letterbooks among the Fonmon Castle archives on
deposit in the Glamorgan Record Office in Cardiff brings to light a wealth of
information about the activities of a virtually unknown Midlands bibliophile
of the late seventeenth century.[1] Sir William Boothby, first Baronet (1636–1707),[2] of
Broadlow Ashe and Ashbourne Hall, Derbyshire, was one of the scions of the Boothby
family before a later generation migrated to Wales, and his letterbooks are chance survival from that earlier period. Besides documenting his day-to-day activities as a rural
landowner, they establish clearly the depth and extent of his personal passion for books;
they document in remarkable detail his dealings with some notable London and
Midlands booksellers, not least Dr Samuel Johnson's father, Michael Johnson of
Lichfield; they illuminate book trade practices of the period; and they incidentally shed
light on a local circle of literate, if not literary, gentlemen in the Dove Dale area on the
Derbyshire–Staffordshire border some thirteen miles or so north-west of Derby,
including the poet and translator Charles Cotton the younger.[3]

The manuscripts themselves, which contain over 1100 pages in all, comprise
Boothby's personal diary, in octavo, for the period from 29 September 1676 until
23 March 1677, and three letterbooks in folio (containing copies of his outgoing letters)
for the periods from 29 March 1683 to 17 September 1686 and from 26 March 1688 to
28 September 1689. Most of the pages are written in Boothby's own distinctive, ungainly

[1] The existence of these letterbooks had been but
imperfectly reported earlier. A thirteen-page transcript,
made in the 1890s, of some of the letters to Michael
Johnson in the third of the volumes (from 3 October 1684
to 11 August 1685) was reported in 1949 to be among items
from the estate of Francis John Cope in the William Salt
Library, Stafford: see Aleyn Lyell Reade, 'Early Career of
Dr. Johnson's Father', *TLS*, 17 June 1949, p. 404. The
whereabouts of this transcript is at present unknown (it is
not in the Salt Library). Reade reported the whereabouts
of the original letterbook itself to be unknown. Then, in
The Times of 14 December 1953 (p. 10), a correspondent
('Some Johnsonian Addenda. Gleanings of American
Scholarship') reported that G. W. Beard and Professor
J. L. Clifford of Columbia University, New York, had
found the letterbook from April [actually March] 1683 to
September 1684 (the second of these volumes) at Fonmon
Castle. These references are cited in J. D. Fleeman's

posthumously published article 'Michael Johnson, the
"Lichfield Librarian"', *Publishing History*, 39 (1996),
23–44. A typed transcript of nineteen letters by Boothby
to Johnson in this letterbook, made by the Glamorgan
Record Office in 1962, may be found in the National
Register of Archives, Quality Court, NRA 21996.

[2] Besides all else, Boothby's diary enables us to establish his birthdate – or at least date of baptism – for he
records on 9 November 1676: 'This day I was happily
dedicated to my God in holy Baptisme 1637'. It should
also be noted that, although sometimes described as the
second Baronet, Boothby was technically the *first*, since
the patent of his father, Sir Henry Boothby, who was
nominated Baronet during the Civil War in 1644, never
passed the Great Seal.

[3] For Boothby's dealings with Cotton, see the
Appendix below.

hand; a portion of the letterbooks by a series of generally more legible amanuenses (including, perhaps, certain of the 'servants', 'scholars' or chaplains – capable of writing 'a very Good hand' – whom he seeks to hire in some of the letters represented in these very manuscripts). With their acquisition in 1995 by the British Library[4] (where they are now classified as Additional MSS 71689–71692), the diary and letterbooks have become readily available to scholars and bibliographers, who are likely to find there a rich source of new information about the book trade in this period. What follows is no more than a brief introduction to some points of interest which happen to have struck me.

Boothby himself was a respectable and wealthy member of the landed gentry of Derbyshire, where, after being knighted at the Restoration, he served as Sheriff in 1661–62 and on the Grand Jury in the Assizes of 1682.[5] He bought Ashbourne Hall and the manor of Ashbourne in 1671 from the minor poet (and friend of Charles Cotton) Sir Aston Cokayne (1608–84).[6] Boothby was twice married, his second wife, Hill Brooke (1640–1704), whom he married in 1657, being occasionally mentioned in his letterbooks ('my wife desires you to subscribe for her to Mr Mantons new Booke', he writes, for instance, on 24 May 1683, and on 6 January 1676/7 he pays an especially warm tribute to what a 'Jewel!' and 'Treasure' she was after nineteen years 'in her sweet and good society'). They had several children, some of whom are also mentioned in the letterbooks, as are various other members of their family, not to mention many of their extensive social connections among the gentry, including, for instance, Sir John Gell, the Earl of Rutland and the Earl of Devonshire (whom Boothby visited at Chatsworth for several days in November 1676).

Among all the estate, financial and family business with which his journal and letterbooks are concerned, not the least of Boothby's preoccupations was bookbuying. 'My Books are the great joy of my life', he tells Cotton on 21 July 1685, and it is a sentiment expressed on more than one occasion. 'My greatest pleasure is in bookes – and indeed my business and I make and keepe collections of all comes out', he said on 29 January 1683/4. And on one occasion, on 18 May 1685, we can almost hear the sigh of relief when he writes: 'My company is Gone so that now I hope to enjoy my selfe & Bookes againe, wch are the true pleasures of my life, all else is but vanity & noyse'.

The result of this passion recorded in these manuscripts is some scores of letters to booksellers, in which he orders, or considers ordering, hundreds of specified books, pamphlets and gazettes between 1676 and 1689. Although inclining especially towards theological subjects, his tastes extend to virtually the whole spectrum of publications in this period – from the classics, philosophy, history, geography, travel, law, medicine,

[4] The four manuscripts were offered for sale by Sir Brooke Boothby at Sotheby's on 25 July 1995, lot 29, and sold to Bernard Quaritch Ltd for £29,900. The British Library subsequently purchased them under Export Licence regulations on 14 September 1995. Sotheby's offered the remainder of the Fonmon Castle archive by private treaty sale to the Glamorgan Record Office.

[5] See the *Complete Baronetage*, ed. G. E. C[okayne], new edn introduced by Hugh Montgomery-Massingberd (Gloucester, 1983), III, 82; Burke's Peerage; John Nichols, *The History and Antiquities of the County of Leicester* (London, 1795–1811), Vol. IV, Part 1 (1807), p. 179; Stephen Glover, *The History and Gazeteer of the*

County of Derby, 2 vols (Derby, 1831–3), II, 35; and Mrs L. Bazeley, *The Family of Boothby* (1915). Nichols and Glover are cited by A. L. Reade, *loc. cit.*

[6] Cokayne was author of three plays, a masque, and a collection of poems, *Small Poems of Divers Sorts* (London, 1658), as well as of an autograph verse notebook now in the Beinecke Library at Yale University (Osborn Collection b 275). His poems give a clear indication of his wide literary circles, both London and provincial, and they include numerous eulogistic tributes to his 'most honoured cousin Mr. Charles Cotton the younger' and other members of Cotton's family.

rhetoric and poetry, through general bibliographical materials (such as Moxon's *Mechanic Exercises* and 'Instructions for a Library by Naudeus') to current miscellaneous social topics (including the likes of 'The Tenne pleasures of marrage' and 'Confession of a maried Couple') and the latest political and ecclesiastical debates, speeches and trials, as well as a variety of prints, maps, atlases and dictionaries – and one could almost draw up a list of topical publications at any particular time from his references alone. Boothby is seen constantly requesting from booksellers their latest catalogues of books available, complete with prices (with occasional references to specific collections, such as the 'Catalogue of the study of Books' Michael Johnson bought in October 1684); pestering them for more information about particular titles he has seen listed or advertised, and for news of forthcoming publications ('I would know what of Eminent there is in the presse', he writes repeatedly); and clamouring no less for [Chiswell's] 'weekely memorialls about Bookes', for regular Term Catalogues, and for catalogues of forthcoming book auctions.

A deeply religious man, who occasionally gives expression to pious meditations, comments on sermons heard, and declares (on 6 January 1676/7) 'I this day finished the reading over the holy *Bible*, oh how great doth my soule delight in it, I find more pleasure in reading it then in any Booke besides', Boothby was often drawn to remark, not surprisingly, on reading matter of a theological nature. Nevertheless, his wide range of tastes, not to mention avid bibliographical curiosity, are more than evident in his frequent comments, requests and criticisms relating to both these and other kinds of books. A brief sampling of them follows:

[24 November 1676] . . . I began Stonhams parable of the Tenne virgins in 4° 1676 – but found it not worth my reading . . .

[11 December 1676] . . . I read over Mr [Anthony] *Hornecks* book of consideration tis an excellent good & pious Booke I intend much to read & meaditate in that . . .

[10 April 1683] . . . *the news letter mentions a new booke of Dryden in Justification of this new play ye D: of Guize pray send it* . . .

[26 June 1683] . . . *the Christian Tutor is a little peace well Expressed I would know whether the Author hath nothing else in print* . . .

[11 December 1683] . . . I would know what the designe of Mʳ [Charles] *Blounts new booke is*, and whether in English or Latine . . .

[29 January 1683/4 . . . Bookes with Cutts must be considered . . . I could wish hee [Blount] would translate Heroditus that antient Greeke Historian . . . I like very well the new Survay the state of vrop [Europe] you sent . . .

[18 September 1688] . . . yᵉ treatice of tradition is done Incomparably: I Long for the 2ᵈ part – pray who is Judged yᵉ Author, and who is meant by R:H: Author of yᵉ Guide – and by Mr M: offten mentioned therein . . .

[26 January 1688/9] . . . send the Rehearsall an old play by the Duke of Buckingham . . . [&] the character of a Trimmer [by George Savile, Earl of Halifax] (this is an Excellent peece) . . .

[5 February 1688/9] . . . Dʳ Caves Large fol: Scriptorum Ecclesiasticarum (be sure to send with all speed, for I very much Longe to see it . . .

As may be seen, his overwhelming desire to be *au courant* by no means excludes 'literary' works, including poetry and publications by women. Among his lists of requests are such items as 'mis An: Ben: [Aphra Behn] Poems new', 'Miltons poems & discourses in 8°', 'Bakers [Jane Barker's] poeticall Recreations 8°', further works by Dryden ('Drydans Poemes on the kings Death', 'History of the League' and 'Xaviers Life'), 'Miscellany poems', and (in early 1689) 'New Booke of Songes & poems about ye government 8°'. In addition he orders 'Baxters Poeticall fragments', Henry Vaughan's *Thalia Rediviva*, John Oldham's *Poems and Translations*, 'Evelins Translation of Lucretius', 'felthams Reso[l]ves', Foxe's Book of Martyrs, Samuel Daniel's *Collection of the History of England* and John Trussell's *Continuation*, Filmer's *Patriarcha*, and Urquhart's Rabelais, as well as a variety of works by Bacon, John Selden, Joseph Hall, George Wither, Thomas Browne, Jeremy Taylor, Dugdale, Rushworth, Tillotson, Stillingfleet, and others. If he refuses to purchase a new volume of works by Margaret Cavendish, Duchess of Newcastle, on 6 November 1683, it is because, as he says on 23 October and 27 November, he has 'allredy three Voll: of them' and 'because her works are very deare'.

Boothby used two booksellers consistently during these years, both of whom he occasionally visited in person. One was Richard Chiswell (1639–1711), at the Rose and Crown, St Paul's Churchyard, London, whom he first mentions in late September 1676, commenting on 2 October: 'I write to *Chiswell*, that his rates for Books were very deere & many bound in sheep[,] to continue *his weekly Gazetts* . . .'. It is characteristic of the diverse roles played by publishers and booksellers in this period, as well as of the nature of Boothby's personal relationship with him, that Boothby did not hesitate to call on Chiswell for other services besides delivering books. As well as wanting him also to supply the common commodities of stationery ('my wife desires you to send her 2 or 3 quire of gilt paper in 8°', he requests on 19 June 1683), he expected Chiswell to act as his virtual money broker. 'I would you could put out the 400^l in yr hands for me', he writes on 6 June 1683, 'for I am desirous to have some moneys to lye ready at London, upon any occasion: nor must it Lye dead for it is my younger childrens portion'. Chiswell acts as his agent to pay a series of bills of others (on 27 July 1683, for example); he is called upon to find cheap lodgings in Lincoln's Inn when Boothby gets ready to come to town in August 1685; and is even enjoined, on 21 May 1684, to buy him tea ('of the best though deare, ffor I cannot drinke bad . . . and I can not live without it'). In one of Boothby's typical haggles over monetary matters, on 17 November 1684, he pays Chiswell the compliment of saying: 'I was resolved you should have had my greatest custome, being a person I have a great respect for and good opinion of, though I allways thought you a deere seller for I have paid for my Experience, so that I cannot be a stranger to bookes'.

His other regular, nearer home (25 miles to the south), was the young Michael Johnson (1656–1731), of Lichfield, Staffordshire, with whom he had dealings from at least April 1683 onwards.[7] Cautiously he enjoined him to 'send no Bookes (onely the Titles & prices) till you have my order', but set up an account with him on 4 August 1683, to pay him quarterly on a regular basis. By the following 29 January he wished to know

---

[7] For the most recent account of Michael Johnson, see Fleeman, *loc. cit.*

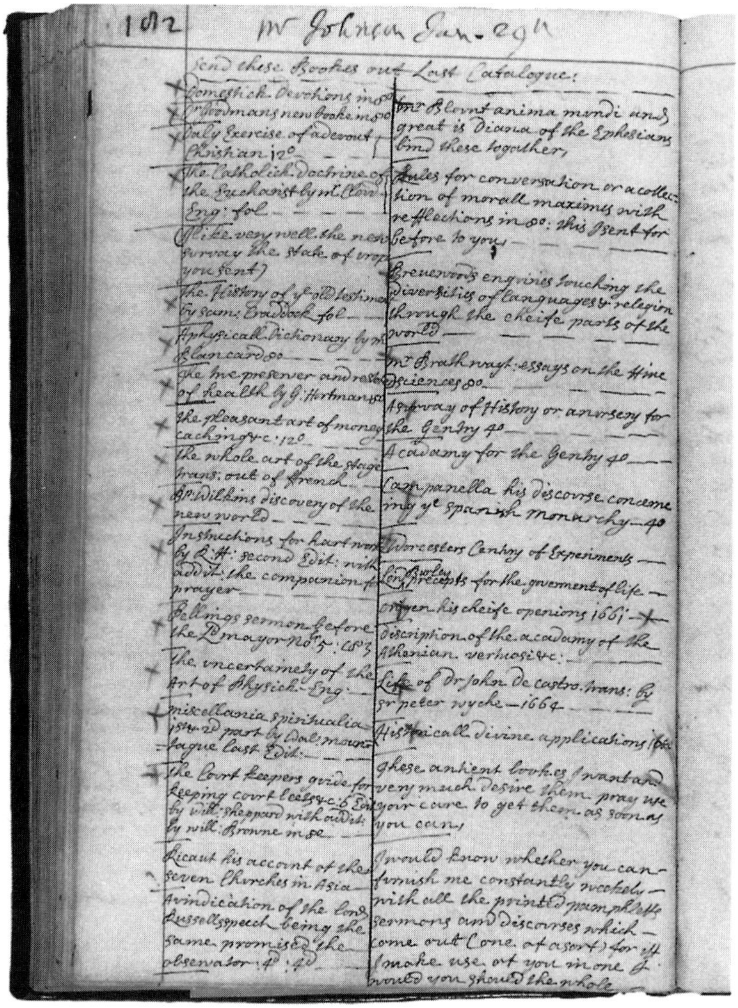
1012 Mr Johnson Jan. 29th

Send these Bookes out Last Catalogue:

Domestick Devotions in 8o
Dr Woodmans new booke in 8o
Daily Exercise of a devout Christian 12o
The Catholick doctrine of the Eucharist by Mr Clon: Eng: fol
(I like very well the new survay the state of Europe you sent)
The History of ye old testament by sam: Craddock fol
A physicall dictionary by Mr Blancard 8o
the true preserver and restorer of health by G: Hartman 8o
the pleasant art of money catching &c 12o
the whole art of the stage trans: out of French
Dr Wilkins discovery of the new world
Instructions for heart worke by R.H: second Edit: with addit: the companion for prayer
Bellings sermon before the Ld mayor Nov 5: 683
The uncertainety of the Art of Physick Eng
miscellanea spiritualia 1st & 2d part by Wal: montague last Edit:
The Court keepers guide for keeping court leets &c: 6 Edit: by will: Sheppard with addit: by will: Browne in 8o
Ricaut his account of the seven Churches in Asia
A vindication of the Lord Russells speech being the same promised the observator 4o 4d

Dr Blount anima mundi and great is Diana of the Ephesians bind these togither,
Rules for conversation or a collection of morall maximes with reflections in 8o: this I sent for before to you
Brerewoods enquiries touching the diversities of languages & religion through the cheife parts of the world
Mr Brathwayt: essays on the five sciences 8o
A survay of History or a nursery for the Gentry 4o
A cadamy for the Gentry 4o
Campanella his discourse concerning ye Spanish monarchy 4o
Worcesters Century of Experiments
Lord Burley Precepts for the government of life
Osborn his cheife opinions 1661
discription of the academy of the Athenian vertuosi &c:
Life of Dr John de castro trans: by sr peter wyche 1664
Historicall divine applications &c
these antient bookes I want and very much desire them pray use your care to get them as soon as you can,
I would know whether you can furnish me constantly weekely with all the printed pamphletts sermons and discourses which come out (one of a sort) for if I make use of you in one I would you should the whole

PLATE I

whether Johnson could furnish him 'constantly weekely with all the printed pamphletts sermons and discourses which come out'. As with Chiswell, Boothby turned to Johnson for a variety of other services besides. He consults him, for instance, on 15 April 1684, about finding a suitable chaplain and tutor for his household ('. . . a truly pious and holy man, learned & ingenious, who knows Bookes and men . . .'); pursues Johnson with queries about the Frenchman teaching in Lichfield who might be engaged to tutor his son Brooke in French (29 November 1684), and, in the following January, about a certain Mr Pike, scholar, in Uttoxeter (ten miles to the south-west of Ashbourne and where Johnson occasionally set up a stall); and, even as late as 13 August 1689, he presses Johnson urgently to find him a suitable 'servant' ('. . . you may very well heare of one at London – a Gentell person civill, a good Scholar & who writtes a very Good hand . . .').

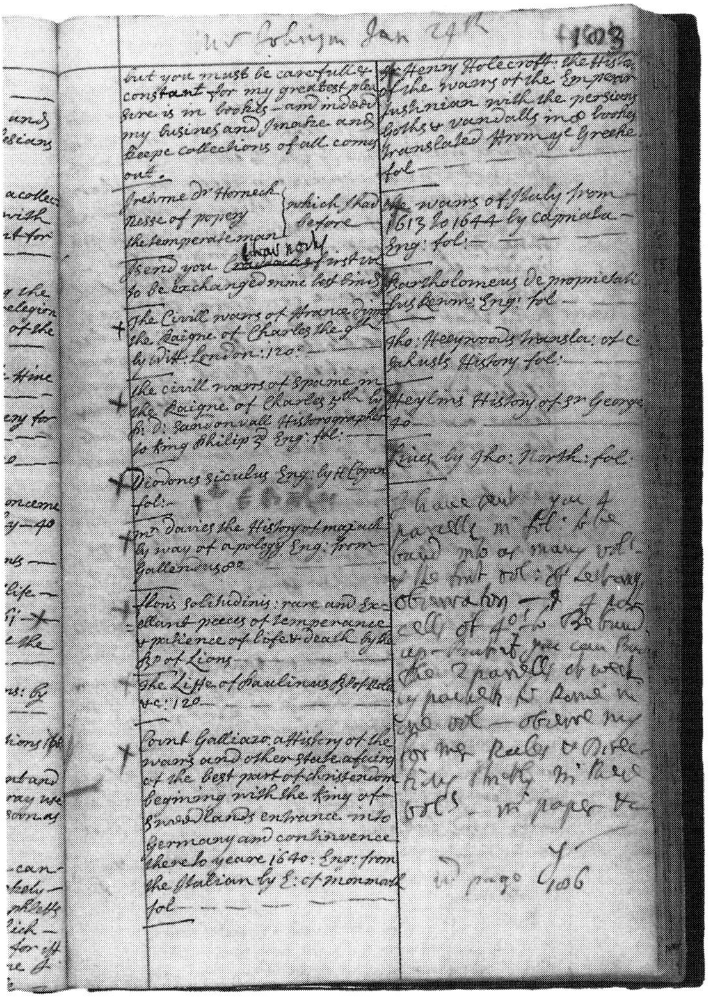

PLATES I–II. Two pages of Boothby's order to Michael Johnson on 29 January 1683/4, chiefly in the hand of an amanuensis, with Boothby's autograph corrections and his additions at the end. British Library, Additional MS 71690, pp. 182–3. Each page *c.* 296 × 191 mm.
Reproduced by Permission of the British Library Board.

By the same token, he gets Johnson to find him lodgings in Lichfield, on 23 October 1683 (but complains they are too near the school where the choristers 'are taught to singe which is a great disturbances'); consults him about picture-framing; and – taking advantage of yet another customary service offered by booksellers – uses him as a postal agent (sending papers to him, for the Irish packet at Lichfield, on 26 June 1683).

Boothby did not, however, restrict his custom to these two booksellers alone – although, for all his complaints to the contrary, they seem to have remained his two most dependable suppliers. Others represented in the letters include, notably, the provincial booksellers John Smith of Coventry, whom he approached on 20 October 1684 ('. . . I have some thoughts of trading with you . . .'), and Richard Davis (*fl.* 1646–88) of Oxford, with whom he placed orders from at least November 1684 onwards. By August 1688 Boothby seems to have depended less upon Chiswell for supplies from London, and to have transferred his regular custom to Joseph Watts, at the nearby Angel in St Paul's Churchyard. In haggling over prices, he cites the terms he had always received from Chiswell (who had charged carriage at the rate of 6*d.* per £1), and enjoins Watts to take care over letters sent to him, and to deliver stationery items as specified, including 'some Black and some Red lead penes of the best sort' and '6 or 8 quier of french paper' ('. . . you may have the rite sort at the french Bookseller in Salisbury Exchange – for that you sent formerly was not rite . . .'). Neither is Watts, as Boothby's new factotum, spared the responsibility of getting chocolate sent to him, or even of having someone call on his French tailor in Long Acre. Nor, indeed, is Watts exempt from implied criticism about his deficient solicitude on Boothby's behalf ([6 November 1688] '. . . I am well pleased in what you sent Last Saterday yet I find in other hands in the Country what I want and desire . . .').

Other dealers who get an occasional mention include Robert Clavell (*fl.* 1658–1711), in St Paul's Churchyard, from 5 March 1688/9 onwards; Richard Bentley (*fl.* 1675–97), of the Post House, Russell Street, from whom he orders the Fourth Folio of Shakespeare on 11 September 1688; and 'the ffrench bookseller in yᵉ Middle Exchange in yᵉ Strand', from whom, on 25 December 1688, he wants 'yᵉ Large ffrench Historicall Dictionary in 2 Vol in folio'.

As for what kind of client Boothby proved to be, his letters are susceptible to more than one interpretation. On the one hand, from a bookseller's point of view, there is every reason to believe that Boothby was both demanding and difficult. From start to finish, his letters provide a litany of complaints about bad service, neglect, and innumerable mistakes on the part of booksellers, not to mention his endless carping about what he considered to be the excessive prices they charged. Some characteristic instances of his quibbles and haggling on this last score are as follows:

[26 June 1683] . . . your little bookes bound onely plaine Calve are very deare, I never paid but 1ˢ apeace for such . . .

[14 July 1683] . . . & againe I take notice yr plane Twelpenny Books are at 16ᵈ wch I will not give . . .

[15 August 1683] . . . The 8° Books are so to deare That I desire them Either in quiers or stich'd – & yr other Books are Dearer then I can have them at my owne Doore . . .

[10 October 1684] . . . you allow :07ˢ:9ᵈ short in those bookes sent in may last, which is very hard consedering the few I returne out of so great a value of bookes bought . . . for – of those many bookes printed by you – I yet never was presented wᵗʰ any in the biying of above 400ˡ worth of books, and the only booke returned in all this trade was only a bible of about :3ˡ odd which I could not get you to accept of but was forced to take it againe or have nothing for my money . . .

Certainly frugality is not the least of Boothby's concerns here ('[Brian] Waltons poliglott (whether you can get me one at second hand cheep . . .)', on 10 November 1684, is a not untypical request). Yet, as we shall see, he was extremely fussy about his requirements, and his constant exhortations amount almost to a form of badgering, so that he might well be seen as a man who wanted things both ways – the maximum quality of service at the very minimum price – and there is more than a hint to be found here that booksellers may have found him somewhat tiring. For one thing, while quick to claim what is due to him, he always seems surprised to learn from booksellers that he owes them money, and we might note the occasional contradiction in his behaviour when, for instance, he claims, in excuse for non-payment – and despite the perpetual urgency of his importunities for new deliveries – that he has not yet had time to examine his latest parcel of books received ([20 May 1684] '. . . yet I cannot get time to Examine it, and my occasions call mee to London for a month . . .'). Despite Boothby's declared insistence that all their accounts should be absolutely clear – if only, as he says on 10 October 1684, to avoid running 'the greatest hazard iff you should dye, and myselfe allso (as wee are both mortall)' – we can sense the degree of Chiswell's uneasiness about the amount of debt outstanding when Boothby retorts, on 17 November: 'others who had my Custome before (as Mʳ Rooper [Abel Roper, *fl.* 1638–80] in fleetstreet) did the same willingly for more yeares then you have done it and never maide any complaint, though great sums of money had passed his hands . . .'. Nor, in his attempts to make them take him seriously, is he entirely averse to playing one bookseller off against another – as when he tells Johnson, on 25 November 1684: 'Mr chiswell is very angry I lye from him – if you could be constant in getting up the pamphletts Every weeke that come out, I rather desire them from you'. Symptomatically, he tells Johnson on 20 January 1684/5, 'I am afraid you grow weary of my custome', reminding him on 18 September 1688, 'if you Expect my Custome you must use me well, for I will make good pay', and there are times when he has to remind most of his suppliers that he is an important, regular, and profitable client, whose 'Custome is great'. The tone and persistency of these reminders do make one wonder whether the dealers entirely shared that view.

On the other hand, it has to be said that he does seem to have had much to complain about. From the – admittedly biased – evidence of these letterbooks, the dealers appear to be somewhat less than models of efficiency. Can they be exonerated altogether from quite so much neglect, inattentiveness, lack of communication, delays in delivery, inadequate packaging, disregard of binding instructions, and mistakes of every kind that we find reported here?

[19 April 1683] . . . I rec: both the parcells yesterday – But the first was *broken* by the carrier – & many Books much injured. some must be bound againe . . .

[26 June 1683] . . . I have much more worke for you – But am discouraged by yr slow returnes of those sent you . . .

[15 August 1683] . . . Those come out constantly weekely or monthly I desire punctually . . . you some times send some onely (as one packet) & other times none & so 'tis a great trouble to looke what is wanting &c & the Gazetts sometimes mistaken . . .

[23 November 1683] . . . you take no notice of the bookes I ordered you to send to my Lady Whitmore, iff your greater occasions will not give you time to looke to such little things, pray let your youngest prentice doe it . . .

[23 September 1684] . . . I find all or most are old Books – new Bound – & so many Leaves not cutt & most cutt narrow – & some Books part of the margett are cutt – all wch are great faults – An ill

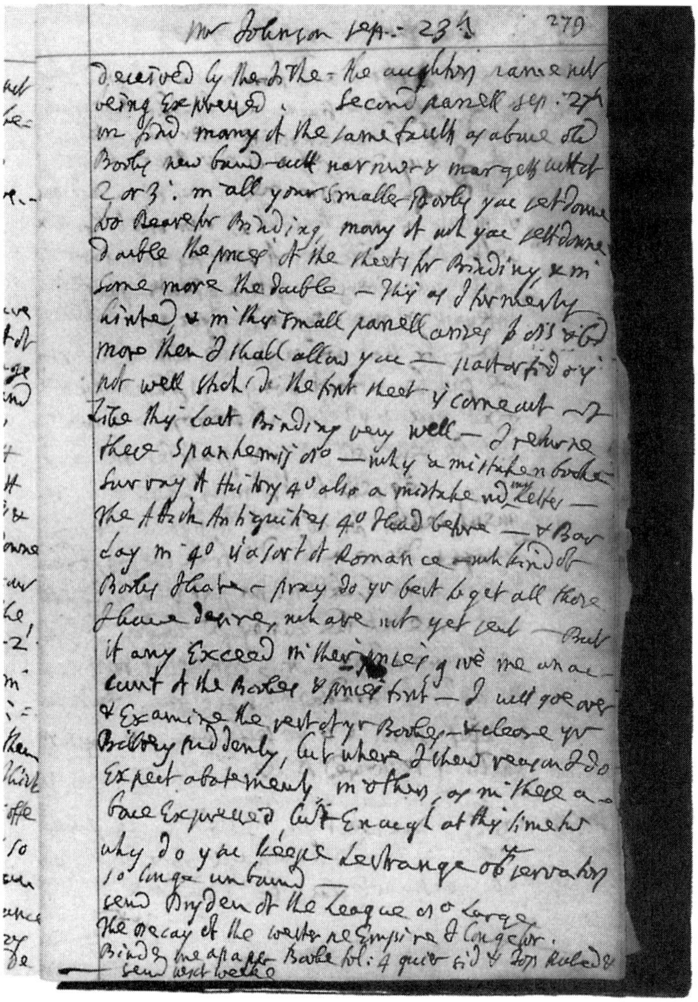

PLATE III. A page of Boothby's autograph letter to Michael Johnson, 23 September 1684.
British Library, Additional MS 71690, p. 279. *c.* 296 × 191 mm.
Reproduced by Permission of the British Library Board.

& weake past board (great fault this) you set downe to deape for binding . . . Helmott hath 2 or 3 leaves misplaced in Binding (you must take great care in Examining & placing things rite, before you send them to me) . . . pastor fido is not well stiched the first sheet is come out . . .

[14 October 1684] . . . yr Books do open very ill, so that it is troublesome reading pray mend this great fault . . .

[18 September 1688] . . . You have Cutt ye Little Bible into ye Letters so that it is much worse then it was, and I had better have given you 4^s Not to have Medled with it, then two shilling for making it of Little use . . .

[19 March 1688/9] . . . your Books are not so well bound as formerly – ye passeboard is very weak (wch is a great fault) and the Leather not well pollished . . .

In the matter of delayed deliveries, besides insisting upon the receipt of at least one parcel every week, Boothby is constantly having to request dealers to get their apprentices to check on his previous letters to 'see what is yet unsent', and more than once he sends the same orders two or three times to make sure that they get through. Indeed, in the frustration clearly expressed in his harangues, we can perceive quite vividly Boothby's sense of what it was to be isolated in the provinces at this time: his sense of detachment from the great world of affairs in London, his more than eager desire to keep up with the current news and debates available to other informed gentlemen of his class, and his reluctant, but unavoidable, dependence on the good will of booksellers, who prove to be so often unreliable.

M^r watts. Jan 26/88 I find that you are in great Bussness so that I cannot Expect you should spare so much time as to Collect prints, or take notice to Answer my letters . . . I will Ease you of the trouble for I am sure I have not a 3^d part of what comes out by what I see in other hands and here of . . . you have noe Excuse – however you know your own Bussness . . . you have omitted sending the weekley Intelligences . . . the above are in most Gentlemens hands and in Coffy houses Long since, and many more wch I have forgott . . .

Whatever the justice of his complaints, we see reflected in Boothby's dealings a variety of trade practices of the period, as well as his own specific requirements as an enthusiastic bibliophile. Indeed, we might observe that it is precisely because he is so isolated in the provinces that we have this extensive recorded witness to his tastes, desires, and assumptions about book buying, which might otherwise have been more readily expressed, in direct personal transactions, by word of mouth.

For one thing, some form of approval system seems to have operated. At least, Boothby did not hesitate to return (presumably after reading in part) books he did not like after all. 'I returne [James Harrington's] occeana as too dense & Du: of newcastles plays fol', he writes to Johnson on 8 January 1683/4, for instance, and on 24 February 1684/5 says: 'I returne Mathers booke, I like not the author'. Indeed, there are a great many returns recorded in these pages – many because of defects ([19 August 1684] '. . . The Historicall account of Varcelles I pray Exchange for 'twas blemished before it came to me . . .'); some because of misunderstandings ([23 September 1684] '. . . Bacons advancement I returne as having it before, I was deceived by the title – the aughtors name not being Expressed . . .'); but a number simply because he seems to have changed his mind about their desirability. In addition – despite his implied and no doubt sincere ambition to build up a great library for posterity – he was prone to occasional culling of duplicates ('. . . I have a great many bookes double &c folios: 4os & 8os unblemished', he tells Johnson on 5 February 1683/4), and was willing to trade in unwanted books for credit ('. . . I would know what you would allow me a sheet for them and consider I have bookes and not ready mony for them . . .').

Improvements to his library included replacing old editions of standard works with more up-to-date ones. So, for instance, on 6 November 1683, he tells Johnson, 'I have sent you my old Josephus, and desire you to send me one of the last and best Edition'; sends him, on 19 August 1684, 'cowells Interpreter in 4° to be Exchanged for that in fol. with manleys Additions'; and, on 19 March 1688/9, informs him: 'I would know

whether their be not a late & Good Edition of Livy with a table, I have the old and Trans:
by Holland and if their be a better I desire to Exchange it'. It is because of his particular-
ity in the choice of editions that he can complain, on 25 November 1684, 'The Theatrum
Historicum you sent is not the Best Edit: That I saw at mr Blunts was printed at
Amsterdam upon larger & better paper a better character'; and, a fortnight later, on
9 December, can return to Johnson 'Burtons maloncoly . . . being deare and there is a
much better Edition'.

In nothing, however, is Boothby more particular than in matters of binding – a subject which occupies a fair amount of discussion in his letters to booksellers. Some of his
special requirements and concerns can be gauged from these typical instructions and
complaints:

[10 April 1683] . . . I haue some thoughtes to haue my Bookes onely Bound well, & plaine)
Because the Guilding on Backs in'hances the price) & to try some Binders what I could get the
Guilding on the Backs done for.

[19 April 1683] . . . I find a great many small Books 10 or 12 in one parcell – I would either have 2
or 3 (of agreing subjects) bound together – or else have such bound onely plaine in calve – for this
Binding doubles the price & more fro[m] 10^d plaine to 1^s 10^d . . . I would have no books bound with
guilt backs but such as are above 2^s or 2^s 6^d price in quires, onely in plaine calve . . .

[24 April 1683] . . . Mr Johnson I have rec: the *Books*, & like the Binding very well – But thinke the
prices very deepe – I would haue all the B. you Bind for me wch are above 2^s price in quires –
Bound as those vol: of playes you did for my sonne James guilt & lettered on the Back – I thinke
them very well done – & cheape at 2^s a vol . . .

[6 November 1683] . . . *I have allso sent you ffive parcells of follio pamphlets to be bound in as many
Vol:* pray be very carefull of them to keep them soe that none be lost or misplaced (other then now
in) bind them strong and plaine and a sheet of white paper sometimes at the end of any large
Pamphlet, and three sheets at the begining and three sheets at the end of Every vol: lettered
behind according to the Notes and papers tyed upon Every parcell (and remember my rule as to
cutting them and leaveing large Margents, though many be not Cutt for the backs stand only to
be seen, *I have allso sent you Eleven parcells of sermons to be bound in as many Vol:* place Halph a
sheet of white paper at the end between Every sermon and 2 sheets at the begining and 2 sheets at
the end of Every Vol: and lettered one the backs according to the notes, be very carefull in these
bindings . . .

[29 January 1683/4] . . . by the by I find your binding not so neat as at the ffirst nor so well polished and I feare that oyle you use will suddenly weare of and prove rather a blemish then a
beauty . . .

[19 August 1684] . . . The Guilding is very apt to come off pray take care to mend this great fault
. . .

[31 July 1688] . . . all books which are under 18^d in Sheets Send unbound, and I after will bind them
2 or 3 together . . .

An interesting recurrent theme in his binding instructions is the specific use of
Boothby's arms and crest.

[5 February 1683/4] . . . you may remember I sent you a booke of Cambridge binding for a pat-
terne, pray mend this for I designe my bookes for posterity, I send you my armes and creast the

next folios you send me asw[ell] 4° put them upon them: vix the armes on the folios and the creast on the 4° – and your lowest rates for it . . .

At one point (on 15 April 1684) he orders 'A Common prayerbooke in 8° best character and my Arms on one side of it and my crest on the otherside (this is for my daughter Boothby)'; but eschews the expense of having his arms on lesser kinds of publication, such as collections of miscellaneous pamphlets.

An example of Boothby's crest stamped in gilt on calf is found on the covers of one of these very letterbooks (the third volume, BL Add. MS 71691: see Plate IV). It comprises, technically, a lion's paw (or jamb) erased and erect, with the shield of Ulster pendant from the surrounding foliage.

Not, of course, that Boothby was always satisfied with binders' workmanship in the execution of these arms. 'The Armes on one Booke are wronge set on – generally all the Armes not well and cleare', he tells Johnson on 23 September 1684, for instance. By 27 June 1688, he learns the disadvantage of this particular bibliophiliac indulgence when he grumbles about not being able to return one book he doesn't want because 'my Armes are on it'. Besides trying to get this job too done on the cheap, he dreams up the scheme, at one point, of getting Johnson to hire a bookbinder to undertake a huge, mass-production, quality – controlled operation *in situ*.

[11 September 1688] . . . I designe to make all my Bookes Sutable by Guilding yᵉ Backs, and Lettering them . . . and puting on my Armes . . . So that I have Some thoughts to have a Booke=binder come ore and do all yᵉ worke under my owne Eye and direction (for those many Mistakes in your binding up of my pamphlets hath discuraged me much) I would know whether you can help me to a Good worke man, and if he Come ore I will a greed with him.

Judging by the continuance of his somewhat reluctant orders to Johnson for further binding tasks, it seems (not altogether surprisingly) that this particular plan did not come to fruition.

Boothby's fastidious directions for binding also extend to other kinds of book. In an order on 19 December 1688, he requests, for instance, 'a Goldsmiths Almanack for my Pockett bound in vellum and Guilt with Clasp'; while earlier, on 26 June 1683, he sends Johnson 'a Reame of paper Ruled, wch I desire you to Bind into one volume, well & han-somely – Guilt Back – & lettered viz – *A Comon place Booke*'. Typically, the execution of this task too proves unsatisfactory:

[6 November 1683] Mr Johnson – yours I Reced . . . *the paperbooke which you bound* (it being use-less becaus of the thicknesse which your o[w]ne reasen might have convinced you of and saved me this Charge) *I desire you will bind it new into two vol:* butt doe not cutt the leaves new (ffor in all my bound bookes be sure to observe this constant rule as to leave as large a margant as possable rather let some leaves be left uncutt then losse a haires breadth ffor the fflatnes and breadth of a booke is very gracefull besides the useffullnes of the margent) . . .

Neither does Boothby seem to have had much luck with other orders for blank writing books. 'The paper booke was not good paper', he writes, on 14 October 1684; it 'will not beare inke well'. Though perhaps, in this regard, we should not discount the relative suc-cess of the very letterbooks under consideration. The third volume (Add. MS 71691), in

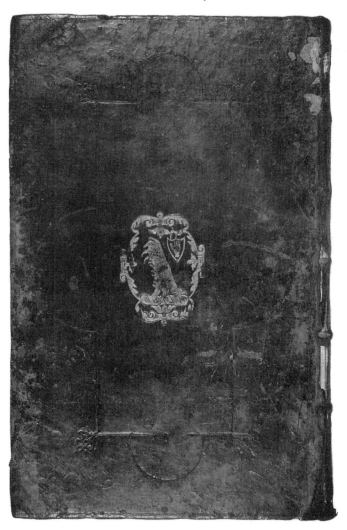

PLATE IV. The lower cover of Boothby's letterbook for 1684–6 with his crest in gilt.
British Library, Additional MS 71691. Cover *c.* 317 × 212 mm. Crest *c.* 75 × 60 mm.
Reproduced by Permission of the British Library Board.

calf gilt, has Boothby's inscription inside the upper cover, 'Will: Boothby 5ˢ 6ᵈ (4 quier) Lichfeild', testifying to Johnson's binding work and charges for a substantial 'paper booke'; while the fourth volume (Add. MS 71692), in vellum boards, has Boothby's inscription: 'October 24ᵗʰ 1687 – ff 3ˢ – Three quier'.

Another kind of order involving manuscript matters throws interesting light on one trade practice. On 6 November 1683 he writes:

Mr Johnson *I have sent a new Testiment to be bound* there are some leaves wanting which I desire you to Examine and make them good (iff you can of printed though not of the same letter but iff not let them be writ out in a ffaire hand as nigh this letter as possable and I will pay for it.

It is interesting to note here his instruction that a made-up copy of a book should be clearly identifiable as such: bound-in printed pages should be 'not of the same letter'. At the same time his comments imply that a service undertaken by booksellers was to mend defective copies by appointing or hiring scribes to replace missing text with neat manuscript copy or even manuscript facsimile. One does indeed encounter the occasional defective seventeenth-century printed volume treated in this way. It is also further evidence that some particularly interesting books that have been found with pages in manuscript – some play texts, for instance – are more likely to have been restored by professional stationers or scriveners than by anyone altogether outside the book trade.[8]

Finally, it may not be coincidental that manuscripts are mentioned more than once in Boothby's later entries in these letterbooks, in the years 1688–89. As we move into the turbulent period of the Glorious Revolution and its aftermath, we can sense vividly the contemporary anxieties and uncertainty, that strong element of political circumspection which affected booksellers as much as anyone else. Boothby writes on 2 December 1688: 'I beleeive you are in a great disorder and disturbance in London, as we are in this County, many great men, and others being up: But my Allegiance and Religion According to ye principles of the Church of England keeps me from Joyning with them . . .'. With his provincial isolation becoming even more pronounced – 'what news at Lichfield about Ireland,' he asks on 9 July 1689, 'for we are much in the Darke' – Boothby's eagerness for every kind of current newsletter, pamphlet, gazette, and proclamation becomes more urgent than ever. And along with his requests for printed materials go, apparently for the first time, importunities for the kind of 'private' information and discussions which are to be found principally in restricted manuscript circulation. Thus, on 14 August 1688, he informs a Mr Horton that he has received all his books

and shall Long for the time when I may be so happy as to injoy your good Company: pray bring what Maniscrips you have, either Verses – or [Halifax's] the Charater of a trimer with your Observations on Dr Burnetts history of the Reformation . . .

But that caution, personal trust and reliability were essential elements in the distribution of 'private' newsletters and manuscript materials – much of which, of course, was satirical or critical of the authorities – is evident from Boothby's indignant response to a 'Mr Rossell' on 30 September 1688: 'I take it ill that you dare not trust me with what Comes in your news Letters, but Blott out so many Lines: So that I have sent you your 9^s pay by the Bearer, and shall give you no further trouble'. On 13 August 1689 he tells Robert Clavell: 'I much desire private things Either prints, or written (you may Trust me)'; and on 27 August instructs Johnson: 'tell mr clavell he doth not make Collection of those most in choice – (he may trust me Either with manuscripts or secrett papers . . .)'. His reference in the same letter to authors who seem to be 'ashamed or afraid to put . . .

---

[8] See, for example, the work of the Inns of Court 'Chute scribe', responsible for the play *Dick of Devonshire* (in BL Egerton MS 1994), for a complete verse miscellany (BL Add. MS 33998), and for the missing pages in printed copies of Middleton's *Blurt Master Constable* (in the Folger) and Chapman's *May-Day* (at Worcester College, Oxford), discussed in Mary Hobbs, 'Early Seventeenth-Century Verse Miscellanies and Their Value for Textual Editors', *English Manuscript Studies*, 1 (1989), 182–210 (pp. 200–1, 209–10).

PLATE V. Boothby's memorial in St Oswald's Church, Ashbourne

their names' to their works provides, nevertheless, a good clue as to why complete confidence in Boothby's discretion might not always be readily forthcoming.

What happened to Boothby's bookbuying activities after 1689 we have little hope of discovering unless, by some miracle, further letterbooks should turn up elsewhere. But we do have a tribute to Boothby's eventual library in the memorial to him which his son Brooke (1670–1727) erected after 1707 in St Oswald's Church, Ashbourne (see Plate V):

. . . Sʳ WILLIAM was a true Son of the Established Church of England, eminent for Piety, Sobriety, & disinterested Loyalty; a Lover of Learning, evident by his Collection of near Six

Thousand Books, now regularly placed in a Convenient graceful Library in Ashborn=Hall, to remain to his Posterity there . . .[9]

According to John Nichols, who cited as his source what he calls the 'Dr. Pegge MS.',[10] Boothby's bibliomania was inherited by his grandson, Brooke Boothby, the fifth Baronet (1710–89), who himself 'collected a large library at Ashbourne hall', and Pegge had heard that 'Mr. Boothby ordered *every* book that was published to be sent to him'.[11] A tribute to this later library is offered by Ellis Farneworth in the Preface to his translation of *The Life of Pope Sixtus the Fifth* . . . *Translated from the Italian of Gregorio Leti* (London, 1754), which, incidentally, is dedicated to William Fitzherbert of Tissington. Farneworth claims that he could not have produced his edition had he not been granted free access by his 'honour'd friend *Brooke Boothby*, Esq. to a large collection of books in his possession at *Ashbourn Hall*', and he lists some of the essential Italian, French and English authors whose works he found there. Nevertheless, according to Pegge, 'This library was sold before the year 1776'.[12]

That, whatever the circumstances, Boothby's library was dispersed is beyond doubt. A handful of his widely scattered books, bearing his signature, can already be identified. A copy of Edward Symmons, *A Vindication of King Charles* ([London], 1648) [Wing S6350], now in the British Library (RB 23. a. 10857), bears Boothby's distinctive signature, 'Will: Boothby'.[13] Four other titles with similar signatures are in a private collection: namely, John Fell, *The Privileges of the University of Oxford, in point of Visitation* (1647) [Wing F619], bound with *The Character of an Oxford-Incendiary* (1645) [Wing C2014] (these were later in the Fairfax Library); Richard Farrar, *An Expedient for the King: or King Charls his Peace-Offering, Sacrificed at the Altar of Peace* (1648) [Wing F520] (this was later in Wigan Public Library); and *State Tracts: Being a Collection of Several Treatises relating to the Government. Privately printed in the Reign of K. Charles II* (London, 1689) [Wing S5329]. This worn folio volume in calf has the remains of its ribbed spine stamped in each compartment with Boothby's lion's-paw crest in gilt, and his inscription on the title-page ('Will: Boothby – 9ˢ Lich:') indicates that this is yet another binding by Johnson. In addition, there is a copy of Ariosto's *Orlando Furioso* (1634) in the Folger Shakespeare Library (STC 748) which belonged to a William Boothby, but possibly a later member of the family.[14] No doubt other examples will come to light in due course.

---

[9] Inscription on Boothby's memorial on the wall of the north transept in the Parish Church of St Oswald, Ashbourne. A version of this inscription is printed in Glover, *History . . . of . . . Derby*, II, 35. The well-preserved monument, in white and black marble, has the full family arms partly illuminated in red and gold: *viz.* *Argent*, on a canton, *Sable*, a lion's paw erased, in bend, *Or*, with the arms of Ulster and a shield of pretence. Brooke, *Gules*, on a chevron, *Argent*, a lion rampant, *Sable*, crowned, *Or*. It is among several monuments relating to the Boothby family from the seventeenth to late eighteenth centuries. They accompany those of the Cokayne family in the same chapel.

[10] Giles Mandelbrote suggests that this may be one of the manuscripts, now in the College of Arms, of the antiquary Dr Samuel Pegge (1704–96), prebendary of Lichfield.

[11] Nichols, *History . . . of . . . Leicester*, IV.i, 179.

[12] ibid.

[13] I am obliged to Giles Mandelbrote for bringing this volume to my attention. I owe Giles my gratitude for other relevant points of information besides and for his kindness in reading through and commenting on the present article.

[14] For this reference I am obliged to Theodore Hofmann.

Otherwise, without so much as a library catalogue to preserve a sense of the integrity of his collection,[15] the present diary and letterbooks must be accounted the only significant monument to a serious bibliophile of remarkable energy, persistence, and resolve, if not of unfailing tact and diplomacy towards those humbler agents who made his pursuit possible.

APPENDIX
Sir William Boothby and Charles Cotton

The record of Sir William Boothby's association with his highly respected friend Charles Cotton ('Dear Brother'), though of no great consequence in itself, provides a rare and tantalizing glimpse of a provincial 'literary' community in the seventeenth century and is thus worth publishing in full. As a new biographical source, it supplements significantly the meagre existing total of four known letters by Cotton himself and six written to him by correspondents.[16] The new material offers an insight into the nature of the day-to-day relationship between the two men and of their domestic, social, business and, just occasionally, bibliographical concerns.

Charles Cotton the younger (1630–87) – notable poet and translator, perhaps best remembered as the angling friend and literary collaborator of Izaak Walton – lived at Beresford Hall, some eight miles north-west of Ashbourne.[17] His second wife, mentioned in the letterbooks, was Mary Russell, widow of Wingfield Cromwell, fifth Baron Cromwell and second Earl of Ardglass (1624–68). Also mentioned several times in the letterbooks is Cotton's second and favourite daughter, Catherine (d. 1710). Catherine's own bibliographical interests are reflected in the fact that a number of extant books from her father's library, as well as a few others (including a Shakespeare Second Folio), were subsequently owned and inscribed by her.[18]

Boothby also makes frequent allusions to their common neighbour, his 'cousin' William Fitzherbert, of Tissington Hall, four miles north of Ashbourne. Among other things, Fitzherbert and his family once owned the important 'Derby Manuscript' of Cotton's poems now preserved in Derby Central Library.[19] Boothby's allusions to social, dining and business (legal document-signing) meetings with Fitzherbert and other members of his family, such as Mary and 'An.' Fitzherbert, indicate the relative closeness of their circle; but no attempt is made to record all these references below.

These allusions and letters to the Cottons (which sometimes amount to rough retained synopses) are written chiefly in Boothby's own cursive script (a hurried scrawl which obliges one sometimes to follow the contour of the word rather than of the individual letter); a few are in the hands of amanuenses. I have transcribed them *literatim*,

---

[15] A four-page list of about a hundred books, dating up to 1757, is preserved among the Fonmon Castle archives in the Glamorgan Record Office (D/DF/F/195), but it does not necessarily relate to Ashbourne Hall.

[16] These letters (only two of which apparently survive in the originals) are recorded in my *Index of English Literary Manuscripts*, Volume II, Part 1 (London & New York, 1987), pp. 213–14.

[17] The only remains of Beresford Hall today are the two original pillars of the gateway to the estate standing some two and a half miles along the road from Hartington to Hulme End.

[18] See my *Index*, II.i, pp. 210, 215–18.

[19] ibid., II.i, pp. 210–11.

including mis-spellings, with pointers to uncertain readings ('[?]'). The distinction between upper and lower case lettering, as well as between normal lettering and super-script abbreviations, is not always clear.

A.

References to Cotton and his daughter in Boothby's diary for 1676–77 are as follows:

a. [late September 1676] . . . rec. by Mr Cotton letter to Dr *Chem:* all about *F Booth* by,[20] dated July and I told Mr Cotton all – noe reason he should have written to me – it wholly concerns F Boothby for I was no party to any Bargaine between them . . . (*Add. MS 71689, f.7r*)

b. [15 October 1676] . . . Mis Cotton (wifes woman) [?red] [?red] with us . . . (*Add. MS 71689, f.25v*)

c. [24 October 1676] . . . Mr Heans spoke to me for Mr *Cotton* desires I would come to him tomorrow to take a fine of his Lady &c . . . (*Add. MS 71689, f.31v*)

d. [26 October 1676] . . . I & franck Boothby went to Mr *Cottons* to dinner – I & Mr H. Jackson tooke my Lady of Ardglasses[21] acknowledgment of a fine – & they [?] Lady & Mr Cotton sealed Deed to Mr Fu[tz]herbert in Trust of some formes & lands in water-fall[22] . . . (*Add. MS 71689, f.32r*)

e. [I January 1676/7] . . . I sent An. Johnson to Mr Cottons with a fat weather[23] . . . (*Add. MS 71689, f.63v*)

f. [13 March 1676/7] . . . I went to Mr *Cottons* to take a fine for him & Lady & Lord Ard glasse[24] – came home – Cousin An. Fu[tz]herbert & will [?Foe] went with me . . . (*Add. MS 71689, f.119v*)

B.

In the later letterbooks there are texts of sixteen letters by Boothby addressed to Cotton, as well as of one (No. xi below) to his daughter Catherine. They are as follows:

i. [5 May 1683]
Mr Cotton found y^r Letter upon my coming home from Derby – I shall Ever be ready to meete you at any time & place – as my very Good friend – & hope you do not doubt it – will meet you on Munday – at Jo Robinsons at Thorp[25] at Two a clock in 'after noone / yrs (*Add. MS 71690, p. 22: f. 12v*)

ii. [16 July 1683] Mr Cotton. D. Broth:
I haue sent you a peece of the first venison I Kill'd – poore Brooke[26] is very unhappy if it might not be a Trouble I would send him to wayt on you for a weeke – as[']t would be to his great

---

[20] '*F Boothby*': Boothby's eldest son Frank (see below).
[21] 'my Lady of Ardglass': Cotton's wife (see above).
[22] Waterfall: a village about seven miles north-west of Ashbourne.
[23] 'weather': i.e. bell-wether, sheep.
[24] 'Lord Ard glasse': Lady Ardglass's son, Thomas

Cromwell, third Earl of Ardglass (1653–82).
[25] 'Thorp', i.e. Thorpe: a village about two and a half miles north of Ashbourne.
[26] 'poore Brooke': Brooke Boothby (1670–1727), seventh child of Sir William Boothby.

advantage – I must begge the opertunity of an houres discourse before our assises, for I am much solicited fro[m] s^r Rob Coke about m^r petite, But I will do nothing without yr advice to yr (*Add MS 71690, p.67: f.35r*)

iii. [30 October 1683] Mr Cotton octob. 30th

D. Brother you shall never want in me a friend ready to serve you upon all occasions: as in gratitude & honour (as well as friendship) I am obliged to: hauing upon the greatest & just reason devoted myselfe in all sincerity & trust / Yr most affec: Bro: friend & serf / W B. (*Add. MS 71690, p. 133: f.68r*)

iv. [5 November 1683] To C.C.

wife hath been ill & hath a great desire to see Brooke – whom I have now sent for – wth 1000 thanks for yor. kindnesse to him & whereby you have obliged for Ever / yrs / o^r. service & hope yor. Daughter will appoint a day that wee may have ye hono^r. of her company (*Add. MS 71690, p. 132: f.67v*)

v. [12 April 1684] Mr Cotton. – Satirday Aprill 12th 1684

deare brother – though I am in great afliction and trouble[27] yet I would not that poore Brooke should suffer by it and look his ffrench, iff m^r. Boulay please to come I shall giue him the same as before, onely at present my house and table is soe ffull by the company of my daughter Boothby, her Sister, and my deare grandson, with her servants, that I cannot aford him those conveniences in my family that I did before; and am willing to doe, but iff hee please to come I will pay for his lodging and diett in the towne or giue him satisfaction for it, I desire by this bearer to know his mind; for I am vneasy for Brooke, and iff hee doe not like of my proposalls I must thinke of some other way to dispose of him, for I am resolved hee shall improue his french, I was in some good hopes off seeing you heare to have returned my thankes for your last Kindnesse to deare ffranke, my service to yovr daughter – / deare brother yovr most / affectionate & reall ffrend, / W: Boothby (*Add. MS 71690, p. 211: f.107r*)

vi. [20 April 1684] Mr Cotton Aprill 20th

D. Brother: I give you my thanks for y^r kind Letter, I am sorry Mr Boullay doth not thinke fitt to comply with my desires: his being heare could be no hinderance to any other preferement – for he should haue his Liberty at a days warning – And the reason why I cannot ingage for aboue a month or two, is that I am taking a person into my family, who is not onely to be as a companion to me, in my studyes: But also a divine to performe all the offices of a chaplaine, & yet one that understands french so as to teach Brooke & I haue ingaged my friends to assist me in procuring such an one; & I know not how soone I may heerein be fitted. & now you haue the truth & reason of it; I am confident you will approve of my designe: But being much troubled that Brooke (who hath already Lat so much) should still Loose more time. I desire (if you please; to get mr woodhouse yr neighbour to board him, & let Either mr Boullay goe over thither to teach him, or he to Come to him to yr house: This I move not But that I raither desire him under y^r owne Eye – But for the trouble thereof to y^r family, whither too he hath given you: Though I should be much more pleased if it were fitt & reaseonable to Expect & desire it – & that I might pay for his Board / y^r (*Add. MS 71690, pp. 218–19: ff.110v–11r*)

vii. [26 July 1684] July 26th C. Cotton.

The coach shall be ready at yr Time, & will meet at Broadlow ash according to yr desire – & desire you will value my friendship, as you find me constant to what I haue, & do really profess my selfe / yr (*Add. MS 71690, p. 261: f.132r*)

---

[27] 'great afliction and trouble': the recent death of Sir William's eldest son, Francis (Frank) Boothby (1654–84), by his first wife.

viii. [2 August 1684] C. Cotton Aug. 2ᵈ

D. Brother I will make no Excuse when I am so happy as to haue an occasion to manifest the Sincerity of my friendship: & though sometimes I am not very well provided, yet all difficulties shall yield & I will find or make a way to give my selfe the highest satisfaction in serving so good & most oblidging a friend: I haue sent the 7ˡ by yʳ servant (sealed up) & you may please to take yʳ owne Time in sending over the Tenant; I shall be proud of An occasion to wayt on you to my Lord Rutland: & Beleive I must goe thither (upon orders fro[m] aboue) this next weeke: I will giue you notice & call on you: poore Brooke is more my Beloved, by yʳ favour & great care of him: my wife Blushes to be put in minde of the Little present. Both our services to yʳ Good Daughter, her company will be very acceptable to us: & I hartily wish I could injoy yours as often as my inclination prompt me to desire it: I am sure it would be greatly to my advantage in all respects – But we must not promise our selves too great happiness in this world; God grant we may be prepared for & injoy that compleat & Blessed happiness of the saints in the next / D. Broth / yr / The inclosed (for mr fox) is a second letter, I received fro[m] a Bookeseller (who I know is an honest sufficient man) he spoke to me when at London about the same Business to have it to yʳ owne consideration who know best yʳ owne concernes (*Add. MS 71690, p. 255 : f.129r*)

ix. [19 September 1684] Mʳ Cotton Sep. 19

D Bro: haue Enquired & can heare of nothing against you, so that I believe you may come home – I If you please shall be glad to see you heere on Sunday – yr Daughter is well & wellcome / yr (*Add. MS 71690, p. 276: f.139v*)

x. [20 October 1684] C. Cotton octob: 20ᵗʰ

D: Brother yr thanks are Larger then I deserve, yr Daughters meritts make her company very agreable – besides the addition of being yr beloved – for Brooke 'tis onely at present delayed (as you mentioned in yʳˢ to me) till you be setled, & when he may be no trouble he shall wayt upon you fro[m] / yr (*Add. MS 71691, p. 12: f.6v*)

xi. [30 October 1684]

Mis K. Cotton madam. This is to begge yr pardon that I did not (as I ought) returne my acknowledgements for the honour you did me with a Letter: & to assure you that I am, & Ever shall be ready to serve you, & my Brother as by a Thousand obligations I am bound to do: or Else should be the most ung[r]atefull of mankind – my most humble service to my Deare Brother fro[m] / yr / 30ᵗʰ octob (84 (*Add. MS 71691, p. 18: f.9v*)

xii. [20 November 1684]

D: Brother (Clotton) I give you many thanks for yr kind Enquiry after us – we haue both been very ill of Colds – But I thanke god are now Better – we shall be hartily glad to see you heere – I haue sent you the Booke Desired (Lucians Dialogues 8°)[28] But will onely lend it; for being yʳˢ I must not be without one – The Tenant you fownd at Markett never came – This I onely lent as beleiving you may have ordered one, & he hath neglected – But if your other occasions haue hindred (wch they may very well do) Take no further trouble in thinking of it – till you haue freedome & leasure, as that it may be no prejudice to you, But to be done with Ease – for I am satisfied that I can serve you in any thing – wch is a reward in it selfe whereof I am ambitious – who am in great truth / D.B / your most affect: / & constant friend (*Add. MS 71691, p. 37: f.19r*)

---

[28] One of Cotton's burlesques had been *Burlesque upon Burlesque: or, The Scoffer Scoft, being some of Lucians Dialogues Newly put into English Fustian* (London, 1675).

xiii. [9 December 1684]

D. Brother (Cotton) I should be much pleased to haue yr company to pay our last respects to that person for whom we both had so great an honour: &, in whom we haue Lost a very good friend: But I dare not advice you to it: however I shall acquaint those who are most concerned of yʳ harty intentions. My Lord Halifax[29] hath been a marquess a good while – his other titles I am ignorant of: But haue sent you the paper desired. mine & wifes service to yʳ good Daughter – she is troubled in the Thoughts Least she should be fallene out with her, but she never hath (knowingly) nor Ever will give her any just occasion for it; hauing so particular & great an hon[ou]r & respect for her. Good Brother I am in great truth / yr / Dec. 9ᵗʰ pray haue a care of the paper (*Add. MS 71691, p. 57: f.29r*)

xiv. [24 January 1684/5] January 24ᵗʰ Coppy to C. Cotton

Dear Brother, Mault was ready against Munday though I had occasion to use it. yet he shall never find me makeing excuses, when to pleasure such a friend / yoʳ (Add. *MS 71691, p. 95: f.47r*)

xv. [26 January 1684/5] January 26ᵗʰ coppy to Charles Cotton

Dear Brother: I onely desire the favour you will send over any tenant that will engage to pay out of his Ladys Day rent the 7ˡ & the 3 Load of Mault, which is all that I expect or desire, who am in great truth/yoʳ (*Add. MS 71691, p. 95: f.47r*)

xvi. [29 January 1684/5] Mʳ Cotton Jan 29

D Bro: I Expected to haue heard fro[m] you on munday (as I sent you word) & set by 6ˡᵇ of mault though I had occasion to haue vsd 6ˡᵇ for my house – yet you shall never find me guilty of making Excuses – when I am capable of serving you &c – (*Add. MS 71691, p. 85: f.42r*)

xvii. [21 July 1685] Mʳ Cotton July 21ᵗʰ

Dear Brother, There is but one Volume of Bishop of Winchester against Baxter,[30] which I have sent you; I desire you will be pleased to returne those books you have perused, for my Books are the great joy of my life. / I am yoʳ (*Add. MS 71691, p. 227: f.94r*)

---

[29] George Savile, Marquess of Halifax (1633–95), the dedicatee of Cotton's translation of Montaigne's *Essays* (1685). The 'paper [i.e., manuscript copy] desired' is probably Halifax's *The Lady's New Year's Gift: or, Advice to a Daughter*, first published in 1688 but originally circu-

lated in manuscript (see my *Index*, II.i, p. 515).

[30] [George Morley], *The Bishop of Winchester's Vindication of Himself from divers False, Scandalous and Injurious Reflexions made upon him by Mr. Richard Baxter in several of his Writings* (London, 1683) [Wing M2797].

A Hilton Manuscript
Once in the Possession of Luttrell Wynne

I N 1970, when I was a graduate student working on Middle English at Keio University, Tokyo, I came across an antiquarian bookshop newly opened in a fashionable department store in Shinjuku, where my earliest acquisition was Robinsons' catalogues of rare books and manuscripts, most of which came from Sir Thomas Phillipps. I had no idea that these literary treasures still found their way to market. Knowing my interest in medieval literature, shop clerks began offering me medieval manuscripts and incunabula. Thus Takamiya MS 1 was a mid-thirteenth century glossed bible on uterine vellum, produced in Paris. I do not know where they found it.

A few months later, when I showed the late Professor Fumio Kuriyagawa, my supervisor at Keio, the newly acquired manuscript, now shelfmarked MS 2, of Boethius, *De Consolatione Philosophiae*, fifteenth-century MS copied in Tuscany, in a contemporary North Italian binding of beech boards, with the bookplates of John T. Jeffcock and Edward F. H. Paget, he immediately identified it, to my surprise, as item 48 of Bernard Quaritch's catalogue, no. 902 (1970). I learned from him that Quaritch was a leading antiquarian book dealer, who once made business transactions based in Yokohama some time after the Meiji Restoration (1868). Professor Kuriyagawa, recognizing my bibliophilic taste, kindly gave me all the back issues of Quaritch's catalogues he owned, which have since formed the basis of my reference library.

I would like to make below a description of MS 3, Walter Hilton's *Scale of Perfection* and *Of Angels' Song*, producing evidence in dialect, text, and later provenance that it was possibly connected with either Syon Abbey or Sheen Charterhouse.

PHYSICAL DESCRIPTION

Walter Hilton, *The Scale of Perfection* and *Of Angels' Song*, English prose manuscript on vellum, 8vo (173 mm × 132 mm; written space approximately 130 mm × 900 mm), ff. 174 (last blank) plus two early vellum flyleaves at beginning and one at end, complete, gatherings of twelve leaves (ff. 171–4 two single leaves and a bifolium) with catchwords and two series of leaf signatures (in brown ink on versos, in red on rectos), an extra bifolium (ff. 161, 162) inserted where a passage was omitted by the original scribe, about thirty lines of text to a full page of single column, written in brown ink by a single scribe in a good but variable English secretary hand with some *anglicana* features, additions and corrections supplied in the margins as well as interlinear positions, with various carets,

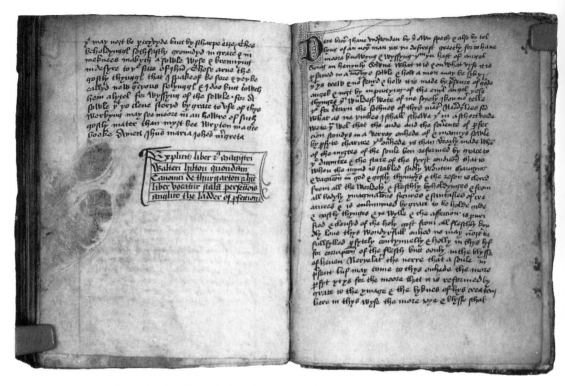

PLATE I. Walter Hilton's *The Scale of Perfection* and *Of Angels' Song*, Takamiya MS 3, ff. 169–70

by more than one fifteenth-century scribe, biblical quotations in Latin underlined in red, three-line chapter initials in blue with red penwork filigree decorations, some edges stained, margins of ff. 102, 108 slightly torn, a few outer margins irregularly cut down, corner of f. 86 defective, upper margins of f. 161 repaired, a large piece of f. 168 missing with the ends of many lines but this leaf evidently to some extent defective before the text was written (possibly this leaf had a piece of vellum pasted over a natural defect and this piece has become detached); natural flaws in some other leaves, but on the whole in good condition, contemporary English binding of what was once white tawed leather, now stained, over wooden boards, spine in raised compartments, nails for clasps and catches, in a blue half-morocco case. [England, probably east Berkshire, fifteenth century].

PROVENANCE

(1) Possibly from Syon Abbey or Sheen Charterhouse: see below.

(2) Belonged probably to the diarist and collector Narcissus Luttrell (1657–1732: see *DNB*, vol. 34, p. 300), but without his stamped monogram or the date of acquisition. Most of his books and manuscripts were inherited in 1732 by his younger son Francis Luttrell, at whose death in 1740 the collection passed to William Wynne (1692–1765), sergeant-at-law. In 1765, when William died, the whole collection was inherited by

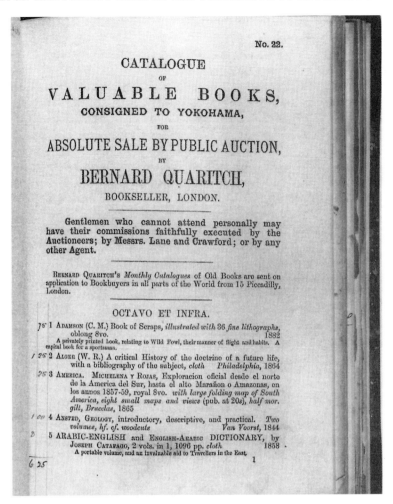

PLATE 11. Consignment of books for sale by auction in Yokohama, 8 May 1886

William's eldest son, Edward Wynne (1734–84: see *DNB*, vol. 63, p. 261), law writer. But the present manuscript, judging from the note on one of the flyleaves, 'Jn. Price/This MS. was given me Dec. 14th 1765, / by Mr Luttl. Wynne Fellow of A.S. Coll. Oxford', was probably given by William to Rev. Luttrell Wynne (1740–1814: see J. Foster, ed., *Alumni Oxonienses*, vol. 4, p. 1622) either during the former's lifetime or at his death. John Price (1734–1813: see *DNB*, vol. 46, p. 332), was Bodley's Librarian and became Rector of Llangattock in Breconshire in 1798.

(3) Note of ownership of S[amuel] Courthope Bosanquet [of Dingestow Court, Monmouthshire, 1832–1925].

(4) Dawsons of Pall Mall, Catalogue, no.102 (1959), item 6. Apparently they bought the present manuscript privately.

(5) Dawsons of Pall Mall, Catalogue, no. 135 (1964), item 361.

(6) Dawsons of Pall Mall, Catalogue, no. 162 (1966), item 54.

(7) Sotheby's, 8th July 1970, lot 71: bought by Bernard Quaritch.

(8) Bernard Quaritch, Catalogue, no. 902 (1970), item 167.

(9) Bought, prior to its reappearance in Quaritch's catalogue, no. 914 (1972), item 6, by Yushodo 11 February 1972 for T. Takamiya: now MS Takamiya 3.

CONTENTS

TEXT AND EDITIONS

Walter Hilton (d. 1396) was an Augustinian canon of Thurgarton Prior near Southwell. His major devotional work, *The Scale of Perfection*, which comprises two books, is extant in no less than sixty-two medieval manuscripts including thirteen Latin versions translated by Thomas Fishlake: a list of English and Latin manuscripts of the *Scale* is published by Takamiya, 'The Luttrell Wynne MS of Walter Hilton', *Reports of the Keio Institute of Cultural and Linguistic Studies*, 7 (1975), pp. 171–91. Despite several early printed editions led by Wynkyn de Worde's *editio princeps*, a few copies of which include at the end of Book II a version of Hilton's *Mixed Life* as Book III, probably printed shortly after the *Scale* and distributed to subscribers later, and several modern English translations, a modern critical edition of *The Scale of Perfection* is yet to be published by the Early English Text Society under the editorship of the late A. J. Bliss and Michael G. Sargent for Book I and S. S. Hussey for Book II.

Of his minor works, *Mixed Life* is now edited by S. J. Ogilvie-Thomson as *Walter Hilton's Mixed Life edited from Lambeth Palace MS 472*, Salzburg Studies in English Literature, 92:15 (Salzburg, 1986). Two of the Middle English tracts convincingly attributed to Hilton, the *Eight Chapters on Perfection* and *Of Angels' Song*, are available in critical editions, by Fumio Kuriyagawa (1958 and 1971) and by T. Takamiya (1977) respectively. They were privately printed in a single volume by Takamiya in 1980. In 'Walter Hilton's *Of Angels' Song* edited from British Museum MS Additional 27592', *Studies in English Literature*, English Number 1977, Takamiya collated six extant manuscripts including the present [Lw] and one black-letter edition of the piece.

Lw belongs to Helen Gardner's Type A in 'The Text of *The Scale of Perfection*', *Medium Ævum*, 5 (1936), pp. 11–30, in that it contains the passage on the Holy Name in *The Scale*, Book I, chapter 44, which she believes to be a part of the original text accidentally omitted from one family of manuscripts, and the numerous brief 'Christocentric' passages which she believes to have been added either at the Bridgettine Abbey of Syon or the neighbouring Charterhouse of Sheen at the beginning of the fifteenth century. Lw evidently belonged to a library where more than one copy of Hilton's works was available, for a long passage near the end of Book II, which was omitted by the original scribe, was later added on two inserted leaves (ff. 161, 162) and this later scribe and others of the fifteenth century have made a large number of minor additions and corrections throughout the text. The longest addition is of eleven lines, on a slip of vellum stitched to f. 84v. Careful correction of a text of this kind at this date is often a sign of Carthusian ownership, as admirably demonstrated by Michael G. Sargent in 'The Transmission by the English Carthusians of Some Late Medieval Spiritual Writings', *Journal of Ecclesiastical History*, 27 (1976), pp. 225–40.

The following is an attempt to make a collation of part of the Holy Name passage in the *Scale*, Book I, chapter 44 in three manuscripts and Wynkyn de Worde's edition of 1494:

Cambridge University Library, Additional MS 6686 [C]: . . . souereyn ioye; þe whilk he þat myȝt in þis life by abundaunce of perfite charite enioye in iesu schal fele and haue / /

Takamiya MS 3 [Lw]: . . . soueren Ioye the which he þat myȝt in thys lyff by abundans of perfytte charite emage in iesu schall fele *and* haue

Trinity College, Cambridge, MS B. 15. 18 (354) [*To*]: . . . ioye souereyn þe which he þat myght in þis life bi abundance of perfite charite [. . . blank . . .] in iesu shall fele and haue

Wynkyn de Worde's Edition of 1494 [W]: . . . souereyne Ioye, the whiche he that myght in thys lyf by aboundance of perfite charyte in Iesu shall fele *and* haue /

In this sentence Lw produces the mysterious 'emage' for the correct 'enioye' in C, the best manuscript for Book I. It seems likely that Lw misunderstood the three minims of '–ni–' in his exemplar by devising a corrupt reading. It looks as though T failed to understand this and left a blank, which W in due course closed up. That is, the readings here could easily be explained by the assumption that T was copied from Lw and W from T. This will not do for the rest of the text, but we have to wait for the publication of the long overdue EETS edition for a full collation of extant manuscripts. It is important to note, however, even at this stage that there is a strong textual affinity between Lw and T, which was owned by Sheen Charterhouse, bearing annotations by James Grenehalgh, a fifteenth-century textual critic at Sheen: see Michael G. Sargent, 'James Grenehalgh as Textual Critic', Ph.D. dissertation, University of Toronto, 1979.

There is also a significant textual relationship between Lw and All Souls College, Oxford, MS 25 [As], which was in the possession of Syon Abbey and later of Narcissus Luttrell, with his stamped monogram and the handwritten date of acquisition, '1693': As was donated to the college in 1786 by Luttrell Wynne. British Library, Harley 6579 [H], from London Charterhouse, was subjected to a series of additions and interpolations; the various stages of this process are reflected in other manuscripts. Stonyhurst College MS A.vi.24 (xxxvi) [St] is very close to the plain text of H; As to H with a first set of additions; Lw T W to H with the first and a second set of additions. Thus Lw is closely related to As. Probably Luttrell ownership is only indirectly connected with this relationship. As and Lw both belong to a group of manuscripts associated with Syon and the London and Sheen Charterhouse; probably the Luttrells succeeded in acquiring books directly or indirectly from these religious foundations at the Dissolution, but there have been no documents to prove it.

WYNKYN DE WORDE'S *SCALE OF PERFECTION*, 1494

In terms of Narcissus Luttrell, one must not forget a splendid royal association copy of Wynkyn de Worde's first edition of the *Scale*, carrying his stamped monogram and the handwritten date of '1693' on the title-page. It was sold by Luttrell Wynne's direction at the sale of Edward Wynne's books at Leigh and Sotheby's 6–18 March 1786, lot 1366. From that date the volume was in the possession of Stanesby Alchorne, the bookseller Thomas Payne, Thomas Johnes, and Earl Spencer, and the Duke of Devonshire. It was sold at the sale of the Duke of Devonshire's books at Christie's on 30 June 1958, lot 63, to Bernard Quaritch. It is now owned by Mr Paul Mellon. It was exhibited and catalogued as item 17 in *Fifty-five Books Printed Before 1525 Representing the Works of England's Printers: An Exhibition from the Collection of Paul Mellon*, 17 January–3 March 1968 at the Grolier Club of New York.

The *Scale* of 1494 was the first book to which Wynkyn de Worde put his name: a rhymed 'enuoye' printed on the last leaf informs us that 'this heuenly boke more precyous than golde' was printed 'in Willyam Caxstons hows' at the special command of Lady Margaret Beaufort, Countess of Richmond and Derby, and mother of King Henry VII. It is the first and most important of the books commissioned by Lady Margaret from de Worde, who was later to style himself 'Prynter unto the moost excellent pryncesse my lady the kynges moder'.

The present copy's unique interest consists in its intimate association with Lady Margaret herself and her daughter-in-law Queen Elizabeth of York, who together presented and personally inscribed the book to Mary Roos, one of the ladies of the queen. The autograph inscriptions of the two royal donors occur on a4 verso in the blank space following the table and facing the first page of text; here, presenting the book, the queen wrote:

> I pray you pray for me / Elysabeth þe quene

and below Lady Margaret added:

> mastres rosse y truste yn your prayeres
> the whyche y pray yow y may be partener
> of Margaret R[ichmond] the kyngs modyr.

ACKNOWLEDGEMENTS

I greatly benefited from correspondence with the late Professor Alan Bliss 1974–76, and from the assistance of Richard Linenthal of Bernard Quaritch Ltd., who kindly placed their files at my disposal.